P9-DFJ-187

THE ORDER OF THINGS

"Let all things be done decently and in order."

—*The New Testament*, I Corinthians 14:40

"All things began in order, so shall they end, and so shall they begin again."

—Sir Thomas Browne, *On Dreams*

"Order and simplification are the first steps toward mastery of a subject—the actual enemy is the unknown."

—Thomas Mann, *The Magic Mountain*

THE ORDER OF THINGS

HOW EVERYTHING IN THE WORLD IS ORGANIZED INTO HIERARCHIES, STRUCTURES, AND PECKING ORDERS

REVISED EDITION

BARBARA ANN KIPFER

RANDOM HOUSE
NEW YORK

New York   Toronto   London   Sydney   Auckland

CONTENTS

OUTLINE OF CONTENTS

Life Sciences   35

Technology   93

Physical Sciences   79

Mathematics & Measurement   117

Religion   135

History 167

OUTLINE OF CONTENTS

Society & Social Institutions   219

Business & Economics   261

Sports & Recreation 323

ACKNOWLEDGMENTS

This book is the result of the some of the unique opportunities and experiences I have had over the past 15 years in my work in artificial intelligence, electronic reference publishing, and reference book publishing. I have been called upon to draw up many hierarchies and subject classifications. This has become one of the skills of which I am most proud.

I have had the opportunity to revise Yellow Pages' headings, to classify huge encyclopedia sets, to write and place a thesaurus within a concept hierarchy, and to study the hierarchies of hundreds of others. The idea for this book evolved because my work led me to notice just how many useful and interesting hierarchies exist in our world.

—Barbara Ann Kipfer, PhD
Essex, Connecticut

This book is dedicated to the guys
who never seem to mind my "order of things":

Paul
Kyle
and *Keir*

(in age order!)

PREFACE

Order is heaven's first law.

—Alexander Pope, *An Essay on Man*

From the inner workings of the smallest things to the complex system of the universe, *The Order of Things* is an attempt to cover all those things that we ourselves have organized, or what we have found naturally organized, into:

hierarchies
structures
orders
classifications
branches
scales
divisions
successions
sequences
rankings.

We know that orders exist, but have you ever tried to look one up? One can easily enough find the plant and animal kingdoms in the encyclopedias, but how about the organization of the Boy Scouts, the Mafia, or the ranks of sumo wrestlers? No one encyclopedia or other reference contains such a collection of hierarchies and structures in hundreds of different areas.

Within a given subject area, the orders included here are basic, important, and informative to the layperson without going so far as to be encyclopedic in coverage. A good cross-section of objects, actions, events, qualities, features, states, and conditions are included for each subject area.

Alphabetically arranged reference books separate and isolate items of information that are actually related to each other—as naturally as leaf, branch, and tree. *The Order of Things* puts these related objects back togther, by organizing them into subject areas and then including essential and interesting orders for each. The book provides enough to make every subject easier to understand and remember.

Francis Bacon, seen by some as the first exponent of the scientific method, endeavored to re-organize all knowledge—from the ancient to the modern—into an unprecedentedly thorough and detailed system. *The Order of Things* offers just that. A comprehensive schema and storyboard of the world.

* * *

This book contains orders from thirteen general areas (see below) which may apply to one's work, studies, or personal interests. In the book, the nearly 400 orders are arranged so that the user may take a wide look at the universe, and at the same time choose to look at narrower views of particular subjects. While examining the way civilization and nature are organized, *The Order of Things* also gives answers and provokes questions.

As a directory to hierarchies, *The Order of Things* can speed access to related information. Its goal is to find the appropriate organizing principle for different subjects. With over 80 illustrations, this book is also a visual reference that can demystify the explicit, and some implicit, hierarchies of the world, and provide a link to encyclopedias, dictionaries, and books on more specific subject matter: the whole reference world. Since many of us are "specialists," but at the same time are curious about other interesting subjects, *The Order of Things* is here to make sense of our detailed, complex world.

The book puts things into clearer focus by presenting the frameworks and orderings of the mass of information in all major subject areas, and may even be utilized as a creativity tool. Its logical structure and word associations can assist in brainstorming, aid in preliminary research, and provide a source of words and facts for writing or fun.

The Order of Things is aimed at all those who need or want to know about the structure of and within a wide range of fields. It addresses both the needs and the curiosities of every one of us. It is neither an encyclopedia, thesaurus, standard dictionary, reverse dictionary, nor visual dictionary. The book can be used for business information, for trivia questions—even for seeking creative nudges when writing a letter or considering a topic for a doctoral dissertation. *The Order of Things* is unique.

* * *

The Order of Things presents thirteen broad subject areas and within those areas the hierarchies, structures, and orders are listed alphabetically. The book is set up so that information is easily found and highly understandable. We have tried to arrange the book's chapters so that they segue/proceed one to the next in a natural "order":

EARTH SCIENCES & GEOGRAPHY
LIFE SCIENCES
PHYSICAL SCIENCES
TECHNOLOGY
MATHEMATICS & MEASUREMENT
RELIGION
HISTORY
SOCIETY & SOCIAL INSTITUTIONS
BUSINESS & ECONOMY
THE ARTS
DOMESTIC LIFE
SPORTS & RECREATION
GENERAL KNOWLEDGE

The Order of Things relies on the hierarchies themselves to tell their specific "stories." Their "levels" are made evident through typography, and descriptions are only added for difficult words. For example, the Boy Scout rankings will tell the names of each level, but will not describe their specific roles in the group. The motion picture crew will list each member, but will not provide definitions of each participant. We do, however, attempt to clarify orders that leave much room for curiosity, such as the major Hindu gods. The mission of *the Order of Things* is to show best the structure of the various parts of the world's civilization and nature.

The Order of Things

Here hills and vales, the woodland and the plain,
Here earth and water seem to strive again, Not
chaos-like together crush'd and bruis'd, But, as
the world, harmoniously confus'd: Where order
in variety we see, And where, though all things
differ, all agree.

—Alexander Pope, *Windsor Forest*

CHAPTER ONE

EARTH SCIENCES & GEOGRAPHY

ATMOSPHERE

ATMOSPHERIC LAYERS

homosphere (lower of two portions of atmosphere, from surface to 50–62 mi (80–100 km))

heterosphere (upper of two portions of atmosphere, above 50–62 mi (80–100 km), closely coinciding with ionosphere and thermosphere)

troposphere (0–11 mi (18 km), densest, where life and weather are concentrated)

tropopause (layer joining tropo- and stratospheres)

stratosphere (11–30 mi (18–50 km)) (includes ozonesphere)

stratopause (layer joining strato-and mesosphere)

mesosphere (31–50 mi (50–80 km)) (also called lower ionosphere; airglow and ozone band)

mesopause (layer joining meso- and thermosphere)

thermosphere (50–250 mi (80–400 km))

thermopause (layer joining thermo- and exosphere)

exosphere or magnetosphere (250 mi to 40,000 mi (400–64,000 km))

ionosphere (30–250 mi (50–400 km); includes mesosphere and thermosphere)

D-layer or D region (35–55 mi (56–88 km)): absorbs energy of shortwave radio waves reflected by other layers

Heaviside-Kennelly layer, E-layer, or E region (55–95 mi (88–154 km)): during the day, reflects radio waves

Appleton layer, F-layer, or F region (95–250 mi (154–400 km)): reflects radio waves of up to 50 Mhz

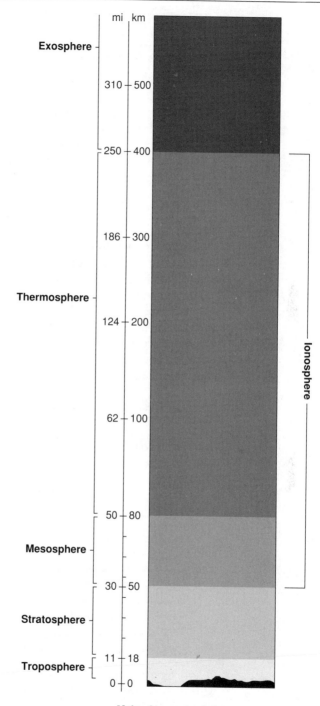

Major Atmospheric Layers

CAVES

CAVE FORMATION

1. Surface of a lava flow cools and solidifies.
2. As molten interior of lava field drains off, it leaves cylindrical cavity.
3. Pressure from hot gases sustains the ceiling of the cavity.

also

1. Naturally acidic rainwater dissolves region made of limestone rock; chemical dissolution of host rock that is weakened by fracturing and erosion.
2. Small cracks form.
3. Cracks widen to create deep holes.
4. Holes become underground caves and rivers as water continues to erode the rock.

TYPES

Primary: lava tubes, cylindrically shaped tunnels along the path of a lava field, e.g. coral cave

Secondary: produced by mechanical and chemical processes, e.g. marine grotto

CITIES

LARGEST CITIES

(by population of city proper and metropolitan area, thousands)

Tokyo, Japan (26,400)
Mexico City, Mexico (18,100)
Mumbai (Bombay), India (18,100)
São Paulo, Brazil (17,800)
New York, NY, US (16,600)
Lagos, Nigeria (13,400)
Los Angeles, CA, US (13,100)
Calcutta, India (12,900)
Shanghai, China (12,900)
Buenos Aires, Argentina (12,600)
Dhaka, Bangladesh (12,300)
Karachi, Pakistan (11,800)
Delhi, India (11,700)

SEVEN HILLS OF ROME

(north to south)

Aventine
Coelian
Palatine
Capitoline
Esquiline
Viminal
Quirinal

CLIMATES AND CLIMATIC REGIONS

BIOMES (ASSOCIATED WITH A PLACE)

tropical rain forest (South America)
tropical seasonal/monsoon forest (Southeast Asia)
giant temperate rain forest (northwest US)
montane rain forest/thicket (tropics)
temperate deciduous forest (eastern US)
temperate evergreen forest (all continents except Antarctica)
taiga/boreal forest (North America)
elfin woodlands (mountainous tropics)
thorn forest/woodlands (tropics)
thorn scrub (tropics)
temperate woodlands (all continents)
temperate shrublands (all continents)
savannas (South America)
temperate grasslands (North America)

alpine meadows (high elevations)
Arctic tundra (northern North
America)
tropical desert (North Africa)
warm-temperate desert (south-
central Asia)
cool-temperate semidesert scrub
(western US)
Arctic-Alpine desert (Greenland)
bog (Ireland, Scotland)
tropical freshwater-swamp forest
(Amazon)
temperate freshwater-swamp forest
(southeastern US)
mangrove swamp (tropical coasts)
marsh (all continents)
marine pelagic (plankton of open
oceans, all continents)
marine benthos (ocean bottom, all
continents)
marine rocky littoral (animals and
algae on rocky coasts, all
continents)
marine sandy littoral (animals and
algae on or in sandy coasts, all
continents)
estuarine and marine mudflat (algae,
animals, plankton in mud, all
continents)
freshwater lentic (lakes and ponds, all
continents)
freshwater lotic (streams and rivers,
all continents)

Rain Forests

Rain Forest Cycles
1. Water, oxygen, minerals, and
nutrients pass through the trees;
water that trees do not need is
given out through the leaves.
2. Oxygen is taken in during
respiration and given out during
photosynthesis.
3. Carbon dioxide is given out during
respiration and taken in during
photosynthesis.

4. Dead leaves (and other organisms)
fall to the ground.
5. Bacteria and fungi in the soil break
down the dead material; trees take
up the nutrients through their roots.
6. Warmth and moisture recycles
nutrients from the soil via the trees
to the forest canopy.

Rain Forest Layers
1. emergent layer, 200 ft above
ground: isolated trees towering
above
2. canopy, 100–165 ft, tall straight
trees form dense, unbroken region
3. lower canopy, 40–100 ft
4. understory, 10–20 ft: young trees,
small conical trees, shrubs
5. ground layer/floor vegetation

CLIMATIC ZONES

polar icecap (South Pole, Antarctica)
polar tundra (western Greenland)
boreal (Siberia)
temperate
  cold temperate (northern Canada)
  cool temperate maritime (London)
    (also cool coastal desert: Lima,
    Peru)
  highland (Quito, Ecuador)
    (also middle-latitude dry: North
    Dakota)
  warm temperate (Greece)
    (also temperate oceanic: Paris)
    (also temperate continental:
    Montreal, New York)
tropical
  subtropical humid (Charleston,
    South Carolina)
  subtropical dry (Perth, Australia)
  tropical-subtropical dry (Phoenix)
  tropical desert (Egypt)
  tropical wet-and-dry (Calcutta)
  tropical wet/monsoon (Myanmar,
    Singapore)

DESERTS

(by area in square miles/square kilometers)

Sahara, Africa (3,500,000/9,000,000)
Great Australian, Australia
  (1,470,000/3,800,000)
Arabian, Arabia (502,000/1,300,000)
Gobi, Asia (400,000/1,036,000)
Kalahari, Africa (201,000/520,000)
Turkestan, Asia (174,000/450,000)
Taklamakan, China (125,000/327,000)

Namib, Africa (120,000/310,000)
Sonoran, U.S./Mexico
  (120,000/310,000)

Somali, Africa (100,000/260,000)
Thar, India/Pakistan
  (100,000/260,000)

ZOOGEOGRAPHICAL REGIONS

Holarctic
  Palaearctic (Europe, northern
    Africa, northern Middle East,
    north and central Asia)
  Nearctic (North America and
    Greenland)
Neotropical (Central and South
  America to central Mexico,
  Caribbean)
Ethiopian (sub-Saharan Africa,
  Madagascar, southern Middle
  East)
Oriental (southern Asia and islands)
Australian/Australasian (Australia,
  Oceania)
Antarctic (Antarctica)

ZOOGEOGRAPHICAL REALMS

Neogea = Neotropical
Notogea = Australia/Australasian
Metagea = Holarctic, Oriental, and
  Ethiopian
Antarctica = Antarctic

CONTINENTS

POPULATION

Asia 3,466,800,000
Africa 760,770,000
Europe 727,464,000
South America 337,094,000
North America 462,051,000
Australia 18,613,087

SURFACE AREA

(largest to smallest)

Asia
Africa
North America
South America
Antarctica
Europe
Australia-Oceania

DEPRESSIONS

WORLD'S DEEPEST

(maximum depth below sea level in feet/meters)

Dead Sea	Jordan-Israel	1,296/395
Turfan Depression	China	505/153
Qattara Depression	Egypt	436/132
Poluostrov Mangyshlak	Kazakhstan	433/131
Danakil Depression	Ethiopia	383/116
Death Valley	California, U.S.	282/86
Salton Sink	California, U.S.	235/71
Zapadnyy Chink Ustyurta	Kazakhstan	230/70
Prikaspiyskaya Nizmennost	Russia-Kazakhstan	220/67
Ozera Sarykamysh	Uzbekistan-Turkmenistan	148/45

EARTHQUAKES

MERCALLI SCALE

(Mercalli number, intensity, effects, Richter number)

   I. Instrumental, Detected by seismographs and some animals, < 3.5
  II. Feeble, Noticed by sensitive people at rest, 3.5
 III. Slight, Similar to vibration from passing truck; hanging objects swing, 4.2
  IV. Moderate, Felt generally indoors; things rattle and parked cars rock; 4.5
   V. Rather strong, Felt generally; most sleepers wake, 4.8
  VI. Strong, Trees shake, chairs fall over, some damage, 5.4
 VII. Very strong, General alarm; walls crack, plaster falls, 6.1
VIII. Destructive, Chimneys, columns, monuments, weak walls fall, 6.5
  IX. Ruinous, Some houses collapse as ground cracks, 6.9
   X. Disastrous, Many buildings destroyed; railway lines bend, 7.3
  XI. Very disastrous, Few buildings survive; landslides and floods, 8.1
 XII. Catastrophic, Total destruction; ground forms waves, > 8.1

RICHTER SCALE

(number, effects)

2.0–2.9 Not felt by many; perceived by sensitive seismographic machines
3.0–3.9 Slight vibration; hanging objects swing

4.0–4.9 Vibration; small objects move and rattle
5.0–5.9 Furniture moves, masonry cracks and falls
6.0–6.9 Difficulty standing; walls and chimneys collapse partially
7.0–7.9 Buildings collapse; cracks in ground, landslides
8.0–8.9 Damage to underground structures; rock masses moved

EARTHQUAKE SEQUENCE

two tectonic plates meet

tectonic plates split or slip by one another (type of contact determines shallow or deep earthquake)

intense forces overcome the friction between the plates

plates become locked, forces build up, and eventually the plates lurch into new positions, creating an earthquake

TECTONIC PLATES

African
Antarctic
Arabian
Carribean
Cocos
Eurasian
Indian-Australian
Juan de Fuca
Nazca
Pacific
Phillipine
North American
Scotia
South American

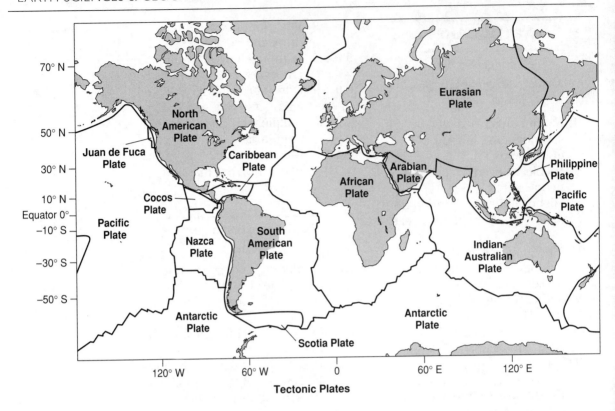

Tectonic Plates

EARTH SCIENCES

ATMOSPHERIC SCIENCES

aeronomy: study of earth's and other planets' atmosphere

meteorology: study of atmosphere and its phenomena

climatology: study of physical state of atmosphere

GEOLOGICAL SCIENCES

astrogeology: application of geology, geochemistry, geophysics to moon and other planets

economic geology: geology applied to engineering and materials usage

engineering geology: geology applied to civil engineering

environmental geology: geology applied to environmental concerns

petroleum geology: geology applied to hydrocarbon fuel technology

urban geology: geology applied to urban concerns

geobotanical prospecting: use of plants to locate ore deposits

geobotany: study of plants in relation to geologic environment

geochemistry: study of chemical makeup of earth and its processes

geochronology: dating of events in earth's history

radiometric dating: using radioisotopes to date events

geochronometry: study of absolute age of rocks by measuring radioactive decay geocosmogony: study of the origin of the earth

geomorphology: study of the origin of secondary topographic features of earth

geophysics: physics of earth and its environment

geodesy: study of size, shape, gravitational field, etc. of earth

glacial geology: study of land features resulting from glaciation

mineralogy: study of minerals

crystallography: study of geometric description of crystals

structural geology: study of form, arrangement, and internal structure of rocks

paleontology: study of life as recorded in fossils

invertebrate paleontology: fossils of invertebrates

micropaleontology: fossils of microfossils

paleobotany: fossils of plants

palynology: fossils of spores, pollen, microorganisms

vertebrate paleontology: fossils of vertebrates

petrology: study of origin, history, structure etc. of rocks

igneous petrology

metamorphic petrology

sedimentary petrology

physical geology: study of composition of earth and its physical changes

seismology: study of earthquakes

stratigraphy: study of rock strata

historical geology: study of bedded rocks

volcanology: study of volcanoes

HYDROLOGIC SCIENCES

glaciology: study of glaciers

hydrology: study of waters of earth

limnology: study of lakes

oceanography: study of oceans

PHYSICAL GEOGRAPHY

analysis, classification, description of features of earth's surface

EARTH STRUCTURES

EARTH LAYERS

1. continental crust: thin layer of hard rock 4–44 mi (6–60 km) thick; temperature at bottom of crust about 1900° F; consists of calcium-iron-magnesium silicates below and aluminum-sodium-potassium silicates above

2. oceanic crust: large, water-filled hollows in crust; average depth 2.2 mi (3.2 km); same composition as lower continental crust

3. mantle: dense, semi-molten layer of iron-magnesium silicates about 1,800 mi (2,896 km) thick, temperature rises to 6700° F; thicker under oceans than continents

4. outer core: molten 90% iron, 9% nickel, and 1% sulfur about 1240 mi (1995 km) thick, temperature approx. 4000° F

5. inner core: dense, hot layer of 90% iron, 9% nickel, and 1% sulfur about 1712 mi (2754 km) thick, temperature approx 8100° F

FOLD CLASSIFICATION

true or flexure fold: formed by compression of strong rock

flow fold: formed in weak rock

shear fold: formed by small movements along cleavagelike fractures

Structure of the Earth

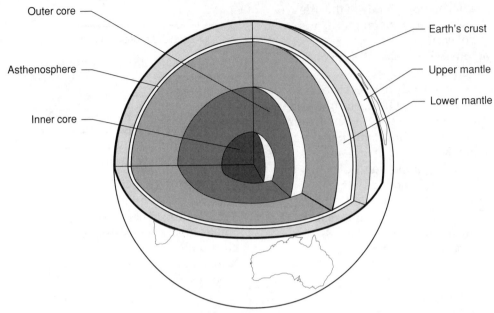

Outer core

Earth's crust

Asthenosphere

Upper mantle

Lower mantle

Inner core

drag fold: formed in weak rock by slip
along sedimentary rock plane

OPENINGS IN EARTH'S CRUST

canyon (very deep valley)
gorge (narrow canyon with steep
walls)
valley/col (depression between
mountains or raised land)
dale (broad valley)
ravine (deep valley)
glen (narrow valley
dell (small valley, often wooded)
dingle (narrow dell)
hollow/notch (small valley)
fissure (narrow opening created by
land mass movement, as from
an earthquake)
trench (long hole or ditch, often
created by running water)
gully (deep trench)

ELEMENTS

CARBON CYCLE IN AIR

1. Carbon dioxide is in the
atmosphere; volcanoes also
release carbon dioxide
2. Green plants (during
photosynthesis) and some
bacteria take in carbon dioxide
and use it to make food
3. Animals eat plants and take in
some of the carbon
4. Carbon dioxide is breathed out as
waste by plants and animals;
animal dung contains carbon
5. Dead plants and animals are
broken down by bacteria in soil
6. Decomposers such as fungi and
bacteria convert the carbon
compounds to carbon dioxide; the
cycle starts again

7. Remains of living organisms that have died form fossil fuels which when burnt release carbon dioxide

CARBON CYCLE IN WATER

1. Carbon dioxide dissolves in seawater
2. Some carbon dioxide evaporates back into air, some taken up by sea creatures' shells
3. After sea creatures die, carbon is locked in sediments for millions of years

CHEMICAL ELEMENTS ON EARTH

(percentage from most to least common)

oxygen, 48.86
iron, 18.84
silicon, 13.96
magnesium, 12.42
sulfur, 1.39
nickel, 1.39
aluminum, 1.31
sodium, 0.64
calcium, 0.46
phosphorus, 0.14
hydrogen, 0.12
chromium, 0.11
carbon, 0.10
potassium, 0.05
manganese, 0.05
cobalt, 0.05
chlorine, 0.04
titanium, 0.03
other, 0.04
Total: 100.00

NITROGEN CYCLE

1. Nitrogen gas is in the atmosphere
2. Nitrogen from the atmosphere is taken in by some plant roots; rain contains nitrogen in form of weak nitric acid
3. Some plants use nitrogen (for making proteins) from bacteria living on their roots
4. Some animals eat plant proteins
5. Manure and decaying plant and animal organisms release nitrogen compounds into the soil; some are converted by bacteria and fungi
6. Nitrifying bacteria convert nitrogen compounds into nitrates
7. Fertilizer/artificial nitrates added to soil
8. Plants absorb the nitrates through roots
9. Denitrifying bacteria break down nitrates and release nitrogen back into atmosphere

PHOSPHORUS CYCLE

1. Phosphorus enters soil when some rocks, such as clay, are weathered
2. Plants get phosphate from soluble phosphorus dissolved in soil water
3. Phosphorus is returned to soil in manure

POTASSIUM CYCLE

1. Plants get potassium from rocks, such as feldspars and micas dissolved in soil water
2. Potassium returns to soil in manure and from decay of plant and animal organisms

FOSSIL FUELS

CLASSIFICATION

coals
petroleum
tar sands and oil shales
natural gas

COAL FORMATION

1. Dying trees and plants fell into water of prehistoric swamps; remains became covered in mud
2. Peat layers formed as plant remains slowly dried out under the mud
3. Over millions of years, weight of overlying mud plus heat and pressure turned peat into lignite (brown coal). Lignite is dug from shallow pits called strip mines.
4. Intense heat and pressure turned deeper layers of peat into soft black (bituminous) coal and anthracite

COAL RANKS

(highest to lowest)

anthracite, greatest carbon content
bituminous coal
lignite/brown coal

COAL SIZES

grain (1/8–1/4 inch)
pea (1/4–1/2 inch)
single (1/2–1 inch)
double (1–2 inch)
treble (2–3 inch)
cobble (2–4 inch)
large cobble (3–6 inch)
large coal (6 inch)

NATURAL GAS FORMATION

1. In the sea, tiny plants sink and dead plants form layers on the sea bed and are buried in mud
2. On land, mud covers dead plants and trees and slowly hardens into rock; more layers of rock form and press down and heat the dead plants below

3. Pressure and heat slowly change sea plants into oil and then into gas [land plants first turn to coal, then become oil and gas]
4. A layer of rock traps the gas deposit
5. Movements of the earth can raise the gas deposit to above sea level.
6. Raw gas must be cleaned and dried before it is used as fuel

PETROLEUM / OIL FORMATION

1. Tiny plants and animals that lived in warm prehistoric seas die and decay and are buried beneath the sea bed.
2. When seabed sediments are lithified into porous rock, the organisms' remains turn gradually into oil.
3. Oil is drawn from ground as crude oil and refined to make fuels.

GEOGRAPHY

CLASSIFICATION

Cartography: mapping
Human geography:
    cultural and social geography: cultural and social values, tools, and organization
    economic geography: how people satisfy their needs and make a living
    historical geography: evolution of present patterns
    linguistic geography: language characteristics
    medical geography: health and diseases, malnutrition, health-care facilities
    political geography: political organization

population geography: distribution of population in relation to certain characteristics

social geography: social characteristics

urban geography: concentration in cities and metropolitan areas

Physical geography:

biogeography: distribution and ecology of plants and animals

ecology: interaction between organisms and their environment

phytogeography: concerning plants

zoogeography: concerning animals

climatology and meteorology: study of state of atmosphere

geomorphology: study of the forms and processes of land's surface

paleogeography: study of the geography of the past

resource management and environmental studies

soil geography: study of distribution and types of soil

Regional geography: associations within regions of all or some of the above elements

---

GEOLOGICAL TIME

Eras and Periods

(formation of earth as a planet till written history)

Precambrian Era

Archeozoic Era (5 billion years ago-1.5 bill)

Proterozoic Era (1.5 bill-600 mill)

Paleozoic Era

Cambrian Period (600–500 mill)

Ordovician Period (500–440 mill)

Silurian Period (440–400 mill)

Devonian Period (400–350 mill)

EARTH COORDINATE SYSTEM

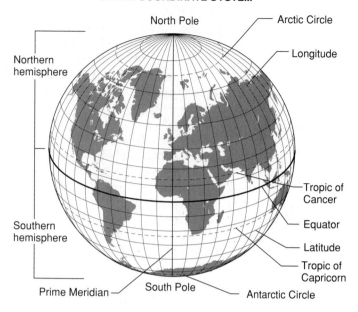

Carboniferous Period:

Mississippian Period/Lower Carboniferous (350–300 mill)

Pennsylvanian Period/Upper Carboniferous (300–270 mill)

Permian Period (270–220 mill)

Mesozoic Era/Secondary Era

Triassic Period (220–180 mill)

Scythian

Anisian

Ladinian

Karnian

Norian

Rhaetian

Jurassic Period (180–135 mill)

Hettangian

Sinemurian

Pliensbachian

Toarcian

Aalenian

Bajocian

Bathonian

Callovian

Oxfordian

Kimmeridigian
Tithonian
[also, Lower Jurassic/Lias
213–183, Middle Jurassic/
Dogger 183–173, Upper
Jurassic/Malm 173–144]
Cretaceous Period (135–70 mill)
Cenozoic Era
Tertiary Period
Paleogene Period
Paleocene Epoch (70–60 mill)
Eocene Epoch (60–40 mill)
Oligocene Epoch (40–25 mill)
Neocene Period
Miocene Epoch (25–10 mill)
Pliocene Epoch (10–1 mill)
Quarternary Period
Pleistocene Epoch (1 mill-10,000)
Holocene or Recent Epoch
(10,000–present)

GEOLOGICAL TIME
(longer to shorter)

aeon/eon (made up of several eras;
largest division of geological time)
era (made up of several periods or
suberas)
subera (division of an era)
period (large division of geological
time, corresponds to a system—a
major stratigraphical division)
epoch (part of a period)
age (part of an epoch, corresponds to
a stage—a stratigraphical division
within a series)
chron (part of an age; smallest
division of geological time)

GEOLOGICAL COLUMN

Stratigraphical Divisions
(time-rock units)

system (corresponds to geological
period)

series (division within a system;
corresponds to an epoch)
stage (division within a series;
corresponds to an age)
chronozone (division within a stage;
corresponds to a chron)

ICE AGES

Glaciations, Interglacials, Interstadials

Gunz (Early Glaciation) Phase I
Gunz (Early Glaciation) Phase II
Prepenultimate Interglacial
Mindel (Prepenultimate Glaciation)
Phase I
Mindel (Prepenultimate Glaciation)
Phase II
Riss (Penultimate Glaciation) Phase I
Riss (Penultimate Glaciation) Phase II
Last Interglacial
Wurm (Last Glaciation) Phase I
First Wurm Interstadial
Wurm (Last Glaciation) Phase II
Final Interstadial
Wurm (Last Glaciation) Phase III
final recession of ice
Arctic or Dryas Phase (flora) with
warmer Allerod oscillation
Preboreal Phase (flora)
Boreal Phase (flora)
Atlantic Phase
Sub-boreal

Major classification

Huronian (1800 million years ago)
Varangian (570 million years ago)
Permo-Carboniferous (more than 30
glacial epochs, 280 million years ago)
Quaternary (at least eight major
glacial and interglacial cycles,
within past 3 million years)

Further classification

Huronian, earliest known
Precambrian ice age

Gnejso, earliest phase of Precambrian
ice age
Sturtian, middle phase of late
Precambrian ice age
Varangian, final phase of late
Precambrian ice age
Cambrian, a mild phase
Ordovician, affecting the Sahara
Desert
Permo-Carboniferous ice age,
glaciers covering much of the
southern hemisphere

Pleistocene ice age, most recent

1. Lower Pleistocene (Nebraskan
glacial phase) 1 million-450,000 yrs
2. Middle Pleistocene (Aftonian
pluvial, Kansanian glacial,
Yarmouthian pluvial, Illinoian
glacial phases) 450,000–100,000 yrs
3. Upper Pleistocene (Sangamonian
pluvial, Early Wisconsin, Mid
Wisconsin, Late Wisconsin glacial
phases) 100,000–10,000 yrs

GLACIATIONS, INTERGLACIATIONS
OF PLEISTOCENE EPOCH

North American Stages
(northern European, central European
stages) approximate end

Late Wisconsin (Weichselian, Wurm)
10,000 years ago
Mid Wisconsin (Eemian, R-W)
Interstadials
Early Wisconsin (Saalian, Riss) 45,000
Sangamonian (Holsteinian, M-R)
Interglacial
Illinoian (Elsterian, Mindel) 125,000
Yarmouth (Cromerian, G-M)
Interglacial
Kansan (Menapian, Gunz) 690,000
Aftonian (Waalian, D-G) Interglacial
Nebraskan (Eburonian, Danube)
1,600,000 years ago

ISLANDS

LARGEST ISLANDS

(by relative area, largest first,
sq mi/sq km in thousands)

Island	Area	Sovereignty
Greenland	840/2,175	Danish
New Guinea	316/818	Papua New Guinean/ Indonesian
Borneo	290/750	Indonesian, Malaysian, Bruneian
Madagascar	227/590	Malagasy
Baffin Island	190/492	Canadian
Sumatra	164/425	Indonesian
Honshu	88/230	Japanese
Great Britain	88/228	British
Victoria Island	80/208	Canadian
Ellesmere Island	76/198	Canadian
Sulawesi	72/189	Indonesian
South Island	58/150	New Zealand
Java	51/132	Indonesian
North Island	44/114	New Zealand
Cuba	44/114	Cuba
Newfoundland	42/110	Canadian
Luzon	40/104	Philippine
Iceland	39/102	Iceland
Mindanao	36/94	Philippine
Novaya Zemlya	35/90	Russian

TYPES

continental island (part of neighboring
continental rock structure: Great
Britain, Manhattan, Long Island,
Bahamas)

barrier islands: made of quartz sand,
where continental shelf is broad
and gently sloping
mangrove islands: form in calm
shallow water in semitropical
regions
channel islands: found in rivers and
deltas

oceanic island (built of lava from submarine volcanoes: Hawaii)

volcanic island (Iceland)
coral island
cay (flat coral island)

MINERALS & ROCKS

CRYSTAL SYSTEMS

(each with different axes of symmetry and distinctive shapes)

cubic: halite
tetragonal: zircon
orthorhombic: staurolite
hexagonal: quartz
monoclinic: orthoclase
triclinic: albite

MINERAL CATEGORIES

abrasives: corundum, diamond, kaolin
ceramics: feldspar, quartz
chemical minerals: halite, sulfur, borax
fertilizers: phosphates
gem minerals: diamond, garnet, opal, zircon
lime, cement, and plaster: calcite, gypsum
natural pigments: hematite, limonite
optical and scientific apparatus: quartz, mica, tourmaline
ores of metals: crhomite, cinnabar, molybdenite, galena, sphalerite
ornamental objects and structural material: agate, calcite, gypsum
refractories: asbestos, graphite, magnesite, mica

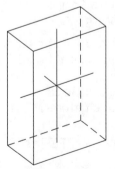

Isometric (Cubic) Crystal

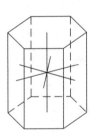

Hexagonal Crystal

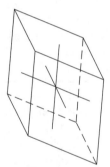

Triclinic Crystal

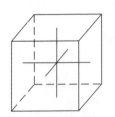

Monoclinic Crystal

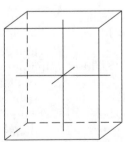

Orthorhombic Crystal

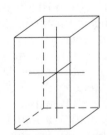

Tetragonal Crystal

Types of Crystals

MINERAL CLASSIFICATION

Nonsilicate minerals

native elements: gold, silver, copper, platinum, iron, diamond, sulfur, graphite
sulfides and sulfarsenides: pyrrhotite, cinnabar, pyrite, molybdenite, galena
sulfosalts: pyrargyrite
oxides and hydroxides: cuprite, corundum, hematite
halides: halite, fluorite, galena, sylvite
carbonates: calcite, dolomite
nitrates: nitratite, nitre
borates: colemanite, borax
sulfates: barite, gypsum, anhydrite
phosphates: turquoise, apatite

Silicate minerals

garnet, zircon, topaz, talc, mica, quartz, feldspar, pyroxene, zeolite and amphibole families

MOHS' SCALE OF MINERAL HARDNESS

(hard to soft)

ADDED ENTRIES TO REVISED SCALE:

15 diamond
14 boron carbide
13 silicon carbide
12 fused alumina
11 fused zirconium oxide

cannot be scratched by knife or file:

10 diamond (revised scale, garnet)
9 corundum, sapphire, ruby (revised scale, topaz)
8 topaz (revised scale, quartz)

can be scratched by streak plate

7 quartz, rock crystal (revised scale, vitreous pure silica)

can be scratched by glass plate or steel needle:

6 orthoclase, feldspar

can be scratched by knife or file:

5 apatite
4 fluorite

can be scratched by copper penny:

3 calcite

can be scratched by fingernail:

2 gypsum, rock salt
1 talc

ROCK CLASSES

magma: molten rock
igneous rock: formed from molten magma
  extrusive: ejected by volcanoes
  intrusive: beneath surface
  pyroclastic: from deposits of explosive volcanic eruptions
  also classified:
  plutonic: mineral grain sizes visible to naked eye
  volcanic/hypabyssal: too fine-grained or glassy to be observed without microscope
sedimentary rock, weathered, eroded, or biologically reconstituted remains of igneous or metamorphic rock

clastic/crystalline: made of broken bits of pre-existing rocks
nonclastic:
  carbonate/organic/biogenic: built up from the remains of living things
  noncarbonate/chemical: forms when salt and other substances dissolved in water are separated from the solution
metamorphic rock: igneous or sedimentary rock reformed under intense heat or pressure
regional/dynamic: deep in crust, at heart of mountain ranges
thermal/contact: made by heat from nearby igneous rock

ROCK CYCLE

deposition: accumulation into beds, veins, masses by natural agent
lithification: conversion of newly deposited sediment into rock; change of coal to shale or other rock
fusion: change of a solid to liquid
solidification: change of a liquid to solid
metamorphism: changes in rock in response to environmental conditions on earth's surface
erosion: loosening and transportation of rock on earth's surface; wearing away by weather and water
intrusion/emplacement of new material from earth's interior

ROCK-FORMING MINERAL GROUPS

Feldspars and feldspathoids
Amphiboles: tremolite
Pyroxenes: augite
Quartz and other silica minerals: quartz, opal

Micas
Olivines: tephroite
Garnets
Clay minerals
Calcite
Dolomite
Other rock-forming minerals: halite, pyrite, gypsum, etc.

ROCKS BY SITUATION

basement rock: igneous or metamorphic, usu. Pre-Cambrian that is overlain by sedimentary rock
bedrock: rock underlying soil or other surface material
country rock: rock that surrounds and is penetrated by mineral veins
source rock: rock from which a sediment is derived

ROCK SIZES

(largest to smallest in size and grain, according to Wentworth-Udden scale)

boulder (10 in; 256 mm)
cobblestone/cobble (2.5–10 in; 64–256 mm)
pebble (1.5–2.5 in; 4–64 mm)
granule/gravel (.75–1.5 in; 2–4 mm)
sand (very coarse, coarse, medium, fine, very fine)(1/16–2 mm)
silt (coarse, medium, fine, very fine) (1/256–1/16 mm)
clay (less than 1/256 mm)
colloid (less than .0024 mm)

ROCK STRATA

(lowest to highest, oldest to youngest)

1. metamorphic rock
2. conglomerate
3. sandstone
4. limestone
5. alluvium

ROCKY SHORE ZONES

(often clearly marked by the types of seaweed)

upper shore: green seaweeds and animals that can survive out of the water the longest

middle shore: darker seaweeds and animals that cannot survive long out of the water

lower shore: brown seaweeds and animals that cannot survive out of water

MOUNTAINS

CLASSIFICATION

dome: comparatively flat, dissected surface that gradually slopes toward lowlands (as in Black Hills, South Dakota)

fault-block: segments uplifted along linear fracture zones (as in Sierra Nevada)

fold: formed by lateral compression and uplift, occurring near basins of sedimentary rock layers (as in parts of Appalachian system)

volcanic: usually in fault zones and subduction zones

built by active volcano (Mount Fuji, Japan)

built by residual products of volcano (Devils Tower, Wyoming)

HIGHEST MOUNTAINS

(by continent, thousands of ft/m)

Everest, Asia (29/8.8)
Aconcagua, South America (22.8/6.9)
McKinley, North America (20.3/6.2)
Kilimanjaro, Africa (19.3/5.9)
Elbrus, Europe (18.5/5.6)

Vinson Massif, Antarctica (16.9/5.1)
Kosciusko, Australia (7.3/2.2)

MOUNTAIN STRUCTURE

(top to bottom)

summit or peak (top)

alpine zone (end of treeline: hardy mosses and some flora)

foothills (at base of mountain, but not part of peak; three altitudes— high, middle, and low where plants and trees grow)

base (lowest point from which horizontal plane can be measured)

MOUNT RUSHMORE PRESIDENTS

(left to right)

Washington
Jefferson
Theodore Roosevelt
Lincoln

RANGES—LONGEST

Range	Locality	Length
Cordillera de Los Andes	South America	4500 mi (7200 km)
Rocky Mountains	North America	3000 mi (4800 km)
Himalaya-Karakoram-Hindu Kush	Central Asia	2400 mi (3800 km)
Great Dividing Range	Australia	2250 mi (3600 km)
Trans-Antarctic Mountains	Antarctica	2200 mi (3500 km)
Brazilian Atlantic Coast Range	Brazil	1900 mi (3000 km)
West Sumatran-Javan Range	Sumatra-Java	1800 mi (2900 km)
Aleutian Range	Alaska-NW Pacific	1650 mi (2650 km)
Tien Shan	Kyrgyzstan-China	1400 mi (2250 km)
Central New Guinea Range (Papua New Guinea)	New Guinea	1250 mi (2000 km)

NATIONS OF THE WORLD

AFRICA

Northern Africa
(largest to smallest by area)

Algeria
Sudan
Libya
Egypt
Morocco
Western Sahara
Tunisia

Central Africa
(largest to smallest)

Democratic Republic of the Congo
Chad
Angola
Central African Republic
Cameroon
Congo
Gabon
Equatorial Guinea
Sao Tome and Principe

Southern Africa
(largest to smallest)

South Africa
Namibia
Botswana
Lesotho
Swaziland

Eastern Africa
(largest to smallest)

Ethiopia
Tanzania
Mozambique
Zambia
Somalia
Madagascar
Kenya
Zimbabwe
Uganda
Eritrea
Malawi
Burundi
Rwanda
Djibouti
Réunion
Comoros
Mauritius
Seychelles

Western Africa
(largest to smallest)

Niger
Mali
Mauritania
Nigeria
Côte d'Ivoire
Burkina Faso
Guinea
Ghana
Senegal
Benin
Liberia
Sierra Leone
Togo
Guinea Bissau
The Gambia
Cape Verde
Saint Helena

THE AMERICAS

North America
(largest to smallest)

Canada
United States
Mexico

Central America
(largest to smallest)

Nicaragua
Honduras
Guatemala
Panama
Costa Rica

Belize
El Salvador

South America
(largest to smallest)

Brazil
Argentina
Peru
Bolivia
Colombia
Venezuela
Chile
Paraguay
Ecuador
Guyana
Uruguay
Suriname
French Guiana

Caribbean
(largest to smallest)

Cuba
Dominican Republic
Haiti
Jamaica
Bahamas
Puerto Rico
Trinidad and Tobago
Guadeloupe
Martinique
Netherlands Antilles
Dominica
St. Lucia
Antigua and Barbuda
Barbados
Turks and Caicos Islands
US Virgin Islands
Grenada
St. Vincent and the Grenadines
St. Kitts and Nevis
Cayman Islands
Aruba
British Virgin Islands
Montserrat
Anguilla

AUSTRALASIA
(largest to smallest)

Australia
Papua New Guinea
New Zealand
Solomon Islands
Fiji
Vanuatu
Samoa
Tonga
Kiribati
Micronesia
Palau
Marshall Islands
Tuvalu
Nauru

Middle East
(largest to smallest)

Saudi Arabia
Iran
Yemen
Iraq
Oman
Syria
Jordan
United Arab Emirates
Israel
Kuwait
Qatar
Lebanon
Bahrain

ASIA

Central Asia
(largest to smallest)

Russian Federation
Kazakhstan
Ukraine
Turkmenistan
Uzbekistan
Belarus

Kyrgystan
Tajikistan
Azerbaijan
Georgia
Moldova
Armenia

Eastern Asia
(largest to smallest)

China
Mongolia
Japan
North Korea
South Korea
Taiwan
Macao

Southeastern Asia
(largest to smallest)

Indonesia
Burma (Myanmar)
Thailand
Malaysia
Vietnam
Philippines
Laos
Cambodia
Brunei
Singapore

Southern Asia
(largest to smallest)

India
Pakistan
Afghanistan
Nepal
Bangladesh
Sri Lanka
Bhutan
Maldives

EUROPE

Eastern Europe
(largest to smallest)

Poland
Romania
Bulgaria
Hungary
Czech Republic
Lithuania
Latvia
Slovakia
Estonia

Northern Europe
(largest to smallest)

Sweden
Norway
Finland
Iceland
Denmark

Southern Europe
(largest to smallest)

Republic of Turkey
Spain
Italy
Greece
Serbia
Portugal
Yugoslavia
Croatia
Bosnia & Herzegovina
Albania
Macedonia
Slovenia
Andorra
San Marino
Holy See (Vatican City)

Western Europe
(largest to smallest)

France
Germany
United Kingdom

Austria
Ireland
Switzerland
Netherlands
Belgium
Luxembourg
Liechtenstein
Monaco

NATIONS WITH LONGEST COASTLINES

Canada, 152,110 mi/244,800 km
Russia, 64,000 mi/103,000 km
Indonesia, 25,000 mi/40,000 km
Australia, 22,826 mi/36,735 km
Japan, 20,684 mi/33,287 km
Norway, 13,264 mi/21,347 km
USA, 12,380 mi/19,924 km
China, 11,500 mi/18,500 km

NATIONS WITH SHORTEST COASTLINES

Monaco, 3.5 mi/5.6 km
Nauru, 12 mi/19 km
Bosnia, 13 mi/20 km
Jordan, 16 mi/25 km
Slovenia, 19 mi/30 km
Zaire, 24 mi/39 km
Iraq, 28 mi/45 km
Togo, 31 mi/50 km
Belgium, 41 mi/66 km

OCEANS & SEAS

CORAL REEF FORMATION

1. Corals grow in shallow water (bright sunlight makes them grow) around island
2. Coral reef builds up as island sinks, due to movements in Earth's surface
3. Island disappears, leaving an atoll (ring of coral reefs)

OCEAN CURRENTS

Warm Currents

North Pacific
Alaska
Kuro Shio
Gulf Stream
North Equatorial
South Equatorial
Counter Equatorial
Brazil
Indian Counter Equatorial
Equatorial
East Australian

Cold Currents

California
Oya Shio
Canaries
Peru
Benguela
West Wind Drift
West Australian

OCEAN FLOOR LAYERS

continental shelf: nearly level part of sea floor, next to land mass, over which the sea is not more than 180–200m deep
continental slope: sloping part of sea floor from outer edge of continental shelf
continental rise: gently sloping surface between continental slope and abyssal plain
neritic zone: part of sea floor from low tide mark to the outer edge of continental shelf
marginal plateau: level part of sea floor, usu. between 240–2400m depth
submarine plateau: generally flat area that is higher than the rest of the ocean floor

NATIONS OF THE WORLD

OCEANS & SEAS

abyssal plain: level area of deep ocean floor

OCEAN ZONES

layers by biological habitat

pelagic (free, active) (water region)
  neritic zone: to 200 m (656 ft.)
  oceanic zone: below 200m
benthic (living on sea bottom)
    (seafloor region)
  intertidal zone: between high and
    low tide
  sublittoral zone: down to 200 m
  bathyal zone: 200–4000 m
    (656–13120 ft.)
  abyssal zone: 4000–5,000 m
    (13120–16400 ft.)
  hadal zone: deeper than 5,000 m

Ocean Zones Addendum

pelagic habitat = ocean from 33 ft
    (10 m) plus, above abyssal and
    beyond littoral (between high-
    and low-water marks) zones
neritic zone: low tide mark to outer
    edge of continental shelf
euphotic zone: sunlight to 300–330
    ft (90–100 m); limit of effective
    light for photosynthesis
inframedian zone: 330–600 ft
    (100–183 m)
bathyal/bathypelagic zone: little or
    no light, to about 5,900 ft
    (1800 m)
abyssal zone: vast depths, below
    5,900 ft (1800 m)
  abyssal plain: smooth floor of
    deep ocean, up to 16,400 ft
    (5000m) deep
benthic habitat=bottom/greatest
    depths of ocean/ocean floor
hadal zone: deep ocean trenches
    (over 4 miles (6.4 Km) in depth)

SEAS

LARGEST SEAS

*(by relative area, largest first,
millions of sq mi/sq km)*

Coral Sea (1.85/4.79)
Arabian Sea (1.49/3.86)
South China Sea (1.42/3.69)
Mediterranean Sea (0.97/2.52)
Bering Sea (0.89/2.30)
Bay of Bengal (0.84/2.17)
Sea of Okhotsk (0.61/1.59)
Gulf of Mexico (0.60/1.54)
Gulf of Guinea (0.59/1.53)
Barents Sea (0.54/1.41)

SEVEN SEAS

Antarctic
Arctic
Indian
North Atlantic
North Pacific
South Atlantic
South Pacific

WAVE CLASSIFICATION

tsunami or seismic waves: result of
    undersea earthquakes; often
    catastrophic
destructive waves: remove more
    material seawards than towards
    land
constructive waves: deposit
    sediments on beaches

CLASSIFICATION BY MOTION

longitudinal wave: direction of some
    vector characteristic of wave is
    along the direction of propagation
standing wave: wave in which ratio of
    instantaneous value does not vary
    with time

transverse wave: direction of disturbance is perpendicular to vector and parallel to surfaces of constant phase

WAVE HEIGHT SCALE

Code 0, 0 ft (0 m), glassy
Code 1, 0–1 ft (.3 m), calm
Code 2, 1–2 ft (.3–.6 m), rippled
Code 3, 2–4 ft (.6–1.2 m), choppy
Code 4, 4–8 ft (1.2–2.4 m), choppy
Code 5, 8–13 ft (2.4–4 m), rough
Code 6, 13–20 ft (4–6 m), very rough
Code 7, 20–30 ft (6–9 m) high
Code 8, 30–45 ft (9–14 m), very high
Code 9, 45+ ft, (14+ m) ultra high

RIVERS & LAKES

CYCLE OF EROSION

youth: river cuts deep V-shaped valleys
maturity: river meanders and wide valley forms
late maturity: floodplain widens, oxbow lakes develop, and meanders are pronounced

LONGEST RIVERS

(longest first, thousands of mi/km)

Nile, Africa (4.1/6.6)
Amazon, South America (4/6.4)
Ob-Irtysh, Russia (3.5/5.5)
Yangtze Kiang, China (3.4/5.5)
Huang Ho/Yellow, China (2.9/4.7)
Congo, Africa (2.9/4.7)
Amur, Russia (2.8/4.5)
Lena, Russia (2.6/4.3)
Mackenzie, Canada (2.6/4.2)
Mississippi, North America (2.5/4.0)

RIVER STAGES

1. Glacier to spring to tributary; vigorous erosion by water cutting downward
2. Floodplain formed by deposit of sediment; meandering and erosion/deposition
3. Delta formed when river sheds much sediment at the mouth

LAKES

Largest

Lake	Locality	Area (sq. mi/sq. km)
Caspian Sea	Asia	169,000/438,000
Superior	Canada-U.S.	31,820/82,415
Victoria	Kenya-Tanzania-Uganda	26,828/69,485
Aral Sea	Kazakhstan-Uzbekistan	26,166/67,770
Huron	Canada-U.S.	23,010/59,595
Michigan	U.S.	22,400/58,015
Baikal	Russian Federation	13,200/34,018
Tanganyika	Zaire-Tanzania	12,700/32,893
Great Bear Lake	Canada	12,275/31,792
Great Slave Lake	Canada	11,172/28,935
Malawi	Malawi-Mozambique-Tanzania	11,000/28,500
Chad	Chad-Niger-Nigeria	10,000/26,000
Erie	Canada-U.S.	9,940/25,745
Winnipeg	S. Manitoba	9,300/24,085
Ontario	Canada-United States	7,540/19,530
Balkhash	Kazakhstan	7,115/18,430
Ladoga	Russian Federation	7,000/18,000
Maracaibo	Venezuela	6,300/16,320
Onega	Russian Federation	3,764/9,750
Turkana	Kenya-Ethiopia	3,500/9,100

Great Lakes mnemonic

Homes

H Huron
O Ontario
M Michigan
E Erie
S Superior

Lake Layers

(freshwater, salt, and volcanic)

Pelagial zone: open-water area with plankton, bacteria, blue-green algae

Littoral zone: shallower area: higher forms of aquatic vegetation

Benthos: organic community of the lake bottom

WATERFALLS

Largest

(by height, ft/m)

Angel Falls, Venezuela (3212/979)
Tugela, South Africa (3110/948)
Utigord, Norway (2625/800)
Mongefossen, Norway (2540/774)
Yosemite, US (2425/739)
Ostre Mardola Foss, Norway (2154/657)
Tyssestrenggane, Norway (2120/646)
Kukenaom, Venezuela (2000/610)
Sutherland, New Zealand (1904/580)
Kjellfossen, Norway (1841/561)

WATERWAYS

river (water flowing downhill in a channel)
stream (small river)
   brook (small, freshwater stream)
   rivulet (small, saltwater stream)
     creek (even smaller)
     rill (smallest)
   streams also have hierarchy according to their tributaries:
   first order stream: from head to the first confluence with another stream
   second order stream: two first order streams converge
   third order stream: two second order streams converge

SOILS

CLASSIFICATION

(also called Seventh Approximation System, US Dept of Agriculture)

Entisol: young soils lacking horizons
Inceptisol: young soils with poor horizons (as in rice paddies)
Histosol: wet soils made of decaying plants
Oxisol: mature, well-leached soils with distinct oxic horizon
Ultisol: red soil, less leached, with clay argillic horizon
Alfisol: soil with clay argillic and ochric epipedon
Spodisol: podozolized soil with albic and spodic horizon
Mollisol: fertile soil with mollic epipedon
Aridisol: dry soil with salic, calcic, and gypsic horizon
Vertisol: dark soil with deep vertical cracks

HORIZONS

Oxic horizon: subsurface layer rich in iron and aluminum oxides
Albic horizon: sandy light horizon from which clay and iron oxides have been leached
Spodic horizon: dark layer below A-horizon from which humus and iron oxides have been leached
Calcic horizon: subsurface layer rich in calcium carbonate or magnesium carbonate
Salic horizon: accumulated mineral salts in desert soil
Gypsic horizon: subsurface layer rich in gypsum
Argillic epipedon: layer of clay, usually beneath A-horizon

Ochric epipedon: pale layer lacking organic matter

Mollic epipedon: dark surface layer rich in humus, calcium, and other minerals

LAYERS

top to bottom:

humus (Horizon O: decaying plant material and leaves)

topsoil (Horizon A: top layer where moisture seeps downward, dissolving chemical elements; minerals in the moisture enter streams, rivers, eventually seas)

subsoil (Horizon B: middle layer including iron oxides, clay, and other insoluble substances, touched by deep-rooted plants (like trees))

parent rock (Horizon C: bottom layer, combination of decomposed rock and shaly materials)

rock zone (Horizon D: underlying bedrock, layer of crumbled rocks)

SOIL CONSTITUENTS

air
humus
mineral salts
water
bacteria
rock particles

SOIL TEXTURES

clay soils (smallest grains)
silty soils (medium-sized)
sandy soils (largest grains)
loam soils (mixture of the three)

VOLCANOES

HIGHEST VOLCANOES

Volcano	Location	Height (ft/m)
Guallatiri	Northern Chile	19,882/6,060
Lascar	Northern Chile	19652/5,990
Cotopaxi	Northern Central Ecuador	19,498/5,943
El Misti	Southern Peru	19,200/5,880
Demavend	Northern Iran	18,606/5,670
Tupungatito	Central Chile	18,504/5,640
Nevado del Ruiz	West Central Colombia	17,720/5,401
Sangay	Central Ecuador	17,159/5,230
Cotocachi	Northern Ecuador	16,197/4,937
Klyechevskaya	Russian Federation	15,912/4,850
Puracé	Southern Colombia	15,420/4,700
Pasto	Southwestern Colombia	13,990/4,265
Mauna Loa	Central Hawaii, U.S.	13,680/4,170
Colima	Western Mexico	12,631/6,850
Fuji	Central Honshu, Japan	12,395/,3778

VOLCANIC ERUPTION

1. Magma chambers (red-hot molten rock) form deep underground
2. Pressure from hot gases forces magma to surface through main pipe and branches
3. Lava melts a hole and flows out or blocks the main pipe and explodes out. Lava, volcanic ash, and often, gas pour out
4. Lava and ash cool and solidify, building up a cone-shaped mountain around the central lava pipe

VOLCANOES
  Volcanic Eruption
    (cont.)
WATER

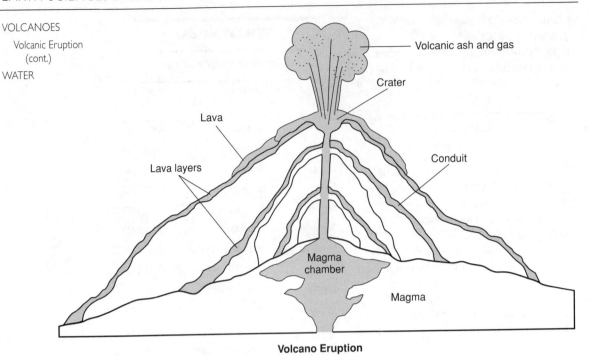

Volcano Eruption

Labels: Volcanic ash and gas · Crater · Lava · Lava layers · Conduit · Magma chamber · Magma

---

WATER

WATER BODIES

ocean: vast body of salt water, stretches between two continents

sea: large body of water with land on two or three sides; sometimes a part of an ocean

gulf: large body of water extending into land from an ocean or sea

bay: arm of body of water extending into land, smaller than a gulf

inlet: narrow passage, often between islands

fjord: sea inlet between cliffs or high banks

sound: an narrow arm of the sea

strait: narrow passage connecting two larger bodies of water

lake: large body of water surrounded by land

lagoon: shallow water separated from a larger body

pond: small body of water surrounded by land, often manmade

pool: still pond

puddle: small pool

WATER (HYDROLOGIC) CYCLE

1. fresh water present as water vapor in atmosphere and as ice and liquid water
2. precipitation as rain
3. surface runoff
4. evaporation of rain in falling
5. ground water flow to rivers and streams
6. ground water flow to the ocean
7. transpiration from plants
8. evaporation from lakes and ponds
9. evaporation from the soil
10. evaporation from rivers and streams

11. evaporation from the oceans
12. flow of rivers and streams to the oceans
13. ground water flow from the ocean to arid land
14. intense evaporation from arid land
15. movement of moist air from the oceans and to them
16. precipitation as snow
17. ice flows from the land into sea

WEATHER & METEOROLOGY

CLOUDS

Cloud Classification

high-level (3–8 mi; 5–13km)
  cirrus: light, fleecy
  cirrocumulus
  cirrostratus
  (also noctilescent: (glowing atmospheric methane at 50,000 ft))
middle-level (1.25–4.3 mi; 2–7 km)
  altocumulus
  altostratus
  nimbostratus
low-level (0–1.25 mi;0–2 km)
  stratocumulus
  stratus: horizontal, misty
  cumulus
  cumulonimbus

Cloud Cover

clear
scattered
broken (or partly overcast) (clouds block sunlight for several minutes at a time)
partly obscured (more clouds than clear sky)
overcast (continual haze)
obscured (complete cloud cover)

POLLUTANTS

Air Quality Standard Index

(Environmental Protection Agency & South Coast Air Quality Management District)

  0: good, no cautionary status
 50: moderate, no cautionary status
100: unhealthful, no cautionary status
200: very unhealthful, alert for elderly or ill to stay indoors and reduce physical activity
300: hazardous, alert for general population to stay indoors and reduce physical activity
400: extremely hazardous, emergency alert, all stay indoors, windows shut, no physical activity
500: toxic, significant harm alert

PRECIPITATION INTENSITY

fog 0.005 inches per hour
mist 0.002
drizzle 0.01
light rain 0.04
moderate rain 0.15
heavy rain 0.60
excessive rain 1.60
cloudburst 4.00

PRECIPITATION TYPES

(warmest air to coldest)

drizzle
rain
freezing drizzle
freezing rain
sleet
hail
snow

SEASONS

Hemisphere

March 20–21, northern=spring
(vernal equinox),
southern=autumn

June 21–22, northern=summer
(summer solstice),
southern=winter

September 22–23, northern=autumn
(autumnal equinox),
southern=spring

December 22–23, northern=winter
(winter solstice),
southern=summer

STORMS

cyclone, 0–50 mph, 500–100 miles
wide, week or more in duration

hurricane, 74–200 mph, 300–600
miles wide, week

tornado, 200–250 mph, 1/8 mile, few
minutes

thunderstorm, 20–30 mph, 1–2 miles,
hour or less

WIND

Force—Beaufort Scale for Wind Strength

Beaufort Number Speed	Description	(mph)
0	calm	1
1	light air	1–3
2	light breeze	47
3	gentle breeze	8–12
4	moderate breeze	13–18
5	fresh breeze	19–24
6	strong breeze	25–31
7	near gale	32–38
8	gale	39–46
9	strong gale	47–54
10	storm	55–63
11	violent storm	64–73
12	hurricane	74+

Hurricane Scale
(Saffir-Simpson)

1. minimal: 74–95 mph (119–153 kph), some plant and home damage
2. moderate: 96–110 mph (154–177 kph), trees down, some roof damage
3. extensive: 111–130 mph (178–209 kph), large trees uprooted; small buildings weakened
4. extreme: 131–155 mph (210–250 kph), signs destroyed; windows, doors, roofs heavily damage; flooding to 6 mi (10 km)inland; major damage to shoreline buildings
5. catastrophic: 156+ mph (250+ kph), shoreline buildings razed; small buildings overturned; roofs and walls of large buildings severely damaged

Small-Craft Advisory System
(National Weather Service; 1 knot = 1.15 mph (1.85 kph))

light wind, 6 knots or less
gust, 7–16 knots
squall, 16–32 knots
special marine warning, 32–34 knots
gale warning, 34–47 knots
tropical storm warning, 47–63 knots
storm warning, 48+ knots
hurricane warning, 64+ knots

Wind Barometer Table
(wind direction, barometer normalized to sea level, weather indication)

SW to NW, 30.10–30.20 and
steady=fair with slight temp.
changes for 1–2 days

SW to NW, 30.10–30.20 and rising
rapidly=fair and followed within 2
days by rain

SW to NW, 30.20 or above and

stationary=fair with no decided temp. change

SW to NW, 30.20 or above and falling slowly=slowly rising temp. and fair for 2 days

S to SE, 30.10–30.20 and falling slowly=rain within 24 hours

S to SE, 30.10–30.20 and falling rapidly=wind increasing and rain within 12–24 hours

SE to NE, 30.10–30.20 and falling slowly=rain in 12–18 hours

SE to NE, 30.10–30.20 and falling rapidly=wind increasing and rain within 12 hours

E to NE, 30.10 or above and falling slowly=light wind, rain anywhere from 24 hours to several days

E to NE, 30.10 or above and falling rapidly=rain (snow in winter) within 12–24 hours

SE to NE, 30.00 or below and falling slowly=rain 1–2 more days

SE to NE, 30.00 or below and falling rapidly=rain with high wind clearing within 36 hours (colder temps. follow in winter)

S to SW, 30.00 or below and rising slowly=clearing within hours and fair for several days

S to E, 29.80 or below and falling rapidly=severe storm coming followed by clearing within 24 hours (colder temps. follow in winter)

E to N, 29.80 or below and falling rapidly=severe gale and heavy precipitation (heavy snow and cold wave in winter)

going to W, 29.80 or below and rising rapidly=clearing and colder

Chaos often breeds life, when order breeds habit.

—Henry Brooks Adams, *The Education of Henry Adams*

CHAPTER TWO

LIFE SCIENCES

ANIMALS

AMPHIBIANS

Trachystomata (sirens)
Gymnophiona (caecilians)
Urodela or Caudata
  Hynobiidae (Asiatic salamanders)
  Cryptobranchidae (giant
    salamanders)
  Sirenidae (sirens and dwarf sirens)
  Proteidae (olm)
  Necturidae (mud puppies)
  Amphiumidae (congo eels)
  Salamandridae (salamanders and
    newts)
  Ambystomatidae (mole
    salamanders)
  Plethodontidae (lungless
    salamanders)
Anura
  Leiopelmatidae (primitive frogs)
  Discoglossidae (fire-bellied and
    midwife toads)
  Rhinophrynidae (burrowing toad)
  Pipidae (tongueless frogs)
  Pelobatidea (spadefoots)
  Myobatrachidae (terrestrial,
    arboreal, and aquatic frogs)
  Rhinodermatidae (mouth-breeding
    frogs)
  Leptodactylidae (terrestrial
    neotropical frogs)
  Bufonidae (true toads)
  Brachycephalidae (terrestrial toads)
  Dendrobatidae (arrow-poison
    frogs)
  Pseudidae (fully aquatic frogs)
  Centrolenidae (leaf frogs)
  Hylidae (tree frogs)
  Ranidae (true frogs)
  Sooglossidae (terrestrial frogs)
  Microhylidae (narrow-mouthed
    frogs)

ANIMAL CLASSIFICATION

Placozoa (simplest animal, no
  tissues, organs, or symmetry)
Porifera (sponges)
Mesozoa (mesozoans)
Cnidaria/Coelenterata (true jellyfish,
  corals, sea anemones,
  coelenterates)
Ctenophora (comb jellies, sea
  gooseberries)
Platyhelminthes (flatworms, flukes,
  tapeworms)
Nemertea (ribbon worms, proboscis
  worms)
Acanthocephala (spiny-headed
  worms)
Aschelminthes (rotifers, nematodes)
  Gastrotricha (gastrotrichs)
  Kinorhyncha (kinorhynchs)
  Nematoda (nematodes,
    roundworms)
  Nematomorpha (horsehair worms,
    Gordian worms)
  Rotifera (rotifers, wheel animals)
Priapulida (priapulids)
Annelida (annelids, segmented
  worms, earthworms, leeches)
Tardigrada (water bears, tardigrades)
Onychophora (velvet worms,
  onychophorans)
Arthropoda
  Insecta (insects)
  Chilopoda (centipedes)
  Diplopoda (millipedes)
  Crustacea (crustaceans)
  Arachnida (spiders)
Mollusca (mollusks, gastropods,
  bivalves, cephalopoda)
Bryozoans (moss animals)
Phoronida (horseshoe worms,
  phoronids)
Brachiopoda (lamp shells)
Sipuncula (peanut worms)
Chaetognatha (arrow worms)
Echiura (spoon worms)

ANIMALS
  Animal Classification
      (cont.)

Echinodermata (echinoderms, starfish, sea urchins, sea cucumbers)
Hemichordata (hemichordates)
Pogonophora (beard worms)
Chordata (chordates)
  Tunicates (sea squirts, appendicularians, thaliaceans)
  Cephalochordata (amphioxus, lancelet)
  Vertebrata (vertebrates)
    Cyclostomata/Agnatha (jawless fish)
    Chondrichthyes (cartilaginous fish)
    Osteichthyes (bony fish)
    Amphibia (amphibians)
    Reptilia (reptiles)
    Aves (birds)
    Mammalia (mammals)

ANIMAL GROUPS

(popular names)

bale of turtles
bed of snakes
bevy of quail
bouquet of pheasants in flight
cete of badgers
charm of finches
clowder of cats
colony of ants, badgers or frogs
confusion of guinea fowls
covert of coots
covey of partridges, pheasants, or quail on the ground
drove of animals moving together; oxen, sheep or swine
exaltation of larks
flight of birds or insects
flock of birds or sheep
gaggle of geese on water or ground
gam of whales
gang of elk
herd of animals grazing together, especially cattle or sheep; elephants

hive of bees
host of sparrows
husk of hares
kennel of dogs
knot of toads
labor of moles
leap of leopards
murmuration of starlings
muster of peacocks
nest of rabbits, wasps, or vipers
pace of asses
pack of wild animals moving together, especially dogs or wolves; grouse
parliament of owls
plague of locusts
pod of seals or whales
pride of lions or peacocks
sault of lions
school of fish
shoal of fish, especially bass
shrewdness of apes
skein of geese in flight
skulk of foxes
sloth of bears
swarm of insects, especially bees
team of ducks in flight; oxen or horses
trace of hares or rabbits
troop of monkeys
watch of nightingales

ANIMAL SPECIES

(from highest number to lowest)

Arthropoda (crustaceans, insects, spiders)
Mollusca (mollusks, snails)
Chordata (chordates, vertebrates)
Protozoa (amoebas)
Annelida (segmented worms)
Coelenterata (jellyfish)
Nematoda (nematode worms)
Platyhelminthes (flatworms)
Echinodermata (starfish)
Porifera (sponges)

BIRDS

(based on work of Linnaeus, 1707–78)
(order, family, common name)

Struthioniformes, Struthionidae, ostrich
Rheiformes, Rheidae, rheas
Casuariiformes
   Casuariidae, cassowaries
   Dromaiidae, emu
Apterygiformes, Apterygidae, kiwis
Tinamiformes, Tinamidae, tinamous
Sphenisciformes, Spheniscidae, penguins
Gaviformes, Gaviidae, divers or loons
Podicipediformes, Podicipedidae, grebes
Procellariiformes
   Diomedeidae, albatrosses
   Procellariidae, petrels and fulmars
   Hydrobatidae, storm petrels
   Pelecanoididae, diving petrels
Pelecaniformes
   Pelecanidae, pelicans
   Sulidae, gannets and boobies
   Phaethontidae, tropicbirds
   Phalacrocoracidae, cormorants
   Fregatidae, frigatebirds
   Anhingidae, darters
Ciconiiformes
   Ardeidae, herons and bitterns
   Scopidae, hammerhead
   Balaenicipitidae, whale-headed stork
   Ciconiidae, storks
   Threskiornithidae, spoonbills and ibises
   Phoenicopteridae, flamingos
Anseriformes
   Anatidae, ducks, geese, and swans
   Anhimidae, screamers
Falconiformes
   Cathartidae, New World vultures
   Sagittariidae, secretary bird
   Pandionidae, osprey
   Falconidae, falcons and caracaras
   Accipitridae, kites, harriers, hawks, eagles, and buzzards

Galliformes
   Megapodidae, megapodes
   Cracidae, curassows
   Tetraonidae, grouse
   Phasianidae, pheasants, quail, and partridge
   Numididae, guineafowl
   Meleagrididae, turkeys
Gruiformes
   Mesitornithidae, mesites
   Turnicidae, buttonquails and hemipodes
   Perdionomidae, plains wanderer
   Gruidae, cranes
   Aramidae, limpkin
   Psophiidae, trumpeters
   Rallidae, rails
   Heliornithidae, finfoots
   Rhynochetidae, kagu
   Eurypygidae, sunbittern
   Cariamidae, seriemas
   Otididae, bustards
Charadriiformes
suborder Charadrii
   Jacanidae, jacanas or lily-trotters
   Rostratulidae, painted snipe
   Haematopodidae, oystercatchers
   Charadriidae, plovers and lapwings
   Scolopacidae, sandpipers
   Recurvirostridae, avocets and stilts
   Phalaropodidae, phalaropes
   Dromadidae, crab plover
   Burhinidae, stonecurlews or thick-knees
   Glareolidae, pratincoles or coursers
   Thinocoridae, seed snipe
   Chionididae, sheathbills
suborder Lari
   Stercorariidae, skuas and jaegers
   Laridae, gulls
   Sternidae, terns and noddies
   Rynchopidae, skimmers
suborder Alcae, Alcidae, auks
Columbiformes
   Pteroclididae, sandgrouse
   Columbidae, pigeons and doves
Psittaciformes, Psittacidae, parrots,

ANIMALS
  Birds (cont.)

lovebirds, and cockatoos
Cuculiformes
  Musophagidae, turacos
  Cuculidae, cuckoos, anis, and
    roadrunners
  Opisthocomidae, hoatzin
Strigiformes
  Strigidae, owls
  Tytonidae, barn owls
Caprimulgiformes
  Caprimulgidae, nightjars or
    goatsuckers
  Podargidae, frogmouths
  Aegothelidae, owlet-nightjars
  Hyctibiidae, potoos
  Steatornithidae, oilbird
Apodiformes
  Apodidae, swifts
  Hemiprocnidae, crested swifts
  Trochilidae, hummingbirds
Coliiformes, Coliidae, mousebirds or
    colies
Trogoniformes, Trogonidae, trogons
Coraciiformes
  Alcedinidae, kingfishers
  Todidae, todies
Momotidae, motmots
  Meropidae, bee-eaters
  Leptosomatidae, cuckoo-rollers
  Upupidae, hoopie
  Phoeniculidae, woodhoopoes
  Bucerotidae, hornbills
Piciformes
  Galbulidae, jacamars
  Bucconidae, puffbirds
  Capitonidae, barbets
  Indicatoridae, honeyguides
  Ramphastidae, toucans
  Picidae, woodpeckers
Passeriformes
suborder Eurylaimi, Eurylaimidae,
    broadbills
suborder Menurae
  Menuridae, lyrebirds
  Atrichornithidae, scrub-birds
suborder Tyranni
  Furnariidae, ovenbirds

Dendrocolaptidae, woodcreepers
Formicariidae, antbirds
Tyrannidae, tyrant flycatchers
Pittidae, pittas
Pipridae, manakins
Cotingidae, cotingas
Conopophagidae, gnateaters
Rhinocryptidae, tapaculos
Oxyruncidae, sharpbill
Phytotomidae, plantcutters
Xenicidae, New Zealand wrens
Philepittidae, sunbird astites
suborder Oscines
  Hirundinidae, swallows and
    martins
  Alaudidae, larks
  Motacillidae, wagtails and pipits
  Pycnonotidae, bulbuls
  Laniidae, shrikes
  Campephagidae, cuckoo-shrikes
  Irenidae, leafbirds
  Prionopidae, helmet shrikes
  Vangidae, vanga shrikes
  Bombycillidae, waxwings
  Dulidae, palmchat
  Cinclidae, dippers
  Troglodytidae, wrens
  Mimidae, mockingbirds
  Muscicapidae subfamilies:
  Prunellidae, accentors
  Turdinae, thrushes
  Timaliinae, babblers
  Sylviinae, Old World warblers
  Muscicapinae, Old World
    flycatchers
  Malurinae, fairy wrens
  Paradoxornithinae, parrotbills
  Monarchinae, monarch flycatchers
  Orthonychinae, logrunners
  Acanthizinae, Australian warblers
  Rhipidurinae, fantail flycatchers
  Pachycephalinae, thickheads
  Paridae, tits
  Aegithalidae, long-tailed tits
  Remizidae, penduline tits
  Sittidae, nuthatches
  Climacteridae, Australasian

treecreepers
Certhiidae, holartic treecreepers
Rhabdornithidae, Philippine
 treecreepers
Zosteropidae, white-eyes
Dicaeidae, flowerpeckers
Pardalotidae, pardalotes or
 diamond eyes
Nectariniidae, sunbirds or
 spiderhunters
Meliphagidae, honeyeaters
Ephthianuridae, Australian chats
Emberizidae subfamilies:
Emberizinae, Old World buntings,
 New World sparrows
Catamblyrhynchinae, plush-
 capped finch
Thraupinae, tanagers and
 honeycreepers
Cardinalinae, cardinal grosbeaks
Tersininae, swallow tanagers
Parulidae, wood warblers
Vireonidae, vireos and pepper
 shrikes
Icteridae, blackbirds
Fringillidae subfamilies:
Fringillinae, fringilline finches
Carduelinae, cardueline finches
Drepanidinae, Hawaiian
 honeycreepers
Estrildidae, waxbills
Ploceidae subfamilies:
Ploceinae, true weavers
Viduinae, widow birds
Bubalornithinae, buffalo weavers
Passerinae, sparrow weavers and
 sparrows
Sturnidae, starlings
Oriolidae, orioles and figbirds
Dicruridae, drongos
Callaeidae, New Zealand
 wattlebirds
Grallinidae, magpie larks
Corcoracidae, Australian
 mudnesters
Artamidae, wood swallows

Cracticidae, bell magpies
Ptilonorhynchidae, bowerbirds
Paradisaeidae, birds of paradise
Corvidae, crows, magpies, and jays

FASTEST ANIMALS

peregrine falcon, 225 mph (362 kph)
golden eagle, 150+ mph (240+ kph)
cheetah, 70 mph (113 kph)
sailfish, 68 mph (109 kph)
pronghorn antelope, 55+ mph (88.5+
 kph)
Grant's gazelle, 47 mph (75.5 kph)
yellowfin tuna, 46.61 mph (75 kph)
ostrich, 45 mph (72 kph)
race horse, 43.26 mph (69.62 kph)
greyhound, 41.72 mph (67.14 kph)
eastern grey kangaroo, 40 mph (64 kph)
American free-tailed bat, 35–40 mph
 (56–64 kph)
blue wildebeeste, 37 mph (59.5 kph)
dragonfly, 36 mph (58 kph)
killer whale, 34.5 mph (55.5 kph)
giraffe, 32 mph (51.5 kph)
black rhinoceros, 28 mph (45 kph)
man, 27.89 mph (44.88 kph)
common dolphin, 24.5 mph (44.4 kph)

FISHES

(order, common name)

Class Agnatha (jawless fishes)
Cyclostomata, lampreys and
 hagfishes
Chondrichthyes (cartilage skeleton
 fishes)
Batoidei, rays, skates, and stingrays
Selachii, sharks
Osteichthyes (bony skeleton fishes)
Acipenseriformes, sturgeons and
 paddlefishes
Anguilliformes, eels
Atheriniformes, flying fishes,
 needlefishes, garfishes, and
 cyprinodonts

Characiformes, tetras and piranhas
Clupeiformes, herrings and
anchovies
Dipnoi, lungfishes
Elopiformes, bonefishes, tarpons,
and ladyfish
Gasterosteiformes, sticklebacks, tub
snout, and sea horses
Ostariophysi, carps, minnows,
suckers, and catfishes
Osteoglossiformes, bony tongues and
freshwater butterfly fish
Paracanthopterygii, toadfishes, trout,
perches, and codfishes
Perciformes, perches, tunas, and
marlins
Pleuronectiformes, flatfishes,
flounders, and soles
Polypteriformes, bichirs or reedfishes
Salmoniformes, salmons, trouts,
smelts, and whitefishes
Scorpaeniformes, scorpion fishes,
rockfishes, redfishes, and gunards
Tetraodontiformes, box fishes, puffer
fishes, and ocean sunfishes

INSECTS

Ants

*(phylum Arthropoda, class Insecta, order
Hymenoptera, superfamily Scolioidea,
family Formicidae)*

Cerapachyinae
Dolichoderinae
Dorylinae (army ants)
Formicinae
Leptanillinae
Myrmeciinae (carpenters and honey
ants)
Myrmicinae (largest subfamily)
Ponerinae (primitive Ponerines)
Pseudomyrmecinae
Sphecomyrminae

Bees

Colony Hierarchy

Queen bee (fertile mated female who
lays all the eggs)
Drones (males who fertilize the
queen)
Workers (sterile females who do all
the work)
Hive workers (stay and work in the
hive)
Foragers (go to the flowers to get
food for the colony)

Family Classification

*(phylum Arthropoda, class Insecta, order
Hymenoptera, suborder Apocrita,
Superfamily Apoidea)*

Adrenidae (burrowing bees)
Anthophoridae (mining bees)
Apidae (bumblebees, digger bees,
cuckoo bees, carpenter bees,
honeybees)
Bombidae (bumblebees)
Ceratinidae (small carpenter bees)
Colletidae (plasterer bees, yellow-
faced bees)
Halictidae (mining bees)
Megachilidae (leaf-cutter bees)
Meliponidae
Melittidae (melittids)
Xylocopidae (large carpenter bees)

Insect Classification

Blattaria, cockroaches
Coleoptera, beetles and weevils
Collembola, springtails
Dermaptera, earwigs
Diplura, diplurans
Diptera, true flies
Embioptera, webspinners
Ephemeroptera, mayflies
Hemiptera, true bugs
Homoptera, cicadas, hoppers,
aphids, and scale insects
Hymenoptera, ants, bees, and wasps
Isoptera, termites or white ants

Lepidoptera, butterflies, moths, and skippers

Mantodea, mantids and mantises

Mecoptera, scorpion flies

Neuroptera, alderflies, dobsonflies, lacewings, and snakeflies

Odonata, dragonflies and damselflies

Orthoptera, grasshoppers, locusts, and crickets

Phasmida or Phasmoptera, stick and leaf insects

Phthiraptera, sucking, biting, book, and bark lice

Protura, proturans

Siphonaptera, fleas

Strepsiptera, stylopids

Thysanoptera, thrips

Thysanura, bristletails and silverfish

Trichoptera, caddisflies

Zoraptera, zorapterans

INVERTEBRATES

Phyla

Protozoa (amoebas and other protozoa)

Mesozoa (tiny parasites)

Porifera (sponges)

Coelenterata/Cnidaria (coelenterates, jellyfish, sea anemones)

Ctenophora (comb jellies)

Platyhelminthes (flatworms, flukes, tapeworms)

Nemertina (ribbon worms)

Aschelminthes (sac worms)

Nematoda (roundworms)

Acanthocephala (spiny-headed worms)

Entoprocta (entoprocts, tube-dwelling aquatic animals)

Bryozoa (tube-dwelling aquatic animals)

Phoronida (tube-dwelling wormlike animals)

Ectoprocta (ectoprocts, microscopic colonizers)

Brachiopoda (lamp shells)

Mollusca (clams)

  Amphineura (chitons)

  Cepalopoda (octopuses and squids)

  Gastropoda (univalves)

  Pelecypoda (bivalves)

  Scaphoda (tooth shells)

true invertebrates:

Sipunculoidea (peanut worms, marine worms)

Annelida (segmented; earthworms)

Echiuroidea (spoon worms)

Oncopoda (segmented, claw-footed worms)

Arthropoda (crustaceans, spiders, ticks, centipedes, insects)

Enterocoelomates (coeloms)

Chaetognatha (arrowworms)

Pogonophora (beard worms)

Echinodermata (spiny-skinned animals, starfish, sea urchins)

Chordata (sea squirts, amphioxus, tunicates, acorn worms)

LIFE CYCLES

Amphibian

(frog, toad, salamander)

sperm cell fertilizes egg cell outside body

eggs spawn

larva forms into tadpole

adult amphibian

Annelid Worm

(earthworm, leech)

sperm cell fertilizes egg cell outside body

eggs produced

larva forms

adult worm

Bird

(robin, sparrow)

sperm cell fertilizes egg cell
shelled egg produced
adult bird

Butterfly, Moth, or Wasp

complete metamorphosis:

adult female is fertilized
female lays eggs
caterpillar hatches from egg as larva
caterpillar grows to full size and
    begins hibernation, developing
    pupal case for protection
pupa or chrysalis (resting insect)
    undergoes metamorphosis while
    hibernating
adult butterfly emerges from pupa

Cnidarian

(jellyfish, anemone, coral)

sperm cell fertilizes egg cell outside
    body
larva forms
polyp develops
medusa (adult form)

Crickets, Grasshoppers, or Lice

incomplete metamorphosis:

adult female is fertilized
female lays eggs
insect hatches from egg as mini-adult,
    without wings (early-stage nymph)
late-stage nymph's skin begins to
    molt and wings begin to bud
fully grown insect

Crustacean

(arthropods: spider, crab, centipede)

sperm cell fertilizes egg cell outside
    body
eggs produced
larva forms
adult crustacean

Echinoderm

(sea star, sand dollar, sea urchin)

sperm cell fertilizes egg cell outside
    body
eggs produced
larva forms
adult echinoderm

Fish

(trout, salmon)

sperm cell fertilizes egg cell outside
    body
eggs produced
adult fish

Frog

female spawns in water
eggs develop in water
tadpole hatches
tadpole metamorphoses into frog

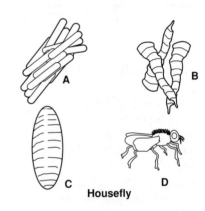

Housefly

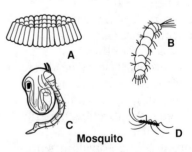

Mosquito

Metamorphosis
A. Eggs; **B.** Larvae; **C.** Pupa; **D.** Adult

Insect

(dragonfly, fly)

sperm cell fertilizes egg cell outside
  body
eggs produced
larva forms
pupa develops
adult insect

Mammal

*(humans, primates, horses,
dogs, etc.)*

sperm cell fertilizes egg cell
fertilized egg develops inside body
adult mammal

Marsupial

(kangaroo, koala)

sperm cell fertilizes egg cell
fertilized egg develops inside body
young born in immature state, in pouch
adult marsupial

Mollusk

(snail, slug)

sperm cell fertilizes egg cell outside
  body
eggs produced
larva forms
adult mollusk

Reptile

(snake, crocodile)

sperm cell fertilizes egg cell
shelled egg produced
adult reptile

MAMMALS

Classification

*(Phylum Chordata, Subphylum
Vertebrata, Class Mammalia)*

*order, family name, common
name/examples*

Monotremes (egg-laying mammals)
  Ornithorhynchidae, platypus
  Tachyglossidae, echidna or spiny
    anteater
Marsupialia (pouched mammals)
  Burramyidae, feathertail gliders
  Caenolestidae, rat opossums
  Dasyuridae, native cats and
    marsupial mice
  Didelphidae, opossums
  Macropodidae, kangaroos and
    wallabies
  Myrmecobiidae, numbat
  Notoryctidae, marsupial moles
  Peramelidae, bandicoots
  Petauridae, gliding phalangers
  Phalangeridae, phalangers,
    cuscuses
  Phascolarctidae, koala
  Tarsipedidae, honey possum
  Thylacinidae, Tasmanian wolf
  Thylacomyidae, burrowing
    banidcoots
  Vombatidae, wombats
Insectivora (insect-eaters)
  Chrysochloridae, golden moles
  Erinaceidae, hedgehogs
  Macroscelididae, elephant shrews
  Potamogalidae, otter shrews
  Solenodontidae, solenodon and
    almiqui
  Soricidae, shrews
  Talpidae, moles
  Tenrecidae, tenrecs
  Tupaiidae, tree shrews
Chiroptera (bats)
  Craseonycteridae, hog-nosed or
    butterfly bats

Desmodontidae, vampire bats
Emballonuridae, sheath-tailed or
  sac-winged bats
Furipteridae, smoky bats
Hipposideridae, Old World leaf-
  nosed bats
Megadermatidae, false vampires
Molossidae, free-tailed bats
Mormoopidae, insectivorous bats
Mystacinidae, New Zealand short-
  tailed bats
Myzopodidae, Old World sucker-
  footed bats
Natalidae, funnel-eared bats
Noctilionidae, bulldog bats
Nycteridae, slit-faced or hollow-
  faced bats
Phyllostomatidae, American leaf-
  nosed bats
Pteropodidae, Old World fruit bats
  and flying foxes
Rhinolophidae, horseshoe bats
Rhinopomatidae, mouse-tailed
  bats
Thyropteridae, disk-wing bats
Vespertilionidae, common bats
Rodentia (gnawing mammals)
  Abrocomidae, abrocomes or
    chinchilla rats
  Anomaluridae, scaly-tailed
    squirrels
  Aplodontidae, mountain beaver or
    sewellel
  Bathyergidae, blesmols or African
    mole rats
  Capromyidae, hutias and coypus
  Castoridae, beavers
  Caviidae, cavies, guinea pigs, and
    maras
  Chinchillidae, chinchillas and
    viscachas
  Cricetidae, field and deer mice,
    voles, and muskrats
  Ctenodactylidae, gundis
  Ctenomyidae, tuco-tucos

Dasyproctidae, pacas and agoutis
Dinomyidae, pacarana or Branick's
  paca
Dipodidae, jerboas
Echimyidae, spiny rats and rock
  rats
Erethizontidae, New World
  porcupines
Geomyidae, pocket gophers
Gliridae, dormice
Heteromyidae, mice and kangaroo
  rats
Hydrochoeridae, capybaras
Hystricidae, Old World porcupines
Muridae, Old World rats and mice
Octodontidae, octodonts and
  degus
Pedetidae, cape jumping hare or
  springhaas
Petromuridae, rock or dassie rat
Rhizomyidae, bamboo rats and
  African mole rats
Scuiuridae, squirrels, chipmunks,
  and marmots
Seleveniidae, jumping dormouse
Spalacidae, mole rats
Thryonomyidae, cane rats
Zapodidae, jumping and birch
  mice
Dermoptera (colugos or flying
  lemurs)
  Cynocephalidae, colugos or flying
    lemurs)
Edentata (toothless)
  Bradypodidae, tree sloths
  Dasypodidae, armadillos
  Myrmecophagidae, anteaters
Hyracoidae (hyrax, dassie)
  Procaviidae, African rock hyrax
Lagomorpha (pikas, hares, rabbits)
  Ochotonidae, pikas
  Leporidae, hares and rabbits
Carnivora (meat-eaters)
  Canidae, dogs, foxes, wolves, and
    jackals

Felidae, cats
Hyaenidae, hyenas
Mustelidae, weasels, otters, skunks, and badgers
Otariidae, eared seals and walrus
Phocidae, earless seals
Procyonidae, raccoons
Ursidae, bears and giant pandas
Viverridae, civets, mongooses, and genet
Cetacea (whales and porpoises)
Balaenidae, right whales
Balaenopteridae, rorquals and humpbacks
Delphinidae, dolphins and killer whales
Eschrichtiidae, grey whale
Hyperoodontidae, beaked whales
Monodontidae, beluga and narwhals
Phocoenidae, porpoises
Physeteridae, sperm whales
Platanistidae, river dolphins
Stenidae, long-snouted dolphins
Proboscidea (elephants)
Elephantidae, African and Asian elephants
Pholidata (pangolins)
Manidae, pangolins
Pinnipedia (seals and walruses)
Odobenidae, walrus
Otariidae, eared seal, sea lion
Phocidae, earless seal
Sirenia (dugongs and manatees)
Dugongidae, dugong
Trichechidae, manatees
Perissodactyla (odd-toed hoofed)
Equidae, horses, asses, zebras, and donkeys
Tapiridae, tapirs
Rhinocerotidae, rhinoceroses
Tubulidentata (aardvarks)
Orycteropodidae, aardvarks
Artiodactyla (even-toed hoofed)
Antilocapridae, pronghorn

Bovidae, cattle, goats, sheep, antelopes, and gazelles
Camelidae, camels and llamas
Cervidae, deer
Giraffidae, giraffe and okapi
Hippopotamidae, hippopotamuses
Suidae, pigs
Tayassuidae, peccaries
Tragulidae, chevrotains
Primates (primates)
Callitrichidae, tamarins and marmosets
Cebidae, New World monkeys
Cercopithecidae, Old World monkeys
Cheirogaleidae, dwarf and mouse lemurs
Daubentoniidae, aye aye
Galagidae, galagos
Hominidae, man
Hylobatidae, gibbons and siamang
Indriidae, indrii, sifaka, and avali
Lemuridae, lemurs
Lepilmuridae, sportive lemurs
Lorisidae, lorises, pottos, and hushbabies
Pongidae, gorilla, chimpanzee, and orangutan
Tarsiidae, tarsiers
Tupaiidae, tree shrews

Dogs

1. working dogs (collies, schnauzers, boxers, sheepdogs, huskies)
2. sporting dogs (pointers, setters, retrievers, weimarers, cocker-spaniel)
3. hounds (bassets, bloodhounds, dachshunds, greyhounds)
4. terriers (fox, Welsh, Scottish, Irish, bull)
5. nonsporting (poodles, dalmatians, bulldogs)
6. toy dogs (Shih Tzu, pug)

Great Dane

Collie

Working Dogs

Boxer

German Shepherd

Weimaraner

Cocker Spaniel

Golden Retriever

Sporting Dogs

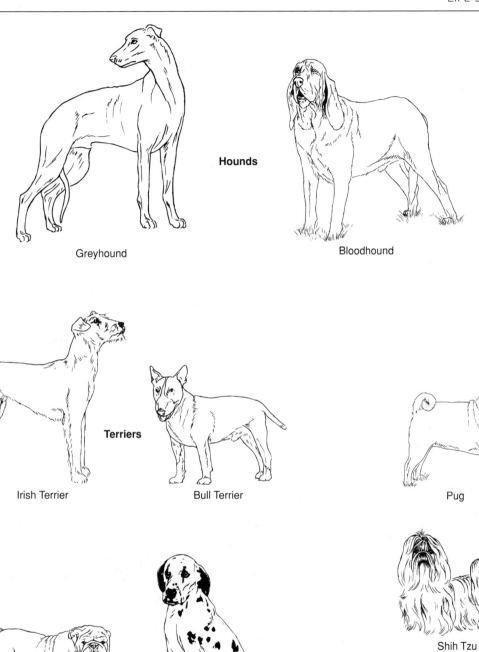

Hounds

Greyhound

Bloodhound

Terriers

Irish Terrier

Bull Terrier

Pug

Shih Tzu

Toy Dogs

Bulldog

Dalmatian

Nonsporting Dogs

ANIMALS
Mammals (cont.)

Long-Haired

Turkish Angora

Persian

Maine Coon

Manx

Short-Haired

Rex

Siamese

Examples of Cat Breeds

Felines

great cats (lions, tigers, leopards,
   jaguars)
lesser cats (ocelots, tabby cats)
miscellaneous (pumas)
lynxes (jungle cats, bobcats)
servals
jaguars
cheetahs

Cats—Major Domestic Breeds

Abyssinian
Balinese
Bombay
Chantilly
Chartreux
Colorpoint Shorthair
Cornish Rex
Exotic Shorthairs
Himalayan
Japanese Bobtail
Javanese
Korat
Maine Coon
Manx
Norwegian Forest Cat
Ocicat
Oriental Longhair
Persian
Ragdoll
Rex
Scottish Fold
Selkirk
Siamese
Somali
Turkish Angora

REPTILES

(order, family, common name)

Chelonia
   Dermatemydidae, American river
      turtle
   Chelydridae, alligator and snapping
      turtles
   Kinosternidae, mud and musk turtles
   Emydidae, common turtle
   Cheloniidae, sea turtles
   Dermochelyidae, leatherback turtles
   Carettochelyidae, New Guinea
      plateless turtle
   Trionychidae, softshell turtles
   Pelomedusidae, side-necked turtles
   Chelyidae, snake-necked turtles
Rhynchocephalia
   Sphenodontidae, tuatara
Squamata
   suborder Sauria
      Gekkonidae, geckos
      Pygopodidae, flap-footed lizards
      Dibamidae, burrowers
      Iguanidae, iguanas
      Agamidae, agamid lizard
      Chameleontidae, Old World
         chameleons
      Scincidae, skinks
      Cordylidae, girdle-tailed lizards
      Lacertidae, Old World terrestrial
         lizards
      Teiidae, whiptail lizards
      Anguidae, glass and alligator
         lizards
      Anniellidae, California legless
         lizards
      Helodermatidae, gila monster
         and bearded lizard
      Varanidae, monitor lizards
      Lanthanotidae, earless monitor
         lizard
      Xantusiidae, night lizards
   suborder Serpentes
      Typhlopidae, blind and worm
         snakes
      Letotyphlopidae, slender blind
         snakes
      Xenopeltidae, sunbeam snake
      Uropeltidae, shieldtail snakes
      Boidae, pythons, boas, and
         woodsnakes
      Acrochordidae, wart snakes
      Colubridae, terrestrial, arboreal,
         and aquatic snakes

Viperidae, vipers, rattlesnakes, moccasins
Elapidae, cobras and coral snakes
Hydrophiidae, sea snakes
  suborder Amphisbaenia
    Amphisbaenidae, worm lizards
Crocodilia
  Alligatoridae, alligators and caiman
  Crocodilidae, true crocodile
  Gavialidae, gavial or gharial

DINOSAURS

Herrerasauria, the earliest dinosaurs
  (named after discoverer V.
  Herrera, an Argentinian
  goatherd)
  Staurikosauridae (stake-like lizard)
  Herrerasauridae
Saurischia (lizard-hipped)
  Theropods (beast feet), carnivorous
    Tyrannosaurus
  Sauropodomorphs (lizard feet),
    herbivorous Apatosaurus
  Segnosaurs (slow lizards)
Ornithischia (bird-hipped)
  Ornithopods (bird feet)
  Scelidosaurs (limb lizards)
  Stegosaurs (roof lizards)
  Ankylosaurs (fused lizards)
  Pachycephalosaurs (thick-headed
    lizards)
  Ceratopsians (horned faces)

VERTEBRATES

Fishes
Reptiles
Amphibians
Birds
Mammals

BIOLOGY

ANIMAL & PLANT KINGDOMS
(Whittaker system)

Prokaryota: monera, bacteria
  (sometimes includes viruses)
Protoctista: algae, protozoans, slime
  molds
Fungi: mushrooms, molds, and
  lichens
Animalia: animals
Plantae: plants

Animal Taxonomy
(extended taxonomy with capitalization guide; intermediate taxonomic levels between each use the prefixes super-, sub,- and infra-)

Kingdom
Subkingdom
Phylum
Subphylum
Superclass
Class
Subclass
Infraclass
Cohort
Superorder
Order
Suborder
Superfamily (suffix -oidea)
Family (suffix -idae)
Subfamily (suffix -inae)
Tribe (suffix -ini)
Genus
Subgenus
species
subspecies

Obligatory Taxonomy

Kingdom
Phylum/Division
Class
Order

Family
Genus
Species

BIOLOGICAL SCIENCES

Biology
  Anatomy
    Cytology (cells)
    Gnotobiosis (organisms or
      conditions free of germs)
    Histology (tissues)
    Microbiology (microscopic
      organisms)
      bacteriology (bacteria)
      virology (viruses)
    Morphology (form and structure
      of organisms)
    Organology (organs)
  Biochemistry
  Bioecology
    Limnology (bodies of fresh water)
    Marine biology (bodies of salt
      water)
    Parasitology (parasites)
    Synecology (relations between
      natural communities and
      environments)
  Biogeography
  Biometry (calculations of human
    life)
  Biophysics
  Ecology
  Embryology
  Eugenics (improving species or
    breeds)
  Evolution
  Exobiology (potential life beyond
    earth's atmosphere)
  Genetics
  Molecular biology (DNA, RNA)
  Physiology
    Biodynamics (energy of living
      organisms)
    Biostatistics (statistics in
      biological and medical data)

Population Biology
  Biogeography
  Population genetics
Taxonomy (classification)
Botany
  Applied Botany
    Agriculture
    Forestry
    Hydroponics (plant cultivation in
      liquid)
    Plant breeding
    Pomology (fruit growing)
  Research Botany
    Algology (algae)
    Bacteriology
    Bryology (bryophytes)
    Dendrology (trees and shrubs)
    Economic botany
    Genetics
    Geobotany
    Mycology (fungi)
    Paleobotany
    Plant cytology (study of cells)
    Plant ecology
    Plant geography
    Plant morphology (structures)
    Plant pathology (plant disease)
    Plant physiology
    Plant taxonomy
    Pteridology (ferns and related
      plants)
Medicine
  Aerospace medicine
  Anesthesiology
  Cardiology (heart)
  Cytotechnology (cell)
  Dentistry
  Dermatology
  Emergency medicine
  Endocrinology (endocrine glands)
  Epidemiology (epidemics)
  Experimental therapeutics
  Family practice
  Forensic medicine (medicine
    applied to law)
  Gastroenterology (digestive organs)

BIOLOGY

Biological Sciences
(cont.)

Geriatrics and gerontology (aged)
Hematology (blood)
Holistic medicine (therapies
    outside orthodox medicine)
    Chiropractic (spine and nervous
        system)
    Homeopathy (symptom causing
        drugs)
    Naturopathy (fasting, diets,
        massage)
Immunology (immune system)
Internal medicine (diseases of
    internal organs)
Medical jurisprudence (medical
    law)
Medical physiology (processes of
    organisms)
Medical records
Medical technology
Nephrology (kidney)
Neurology (nervous system)
Nursing
Nutrition
Obstetrics and gynecology
    (pregnancy and childbirth)
Occupational medicine (work-
    related medicine)
Ophthalmology (eye disease)
Oral surgery
Orthodontics (tooth correction)
Orthopedics (skeletal system)
Osteopathy (manipulation of
    muscles and bones)
Otolaryngology/otorhinolaryn-
    gology (ear, nose, throat)
Pathological physiology (diseases
    of organism processes)
Pathology (disease)
Pediatrics (children)
Pharmacology (preparation, uses,
    effects of drugs)
Pharmacy (preparing and
    dispensing drugs and
    medicines)
Plastic surgery
Podiatry (feet)

Psychiatry
Public health (community health
    services)
Radiology (radiation for diagnosis
    and treatment)
Sports medicine
Surgery
Toxicology (poisons)
Tropical medicine
Urology (urinary tract)
X-ray technology

Zoology

Applied Zoology
    Animal genetics
    Apiculture (beekeeping)
    Veterinary medicine
    Wildlife management
Research Zoology
    Arachnology (spiders)
    Comparative anatomy
    Comparative physiology
    Conchology (shells of mollusks)
    Embryology
    Entomology (insects)
    Helminthology (worms, esp.
        parasitic)
    Herpetology (reptiles and
        amphibians)
    Ichthyology (fishes)
    Malacology (mollusks)
    Mammalogy
    Ornithology (birds)
    Protozoology (earliest forms)
    Zoogeography

CELLS, VIRUS AND TISSUE

Classification

absorptive cells
cells in supporting tissues
circulating cells
muscle cells
nerve cells
reproductive cells

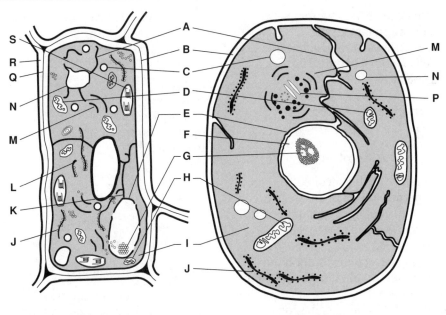

Plant Cell **Animal Cell**

A. Smooth endoplasmic reticulum; **B.** Cell membrane; **C.** Lysosome; **D.** Microfibril;
E. Nuclear envelope; **F.** Chromatin; **G.** Nucleolus; **H.** Mitochondrion; **I.** Cytoplasm;
J. Ribosome; **K.** Rough endoplasmic reticulum; **L.** Microtubule; **M.** Golgi body; **N.** Vacuole;
O. Microvilli; **P.** Centrioles; **Q.** Cell wall; **R.** Lamella; **S.** Chloroplast

secretory cells
sensory cells

Reproduction

1. single cell
2. chromosomes double (DNA copies itself) and form pairs
3. nuclear membrane dissolves and centrioles move and make fibers
4. pairs of chromosomes line up in center, then separate into identical halves
5. membrane forms around each chromosome set, each with its own nucleus
6. furrow forms, then cytoplasm pinched into two halves
7. two new cells complete, each containing exactly the same DNA as the parent cell and each other

Mitosis and Meiosis

prophase
metaphase
anaphase
telophase
lepotene
zygotene
pachytene
diplotene
diakinesis

Tissue Classification

anatomical
embryological
functional

Virus Reproduction

1. Virus approaches cell
2. Virus attaches to cell

3. Virus injects its DNA for replication inside cell
4. New viruses form inside cell
5. Cell explodes and new viruses disperse

ECOLOGY

Areas of Study

community ecology (collective properties of organisms in an area)

ecosystem ecology (regulation of energy flow and material in ecosystems)

physiological ecology (interactions between individual organisms and environment)

population biology (regulation of population growth and population size, and interactions among populations)

Biosphere

1. biosphere: total assemblage of plants, animals, and other living things on earth
2. biome: large biogeographical area containing plants and animals adapted to survive there
3. ecosystem: distinct area of interacting living organisms and their surroundings, e.g. forest; largest ecosystems are called biomes, e.g. rain forests and deserts
4. habitat/address: natural home of a group of plants and animals (community)
5. species: group of living things that can breed together in the wild and produce offspring
6. flora: vegetation of a particular area
7. niche/profession: the role of a living thing within an ecosystem (where it lives, what it absorbs or eats, how it behaves, how it relates to other living things)

Biosphere Levels

biosphere
ecosystems
communities
populations (species)
organisms
  organ systems
  organs
  tissues
cells
molecules
atoms and energy

Ecological Classification of Organisms

autotrophs: self-nourishers or producers such as green plants

heterotrophs: herbivores, carnivores, omnivores, scavengers, bacteria, fungi, parasites

Food Chain

plant uses sun's energy to grow
herbivore (plant eater) eats plant
carnivore (meat eater) or omnivore (plant and meat eater) then eats the herbivore

examples:

first level, algae (food producer)
second level, animal plankton (primary consumer)
third level, herring (secondary consumer)
fourth level, cod (tertiary consumer)
fifth level, humans (quaternary consumer)

first level, insects feeding on plants
second level, beetles and other arachnids
third level, insect-eating birds
fourth level, bird-eating carnivores
fifth level, parasites

Food Pyramid

(food-producing plants supporting successively higher stages of consumers)

[example is African grassland]

top predator/secondary consumer
(e.g. lions, hyena, wild dogs)
large consumer (e.g. wildebeest,
antelope)
plants

Food Web

(example is lake community)

producers: water plants and plant
plankton
predators: herbivores (plant eaters)
such as animal plankton, snails,
some insects, and some fish
predators: carnivores (meat eaters)
such as some insects, fish, and
mammals

Nutrient Cycle

example: grassland

1. animals, bacteria, and fungi feed
on dead plants, animals, or animal
waste
2. nutrients they eat become part of
their bodies and enrich the soil
when waste is produced or when
they die and decay
3. nothing is wasted and nutrients go
around in an endless cycle

Oxygen Cycle

1. oxygen is in the air
2. oxygen breathed in by animals
3. carbon dioxide (a carbon-oxygen
compound) is breathed out
4. carbon dioxide is absorbed by
plants which combine it with
water to make food
5. plants release surplus oxygen into
the air

Trophic Levels Pyramid

(steps on a food chain or food pyramid; trophic level is based on the numbers or mass of living things at the same level in a food web or on the amount of energy stored by a group of living things at one level)

Trophic level 1: plants, flowers, fungi
(producers)
Trophic level 2: animals, butterflies,
worms (primary consumer)
Trophic level 3: reptiles, arthropods,
birds (secondary consumer)
Trophic level 4: owl, fox, weasel
(tertiary consumer)

EVOLUTION

Events

Earth formed (4.6 billion years ago)
first life (3.5 b)
first plants (1 b)
first animals (1 b)
crustaceans (650 million years ago)
fossils formed (590 m)
fish (510 m)
land plants (420 m)
insects (380 m)
amphibians (360 m)
seed plants (360 m)
reptiles (340 m)
mammals (213 m)
birds (150 m)
flowering plants (140 m)
humans (2 m)

GENETICS

Areas of Study

anthropologic genetics
behavioral genetics
clinical genetics
developmental genetics
evolutionary genetics

formal genetics
genetic epidemiology
immunogenetics
population genetics
statistical genetics

ORGANISMS

Five Kingdoms of Living Things

Living things
  Protists
    amoebas
    diatoms
    euglena
    paramecia
  Monera
    bacteria
    blue-green algae
  Animals
  Plants
  Fungi
    mildews
    molds
    mushrooms
    yeasts

Organism Characteristics

nutrition
respiration
excretion
growth
reproduction
irritability (response to conditions)
movement

Organism Structure

(single-cell organisms do not have organs)

cell (made of protoplasm)
tissue (made of cells)
organ (made of tissues)
system (made of organs)
organism (made of systems)

HUMAN LIFE

BIOLOGICAL CLASSIFICATION

Kingdom—Animalia
Subkingdom—Metazoa
Phylum—Chordata
Subphylum—Vertebrata
Superdivision—Gnathostomata
Division—Osteichthyes
Superclass—Tetrapoda
Class—Mammalia
Subclass—Theria
Infraclass—Eutheria
Order—Primates
Superfamily—Hominoidea
Family—Hominidae
Genus—Homo
Species—sapiens
Subspecies—sapiens

BLOOD TYPES

A
B
AB
O

HUMAN BRAIN STRUCTURE

forebrain
  cerebrum
    frontal lobe
    parietal lobe
    occipital lobe
    temporal lobe
  corpus callosum
  basal ganglia
  thalamus
  hippocampus
  hypothalamus
  cerebellum
  pituitary gland
midbrain

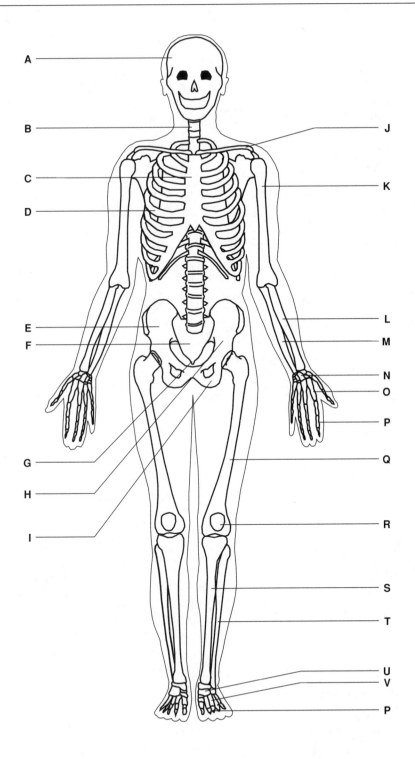

Skeleton
(human)

A. Cranium
B. Vertebrae
C. Sternum
D. Ribs
E. Ilium
F. Sacrum
G. Coccyx
H. Pubis
I. Ischium
J. Clavicle
K. Humerus
L. Radius
M. Ulna
N. Carpus
O. Metacarpus
P. Phalanges
Q. Femur
R. Patella
S. Tibia
T. Fibula
U. Tarsus
V. Metatarsus

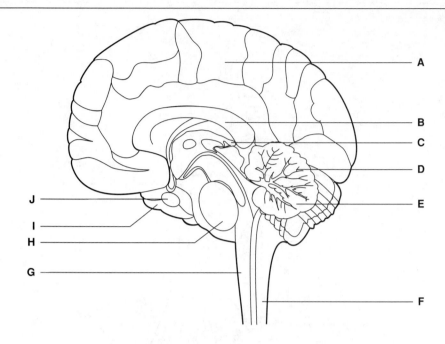

Human Brain (cross section)
A. Cerebrum; **B.** Corpus callosum; **C.** Pineal gland;
D. Vermis; **E.** Cerebellum; **F.** Spinal cord; **G.** Medulla
oblongata; **H.** Pons; **I.** Oculomotor nerve; **J.** Pituitary gland

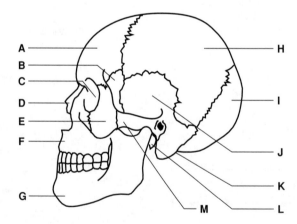

Human Skull (lateral view)

A. Frontal bone	**H.** Parietal bone
B. Sphenoid bone	**I.** Occipital bone
C. Eye socket	**J.** Temporal bone
D. Nasal bone	**K.** Mastoid process
E. Zygomatic bone	**L.** Styloid process
F. Maxilla	**M.** Zygomatic arch
G. Mandible	

hindbrain
  pons
    medulla oblongata
    cerebellum
brain stem / spinal cord

CRANIUM

Cranial Nerves

olfactory
optic
oculomotor
trochlear
trigeminal
abducens
facial
auditory
glossopharyngeal
vagus
spinal accessory
hypoglossal

CHOLESTEROL

Classification

high density lipoprotein (HDL; "good" cholesterol)
low density lipoprotein (LDL; "bad" cholesterol)

Levels

(total cholesterol to high density lipoprotein levels in blood)

220/60 (3.67)   High
200/60 (3.33)   Medium

DIGESTIVE SEQUENCE

1. teeth crush food in mouth, saliva moistens food for ease of chewing and swallowing
2. tongue tastes flavors
3. esophagus pushes swallowed food down behind windpipe and heart, into stomach
4. muscular walls of stomach churn food and mix it with digestive juices produced by pancreas
5. broken-down nutrients seep through lining in small intestine into the blood vessels of its walls (and then are circulated through the body)
6. large intestine absorbs water from undigested food and solidifies and passes waste through to rectum

HUMAN EVOLUTION

Ramapithecus
Australopithecus
    Australopithecus afarensis (3.7 to 2.6 million yrs ago)

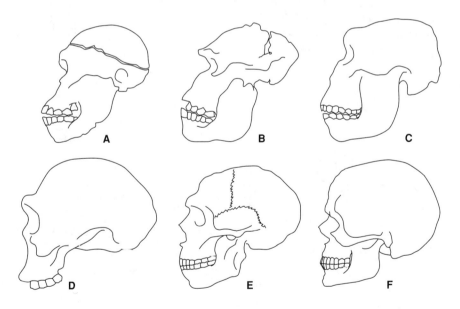

Hominid Evolution

A. *Australopithecus africanus*
B. *Australopithecus robustus*
C. *Australopithecus boisei*
D. *Homo erectus*
E. *Homo sapiens neanderthalensis* (Neanderthal man)
F. *Homo sapiens sapiens* (Cro-Magnon)

Australopithecus africanus (3.0 to 2.3 mya)
Australopithecus boisei (2.5 to 1.3 mya)
Australopithecus robustus (1.9 to 1.6 mya)
Homo habilis (2 to 1.8 mya)
Homo erectus (1.6 to 0.4 mya)
Homo sapiens 400,000 to 125,000 years ago)
Homo sapiens neanderthalensis (125,000 to 30,000 years ago)
Homo sapiens sapiens (125,000 years ago to present)

HEART PUMPING SEQUENCE

1. blood from veins flow into atrium (upper chamber)
2. blood then flows into ventricle (lower chamber) and thick walls force blood into arteries; left pump sends oxygenated blood around
3. blood passes oxygen to body parts, becomes deoxygenated and returns to right pump

4. right pump sends it to lungs for oxygen, then through left pump again before being sent around the body in veins

INTESTINAL TRACT SECTIONS

duodenum
jejunum
ileum
appendix
colon
sigmoid flexure
rectum

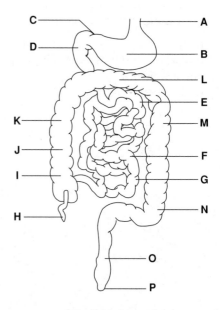

Intestines (human)
A. End of esophagus; B. Stomach; C. Pylorus;
D. Duodenum; E. Jejunum; F. Small intestine;
G. Ileum; H. Vermiform appendix; I. Cecum;
J. Large intestine; K. Ascending colon;
L. Transverse colon; M. Descending colon;
N. Sigmoid flexure; O. Rectum; P. Anus

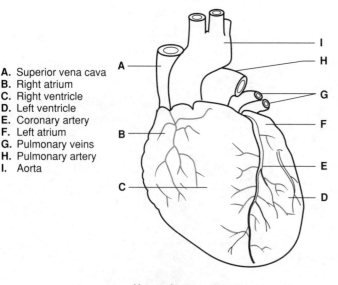

Human heart
(external view)

A. Superior vena cava
B. Right atrium
C. Right ventricle
D. Left ventricle
E. Coronary artery
F. Left atrium
G. Pulmonary veins
H. Pulmonary artery
I. Aorta

LIFE CYCLE

fertilization: beginning of life
prenatal development

birth
postnatal development
reproduction
aging
dying and death

sarcomas: involve bones, muscles, cartilage, and fat
leukemias: involve white blood cells
lymphomas: involve lymphatic system

MEDICAL KNOWLEDGE

Blood Pressure Levels

diastolic (minimum during cardiac cycle)
normal: less than 85 (mm Hg)
high normal: 85–89
mild hypertension: 90–104
moderate hypertension: 105–114
severe hypertension: 115+
systolic (ventricle contraction) [when diastolic is less than 90]
normal: less than 140
borderline isolated systolic hypertension: 140–159
isolated systolic hypertension: 160+

Burns by Degree

first degree (affects epidermis; as from sunburn, steam)
second degree (affects dermis; from scalding water, holding hot metal)
third degree (full layer of skin destroyed; fire burn)

Burns by Type

circumferential (completely encircle limb or body region, possibly impairing circulation or respiration; often from electrical burn)
chemical (from acid or alkali)
electrical (destroys tissues below the skin)

Cancer Classification

carcinomas: involve skin and skin-like membranes of internal organs

Cancer Survival rates
(for five years following diagnosis)

Thyroid	95%
Prostate	92%
Melanoma	88%
Breast	85%
Uterus	84%
Urinary Bladder	81%
Cervix	70%
Larynx	65%
Colon & Rectum	61%
Kidney	60%
Lung & Bronchus	14%
Liver	5%

Carcinogen Classification—EPA

Group A, human carcinogen (cause-effect relationship between substance and cancer established)
Group B, probable human carcinogen
B1: evidence from animal studies, limited epidemiological data
B2: evidence from animal studies, inadequate epidemiological data
Group C, possible human carcinogen (limited evidence from animal studies, no epidemiological data)
Group D, not classifiable (data inadequate or completely lacking)
Group E, noncarcinogenicity for humans (substances testing negative in two adequate animal studies)

Drugs—Addiction Potential

1.	Nicotine	100%
2.	Ice, glass (methamphetamine smoked)	98.5%
3.	Crack	97.6%
4.	Crystal meth (methamphetamine snorted)	94.0%
5.	Valium (diazepam)	85.6%
6.	Quaalude (methaqualone)	83.4%
7.	Seconal (secobarbital)	82.1%
8.	Alcohol	81.8%
9.	Heroin	81.8%
10.	Crank (amphetamine taken orally)	81.1%
11.	Cocaine	73.1%
12.	Caffeine	72.0%
13.	PCP (phencyclidine)	55.7%
14.	Marijuana	21.1%
15.	Ecstasy (MDMA)	20.1%
16.	Psilocybin mushrooms	17.1%
17.	LSD	16.7%
18.	Mescaline	16.7%

DRUG TYPES

Autonomic nervous system
Central nervous system
  anesthetics
    general anesthetics
    local anesthetics
    analgesics and narcotics
    anti-inflammatory analgesics
    opioid analgesics
  drugs affecting mood and behavior
    antianxiety drugs
    antidepressants
    antimanics
    antipsychotic drugs
    sedative-hypnotic drugs
    antiepileptic drugs
    anti-Parkinson drugs
Cardiovascular system
  inotropic agents
  chronotropic agents
  antidysrhythmic drugs
  drugs affecting blood vessels
  cardiovascular disease
Drugs affecting blood
  anticoagulant drugs
  drugs affecting platelets
  fibrinolytic drugs
Drugs affecting muscle
  smooth muscle
  skeletal muscle
Digestive system
  drugs affecting gastrointestinal motility
  diarrhea
  constipation
  vomiting
  drugs affecting digestive juices
  acid secretion
  neutralization
  mucosal barrier
Reproductive system
  female reproductive system
  oral contraceptives
  oxytocin drugs
  teratogenicity
  male reproductive system
Kidney
  proximal tubule
  the loop of Henle
  distal tubule
Dermatological
  topically applied drugs
  steroids
  anticancer agents
  photosensitizing
  transdermally applied drugs
  mucous membranes
  antibiotics
Endocrine
  anterior pituitary gland
  growth hormone
  Prolactin
  thyrotropin
  Adrenocorticotropin
  luteinizing hormone
  follicle-stimulating hormone

posterior pituitary gland
Vasopressin
Oxytocin
adrenal gland
thyroid and parathyroid glands
parathyroid hormone
calcitonin
thyroxine and triiodothyronine
pancreas
Histamine and antihistamines
Chemotherapy
   antibacterial drugs
   antifungal drugs
   antiparasitic drugs
   antiviral drugs
Cancer chemotherapy
   alkylating agents
   antimetabolites
   antineoplastic antibiotics
   hormones
Immunosuppressants

FRACTURE SEVERITY SCALE

(from least severe to worst)

hairline (bone splits in a line, often
   lengthwise)
pathological (caused by disease)
greenstick (incomplete, often
   lengthwise)
fatigue (bone splits)
depressed (bone splits, is pushed
   inward)
simple/closed (bone snaps, does not
   break skin)
comminuted (part of bone shattered)
compound (broken bone pushes
   through skin)

LIFESAVING PROCEDURES

*(AMA recommends priority be given to
these when a person is injured or
suddenly becomes ill:)*

1. Maintain breathing
2. Maintain circulation
3. Prevent loss of blood
4. Prevent further injury
5. Prevent shock
6. Summon professional medical
   services

POISON CLASSIFICATION

Microbial (produced by bacteria or
   fungi)
Plant
Animal
Synthetic (manufactured chemicals)
Solid
Liquid
Gas
Vapor
Aerosol
Metallic /Nonmetallic
Organic / Inorganic
Acidic / Alkaline
Electrophilic (literally meaning
   electron-loving)
Nucleophilic (literally meaning
   nucleus-loving)

NERVE PROCESS

(in reaction to pain)

1. pain triggers sensory neuron to produce a signal
2. signal races along neuron's axon (fiber)
3. signal is passed to an association neuron in the spinal cord; the signal reaches the association neuron by jumping across a synapse (tiny gap)
4. association neuron passes the signal across a synapse to a motor neuron
5. motor neuron makes muscles contract, e.g. making you pull yourself away from the source of pain

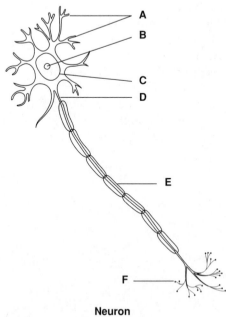

Neuron

A. Dendrites; **B.** Nucleus; **C.** Cell body;
D. Axon; **E.** Myelin sheath; **F.** Axon terminals

HUMAN REPRODUCTION

1. female egg ripens during menstrual period, leaves ovary and goes into Fallopian tube
2. male sperm cells cluster around egg; only one sperm penetrates egg to fertilize it
3. fertilized egg divides into two cells within 36 hours, then into four by 48 hours, then eight, etc. Barrier keeps out other sperm cells.
4. About three days after fertilization, there is a ball of 16–32 cells that enters the uterus as an embryo.

SENSES CLASSIFICATION

deep senses: muscle, tendon, joint, deep pain and pressure
skin senses: touch, skin pain, temperature
special senses: vision, hearing, smell, taste, vestibular/equilibrium
visceral senses: conveyance of information about organic and visceral events

SENSING ORDER OF THE EARS

1. sound waves are gathered by the ear and passed to the auditory canal
2. sound waves cause eardrum to vibrate
3. vitrations are passed on and strengthened by the three ossicles: malleus (hammer), incus (anvil), and stapes (stirrup)
4. the oval window vibrates and vibrations pass into the fluid of the cochlea
5. vibrations are detected by special cells in the cochlea
6. information is sent via the auditory nerve to the brain

SENSING ORDER OF THE EYES

1. Light rays pass through cornea, pupil lens, aqueous humor, and vitreous humor and are bent and partially focused
2. Iris dilates in dim light and contracts in bright light, controlling size of pupil
3. Light focused onto retina by lens produces an image; rods and cones on retinal surface produce nerve signals
4. Optic nerve carries signals to the brain

SENSING ORDER OF THE NOSE

1. Molecules are breathed into roof of nasal cavity
2. Molecules dissolved on olfactory membrane made up of receptor cells with tiny sensitive "hairs"
3. Scent molecules react with hairs to stimulate nerve impulses in receptor cells
4. Factory nerves transmit these signals to olfactory bulbs, then via olfactory tracts to the front part of the cerebrum of the brain

SENSORY SYSTEM CLASSIFICATION

According to Location of Receptors
exteroceptors
interoceptors
According to Type of Stimulus
photoreceptors
thermoreceptors
chemoreceptors
mechanoreceptors
electroreceptors
sound receptors

SEXUAL RESPONSE PHASES

(Masters and Johnson)

1. excitement phase
2. plateau phase
3. orgasm phase
4. resolution phase

SKIN LAYERS

epidermis (outer layer)
  comeum: dead cells on surface
  granular: rough layer just under surface
  spinous: spiny, tight-knit layer
  basal: base cells
dermis (inner layer): blood vessels, hair follicles, nerve endings, sweat glands

SLEEP PERIODS

light sleep: short periods between the longer periods of deep sleep
deep sleep: 1½–2 hours after falling asleep
REM sleep: within deep sleep, time of dreams and "rapid eye movement"

HUMAN BODILY SYSTEMS

cardiovascular system
digestive system
endocrine system
lymphatic system
muscular system
nervous system
reproductive system
respiratory system
skeletal system
urinary system

TASTING AREAS OF TONGUE

(saliva carries food particles to taste buds which register the different flavors)

back: bitter
right middle: sour
right front: salt
front: sweet
left front: salt
left middle: sour

TOOTH ARRIVAL/GROWTH

central incisors, 6–8 months
lateral incisors, 7–8 months
first molars, 1 year
cuspids/canines, 16 months
second molars, 20–24 months
second incisors, 7–9 years
cuspids or canines, 9–12 years
first and second premolars or
    bicuspids, 10–12 years

second molars, 11–13 years
third molars/wisdom teeth, 20 years

baby teeth:

8 incisors
4 cuspids/canines
8 molars

TOOTH LOSS—CHILDHOOD

(in usual order of loss)

central incisors
lateral incisors
first molars
second molars
first molars

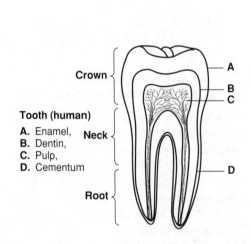

Crown

Tooth (human)
A. Enamel,   **Neck**
B. Dentin,
C. Pulp,
D. Cementum

Root

A
B
C

D

Upper Teeth

A
B
C

**Permanent
teeth of an
adult human**

A. Incisors,
B. Canines,
C. Premolars,
D. Molars

D

C
B
A

Lower Teeth

PLANTS AND NON-ANIMAL ORGANISMS

EDIBLE PLANT PARTS

Vegetative parts
  bulbs: onion, garlic
  entire plant: green onion, carrot, bunched radish
  floral parts and stem: broccoli, cauliflower, globe artichoke
  leaf blades: spinach, lettuce, cabbage, Brussels sprouts
  leaf petioles: rhubarb, celery
  roots: carrot, beet, turnip, sweet potato
  stems: asparagus, kohlrabi
  tubers: potato
Fruit parts
  immature fruits: cucumber, summer squash, eggplant, okra, green bean, lima bean, pea, sweet corn
  mature fruits: tomato, muskmelon, watermelon, pumpkin, squash

FRUITS

Classification

Accessory Fruits (derived from other parts of the flower or from stalk in addition to ovary)
Compound Fruits
  Aggregate (raspberry)
  Multiple (pineapple, mulberry)
Simple Fruits
  Fleshy
    Berry
      true berry (tomato, blueberry)
      hesperidium (orange, grapefruit)
      pepo (watermelon, squash, cucumber)
    Drupe (peach, cherry)
    Pome (apple, pear)

Dry Fruits
  Dehiscent (splitting to emit seeds or spores)
    follicle (milkweed, columbine)
    legume (pea, bean)
    capsule (lily, iris)
    silique (mustard)
    silicle (sweet alyssum)
    schizocarp (carrot, parsnip)
  Indehiscent (not splitting to emit seeds or spores)
    achene (buttercup, grasses, sunflower, elm, maple)

also

1. berries (fleshy with many seeds): tomatoes, grapes
2. hesperidium/citrus (leathery rind and juice sacs): oranges, lemons, grapefruits
3. pepos (hard outer covering): pumpkins, cucumbers, squash
4. drupes (fleshy with thin outer skin and a pit or stone: cherries, plums, peaches
5. aggregates (cluster of small fruitlets): blackberries, strawberries, raspberries
6. multiple fruits (formed from individual ovaries of multiple flowers): pineapple, fig
7. pomes (fleshy with thin skin and seeds in center): apples, pears
8. legumes (seeds in single pod): peas, lima beans, peanuts
9. capsules (more than one compartment of seeds): okras
10. caryposis (tough outer layer attached to seed coat): corn
11. nuts (hard dry fruit with single seed in husk): chestnuts, filberts
12. dry fruits: fruits of grains, flowers, and other plants

Designs

pomes (apple)
drupes (cherry)
nuts (almond)
berries (blueberry)
citrus (orange)
tropical (banana)

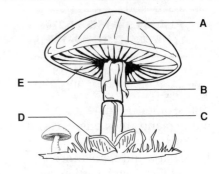

Mushroom
A. Pileus
B. Annulus
C. Stem
D. Volva
E. Gills

FUNGI CLASSIFICATION

(phylum, class, examples)

Zygomycota
  Mucorales, black bread mold
  Entomophthorales, Basidiobolus
  Zoopagales, Cochlonema
    Endocochlus
Ascomycota
  Hemiascomycetae, yeasts
  Euascomycetae, morels and truffles
  Loculoascomycetae,
    Mycosphaerella Elsinoe
  Laboulbeniomycetae, Rhizomyces
    Amorphomyces
Basidiomycota
  Heterobasiciomycetae, jelly fungi,
    rusts, and smuts
  Homobasidiomycetae,
    mushrooms, puffballs,
    stinkhorns, and coral fungi
Deuteromycota
  Sphaeropsida, Clypeoseptoria
    aparothospermi
  Melanconia, Cryptosporium
    lunasporum
  Monilia, Penicillium Candida
    albicans
  Mycelia Sterilia, Rhizoctonia

Typical Mushroom Structure
(from bottom up)

volva
stem (or stipe)
annulus
gills
pileus (or cap)

HORTICULTURE CLASSIFICATION

floriculture (flower growing)
olericulture (vegetable growing)
ornamental horticulture
  (landscaping)
pomology (fruit growing)

INSECTIVOROUS PLANTS

Families

Sarraceniacea (pitcher plants)
Droseracea (sundew)
Lentibulariaceae (butterworts)

Venus' Flytrap Digestion Sequence
1. leaf lobes open
2. insects crawls across leaf, touches
   base of trigger hair
3. lobes snap shut, pressing tightly
   on insect
4. protein-processing enzymes digest
   insect in 5–10 days, lobes open
   wide again

LIFE CYCLES

Algae

(three types)

Sargassum:
   fertilization (union of two
      gametes that starts
      development)
   zygote (cell formed by union of
      two gametes)
   sporophyte stage (spore-bearing,
      diploid, multicelled stage)
   meiosis (diploid divided to
      haploid)
   gametes (mature cell, egg or
      sperm)
Ectocarpus:
   fertilization
   zygote
   sporophyte stage
   meiosis
   gametophyte stage (gamete-
      bearing, haploid, multicelled
      stage)
   gametes
Spirogyra:
   fertilization
   zygote
   meiosis
   gametophyte stage
   gametes

Conifer

(spruce, pine)

ovule meets pollen and is fertilized
cone develops from seed
adult tree

Flowering Plant

(daisy, poppy)

ovule meets pollen and is fertilized
seed forms
adult plant

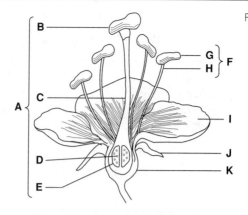

Flower
(in cross section)

A. Pistil	**G.** Anther
B. Stigma	**H.** Filament
C. Style	**I.** Petal
D. Ovule	**J.** Sepal
E. Ovary	**K.** Receptacle
F. Stamen	

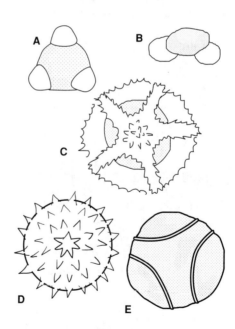

Pollen Grains

A. Evening primrose, *Oenothera biennis*;
B. Scotch pine, *Pinus sylvestris*; **C.** Chicory,
Chicorium intybus; **D.** Hibiscus, *Hibiscus
moscheutos*; **E.** Passionflower,
Passiflora caerulea.

Fungus

(mushroom, toadstool)

spore formed by fertilization inside
    fruiting body
spores released
spores grow into hypha
hypha grows into fruiting body

Non-Flowering Plant

(kelp, liverwort)

spores released by plant
prothallus forms (gametophyte)
sperm cell fertilizes egg cell
zygote beneath gametophyte
sporophyte plant

NON-ANIMAL CLASSIFICATION

Monerans (bacteria, algae, viruses)
Protists (one-celled organisms)
  Algae
  Protozoans
  Slime molds
Fungi
Plants
  Bryophytes (simple nonvascular
    plants)
    Hornworts
    Liverworts
    Mosses
  Psilotophytes (whisk ferns)
  Lycophytes (club mosses and allies)
  Sphenophytes (horsetails)
  Filicophytes (ferns)
    Filicopsids (thin-walled
      sporangia, more strengthening
      tissues)
    Marattiopsids (terrestrial with
      huge sporangia)
    Ophioglossopsids (adder's
      tongue ferns)
  Conifers (cone-bearing trees)
  Ginkgos (ginkgo and maidenhair
    trees)

Cycads (gymnosperms)
Gnetophytes
Angiosperms (flowering plants)
  Liliopsids (monocots)
  Magnoliopsids (dicots)

PLANT TAXONOMY

*(the prefixes myc- = fungi and phyc- =
algae)*

Kingdom
Division (-phyta)
Subdivision (-phytina)
Class (-opsida)
Subclass (-idae)
Order (-ales)
Suborder (-ineae)
Family (-aceae)
Subfamily (-oideae)
Tribe (-eae)
Subtribe (-inae)
Genus
Subgenus
Section
Subsection
Series
Subseries
Species
Subspecies
Variety
Subvariety
Form
Subform

POISONOUS PLANTS

banewort
belladonna
black nightshade
castor oil plant
deadly nightshade
death camass
death cup
foxglove

Bacteria (greatly magnified)
A. Cocci (spherical): **1.** Staphylococcus pyogenes aureus; **2.** Streptococcus pyogenes;
B. Bacilli (rod): **3.** Bacillus sporogenes; **4.** Bacillus proteus; **5.** Bacillus subtilis;
6. Bacillus typhosus; **C.** spirilla (spiral): **7.** Vibrio cholerae asiaticae; **8.** Spirillum undulum;
9. Theospirillum; **10.** Spirochaeta

gastrologium
greyana
hellebore
hemp
henbane
Indian hemp
jimson weed
locoweed
May apple
mescal
monkshood
mushroom, wild
nightshade
nux vomica
opium poppy
poison bean
poisonberry
poisonbush
poison grass
poison hemlock
poison ivy

poison laureal
poison oak
poison rhubarb
poison sumac
poison tobacco
poisonweed
pokeweed
sheep laurel
upas
water hemlock

TREES

Tree Classifications

angiosperms (flowering, broad-
    leaved trees)
    monocotyledons (one-seed
        leaf)(palms, aloes, yuccas)
    dicotyledons (two-seed leaf)(birch,
        elms, magnolias, maples,
        poplars, willows)

catkin-bearing trees
  (Amentiferae)
beech, chestnut, oak
  (Fagaceae)
birch, alder, hornbeam, hazel
  (Betulaceae)
corkwood (Leitneriaceae)
sweet gale, bayberry
  (Myricaceae)
walnut, hickory, pecan
  (Juglandaceae)
willow, poplar, aspen,
  cottonwood (Salicaceae)
flower-bearing trees (Floriferae)
apetalous: lacking petals
  elm, hackberry (Ulmaceae)

mulberry, osage orange, fig
  (Moraceae)
sympetalous/gamopetalous:
  petals united in a tube
  olive, ash (Oleaceae)
  persimmon (Ebenaceae)
  sourwood (Ericaceae)
polypetalous: many-petaled
  flowers
  apples, pears, peaches,
    plums, cherries, almonds,
    mountain ashes,
    hawthorns (Rosaceae)
  buckeye (Hippocastanaceae)
  dogwood (Cornaceae)
  holly (Aquifoliaceae)
  laurel, sassafras (Lauraceae)
  locust (Leguminosae)
  magnolia, tulip tree
    (Magnoliaceae)
  mahogany (Meliaceae)
  maple (Aceraceae)
  sycamore (Platanaceae)
  witchhazel, red gum
    (Hamamelidaceae)
gymnosperms (cone-bearing)
  conifers (Coniferales)
    cedar and cypress
      (Cupressaceae)
    pine, larch, spruce, fir,
      hemlock, Douglas fir
      (Pinaceae)
    redwood, sequoia, bald cypress
      (Taxodiaceae)
    yew (Taxaceae)
  cycads (Cycadales)
  desert shrubs, woody climbers, and
    small trees of tropical forests
    (Gnetales)
  ginkgo and maidenhair trees
    (Ginkgoales)
  pteridophytes (seedless vascular
    plants)

OR

Hardwoods/broadleaf trees
  dicotyledons

Structure of a Tree

top

limb

twig

branch

bole

trunk

tap root

radicle

root-hair zone

Softwoods
  conifers

OR

Deciduous (loses leaves once during
  the year)
Evergreen (retains foliage year-
  round)

Tree Layers

(inner to outer)

heartwood (core of inactive cells)
sapwood (food for seed production
  and tree growth)
annual rings (reveal tree age)
cambium (cells that produce new
  layer of bark and wood between old
  bark and wood each year)
inner bark (carries food made in
  leaves)
outer bark (protects tree)

Woody Stem Layers

(inner to outer)

xylem (cells that carry water to leaves)
cambium (makes phloem and xylem
  cells)
phloem (cells carrying food from
  leaves to roots)

Cross Section of a Trunk

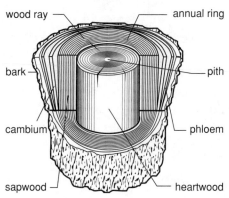

cortex (food-storing cells)
cork (dead outer protection)
heartwood (cell pipes that are
  discarded and pushed in to form
  the tree's core)
sapwood (cells that form pipes that
  carry sap)
cambium (outside generates new
  bark; inside makes sapwood)
bark (hard, dead exterior protection)

VEGETABLES

Families

Amaryllis (Amaryllidaceae): onion,
  leek, garlic, shallot, chive
Buckwheat (Polygonaceae): rhubarb
Carpetweed (Aizoaceae): New
  Zealand spinach
Composite (Compositae): lettuce,
  chicory, endive, dandelion,
  artichoke
Goosefoot (Chenopodiaceae): beet,
  chard, spinach
Gourd (Cucurbitaceae): muskmelon,
  watermelon, pumpkin, squash,
  cucumber
Grass (Gramineae): sweet corn
Lily (Liliaceae): asparagus
Mallow (Malvaceae): okra
Morning Glory (Convolvulaceae):
  sweet potato
Mustard (Cruciferae): mustard,
  turnip, rutabaga, cabbage,
  cauliflower, Brussels sprouts,
  broccoli, watercress, radish)
Nightshade (Solanaceae): potato,
  tomato, eggplant, pepper
Parsley (Umbelliferae): parsley,
  carrot, celery, fennel
Pea (Leguminosea): lima bean, pea,
  broad bean, snap bean, soybean

PLANTS AND
   NON-ANIMAL
   ORGANISMS
    Vegetables (cont.)

COMMON LEAF SHAPES AND MARGINS

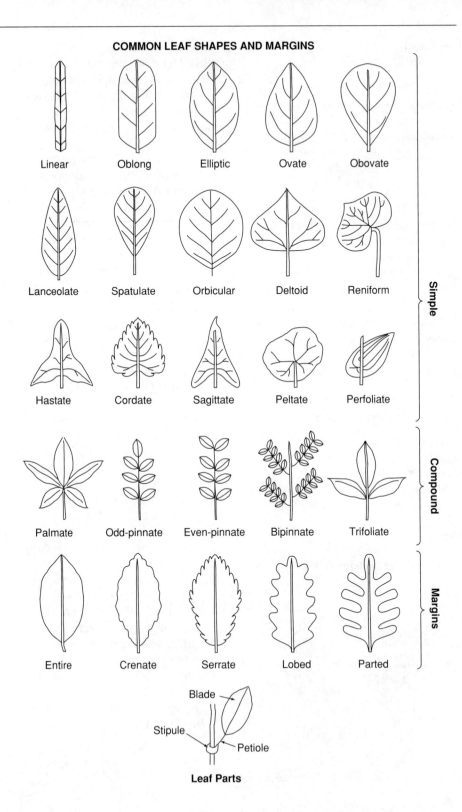

Leaf Parts

Vegetable Types

bulb and stalk vegetables (celery)
cabbage family (cauliflower)
leaf vegetables (lettuce)

root and tuber vegetables (carrot)
seed vegetables (beans)
vegetable fruits (cucumber)

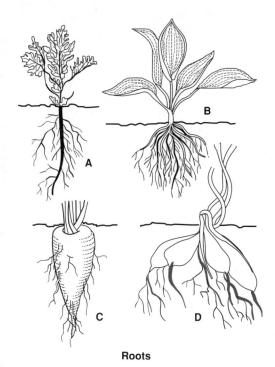

Roots

A. Tap (ragweed, *Ambrosia trifida*); **B.** Fibrous (plantain, *Plantago major*);
C. Fleshy (carrot, *Daucus carota*); **D.** Tuberous (rue anemone,
Anemonella thalictroides)

Physics is experience, arranged in economical order.

—Ernst Mach, *The Economical Nature of Physical Inquiry*

CHAPTER THREE

PHYSICAL SCIENCES

ASTRONOMY

BRANCHES OF ASTRONOMY

Research Astronomy

Astrometry (measurements of
    celestial bodies)
Astronautics
Astrophysics
Celestial mechanics
Chronometry (time measurement)
Cosmology (origin of universe)
Radar astronomy
Radio astronomy
Theoretical astronomy

Applied Astronomy

Celestial navigation
Nautical astronomy

BIG BANG SEQUENCE

*(The Big Bang was a rapid expansion,
not a violent explosion.)*

1. Gravity separates from three other
   forces—electromagnetic, strong
   nuclear, and weak interaction at
   10^{-43} seconds
2. Three forces operating—
   electromagnetic, strong nuclear,
   and gravitational—at 10^{-33} seconds
3. Weak interaction and
   electronmagnetic force separate
   shortly thereafter
4. Quarks combine to form protons
   and neutrons at 10^{-5} seconds
5. The nuclei of helium atoms
   formed (3 minutes)
6. Changeover from dominance of
   energy in the form of radiation to
   energy in the form of matter (1,000
   years)

7. Temperature of matter decreases
   more rapidly than that of radiation
   (100,000 years)
8. The first true complex atoms
   formed (500,000 years)
9. Gaseous clouds of hydrogen and
   helium began to condense into
   protogalaxies and stars (one
   hundred million to a billion years)

GALAXIES

Hubble Classification

elliptical (disk with no arms)
    (further divided into E0–7,
        according to their aspect in the
        sky)
spiral (nucleus with arms spiraling
    outward)
    normal spiral (S) (further divided
        into types a, b, c, depending on
        extent of arms)
    lenticular (SO)
    barred spiral (spiral with a bright
        bar slicing across nucleus) (SB)
irregular (no definite structure)
    (two types, Irr I and Irr II)

MOON

Phases

new moon
waxing crescent moon
half moon, first quarter
waxing gibbous moon
full moon
waning gibbous moon
half moon, last quarter
waning crescent moon
new moon

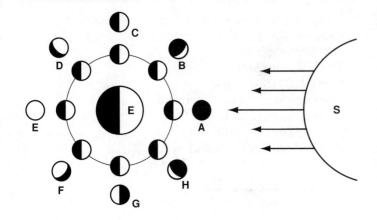

Phases of the Moon

Figures on the inner circle show the moon in its orbit; those on the outer circle represent the moon's corresponding phases as seen from the earth; **A.** New moon (invisible); **B.** Crescent (waxing moon); **C.** First quarter (half-moon; **D.** Gibbous; **E.** Full-moon; **F.** Gibbous; **G.** Last quarter (half-moon); **H.** Crescent (waning moon); **S.** Sun; **E.** Earth

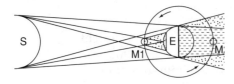

Eclipse
S. Sun, **E.** Earth,
M1. Eclipse of the sun,
M2. Eclipse of the moon

PLANETS

Order from the Sun

(closest to farthest in astronomical units (93 million miles))

Mercury (.39 astronomical units)
Venus (.72 AU)
Earth (1 AU)
Mars (1.52 AU)
Jupiter (5.20 AU)
Saturn (9.54 AU)

Uranus (19.18 AU)
Neptune (30.06 AU)
Pluto (39.36 AU)

Planets in order by size

(diameter in miles)

Jupiter—88,700
Saturn—74,000
Uranus—32,500
Neptune—30,700
Earth—7,921
Venus—7,516
Mars—4,220
Mercury—3,029
Pluto—680

SATELLITES (MOONS) & RINGS

(closest to farthest; with year of first observation)

Jupiter's Satellites

Inner satellites
 Metis (1979)
 Adrastea (1979)
 Amalthea (1892)
 Thebe (1979)
Galilean satellites
 Io (1610)
 Europa (1610)
 Ganymede (1610)
 Callisto (1610)
Outer satellites
 S/1999J1 (1999)
 Leda (1974)
 Himalia (1904)
 Lysithea (1938)
 Elara (1905)
 Ananke (1951)
 Carme (1938)
 Pasiphae (1908)
 Sinope (1914)

Mars' Satellites

Phobos (1877)
Deimos (1877)

Neptune's Satellites

Naiad (1989)
Thalassa (1989)
Despina (1989)
Galatea (1989)
Larissa (1989)
Proteus (1989)
Triton (1846)
Nereid (1949)

Saturn's Rings

D-Ring
C-Ring
B-Ring
A-Ring
F-Ring
G-Ring
E-Ring

Saturn's Satellites

Pan (1990)
Atlas (1980)
Prometheus (1980)
Pandora (1980)
Epimetheus (1980)
Janus (1966)
Mimas (1789)
Enceladus (1789)
Tethys (1684)
Telesto (1980)

Calypso (1980)
Dione (1684)
Helene (1980)
Rhea (1672)
Titan (1655)
Hyperion (1848)
Iapetus (1671)
Phoebe (1898)

(It is now likely that there are an additional six satellites, though not yet confirmed.)

Uranus's Satellites

Cordelia (1986)
Ophelia (1986)
Bianca (1986)
Cressida (1986)
Desdemona (1986)
Juliet (1986)
Portia (1986)
Rosalind (1986)
Belinda (1986)
1986 UIO (1999)
Puck (1985)

Miranda (1948)
Ariel (1851)
Umbriel (1851)
Titania (1787)
Oberon (1787)
Caliban (1997)
Stephano (1999)
Sycorax (1997)
Properso (1999)
Stebos (1999)

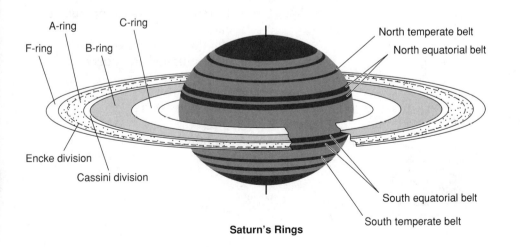

Saturn's Rings

A-ring
C-ring
F-ring
B-ring
North temperate belt
North equatorial belt
Encke division
Cassini division
South equatorial belt
South temperate belt

SPACE

Distances

astronomical unit/AU = 92,955,630 mi (avg. distance from Earth to Sun)

light year = 62,240 AU

parsec = 3.26 light years

kiloparsec = 1,000 parsecs

megaparsec = 1,000,000 parsecs

COMET

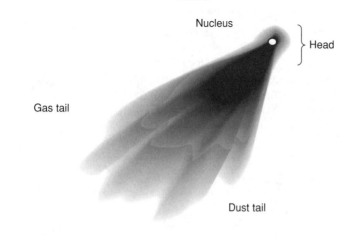

Nucleus

Head

Gas tail

Dust tail

GALAXY

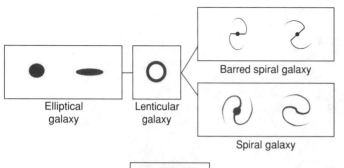

Elliptical galaxy

Lenticular galaxy

Barred spiral galaxy

Spiral galaxy

Irregular galaxy

Layers / Areas

Earth

Earth's atmosphere, approx 100 miles

cislunar space, approx 11,000 miles

translunar space, approx 100,000 miles

interplanetary space, approx 1 million miles (solar wind radiation, meteoroids, micrometeorites, comets)

interstellar space, approx 11 billion miles (cosmic rays, protons, hydrogen, helium, and other gases)

intergalactic space

STARS

Big Dipper's Stars

(from tip of the handle to the end of the cup)

1. Alkaid
2. Mizar and Alcor (double star)
3. Alioth
4. Megrez
5. Phecda
6. Merak
7. Dubhe

Brightness / Magnitude

(brightest to dimmest)

0, extremely luminous supergiant star

Ia, luminous supergiant

Ib, lower luminosity supergiant

II, bright giant

III, ordinary giant

IV, subgiant

V, dwarf

VI, subdwarf

Brightest Stars by Rank
(with constellation)

Sirius	(Canis Major)
Canopus	(Carina)
Rigil Kentaurus	(Centaurus)
Arcturus	(Boötes)
Vega	(Lyra)
Capella	(Auriga)
Rigel	(Orion)
Procyon	(Canis Major)
Achernar	(Eridanus)
Betelgeuse	(Orion)

Closest Stars
(distance in light years)

Proxima Centauri, 4.22
Alpha Centauri, 4.35
Barnard's Star, 5.98
Wolf 359, 7.75
Lalande 21185, 8.22
Luyten 726.8, 8.43
Sirius, 8.65
Ross 154, 9.45
Ross 248, 10.4
Epsilon Eridani, 10.8

Temperature of Stars

Classification

(warm to cool)

[each spectral type is subdivided into ten grades or subclasses, from 0 (early) to 9 (late)]

[luminosity may also be classified from I-VII]

O, super-hot blue star, 25,000 degrees Kelvin
B, hot blue star, 11,000–25,000
A, blue-white star, 7500–11,000
F, white star, 6,000–7,500
G, yellow star (Sun is G2), 5,000–6,000
K, orange star, 3,500–5,000
M, cool red star, 3,500

CELESTIAL COORDINATE SYSTEM

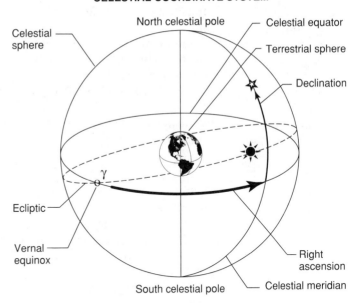

Hertzprung-Russell Spectral Evolution

(evolution of stars plotted on a luminosity-versus-surface temperature graph)

(Chandrasekhar limit is maximum mass that a star can attain without collapsing to become a neutron star or black hole.)

stars with cores below the
    Chandrasekhar limit evolve:
red giants
red supergiants
white dwarfs
dark dwarfs
stars with cores above the
    Chandrasekhar limit evolve:
red giants
supernovae

Types of Stars

1. red supergiant, 400 times larger and 15,000 times brighter than Sun

2. blue-white giant, 80 times larger and 60,000 times brighter than Sun
3. yellow giant, 16 times larger and 150 times brighter than Sun
4. yellow dwarf, as the Sun
5. red dwarf, 10 times smaller than Sun
6. white dwarf, 100 times smaller than Sun

Life Cycle of a Star

1. Nebula, born from clouds of gas and dust
2. Parts of cloud collapse under gravity, making it dense at center where heat is trapped, forming a protostar
3. Hot protostar undergoes nuclear fusion and energy is released, forming a T. Tauri type star
4. Gravity pulls hydrogen atoms toward the center, where they smash and fuse to form helium and energy; pressure at center keeps the star from collapsing, forming main sequence star (Earth's Sun is now in the middle of its main sequence life.)
5. Star's luminosity increases and core becomes denser and hotter; hydrogen is used up, star expands, surface cools and turns red, forming a red giant
6. Helium remaining begins to fuse with itself to form carbon, forming a Cepheid, which continually shrinks and expands, losing outer layers of material
7. Outer layers of the star become unstable and inner layers do not have enough energy to keep them from collapsing; white dwarf forms
8. White dwarf fades to become black dwarf

Sun's Layers

(outermost to innermost)

outer layers:
corona, average temperature 4 million° (outer and inner layers)
transition region, a few hundred km thick, around 100,000° F
chromosphere, reddish layer above sun's surface, around 50,000° F
photosphere, the sun's surface, around 10,000° F
inner layers:
convection zone, temperature about 2 million° F (hot gas currents rise to photosphere)
radiation zone, temperature about 4.5 million° F (radiation passes through this zone)
core, temperature about 27 million° F (nuclei of atoms fuse, releasing high-energy radiation)

CHEMISTRY

ATOMS

Properties

Atomic mass number
Atomic number
Atomic weight
Chemical behavior
Electric charge
Electron shells
Nuclear properties

BRANCHES OF CHEMISTRY

Research Chemistry

Analytical chemistry
  Qualitative analysis
  Quantitative analysis

Parts of the Atom

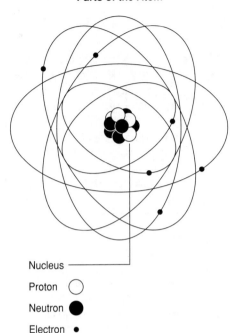

Nucleus ————

Proton ○

Neutron ●

Electron •

Biochemistry
Inorganic chemistry
Organic chemistry
Physical chemistry
  Electrochemistry
  Nuclear chemistry
  Photochemistry
  Thermochemistry

Applied Chemistry

Agricultural chemistry
Chemical engineering
Petroleum chemistry
Pharmaceutical chemistry
Synthetic chemistry
Textile chemistry

OILS CLASSIFICATION

1. petroleum and similar oils, resulting from distillation of crude oil, shale oil, or coal
    principal products: naphtha, gasoline, kerosene, paraffin, fuel oil, pitch, asphalt
2. fixed oils, fats, and waxes
    fixed or fatty oils (glycerides, olive oil)
    vegetable fatty oils (linseed oil)
    animal oils (sardine, salmon)
    vegetable fats (cocoa butter)
    animal fats (lard, tallow, beeswax)
    hydrogenated and special oils (cottonseed oil)
    commercial oils (eucalyptus, citronella)
    artificials and synthetics (apricot, amyl salicylate)
3. essential and volatile oils
    chiefly used in perfumes, as: camphor, musk, rose, sandal

PERIODIC TABLE—CHEMICAL GROUPS

1. Alkali metals/sodium family: Li, Na, K, Rb, Cs, Fr
2. Alkaline earth metals/calcium family: Be, Mg, Ca, Sr, Ba, Ra
3. Nonmetals: C, N, O, F, P, S, Cl, Br, I, At
4. Semimetals: B, Si, Ge, As, Se, Sb, Te
5. Halogen family: F, Cl, Br, I, At
6. Inert/noble gases: He, Ne, Ar, Kr, Xe, Rn
7. Lanthanide series: La, Ce, Pr, Nd, Pm, Sm, Eu, Gd, Tb, Dy, Ho, Er, Tm, Yb, Lu
8. Actinide series: Ac, Th, Pa, U, Np, Pu, Am, Cm, Bk, Cf, Es, Fm, Md, No, Lr

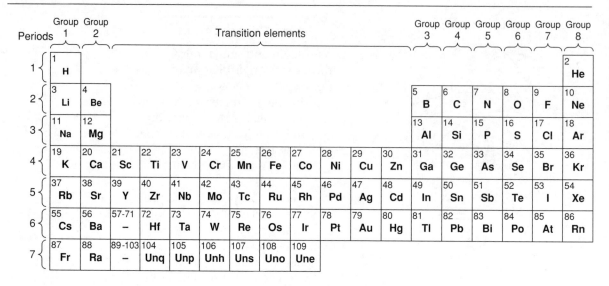

Periodic Table of the Elements

---

pH VALUES

(acid to base)

0 = hydrochloric acid
1 = stomach acid
2 = lemon juice, soda pop, vinegar
3 = apple, grapefruit, orange juice, or wine
4 = tomato, shampoo
5 = bread, black coffee, acid rain, beer
6 = cow's milk, unpolluted rain
7 = pure water
8 = sea water, human blood, egg white
9 = soap
10 = milk of magnesia
11 = ammonia
12 = cleaning fluids
13 = caustic soda, lye
14 = drain cleaner, potassium hydroxide

RADIOACTIVITY

Types

Alpha decay
Beta-minus decay
Beta-plus decay
Electron capture
Gamma decay
Heavy-ion radioactivity
Isomeric transitions
Proton radioactivity
Special beta-decay processes
Spontaneous fission

CHEMICAL REACTION TYPES

aergic (or athermic; i.e., without energy change)
endoergic (or endothermic; with energy change)
exoergic (or exothermic; energy is evolved)

SULFUR CYCLE

1. Sulfates (sulfur-oxygen compounds) absorbed by plant roots
2. Oxygen in sulfates is replaced by hydrogen when plants make amino acids
3. Animals eat plants
4. Amino acids in dead plants and animals are broken down by microorganisms to obtain hydrogen sulfide
5. Bacteria take sulfur from sulfides
6. Other bacteria combine sulfur with oxygen to produce sulfates

MATTER

CLASSIFICATION

gas: particles far apart
liquid: particles attract and stick together
solid: particles tightly packed together

STATES OF MATTER

mixture (two or more elements not chemically bonded)
compound (two or more elements chemically bonded to form a new substance)
element (single substance that cannot be broken down chemically into simpler substances)
molecule (two or more atoms joined together)
atom (made up of subatomic particles, the stable particles being protons, neutrons, electrons)
plasma (mixture of free electrons and ions or atomic nuclei)

PHYSICS

BRANCHES OF PHYSICS

acoustics (sound)
  ultrasonics
astrophysics (the physics of stars and nebulae)
atomic physics (atomic attributes of matter)
biophysics (the physics of biological structures)
chemical physics (chemical attributes of matter)
condensed-matter physics (properties of solid and liquid substances)
electromagnetism (interaction of magnetism and electricity)
  electronics/solid state physics (electrical charges in various media)
  optics (light)
geophysics (physics of earth, air, and waters)
health physics (protection from hazards)
mechanics (motion; internal and external forces)
  dynamics (action of forces in motion or equilibrium)
    aerodynamics
    hydrodynamics
    statics (matter at rest)
      aerostatics
      hydrostatics

kinematics (description of motion)
molecular physics (physics of
molecules)
nuclear physics (structure of atomic
nucleus and radiation from
unstable nuclei)
particle physics (fundamental
subatomic constituents of
matter)
quantum mechanics (atomic and
subatomic characteristics of
energy and momentum)
statistical mechanics (macroscopic
behavior of systems)
thermal physics (interrelation of
matter and temperatures)
cryogenics (processes at extremely
low temperatures)
high-temperature research
thermodynamics (energy and heat
transfer)
tribology (friction, lubrication, and
wear)

types:
chemical
electrical
geothermal
hydraulic
internal
magnetic field energy
nuclear
solar
steam
thermal/heat
tidal
water
wind
OR:
non-renewable energy (fossil fuels)
renewable energy (wind, water,
solar, heat from inside earth)

BOILING—FIVE STAGES

*(first three seen in water boiling in pan or
teakettle; last two only seen in special
cases)*

convection
bubble collapse
smooth boiling
bumping
radiation boiling

ENERGY CLASSIFICATION

forms:
free
kinetic/dynamic
potential/static
radiant/electromagnetic
zero-point

LAWS OF MOTION

(Isaac Newton, 1687)

1. Inertia: if a body is at rest or
moving at a constant speed in a
straight line, it will remain so until
acted on by a force
2. The rate of change of momentum
is directly proportional to the
force, taking place in the direction
of the force
3. The actions of two bodies on each
other are always equal and
opposite ("For every action there is
an equal and opposite reaction)

LAWS OF THERMODYNAMICS

1. Conservation of energy (the
change in the internal energy of a
system is equal to the sum of the
heat added to the system and the
work done on it)
2. Heat always flows from a higher

temperature to a lower (law that it is impossible for any self-acting machine, without any other agent, to transfer heat to another body at a higher temperature)

3. Entropy (measure of disorder of molecules and atoms) of disordered solids reaches zero at absolute zero, i.e., there will be no disorder at all

VISIBLE COLOR SPECTRUM

(light hitting prism for picture)

red (740–620 nanometer (nm) wavelength)
orange (620–585 nm)
yellow (585–575 nm)
green (575–500 nm)
blue (500–445 nm)
indigo (445–425 nm)
violet (425–390 nm)
(Mnemonic: ROY G. BIV)

There is nothing more perilous to take in hand, more perilous to conduct, or more uncertain in its success, than to take the lead in the introduction of a new order of things.

—Niccolò Machiavelli, *The Prince*

CHAPTER FOUR

TECHNOLOGY

AERONAUTICS

SPACE FLIGHTS
Order of First 50

Vostok I (USSR) April 12, 1961
Freedom 7 (USA) May 5, 1961
Liberty Bell 7 (USA) July 21, 1961
Vostok 2 (USSR) August 6, 1961
Friendship 7 (USA) February 20, 1962
Aurora 7 (USA) May 24, 1962
Vostok 3 (USSR) August 11, 1962
Vostok 4 (USSR) August 12, 1962
Sigma 7 (USA) October 3, 1962
Faith 7 (USA) May 15, 1963
Vostok 5 (USSR) June 14, 1963
Vostok 6 (USSR) June 16, 1963
Voskhod 1 (USSR) October 12, 1964
Voskhod 2 (USSR) March 18, 1965
Gemini 3 (USA) March 25, 1965
Gemini 4 (USA) June 3, 1965
Gemini 5 (USA) August 21, 1965
Gemini 7 (USA) December 4, 1965
Gemini 6 (USA) December 15, 1965
Gemini 8 (USA) March 16, 1966
Gemini 9 (USA) June 3, 1966
Gemini 10 (USA) July 18, 1966
Gemini 11 (USA) September 12, 1966
Gemini 12 (USA) November 11, 1966
Apollo 1 (USA) January 27, 1967
Soyuz 1 (USSR) April 23, 1967
Soyuz 2 (USSR) April 24, 1967
Apollo 7 (USA) October 11, 1968
Soyuz 3 (USSR) October 26, 1968
Apollo 8 (USA) December 21, 1968
Soyuz 4 (USSR) January 14, 1969
Soyuz 5 (USSR) January 15, 1969
Apollo 9 (USA) March 3, 1969
Apollo 10 (USA) May 18, 1969
Apollo 11 (USA) July 17, 1969
Soyuz 6 (USSR) October 11, 1969
Soyuz 7 (USSR) October 12, 1969
Soyuz 8 (USSR) October 13, 1969
Apollo 12 (USA) November 14, 1969
Apollo 13 (USA) April 11, 1970
Soyuz 9 (USSR) June 1, 1970

Apollo 14 (USA) January 31, 1971
Soyuz 10 (USSR) April 23, 1971
Soyuz 11 (USSR) June 6, 1971
Apollo 15 (USA) July 26, 1971
Apollo 16 (USA) April 16, 1972
Apollo 17 (USA) December 7, 1972
Skylab 2 (USA) May 25, 1973
Skylab 3 (USA) July 28, 1973
Soyuz 12 (USSR) September 27, 1973
Skylab 4 (USA) November 16, 1973
Soyuz 13 (USSR) December 18, 1973

AGRICULTURE

AGRICULTURAL SCIENCES

agricultural economics and
    management
    agricultural finance
    agricultural law
    agricultural marketing
    agricultural policy
    farm and agribusiness
        management
    rural sociology
agricultural engineering
    (areas of mechanical, electrical,
    environmental, and civil
    engineering, construction
    technology, hydraulics, and soil
    mechanics)
agricultural meteorology
animal production
animal sciences
    animal ecology and ethology
    animal health/veterinary science
    animal nutrition
    applied animal physiology
    breeding and genetics
    food animal pathology
    livestock and poultry management
ergonomics research (study of
    adjustment/adaptation)
food sciences and post-harvest
    technologies
    (processing, storage, distribution,

and marketing of agricultural commodities and by-products)
plant production
  applied plant physiology
  breeding and genetics
  crop management
  plant ecology
  plant nutrition
  plant pathology
  weed science
soil and water sciences
  geological generation of soil
  soil and water physics
  soil and water chemistry
  soil fertility

FARM MACHINERY USE

Example of order of use in grain farming

1. Plow breaks soil into furrows for planting in spring
2. Seed drill puts measured amounts of seed into prepared soil and covers the seed
3. Sprayer covers crops with pesticides to kill diseases and pests
4. Combine harvester cuts crop and prepares it for storage

FARMING SPECIALTIES

animal husbandry
  animal breeding
  animal nutrition
crop farming
  beekeeping
  cereal farming
  dairy farming
  fruit farming
  livestock farming
  poultry farming
  specialty crop farming
  vegetable farming
plant cultivation
  harvesting and crop processing

irrigation and drainage
plant breeding
soil preparation
weather and pollution (effects of weather and pollution on farming)

AIRCRAFT

AIRCRAFT

(smallest to largest)

glider
sailplane
commercial helicopter
single-engine piston
multi-engine piston
multi-engine turboprop (airliners of 20–99 seats; commuter aircraft)
multi-engine turbofan (business jets)
commercial turbojet (DC-10, 747, 757, etc.)
supersonic transport

AIR FORCE AIRCRAFT

(largest to smallest in size)

bomber
transport aircraft
fighter
transport helicopter
helicopter gunship

MACH NUMBERS

(dry air at sea-level)

Mach 1 = 763.67 mph (speed of sound)
Mach 2 = 1,527.3 mph (twice speed of sound)
Mach 3 = 2,291 mph (3 times speed of sound)

PILOT CHECKLIST STEPS

Single-Engine Plane

Exterior preflight walk-around
  (various things at each position)
Interior preflight before starting
  engine
Starting engine
Run-up and ground check
Before take-off
Normal take-off
After take-off
Before landing
After landing
Stopping engine

Parachute: Stages of Descent

free fall
canopy opens
canopy retards descent
deceleration

AUTOMOBILES

AUTOMOBILE CLASSIFICATION

(smallest to largest)

mini-compact
subcompact
compact
midsize
full size
luxury
limousine
stretch limousine
minivan

BRAKING AN AUTOMOBILE

1. Driver presses on brake pedal.
2. A hydraulic system transfers this force equally to the wheels on both sides of the car so that the car slows without swerving. The brake pedal pushes a master piston into a set of pipes that contain brake fluid and go to the brakes. The piston increases the pressure of fluid equally throughout the pipes.
3. The brake fluid pushes out a pair of pistons that force the brake against a disk or drum fixed to the wheel to slow the car down.

AUTOMOBILE STRUCTURE AND SUBSYSTEMS

body
  engine compartment
  passenger compartment
  trunk or storage space
braking system
chassis (framework, underbody)
cooling system
electrical system
  alternator
  battery
  devices for starting engine
  devices for vehicle operation (e.g.,
    headlights)
exhaust system (including catalytic
  converter and muffler)
fuel system
lubrication system
power plant
  engine
  transmission or transaxle (shafts,
    gears, clutch)
steering system
suspension system
wheels/tires

BOATS & NAVIGATION

BOATS BY LENGTH

(U.S. Coast Guard)

Class A: under 16 feet
Class 1: 16–26 feet

Class 2: 26–40 feet
Class 3: 40–65 feet
Class 4: 65+ feet

SHIPS AND BOATS BY SIZE

(largest to smallest)

aircraft carriers
battleships
tankers
passenger liners
cargo vessels
destroyers
submarines
icebreakers
dredgers
barges
riverboats
ferries
hydrofoils
tugboats
yachts
junks
sailboats
rowboats
canoes
kayaks

NAVAL VESSELS

(largest to smallest)

aircraft carrier
battleship
battle cruiser
destroyer
frigate
submarine
patrol craft

SHIP'S BELLS

1 bell, 12:30 am
2 bells, 1 am
3 bells, 1:30 am
4 bells, 2 am
5 bells, 2:30 am
6 bells, 3 am
7 bells, 3:30 am
8 bells, 4 am
1 bell, 4:30 am
2 bells, 5 am
3 bells, 5:30 am
4 bells, 6 am
5 bells, 6:30 am
6 bells, 7 am
7 bells, 7:30 am
8 bells, 8 am
1 bell, 8:30 am
2 bells, 9 am
3 bells, 9:30 am
4 bells, 10 am
5 bells, 10:30 am
6 bells, 11 am
7 bells, 11:30 am
8 bells, 12 noon
—-
1 bell, 12:30 pm
2 bells, 1 pm
3 bells, 1:30 pm
4 bells, 2 pm
5 bells, 2:30 pm
6 bells, 3 pm
7 bells, 3:30 pm
8 bells, 4 pm
1 bell, 4:30 pm
2 bells, 5 pm
3 bells, 5:30 pm
4 bells, 6 pm
5 bells, 6:30 pm
6 bells, 7 pm
7 bells, 7:30 pm
8 bells, 8 pm
1 bell, 8:30 pm
2 bells, 9 pm
3 bells, 9:30 pm
4 bells, 10 pm
5 bells, 10:30 pm
6 bells, 11 pm
7 bells, 11:30 pm
8 bells, 12 midnight

WATCHES AT SEA

8pm-midnight, first watch
midnight-4am, middle watch or
  midwatch
4–8am, morning watch
8am-noon, forenoon watch
noon-4pm, afternoon watch
4–6pm, first dog watch
6–8pm, second dog watch (dog
  watches combined are called
  evening watch)

COMMUNICATIONS & TELECOMMUNICATIONS

COMMUNICATIONS CHAIN

information source
message
transmitter
transmitted signal
channel (with noise source)
received signal
receiver
message
destination

LONG-DISTANCE SYSTEM SETUP

message source
transmitter
  coder
  modulator
channel (transmission medium)
receiver
  demodulator
  decoder
  destination (processor)

TELECOMMUNICATIONS DIVISIONS

broadcast systems (radio, television,
  and cable television)
data communications, teleprocessing

Morse Code

Alphabet

A ● ▬	J ● ▬ ▬ ▬	S ● ● ●
B ▬ ● ● ●	K ▬ ● ▬	T ▬
C ▬ ● ▬ ●	L ● ▬ ● ●	U ● ● ▬
D ▬ ● ●	M ▬ ▬	V ● ● ● ▬
E ●	N ▬ ●	W ● ▬ ▬
F ● ● ▬ ●	O ▬ ▬ ▬	X ▬ ● ● ▬
G ▬ ▬ ●	P ● ▬ ▬ ●	Y ▬ ● ▬ ▬
H ● ● ● ●	Q ▬ ▬ ● ▬	Z ▬ ▬ ● ●
I ● ●	R ● ▬ ●	

Numerals

1 ● ▬ ▬ ▬ ▬	5 ● ● ● ● ●	9 ▬ ▬ ▬ ▬ ●
2 ● ● ▬ ▬ ▬	6 ▬ ● ● ● ●	10 ▬ ▬ ▬ ▬ ▬
3 ● ● ● ▬ ▬	7 ▬ ▬ ● ● ●	
4 ● ● ● ● ▬	8 ▬ ▬ ▬ ● ●	

Punctuation

Comma ▬ ▬ ● ● ▬ ▬	Question Mark ● ● ▬ ▬ ● ●	Error ● ● ● ● ● ● ●
Semicolon ▬ ● ▬ ● ▬ ●	Quotation Marks ● ▬ ● ● ▬ ●	Understand ● ▬ ●
Colon ▬ ▬ ▬ ● ● ●	Wait ● ▬ ● ● ●	Hyphen ▬ ● ● ● ● ▬
Period ● ▬ ● ▬ ● ▬	End of message ● ▬ ● ▬ ●	Apostrophe ● ▬ ▬ ▬ ▬ ●

In 1838 Samuel Morse invented Morse Code, the first successful
long-distance communication system that uses dots and dashes
of sound in combinations to communicate via telegraph.

**Typewriter Keyboard
(QWERTY)**

**Typewriter Keyboard
(Dvorak)**

narrow and broad bandwidth
systems
switched communications systems
telegraph
telephone, facsimile, modem, and
electronic mail

COMPUTERS

COMPUTER LANGUAGE CATEGORIES

algorithmic and procedural
languages (languages with sets of
simple rules for the solution of
mathematically expressed
problems, or for evaluating
functions)
interactive languages (languages that
perform a series of operations
repeatedly until a specific end
condition is reached)
nonnumerical languages (languages
that control via alphabetic or other
nonnumeric instructions)
process and numerical-control
languages (languages that
automatically control machinery
by numerical instructions)
simulation languages (languages that
run operations which simulate
processes)

COMPUTER SIZE AND CAPACITY

(largest to smallest)

supercomputer
mainframe
minicomputer
tower
microcomputer/personal computer
laptop
notebook
subnotebook
palmtop

DATA STORAGE

1 bit (equal to 0 or 1, on or off, true or
false)
1 byte = 8 bits
1 kilobyte = 1,024 bytes
1 megabyte = 1,048,576 bytes
1 gigabyte = 1 billion bytes
1 terabyte = 1 trillion bytes
1 petabyte = 1 quadrillion bytes
8-bit computer (8088) moves data in
1-byte (8 bit) chunks
16-bit computer (286) moves data in
2-byte chunks
32-bit computer (386) moves data in
4-byte chunks
64-bit computer (Pentium) moves
data in 8-byte chunks

GENERATIONS OF COMPUTERS

first generation: earliest, most
primitive machines or equipment;
of computers, those built between
1948–1956
second generation: improved
version, those built between mid-
1950s and mid-1960s
third generation: built between
1966–1979; integrated circuits
replaced transistors
fourth generation: built during the
1980s, with microprocessors
fifth generation: built after mid-
1980s, more advanced and capable
of performing several functions
simultaneously
sixth generation: built since late 1980s,
employing artificial intelligence

INTERNET

E-mail message—generic sequence

1. composed at computer
2. sent to domain name server

3. resolve stage—server takes domain name and turns it into a four-digit number called the IP address
4. larger domain server receives
5. routes to destination server
6. message sorted by name, placed in mailbox as new message.

E-mail: Order of Priority of Messages sorted by servers

First Priority: addresses ending with these abbreviations:
.mil—military institution
.gov—government institution
.edu—educational institution
Second Priority:
.com—commercial organization
.net—non-commercial, community organization
.org—usually non-profit organizations

Sections of Internet most widely used

Usenet—newsgroups
e-mail—electronic messages
bbs—bulletin board services, individual dialogue
TCP: Transfer control protocol, on which the following four run:
http: graphic pages
ftp: file transfer protocol, for downloading files
gopher: search tools
telnet: individual dialogue

CONSTRUCTION

Mortar Grades

M, vigorous exposure, load-bearing, below grade, 2,500 psi
S, severe exposure, load-bearing, below grade, 1,800 psi
N, mild exposure, light loads, above grade, 750 psi.

O, interiors, light loads, 350 psi
K, non-bearing walls, or very light loads, 75 psi

STEEL SKYSCRAPER CONSTRUCTION (FROM BOTTOM TO TOP)

Footings
Concrete foundation
Base Plate
Anchor Bolt
Column
Girder
Floor beams
Poured Concrete Floors
Roof

ELECTRICITY & POWER

BATTERY VOLTAGE

(Carbon zinc)
AAA—1.5 volt
AA—1.5 volt
C—1.5 volt
D—1.5 volt
N—1.5 volt
WO—1.5, 3.0, 4.5, 6.0 volt
109 or 127—9 volt
117—9, 12, 22.5, 45, 90 volt
(Alkaline)
AAA—1.5
AA—1.5
C—1.5
D—1.5
G—6.0
N—3, 4.5, 6, 9 volt

ELECTRIC SHOCK

(current in milliamperes/60 Hz)

(AC, DC, effect)

0–1, 0–4, perception
1–4, 4–15, surprise (over 5 mA can be lethal)

4–21, 15–80, reflex action
21–40, 80–160, muscular inhibition
41–100, 160–300, respiratory block
over 300 usually fatal

ELECTRONIC RESISTOR COLOR CODE

B: black, 1
B: brown, 2
R: red, 3
O: orange, 4
Y: yellow, 5
G: green, 6
B: blue, 7
V: violet, 8
G: gray, 9
W: white, 0

ENGINEERING

AREAS OF STUDY

acoustical engineering
  architectural acoustics
  communication engineering
  instrumentation engineering
  musical acoustics
  noise and vibration control
  shock and vibration engineering
  ultrasonics
  underwater acoustics
aeronautical engineering
aerospace engineering
bioengineering
  agricultural engineering
  biochemical engineering
  bionics (application of biological
    principles to study and design of
    engineering)
  environmental health engineering
  human factors engineering
    (equipment design for the
    workplace)
  medical engineering

chemical engineering
  fiber
  fuel
  metals
  nuclear
  pharmaceuticals
  plastics, polymers, synthetic fibers
  pulp and paper
civil engineering
  construction
  maritime and hydraulic
    engineering
  power
  public health
  transportation
electrical and electronics engineering
  communications
  computer science and engineering
  electric light and power
  electronic systems
industrial engineering
mechanical engineering
  environmental control
  machines for goods production
  machines for power production
  military weapons
military engineering
naval engineering
nuclear engineering
  fusion (combination of nuclei to
    form energy)
  naval nuclear propulsion
  nuclear power
  nuclear waste management
  radioisotopes
optical engineering
petroleum engineering
  drilling engineering
  petrophysical engineering
  reservoir engineering
production engineering
safety engineering

ENGINES

GASOLINE ENGINE CYCLE

Four-Stroke

induction stroke (fuel and air mixture drawn into cylinder)

compression stroke (mixture compressed by piston)

power/combustion stroke (mixture ignited by spark plug; explosion pushes piston downward)

exhaust stroke (burned gases forced out of cylinder)

FIRE AND EXPLOSIVES

EXPLOSIVES

1. mechanical (depends on physical reaction, e.g. overloading container with compressed air)
2. nuclear (sustained nuclear reaction with instant rapidity)
3. chemical
    a. detonating or high explosives (TNT, dynamite)
        1. primary (denote by ignition from some other source)
        2. secondary (require detonator and supplementary booster)
    b. deflagrating or low explosives (gun powder, black powder)

FIRE EXTINGUISHERS

Type A (for wood, cloth, trash, common materials)

Type B (for oil, gas, grease, paints, flammable liquids)

Type C (for "live" electrical equipment)

Type D (for combustible metals, as magnesium)

FIRE RATING SYSTEM

Flammability (depicted as red, top square of diamond on buildings and trucks)

4 very flammable gases or very volatile flammable liquids

3 can be ignited at all normal temperatures

2 ignites if moderately heated

1 ignites after considerable preheating

0 will not burn

Health (depicted as blue, left square of diamond)

4 can cause death or major injury despite medical treatment

3 can cause serious injury despite medical treatment

2 can cause injury; requires prompt treatment

1 can cause irritation if not treated

0 no hazard

Reactivity (depicted as yellow, right square of diamond)

4 readily detonates or explodes

3 can detonate or explode but requires strong initiating force or heating under confinement

2 normally unstable but will not detonate

1 normally stable; unstable at high temperature and pressure; reacts with water

0 normally stable; not reactive with water

Specific Hazard (depicted as white, bottom square of diamond)

OX oxidizing agent

water reactive

radioactive

biohazard

LUMBER

LUMBER GRADES

Softwood (trees with cones)
Hardwood (trees with leaves)
Lumber (more than 2 inches thick)
Boards (less than 2 inches thick)

White Pine Wood Grades:

Clear Grades
 A select = no knots or blemishes
 B select = a few spots with slightly
  inconsistent texture
 C select = a few blemishes on one
  side
 D select = slight blemishes on both
  sides
Common Grades
 No. 1 common = slight blemishes
  on both sides
 No. 2 common = some knots and
  blemishes
 No. 3 common = has knots and holes
 No. 4 common = unsightly wood
 No. 5 common = extremely
  unsightly wood

Lumber Grading—Construction

No. 1 (construction) many knots, all
 under 2 inches
No. 2 (standard) many knots, up to
 3 ½ inches
No. 3 (utility), allows open knots,
 splits, pitch
No. 4 (economy), lowest grade

Lumber Grading—Hardwood

*(National Hardwood Lumber
Association)*

First and Second (FAS) (at least 6
 inches wide, 8–16 feet long)
Select-No. 1 Common (at least 3
 inches wide, 4–16 feet long)
Select-No. 2 Common
Select-No. 3 Common

Lumber Grading—
Plywood and Paneling

*(American Plywood Association
Veneer Grades)*

(Each side is graded, exterior and interior. An exterior piece with no blemishes would be A-A Exterior. An interior piece with no blemishes on one side and small knots on the other would be A-C Interior. G1S means one good side, one utility side. G2S means both sides good. AC1 is one side A, one side C, for interior use.)

Grade N = smooth surface "natural
 finish"
Grade A = no blemishes, smooth,
 paintable
Grade B = few blemishes, knots
 plugged and sanded; solid surface
Grade C Plugged = splits and small
 knots and knotholes; improved
 veneer, some broken grain
Grade C = splits and small knots and
 knotholes; tight knots to ½ inch
Grade D = large knots and knotholes
 to 2 ½ inch
also may be marked:
G = good side for finishing
I = for interior use
S = side
SH = sheathing
WB = wallboard
U = underlaying material
X = for exterior use

Lumber Grading—Softwood

*(US Department of Commerce American
Lumber Standards)*

rough lumber (sawn, trimmed, edged
 but rough faces)
surfaced lumber (dressed rough
 lumber that has been smoothed)
worked lumber (surfaced lumber that
 has been matched, patterned, or
 shiplapped)

shop and factory lumber (millwork lumber for doors, windows, etc.)
yard or structural lumber (for house framing, concrete forms, etc.)
    boards (no more than 1 inch thick and 4–12 inches wide)
    planks (over 1 inch thick and more than 6 inches wide)
    timbers (width and thickness greater than 5 inches)
select and finish materials (for trim, cabinets, etc.)
boards (general building, crafts, flooring, etc.)
    select merchantable
    construction
    standard
    utility
    economy
dimension lumber (surfaced 2–4 inch thick for framing components)
    light framing
    structural light framing
    studs
    structural joists and planks
    timber
    appearance framing

WOOD DURABILITY CLASSIFICATION

very durable: black locust, red cedar, live oak, black walnut, cypress, redwood, white cedar, Lawson cypress
durable: white oak, black ash, cherry, red elm, persimmon, longleaf pine, larch, slash pine, ironwood
intermediate: white pine, Norway pine, shortleaf pine, red oak, red ash, yellow poplar, butternut, sugar pine
perishable: white elm, beech, hickory, hard maple, red gum, white ash, Loblolly pine, hemlock, spruce, yellow birch
very perishable: black gum, basswood, buckeye, paper birch, aspen, willow, sycamore, lodgepole pine, balsam fir, jack pine

WOOD TYPES

By Hardness

very hard: hickory, hard maple, black locust, rock elm, persimmon, Osage orange
hard: oak, beech, birch, black gum, longleaf pine, ash
intermediate: Douglas fir, red gum, tamarack, white elm, cottonwood
soft: Ponderosa pine, hemlock, chestnut, yellow poplar, cypress, cedar
very soft: white pine, sugar pine, spruce, redwood, basswood, willow

By Splitting

difficult to split: elm, black gum, beech, sycamore, dogwood, red gum
intermediate: birch, maple, hickory, oak, ash, cottonwood
easy to split: chestnut, all pines, redwood, cedar, fir, western larch

MACHINE OPERATION

COMPACT DISK PLAYER OPERATION

1. Light reflects off a layer of aluminum inside the disk.
2. Indentations in the layer alter the distance the light travels, causing the reflected light to vary in brightness.
3. The light is detected by four photodiodes (light-sensitive electronic devices) and converted to sound.
4. The player keeps the laser in focus and on track by adjusting the reading head.

FAX MACHINE OPERATION

1. The document is placed in the feeder tray of the transmitting fax machine and the receiver's number is entered on the keypad.
2. When the receiving machine answers, a roller in the first machine pulls in the pages one-by-one and passes them over a scanner.
3. Electric signals representing each page go to the second machine, which prints a copy on paper. A row of tiny electric heating elements heats areas of the paper as it passes from the roll under the head.
4. Rows of dark dots form where the paper is heated, to produce a copy of the document.

MECHNICAL CLOCK OPERATION

1. A weight on the end of a line turns gear wheels that move the hands of the clock and make the hour hand revolve 12 times slower than the minute hand.
2. The gears are connected to an escape wheel, which is controlled by the clock's pendulum.
3. As it swings, the pendulum rocks an anchor—allowing the escape wheel to turn at a constant rate.

MICROWAVE OVEN OPERATION

1. Magnetron inside oven produces a beam of microwaves and scatters them in all directions by a fan.
2. Microwaves hit water molecules in food.
3. Water molecules rotate as they reverse their alignment within the food.
4. Constant rotating movement of the microscopic molecules in food produces the heat that cooks the food.

MOTION PICTURE CAMERA OPERATION

1. Light from the object being filmed produces an image on the piece of film exposed at the film gate.
2. Exposure ends as the revolving shutter stops light from reaching the film.
3. The feeding claw advances the film to bring unexposed film to the film gate. The shutter will move out of the way, allowing a second exposure.

PHONOGRAPH OPERATION

1. A record player replays sounds stored on disks by using the vibration of a stylus in the groove of a record.
2. As the stylus moves along the record, it is vibrated by the sides of the groove which provide separate stereo channels.
3. The vibrations travel to a magnet which produces electrical signals in fixed coils in the stylus.
4. The separate stereo signals are sent to an amplifier and speakers.

PHOTOCOPIER OPERATION

1. A metal plate is wrapped around a cylinder. It conducts electricity only when exposed to light.
2. The plate is given an electric charge.
3. The image to be copied is focused on the plate.
4., The electric charge is conducted away where light falls.

5. Toning powder is dusted over the plate and adheres only to the charged image area.
6. Paper is pressed against the plate.
7. The powder image adheres to the paper, fixed with heat.

POLAROID PROCESSING OPERATION

1. Light passes through a clear plastic surface, acid layer, timing layer, and image layer to nine chemical layers, including developer alternating with layers sensitive to red, green, or blue light, all above a black base.
2. The exposed film, upon leaving the camera, passes through rollers that squeeze reagent from the film's edge between its image and chemical layers. The reagent shuts out light long enough to activate developers.
3. The developers dissolve the dyes which then mix to form a color image in the image layer.

QUARTZ WATCH OPERATION

1. Electric current from the battery passes to a quartz crystal oscillator, which vibrates and produces electric pulses at a fast but very precise rate.
2. This signal goes to a microchip, which reduces the signal to one pulse a second.
3. The regulated signal goes to a coil, which powers an electromagnet.
4. The electromagnet turns a rotor that drives the hands of the watch by means of a set of gear wheels, causing the second hand to advance once per second.

RADAR OPERATION

1. The rotating antenna of a radar alternately sends out short pulses of radio waves and listens for their echoes.
2. After each pulse, a spot on the display sweeps from the center to the edge at an angle matching that of the antenna. Echoes from near objects come back sooner and appear closer to the center of the display.

RADIO OPERATION

1. At a radio transmitter, a microphone converts sounds into electrical signals.
2. A modulator imposes these on a carrier wave, which is produced by a radio frequency oscillator and beamed out by a transmitting antenna.
3. At a receiver, an antenna, tuned circuit, demodulator, amplifier, and loudspeaker reconvert the radio waves to sounds.

REFRIGERATOR OPERATION

1. Air circulates by convection: cold air sinks, takes heat from food, and slightly warmer air then rises before being cooled again at the top of the refrigerator.
2. Freon gas in the pipes evaporates in the evaporator, absorbing heat from the freezer and lowering the temperature at the top of the refrigerator.
3. The gas flows to an electrically driven compressor which compresses the gas and turns it back to a liquid. As this happens heat is released into the room

outside the refrigerator and the cycle starts again.

TAPE RECORDER OPERATION

Recording

1. A microphone converts the sound to an electric current flowing via an amplifier to a recording head.
2. This action produces a varying magnetic field that aligns particles in a magnetic tape.

Playback

1. The tape affects the current flowing via an amplifier to a loudspeaker.
2. The loudspeaker converts current to sound.

TELEPHONE OPERATION

1. A speaker's voice produces sound waves that vibrate a diaphragm.
2. The vibrations cause variations in an electric current sent out from the transmitter.
3. The electric current travels through wires to a receiver.
4. In the receiver, the varying currrent creates a varying magnetic field that vibrates another diaphragm, producing audible sound waves.

VIDEO RECORDER OPERATION

1. The picture and sound are picked up from the television antenna signal.
2. The picture is recorded onto tape by a record/playback head and the sound by another head.
3. Picture signals are recorded as a series of sloping tracks and the sound signals are recorded along one edge.
4. In playback, magnetic patterns in the tape affect the current, which is converted into video and audio signals.

MANUFACTURING PROCESSES

GLASSMAKING

1. Sand, limestone, soda ash, and recycled glass heated in furnace to create molten glass
2. Molten glass poured onto a pool of molten tin, making glass spread into flat sheet (as for windows)
3. Glass sets and hardens

MICROCHIP MAKING PROCESS

(Silicon wafers are turned into integrated circuits by a sequence of operations that includes masking, etching, diffusion, ion implantation (bombarding the wafer with electrically charged atoms), and metallization (creating tracks to link the components))

1. The many superimposed patterns that form the chip need to be lined up accurately. Extensive checking of the logical design and electrical characteristics show whether there are any weaknesses.
2. A photomask is used to create a microscopic stencil on the wafer. The wafer is first exposed to oxygen to coat it with impermeable oxide. The photographic process then creates the stencil through which the oxide is etched away. This leaves areas of silicon ready to receive the next treatment.

The Brewing of Beer

1. Grains are malted by soaking in water
2. Malt is transferred to mash tub, water and mixtures of other grains are combined, preparing for fermentation process.
3. Filtering of unfermented malt, or "wort."
4. Wort is boiled in brew kettles. In the beginning of this step, hops are added for flavor, and removed at the end.
5. Yeast added in Starter tank.
6. Brew ferments in fermentation tank for about a week.
7. After fermentation yeast is removed, and brew is transferred to aging tank for several weeks of storage.
8. Final Filtering.
9. Packaging. Beer is pasteurized for cans and bottles.

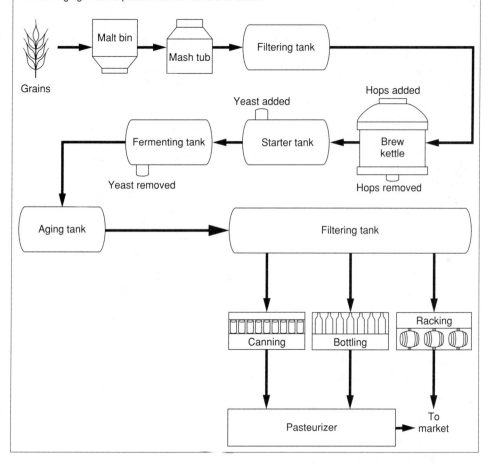

3. Wafers are heated to high temperatures and exposed to chemical compounds that contain the impurity atoms needed to form parts of the circuit being made. Batches of wafers are fed into a furnace where the atoms will diffuse only into those parts of the surface left exposed by the masking and etching. The wafers will go through repeated masking, etching, and diffusion steps before

the circuit is complete.

4. After all those steps and metalization, the finished wafers are tested. Every wafer has a number of control chips that can be tested and individual chips are put through a test cycle. The tests are carried out by delicate probes operated by a computer.

5. Individual chips cut from the wafer now undergo cold welding, where extremely fine gold wires are bonded onto tiny pads formed around the edges of the chip during metallization. A microscope is needed to line up the chip with the microscope on a television screen. The other ends of the wires will be bonded to the pins that connect the chip to a circuit board.

6. The chip and connecting wires are enclosed in a tough plastic or ceramic package.

7. The packaged chips are sent out to manufacturers.

PAPERMAKING

1. Trees cut into logs
2. Logs cut into wood chips
3. Chips heated, either with acids or alkalis, to release fibers
4. Wood chips cooked into pulp
5. Fibers mixed with filings, sizing, pigments, and dyes and made into smooth pulp
6. Pulp drained
7. Water removed, paper pressed and smoothed into rolls

PLASTIC MAKING PROCESS

1. Ethylene is heated under pressure.
2. Groups of 30,000 or more molecules join to make long-chain molecules of polyethylene.
3. Another plastic made from ethylene is polystyrene, produced by mixing benzene with ethylene. Polystyrene is used for toymaking.
4. Ethylene and chlorine make polyvinyl chloride (PVC).

PAPER

PAPER SIZES, STANDARD NON-ISO

atlas, 26×34 inches
imperial, 22×30 inches
elephant, 20×27 inches
royal, 20×25 inches
small royal, 19×25 inches
medium, 18×23 inches
demy, $17\frac{1}{2} \times 22\frac{1}{2}$ inches
crown, 15×20 inches
foolscap, $17 \times 13\frac{1}{2}$ inches
pot, $12\frac{1}{2} \times 15\frac{1}{2}$ inches

PAPER, AMERICAN PRINTING

bond, 17×22 inches (with stardard sizes of $8\frac{1}{2} \times 11$, $8\frac{1}{2} \times 14$, 11×17, 17×22, 17×28, 19×24, 19×28, 22×34)
book, 25×38 inches
text, 25×38 inches
cover, 20×26 inches
bristol, $22\frac{1}{2} \times 28\frac{1}{2}$ inches (also called printing bristol)
index, $25\frac{1}{2} \times 30\frac{1}{2}$ inches (also called index bristol)
tag, 24×36 inches

PAPER SIZES, U.K.

A0, $33\frac{1}{8} \times 46\frac{3}{4}$ inches
A1, $23\frac{3}{8} \times 33\frac{1}{8}$ inches
A2, $16\frac{1}{2} \times 23\frac{3}{8}$ inches
A3, $11\frac{3}{4} \times 16\frac{1}{2}$ inches

A4, 8¼ × 11¾ inches
A5, 5⅞ × 8¼ inches
A6, 4⅛ × 6 inches
A7, 2⅞ × 4⅛ inches
A8, 2 × 2⅞ inches
A9, 1½ × 2
A10, 1 × 1½
B0, 39⅜ × 55⅝
B1, 27⅞ × 39⅜
B2, 19⅝ × 27⅞
B3, 13⅞ × 19⅝
B4, 9⅞ × 13⅞
B5, 7 × 9⅞
B6, 4⅞ × 7
B7, 3½ × 4⅞
B8, 2½ × 3½
B9, 1¾ × 2½
B10, 1¼ × 1¾

PAPER WEIGHTS

9 lb., onionskin
16 lb., mimeograph paper
20 lb., standard typing paper
24 lb., standard letterhead paper
60 lb., good for printing on both sides
65 lb., business cards and postcards
100 lb., coated magazine stock
120 lb., poster board

art paper:

8–48 lb., tracing paper
13–20 lb., bond paper
28–32 lb., ledger paper
65–80 lb., commercial cover paper
90–400 lb., watercolor paper

RADIO TRANSMISSION

FREQUENCIES

EHF, extremely high frequency (30–300 GHz, experimental and amateur radio)
SHF, super high frequency (3–30 GHz, satellite communication)
UHF, ultra high frequency (300–3000 MHz, radar and UHF television)
VHF, very high frequency (30–300 MHz, FM broadcast, police radio)
HF, high frequency (3–30 MHz, CB and shortwave radio)
MF, medium frequency (300–3000 kHz, AM broadcast)
LF, low frequency (30–300 kHz, maritime and aeronautical communication)
VLF, very low frequency (3–30 kHz)

TYPES OF RADIO WAVES

(from highest frequency (hertz) and shortest wavelength to longest)

microwaves (communication devices)
microwave radar (communication and detection devices)
radar (communication and detection devices)
video, FM (television, FM radio)
short wave (short-wave radio)
AM (AM radio)
long wave (long-wave radio)

RECYCLING

ALUMINUM RECYCLING PROCESS

1. Collected cans go to dealers, who crush them into bales that are sold to the recycling plant.
2. At the recycling plant, metal is shredded into small pieces and paint removed with hot air.
3. The metal is passed through a magnetic separator to remove any steel and then is plunged into a pool of molten aluminum in a furnace.

4. After the impurities have been skimmed, the melt is poured into a giant mold.

5. When the melt is cooled, it is ready for rolling into aluminum sheets for making new cans.

PLASTIC PRODUCT RECYCLING CODES

1, PETE polyethylene terephthalate (most valuable of recycled plastics)
2, HDPE high-density polyethylene
3, V vinyl or polyvinyl chloride
4, LDPE low-density polyethylene
5, PP polypropylene
6, PS polystyrene

ROADS & HIGHWAYS

CLASSIFICATION

superhighway (interstates and high-capacity highways)
expressway or highway (divided and undivided)
  urban (such as tollroads, turnpikes, parkways)
  rural
surface road (undivided)
secondary road
collector route
street
unsurfaced road
pathway

Bridge Types

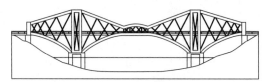
Cantilever bridge

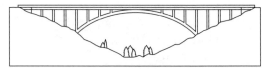
Deck arch bridge

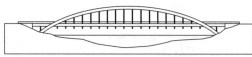
Half-through arch bridge

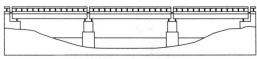
Multiple-span beam bridge

Portal bridge

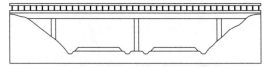
Simple-span beam bridge

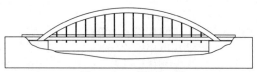
Through arch bridge

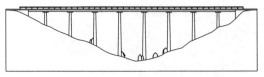
Viaduct

ROAD / HIGHWAY FUNCTIONS

1. expressways that serve major traffic flows
2. primary highways that carry relatively high volumes of traffic between population centers
3. collector and feeder roads, and secondary rural highways
4. local roads and city streets

ROAD LAYERS

1. drains installed
2. compressed soil
3. one or more layers of crushed stone
4. concrete or blacktop (tar and stone chips)

also

(from bottom to top)

1. granular sub-base (rolled aggregate 12–24 inches thick)
2. lower road base (10-inch layer of concrete)
3. upper road base (3-inch layer of rolled macadam (tar and stones))
4. wearing surface (1.5-inch layer of rolled asphalt)
5. concrete haunch (finishes and supports edge of road surface)
6. hard shoulder (for breakdown lane)

TELEVISION

TELEVISION OPERATION

1. Television cameras turn light into electronic video signals that are broadcast by a transmitter and received by the antenna of a television receiver.
2. The television tuner selects a station.
3. A decoder converts video signals into primary color signals.
4. In the picture tube, three electron guns (one for each color) rapidly scan the screen, causing colored dots in the screen to glow— forming the picture seen on the screen.

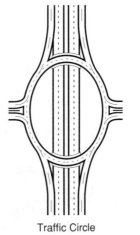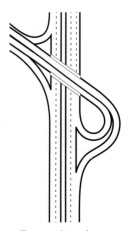

| Cloverleaf | Diamond Interchange | Traffic Circle | Trumpet Interchange |

Major Types of Interchanges

TELEVISION DISH OPERATION

1. The dish gathers microwaves from space and concentrates them into a low-noise block at the top of the cable.
2. There a sophisticated amplifier boosts the very weak signal without adding noise.
3. The block then reduces the frequency of the signal before sending it down the cable to the indoor receiver.

TRANSPORTATION CLASSIFICATION

Air
   air-cushion machines
   aircraft
Ground/underground
   freight pipelines (for water, sewage, oil, natural gas, etc.)
   motor vehicles
   railroads
   urban mass transportation
Water
   ships
   submarines

TRUCKS

TRAILER HITCH CLASSIFICATION

Class I, less than 2000 lbs
Class II, less than 3500 lbs
Class III, less than 5000 lbs
Class IV, less than 10,000 lbs

WEAPONS

NUCLEAR WEAPON RANGE

(farthest to shortest range)

Intercontinental Ballistic Missiles (ICBMs)
Long-range bombers
Medium-range bombers
Submarine Launched Ballistic Missiles (SLBMs)
Intermediate/Medium-Range Ballistic Missiles (IRBMs)
Short-range aircraft
Short-Range Ballistic Missiles (SRBMs)
Artillery

A violent order is disorder and . . . a great disorder is an order. These two things are one.

—Wallace Stevens, *Connoisseur of Chaos*

CHAPTER FIVE

MATHEMATICS & MEASUREMENT

ANCIENT MEASURES

BIBLICAL

cubit=21.8 inches
omer=0.45 peck=3.964 liters=4.188
   quarts
ephah=10 omers
bath=9.4 omers
shekel=0.497 ounce=14.1 grams

EGYPTIAN

shekel=60 grains
great mina=60 shekels
talent=60 great minas

GREEK

cubit=18.3 inches
stadion=607.2 or 622 feet=408 cubits
obol=715.38 milligrams=0.04 ounces
drachma=4.2923 grams=6 obols
mina=0.9463 pound=94 drachmas
talent=60 mina

ROMAN

cubit=17.5 inches
stadium=202 yards=415.5 cubits
as, libra, pondus=325.971
   grams=0.71864 pound

APOTHECARY MEASURES

1 grain=0.0020833 troy
   ounce=0.06479891 gram
20 grains=1 scruple = 0.04166 troy
   ounce
3 scruples=1 drachm(US dram)=0.125
   troy ounce
24 scruples=1 troy ounce=480 grains
1 ounce apoth. =1.09709 avoirdupois
   ounce=437.5 grains=31.103475 grams
1 ounce avdp=0.9115 ounce
   apoth.=437.5 grains
12 ounces apoth=1 pound
   apoth.=373.2417 grams=13.1657
   ounces avdp.=0.82286 pound avdp.

DECIBEL SCALE

0 decibels (absolute silence)
10 decibels (light whisper, leaves
   rustling)
20 decibels (quiet conversation, 10
   times louder than 10 decibels)
30 decibels (normal conversation,
   100 times louder than 10 decibels)
40 decibels (light traffic, quiet room
   in home)
50 decibels (restaurant, office, loud
   conversation)
60 decibels (noisy office or
   restaurant)
70 decibels (normal traffic, loud
   telephone ring, quiet train, lawn
   mower)
80 decibels (automobile interior,
   subway)
90 decibels (bus or truck interior,
   heavy traffic, thunder)
100 decibels (chain saw)
110 decibels (loud orchestra music)
120 decibels (amplified rock music,
   very close thunder clap)
130 decibels (artillery fire at close
   range, air raid siren)
140+ decibels (jet taking off)

EQUIVALENTS TABLES

LENGTHS

1 angstrom=0.1 nanometer=0.0001
   micrometer=0.0000001
   millimeter=.000000004 inch
1 cable's length=120 fathoms=720
   feet=219 meters

1 centimeter=0.3937 inch

1 chain (Gunter's or surveyor's)=66 feet=20.1168 meters

1 chain (engineers)=100 feet=30.48 meters

1 decimeter=3.937 inches

1 degree (geographical)=364,566.929 feet=69,047 miles=111.123 kilometers

1 degree of latitude=68.708 miles at equator=69.403 miles at poles

1 degree of longitude=69,171 miles at equator

1 dekameter=32.808 feet

1 fathom=6 feet=1.8288 meters

100 fathoms=1 cable length

1 foot=0.3048 meters

1 furlong=10 chains (surveyors)=660 feet=⅛ statute mile=201.168 meters

1 hand=4 inches

1 inch=2.54 centimeters

1 kilometer=0.621 mile=3,281.5 feet

1 league=3 survey miles = 4.828 kilometers

1 link (Gunter's or surveyor's)=7.92 inches=0.201 meter

1 link engineers=1 foot=0.305 meter

1 meter=39.37 inches=1.094 yards

1 micrometer=0.001 millimeter=0.00003937 inch

1 mil=0.001 inch = 0.0254 millimeter

1 mile=5,280 feet=1.609 kilometers

1 international nautical mile=1.852 kilometers=1.150779 survey miles=6,076.11549 feet

1 millimeter=0.03937 inch

1 nanometer=0.001 micrometer=0.00000003937 inch

1 pica=12 points

1 point=0.013837 inch=0.351 millimeter

1 rod, pole, or perch=16½ feet=5.029 meters

1 yard=0.9144 meter

AREAS OR SURFACES

1 acre=43,560 square feet=4,840 square yards=0.405 hectare

1 are=119.599 square yards=0.025 acre

1 bolt length=100 yards

1 bolt width=45 or 60 inches

1 hectare=2.471 acres

1 square (building)=100 square feet

1 square centimeter=0.155 square inch

1 square decimeter=15.500 square inches

1 square foot=929.030 square centimeters

1 square inch=6.4516 square centimeters

1 square kilometer=247.104 acres=0.386 square mile

1 square meter=1.196 square yards=10.764 square feet

1 square mile=258.999 hectares

1 square millimeter=0.002 square inch

1 square rod, square pole, or square perch=25.293 square meters

1 square yard=0.836 square meter

CAPACITIES OR VOLUMES

1 barrel liquid=31 to 42 gallons

1 barrel, standard, for fruits, vegetables, and other dry commodities except dry cranberries=7,056 cubic inches=105 dry quarts=3.281 bushels, struck measure

1 barrel, standard, cranberry=5,826 cubic inches=86 ⁴⁵⁄₆₄ dry quarts=2.709 bushels, struck measure

1 board foot=a foot-square board 1 inch thick

1 bushel (U.S.) (struck measure)=2,150.42 cubic inches=35.239 liters

1 bushel, heaped (U.S.)=2,747.715 cubic inches=1.278 bushels, struck measure

1 bushel (British Imperial) (struck measure)=1.032 U.S. bushels struck measure=2,219.36 cubic inches

1 cord firewood=128 cubic feet

1 cubic centimeter=0.061 cubic inch

1 cubic decimeter=61.024 cubic inches

1 cubic inch=0.554 fluid ounce=4.433 fluid drams=16.387 cubic centimeters

1 cubic foot=7.481 gallons=28.317 cubic decimeters

1 cubic meter=1.308 cubic yards

1 cubic yard=0.765 cubic meter

1 cup, measuring=8 fluid ounces=½ liquid pint

1 dram, fluid (British)=0.961 U.S. fluid dram=0.217 cubic inch=3.552 milliliters

1 dekaliter=2.642 gallons=1.135 pecks

1 gallon (U.S.)=231 cubic inches=3.785 liters=0.833 British gallon=128 U.S. fluid ounces

1 gallon (British Imperial)=277.42 cubic inches=1.201 U.S. gallons=4.546 liters=160 British fluid ounces

1 gill=7.219 cubic inches=4 fluid ounces=0.118 liter

1 hectoliter=26.418 gallons=2.838 bushels

1 liter=1.057 liquid quarts=0.908 dry quart=61.025 cubic inchs

1 milliliter=0.271 fluid dram=16.231 minims=0.061 cubic inch

1 ounce liquid (U.S.)=1.805 cubic inches=29.573 milliliters=1.041 British fluid ounces

1 ounce, fluid (British)=0.961 U.S. fluid ounce=1.734 cubic inches=28.412 milliliters

1 peck=8.810 liters

1 pint, dry=33.600 cubic inches=0.551 liter

1 pint, liquid=28.875 cubic inches=0.473 liter

1 quart dry (U.S.)=67.201 cubic inches= 1.01 liters=0.969 British quart

1 quart liquid (U.S.)=57.75 cubic inches=0.946 liter=0.833 British quart

1 quart (British)=69.354 cubic inches=1.032 U.S. dry quarts=1.201 U.S. liquid quarts

1 tablespoon=3 teaspoons=4 fluid drams=½ fluid ounce

1 teaspoon=⅓ tablespoon=1⅓ fluid drams

WEIGHTS OR MASSES

1 assay ton=29.167 grams

1 bale=500 pounds in U.S.=750 pounds in Egypt

1 carat=200 milligrams=3.086 grains

1 dram avoirdupois=27 $11\frac{1}{32}$ or 27.344 grains=1.772 grams

1 gamma=1 microgram

1 grain=64.799 milligrams

1 gram=15.432 grains=0.035 ounce, avoirdupois

1 hundredweight, gross or long=112 pounds=50.802 kilograms

1 hundredweight, net or short=100 pounds=45.359 kilograms

1 kilogram=2.205 pounds

1 microgram=0.000001 gram

1 milligram=0.015 grain

1 ounce, avoirdupois=437.5 grains=0.911 troy ounce=28.350 grams

1 ounce, troy=480 grains=1.097 avoirdupois ounces=31.103 grams

1 pennyweight=1.555 grams

1 pound, avoirdupois=7,000 grains=1.215 troy pounds=453.59237 grams

1 pound, troy=5,760 grains=0.823 avoirdupois pound=373.242 grams

1 ton, gross or long=2,240 pounds=1.12 net tons=1.016 metric tons

1 ton, metric=2,204.623 pounds=0.984 gross ton=1.102 net tons

1 ton, net or short=2,000 pounds=0.893 gross ton=0.907 metric ton

---

FOOD

CAN SIZES

No. 300, 14–16 fluid oz.
No. 303, 16–17 fluid oz.
No. 1 tall, 16 oz. fluid oz.
No. 2, 1 lb. 4 oz. or 1 pint 2 fluid oz.
No. 2½, 1 lb. 13 oz. or 28 fluid oz.
No. 3, 46 fluid oz.
No. 10, 96 fluid oz.

CONTAINER SIZES

8 ounce can=1 cup
10½ to 12 ounce can=1¼ cups
12 ounce vacuum packed can=1½ cups
14 to 16 ounce can (No. 300)=1¾ cups
16 to 17 ounce can (No. 303)=2 cups
20 ounce can (No. 2)=2½ cups
29 ounce can (No. 2½)=3½ cups
46 fluid ounce can (No. 3 cylinder) =5¾ cups
6½ pound or 7 pound, 5 ounce can (No. 10)=12 to 13 cups
6 ounce can frozen juice concentrate=¾cup
10 ounce package frozen vegetables=1½ to 2 cups
16 ounce package frozen vegetables=3 to 4 cups
1 pound package brown sugar (packed)=2⅓ cups

1 pound package powdered sugar (unsifted)=3¼ cups
5 pound bag sugar=11¼ cups
1 pound can coffee=5 cups

COOKING CONVERSIONS

U.S.-Metric

⅕ teaspoon=1 milliliter
1 teaspoon=5 milliliters
1 tablespoon=15 milliliters
⅕ cup=50 milliliters
1 cup=240 milliliters
2 cups (1 pint)=470 milliliters
4 cups (1 quart)=0.95 liter
4 quarts (1 gallon)=3.8 liters

Metric—U.S.

1 milliliter=⅕ teaspoon
5 milliliters=1 teaspoon
15 milliliters=1 tablespoon
34 milliliters=1 fluid ounce
100 milliliters=3.4 fluid ounces
240 milliliters=1 cup
1 liter=34 fluid ounces=4.2 cups=2.1 pints=1.06 quarts=0.26 gallon

---

COOKING EQUIVALENTS TABLE

1 teaspoon= ⅓ tablespoon=60 drops
3 teaspoons=1 tablespoon
48 teaspoons=1 cup
½ tablespoon=1½ teaspoons
1 tablespoon=3 teaspoons=½ fluid ounce=¹⁄₁₆ cup
2 tablespoons=⅛ cup=1 fluid ounce
3 tablespoons=1½ fluid ounces=1 jigger
4 tablespoons=¼ cup=2 fluid ounces
5⅓ tablespoons=⅓ cup
8 tablespoons=½ cup=4 fluid ounces
10⅔ tablespoons=⅔ cup
12 tablespoons=¾ cup
16 tablespoons=1 cup=8 fluid ounces=½ pint

⅛ cup=2 tablespoons=1 fluid ounce
¼ cup=4 tablespoons=2 fluid ounces
⅓ cup=5 tablespoons plus 1
   teaspoon
⅜ cup=¼ cup plus 2 tablespoons
½ cup=8 tablespoons=4 fluid ounces
⅔ cup=10 tablespoons plus 2
   teaspoons
⅝ cup=½ cup plus 2 tablespoons
¾ cup=12 tablespoons=6 fluid ouncs
⅞ cup=¾ cup plus 2 tablespoons
1 cup=16 tablespoons=½ pint=8 fluid
   ounces
2 cups=1 pint=16 fluid ounces
4 cups=1 quart=2 pints=32 fluid
   ounces
1 pint=2 cups=16 fluid ounces
2 pints=1 quart=4 cups=32 fluid
   ounces
1 quart=2 pints=4 cups=32 fluid
   ounces
2 quarts=½ gallon=4 pints=8 cups=64
   fluid ounces
4 quarts=1 gallon=8 pints=16
   cups=128 fluid ounces
8 quarts=1 peck
1 gallon=4 quarts=8 pints=16
   cups=128 fluid ounces
2 gallons=1 peck
4 pecks=1 bushel
1 ounce=28.35 grams
1 pound=453.59 grams
1 gram=0.035 ounce
1 kilogram=2.2 pounds
1 liter=1.06 quarts

GEOMETRY

ANGLES BY DEGREE

acute (1–89 degrees)
right (90 degrees)
obtuse (91–179 degrees)
straight (180 degrees)
reflex (180–359 degrees)

CIRCULAR MEASURE UNITS

Minute=60 seconds
Degree=60 minutes
Right angle=90 degrees
Straight angle=180 degrees
   (semicircle)
Circle=360 degrees

Conic Sections

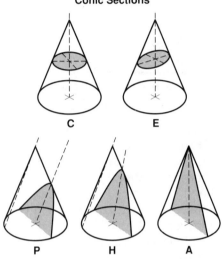

The two principal forms are
E. Ellipse, and **H.** Hyperbola;
P. Parabola, is an intermediate case;
C. Circle, is an ellipse perpendicular
   to the axis of the cone;
A. Angle, is a hyperbola whose axis
   coincides with that of the cone

Hyperboloids

Two-sheet   One-sheet
Two-sheet hyperboloid;
One-sheet hyperboloid

POLYGONS

by Number of Sides

triangle (3 sides)
quadrilateral (4 sides)
pentagon (5 sides)
hexagon (6 sides)
heptagon (7 sides)
octagon (8 sides)
nonagon (9 sides)
decagon (10 sides)
dodecagon (12 sides)
quindecagon (15 sides)

SEMI-REGULAR SOLIDS

by Number of Sides

cuboctahedron or **dymaxion** (12 corners, 14 faces)
truncated octahedron or **mecon** (24 corners, 14 faces)
rhombicuboctahedron or **square spin** (24 corners, 26 faces)
snub cube (24 corners, 38 faces)
icosidodecahedron (30 corners, 32 faces)
truncated cuboctahedron (48 corners, 26 faces)
truncated icosahedron (60 corners, 32 faces)
rhombicosidodecahedron (60 corners, 62 faces)
snub dodecahedron (60 corners, 92 faces)
truncated icosidodecahedron (120 corners, 62 faces)

SOLIDS

(polyhedrons/polyhedra)

by Number of Sides

tetrahedron (4 faces)
hexahedron or cube (6 faces)
octahedron (8 faces)
dodecahedron (12 faces)
icosahedron (20 faces)

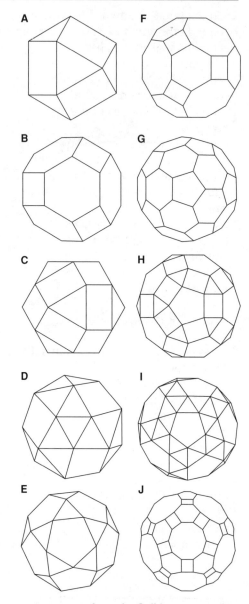

Irregular Solids

A. Dymaxion; **B.** Mecon; **C.** Square spin; **D.** Snub cube; **E.** Icosidodecahedron; **F.** Truncated cuboctahedron; **G.** Truncated icosahedron; **H.** Rhombicosidodecahedron; **I.** Snub dodecahedron; **J.** Truncated icosidodecahedron

Regular Solids

Tetrahedron
(4 sides)

Hexahedron
or cube
(6 sides)

Octahedron
(8 sides)

Dodecahedron
(12 sides)

Icosahedron
(20 sides)

LIQUOR MEASURES

TRADITIONAL BEER MEASURES

1 nip=¼ pint
1 small=½ pint
1 large=1 pint
1 flagon=1 quart
1 anker=10 gallons
1 firkin=9.8 gallons
1 barrel=31½ gallons
1 hogshead=2 barrels=63 gallons
1 butt=2 hogsheads=126 gallons
1 tun=2 butts=252 gallons

CHAMPAGNE BOTTLE SIZES

Split, ¼ bottle
Pint, ½ bottle
Bottle (.75 l, 26 fl oz)
Magnum (1.5 l, 2 bottles)
Jeroboam (3 l, 4 bottles)
Rehoboam (4.5 l, 6 bottles)
Methuselah (6 l, 8 bottles)
Salmanazar (9 l, 12 bottles)
Balthazar (12 l, 16 bottles)
Nebuchadnezzar (15 l, 20 bottles)

DRINKING GLASS MEASURES

stein/liter mug (33.8 fl. oz)
pint mug (16.9 fl. oz)
burgundy (14 fl. oz)
highball glass (13.9 fl. oz)
water (13 fl. oz)
white wine glass (from 8–12 fl. oz)
red wine glass (9.6 fl. oz, also up to
    14 fl. oz)
half-pint mug (9.6 fl. oz)
old-fashioned glass (9.6 fl. oz)
short glass (7.7 fl. oz)
champagne flute (6–7 fl. oz)
sherry schooner (5.75–7.7 fl. oz)
port glass (2.875–5.75 fl. oz)
cordial glass (2 fl. oz)
liqueur glass (1.92–3.8 fl. oz)

SPIRITS MEASURES

1 Pony=0.5 jigger
1 Shot=0.666 jigger=1.0 shot
1 Jigger=1.5 shot
1 Pint=16 shots=0.625 fifth
1 Fifth=25.6 shots=1.6 pints=0.8
   quart=0.75706 liter
1 Quart=32 shots=1.25 fifth
1 Wine bottle (standard)=0.800633
   quart=0.7576778 liter

WINE BOTTLE SIZES

miniature=100 mL
small=187 mL (split)
medium=375 mL
regular=750 mL
large=1 L
magnum=1.5 L
extra large=3 L

TRADITIONAL WINE MEASURES

10 gallons=1 anker
1 hogshead=63 gallons

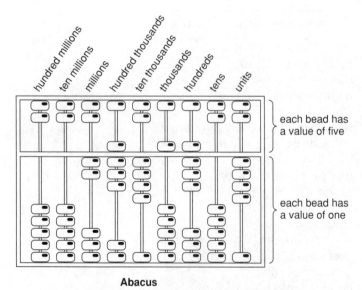

Abacus
The number shown here is 2,845,804.

2 hogsheads=1 pipe
2 pipes=1 tun
1 puncheon=84 gallons
1 butt=126 gallons

MATHEMATICS

ABACUS

(from left to right across the long side)

billions, hundred millions, ten
   millions, hundred thousands, ten
   thousands, thousands, hundreds,
   tens, ones/units
fives=2-bead side
singles=5-bead side

BRANCHES

Pure Mathemathics
   Arithmetic (fundamental
      operations)
   Algebra (operations of arithmetic)
      Algebraic topology
   Calculus (calculating with special
      system of algebraic notations)
   Geometry (sets of points in a plane or
      in space)
      Analytical geometry (geometry
         through algebraic methods)
      Differential geometry (geometry
         through methods of calculus)
      Euclidean geometry
      Non-Euclidean geometry
      Fractal geometry
      Topology (generalized elements
         and properties)
   Logic
   Number theory (integers and
      prime numbers)
   Set theory
   Trigonometry (computing
      distances)
Applied Mathematics
   Chaos theory

Computer science
Operations research (mathematical
analysis of problems for
improving efficiency)
Probability
Statistics

METRIC

LINEAR MEASURE

10 angstroms=1 nanometer
1000 nanometers=1 micrometer
1000 micrometers=1 millimeter
10 millimeters=1 centimeter
10 centimeters=1 decimeter=100
millimeters
10 decimeters=1 meter=1,000
millimeters
10 meters=1 dekameter
10 dekameters=1 hectometer=100
meters
10 hectometers=1 kilometer=1,000
meters

AREA MEASURE

100 square millimeters=1 square
centimeter
10,000 square centimeters=1 square
meter=1,000,000 square
millimeters
100 square meters=1 are
100 ares=1 hectare=10,000 square
meters
100 hectares=1 square
kilometer=1,000,000 square meters

FLUID VOLUME MEASURE

10 milliliters=1 centiliter
10 centiliters=1 deciliter=100
milliliters
10 deciliters=1 liter=1,000 milliliters
10 liters=1 dekaliter

10 dekaliters=1 hectoliter = 100 liters
10 hectoliters=1 kiloliter=1,000 liters
1 kiloliter=1 cubic meter

CUBIC MEASURE

1,000 cubic millimeters=1 cubic
centimeter
1,000 cubic centimeters=1 cubic
decimeter=1,000,000 cubic
millimeters
1,000 cubic decimeters=1 cubic
meter=1 stere=1,000,000 cubic
centimeters=1,000,000,000 cubic
millimeters

DISTANCE

kilometer
hectometer
dekameter
meter
decimeter
centimeter
millimeter

WEIGHT

10 milligrams=1 centigram
10 centigrams=1 decigram=100
milligrams
10 decigrams=1 gram=1,000
milligrams
10 grams=1 dekagram
10 dekagrams=1 hectogram=100
grams
10 hectograms=1 kilogram=1,000
grams
1,000 kilograms=1 metric ton

MILES

Swedish mile: 10,698 meters
German long mile: 9,259 meters
Swiss mile: 8,370 meters

Danish mile: 7,538 meters
Old Prussian mile: 7,532 meters
German new imperial mile: 7,500 meters
German geographical mile: 7,419 meters
Spanish league (common): 6,781 meters
Flanders league: 6,276 meters
German short mile: 6,272 meters
Portuguese league: 6,181 meters
French league: 4,444 meters
Spanish league (judicial): 4,238 meters
French posting league: 3,898 meters
Irish mile: 2,048 meters
Italian mile: 1,855 meters
geographical mile: 1,855 meters
ancient Scottish mile: 1,914 meters
Tuscan mile, 1,653 meters
English statute mile: 1,609 meters (1,760 yards; 5,280 feet)
modern Roman mile: 1,489 meters
ancient Roman mile: 1,476 meters

hex-, hexa-, sex-, sexi- (6)
hept-, hepta-, sept-, septem-, septi- (7)
oct-, octa-, octo- (8)
ennea-, non-, nona- (9)
dec-, deca-, deka- (10)
hendeca-, undec-, undeca- (11)
dodeca- (12)
quindeca- (15)
icos-, icosa-, icosi- (20)
hect-, hecti-, hecto- (100)
kilo- (1000)
myria- (10,000)
mega- (1,000,000)
giga- (1,000,000,000)
tera- (trillionfold)
peta- (quadrillionfold)
exa- (quintillionfold)
zetta- (septillionfold)
yotta- (sextillionfold)

NUMERALS

NUMBER PREFIXES

yocto- (one-septillionth)
zepto- (one-sextillionth)
atto- (one-quintillionth)
femto- (one-quadrillionth)
pico- (one-trillionth)
nano- (one-billionth)
micro- (one-millionth)
milli- (one-thousandth)
centi- ($\frac{1}{100}$)
deci- ($\frac{1}{10}$)
demi-, hemi-, semi- ($\frac{1}{2}$)
uni- (1)
bi-, di- (2)
ter-, tri- (3)
quadr-, quadri-, tetr-, tetra-, tessera- (4)
pent-, penta-, quinqu-, quinque-, quint- (5)

POWERS OF TEN

Numeral System by Zeros

$\frac{1}{1,000,000,000}$, one billionth, 10^{-9}
$\frac{1}{1,000,000}$, one millionth, 10^{-6}
$\frac{1}{1000}$, one thousandth, 10^{-3}
$\frac{1}{100}$, one hundredth, 10^{-2}
$\frac{1}{10}$, one tenth, 10^{-1}
one, 10^{0}
ten (one zero)
hundred (2 zeroes)
thousand (3 zeroes)
million (6 zeroes)
billion (9 zeroes)*
trillion (12)
quadrillion (15)
quintillion (18)
sextillion (21)
septillion (24)
octillion (27)
nonillion (30)
decillion (33)
undecillion (36)
duodecillion (39)
tredecillion (42)

quattuordecillion (45)
quindecillion (48)
sexdecillion (51)
septendecillion (54)
octodecillion (57)
novemdecillion (60)
vigintillion (63)
googol (100)
quintoquadagintillion (138)
centillion (303)
googolplex (googol)

Note: British billion is a million mil-lion, or 1 followed by 12 zeroes, the same as a U.S. trillion.

ROMAN NUMERAL SYSTEM

I one
II two
III three
IV four
V five
VI six
VII seven
VIII eight
IX nine
X ten
XX twenty
XXX thirty
XL forty
L fifty
LX sixty
LXX seventy
LXXX or XXC eighty
XC ninety
C one hundred
CC two hundred
CCC three hundred
CCCC four hundred
D five hundred
DC six hundred
DCC seven hundred
DCCC eight hundred
CM nine hundred
M one thousand
MM two thousand

(Mnemonic)

X shall stand for playmates ten
V for five stout stalwart men
I for one as I'm alive
C for hundred,
D for five (hundred)
M for a thousand soldiers true, and
L for 50, I'll tell you.

SPEED

Speed Equivalencies
10 mph=16.1 km/h
15 mph=24.1 km/h
20 mph=32.2 km/h
30 mph=48.3 km/h
40 mph=64.4 km/h
50 mph=80.4 km/h
60 mph=96.5 km/h
70 mph=112.6 km/h
80 mph=128.7 km/h

20 km/h=12.4 mph
30 km/h=18.6 mph
40 km/h=24.9 mph
50 km/h=31.1 mph
55 km/h=34.2 mph
60 km/h=37.3 mph
70 km/h=43.5 mph
80 km/h=49.7 mph
100 km/h=62.1 mph
110 km/h=68.4 mph
120 km/h=74.6 mph

TIME

Periods of Time
Millennium (1000 years)
Half-millennium (500 years)
Century (100 years)
Half-century (50 years)
Score (20 years)
Decade (10 years)
Lustrum, half-decade (5 years)
Quadrennium or Olympiad (4 years)

TIME
Periods of Time
(cont.)

Triennium (3 years)
Biennium (2 years)
Leap year (366 days)
Year (12 months, 52 weeks, 365 days)
Trimester (3 months)
Month (28–31 days)
Fortnight (2 weeks)
Week (7 days)
Day (24 hours)
Hour (60 minutes)
Minute (60 seconds)
Second (1/60 minute)

Seconds

terasecond (31,689 years)
gigasecond (31.7 years)
megasecond (11.6 days)
kilosecond (16.67 minutes)
millisecond (0.001 or 10^{-3} seconds)
microsecond (0.000001 or 10^{-6} seconds)
nanosecond (0.000000001 or 10^{-9} seconds)
picosecond (0.000000000001 or 10^{-12} seconds)
femtosecond (0.000000000000001 or 10^{-15} seconds)
attosecond (0.000000000000000001 or 10^{-18} seconds)

TIMES OF THE DAY

midnight: 12 a.m., official beginning of new day
twilight: first glow of sunlight
daybreak: first appearance of sun
dawn: gradual increase of light after daybreak
morning
noon: 12 p.m.
afternoon
dusk: gradual decrease of light
sunset: last sight of sun
twilight: last glow of sunlight
evening: approx. between sunset and midnight
night: darkness after twilight

DAYS OF THE WEEK

(with origins of names)

Sunday (sun day)
Monday (moon day)
Tuesday (Tiw's day, god of battle)
Wednesday (Woden's or Odin's day, god of poetry and the dead)
Thursday (Thor's day, god of thunder)
Friday (Freya's day, goddess of married love)
Saturday (Saturn's day, god of fertility and agriculture)

MONTHS

Poems to Remember Number of Days

Thirty days hath September,
April, June, and November.
All the rest have thirty-one,
Except February,
Which has four and twenty-four
And every leap year one day more.

INTERVALS OF TIME

semidiurnal (twice a day)
diurnal (daily)
biweekly (twice a week or every 2 weeks)
semiweekly (twice a week)
weekly (once a week)
bimonthly (twice a month or every 2 months)
triweekly (three times a week or every 3 weeks)
semimonthly (twice a month)
monthly (once a month)
trimonthly (every 3 months)
quarterly (four times a year)
biannual (twice a year)
semiannual (every 6 months)
annual (yearly)
perennial (occurring year after year)

biennial (2 years)
triennial (3 years)
quadrennial (4 years)
quinquennial (5 years)
sexennial (6 years)
septennial (7 years)
octennial (8 years)
novennial (9 years)
decennial (10 years)
undecennial (11 years)
duodecennial (12 years)
quindecennial (15 years)
vicennial (20 years)
tricennial (30 years)
quadricennial (40 years)
semicentennial (50 years)
centennial (100 years)
sesquicentennial (150 years)
bicentennial (200 years)
quadricentennial (400 years)
quincentennial (500 years)
millennial (1000 years)

CALENDARS

Chinese Calendar/Animal Years

*(assigns an animal to each year,
according to zodiacal cycles)*

1996 Rat, year of the
1997 Ox
1998 Tiger
1999 Hare
2000 Dragon
2001 Serpent/Snake
2002 Horse
2003 Sheep
2004 Monkey
2005 Fowl/Cock/Rooster
2006 Dog
2007 Boar/Pig

Gregorian Calendar

months (with Roman name)

January (Januarius or Ianuarius)
February (Februarius)

March (Martius; originally the first
month in the old Roman calendar)
April (Aprilis)
May (Maius)
June (Junius)
July (Julius)
August (Augustus)
September (Latin for seven, as it was
originally the seventh month)
October (L. for eight)
November (L. for nine)
December (L. for ten)

Hebrew Calendar

*(lunar beginning around mid-September
on the Gregorian calendar)*

Tishri (September/October)
Cheshvan or Heshvan
Kislev
Teveth or Tebet
Shevat or Shebat
Adar
(Veadar, 13th month in 3rd, 6th, 8th,
11th, 14th, 17th year of a 19-yr cycle)
Nisan
Iyar
Sivan
Tammuz
Av or Ab
Elul (August/September)

Inca Calendar

Capac Raimi/Capac Quilla (=
December) (month of rest; the lord
festival)
Zarap Tuta Cavai Mitan (time to
watch corn growing)
Paucar Varai (time to wear loincloths)
Pacha Pucuy Quilla (month of land's
maturation)
Camai Quilla/Inti Raymi (month of
harvest and rest)
Zara Muchuy Quilla Aymoray Quilla
(dry corn is stored)
Papa Allai Mitan Pacha (potato
harvest)

Haucai Cusqui (rest from harvesting)
Chacra Conaqui Quilla (month of land redistribution)
Chacra Yapuy Quilla Hailly (month to open lands coming into cultivation with songs of triumph)
Zara Tarpuy Quilla/Coia Raymi Quilla (month for planting; Festival of the Queen)
Chacramanta Pisco Carcoy (time to scare birds from newly planted fields)
Chacra Parcay (time to irrigate fields)

Maya Calendar

tzolkin: 260-day sacred year of a combination of the numbers 1–13 with 20 day names
haab: solar year of 18 20-day months (numbered 0–19) followed by a five-day unlucky period (Uayeb)
series of cycles
   uinal (20 days)
   tun (360 days)
   katun (7,200 days)
   baktun (144,000 days)
   alautun (23,040,000,000 days)

U.S. MEASURES

LINEAR MEASURE

12 inches=1 foot
3 feet=1 yard
5½ yards=1 rod, pole, or perch (16½ feet)
4 rods=1 chain 40 rods=1 furlong=220 yards=660 feet
8 furlongs=1 statute mile=1,760 yards=5,280 feet
3 miles=1 league=5,280 yards=15,840 feet
6076.11549 feet=1 International Nautical Mile

LIQUID MEASURE

4 gills=1 pint=28.875 cubic inches
2 pints=1 quart=57.75 cubic inches
4 quarts=1 gallon=231 cubic inches=8 pints=32 gills

AREA MEASURE

144 square inches=1 square foot
9 square feet=1 square yard=1,296 square inches
30¼ square yards=1 square rod=272 ¼ square feet
40 square rods=1 rood
160 square rods=1 acre=4,840 square yards=43,560 square feet
640 acres=1 square mile
1 mile square=1 section (of land)
6 miles square=1 township=36 sections=36 square miles

CUBIC MEASURE

1 cubic foot=1,728 cubic inches
27 cubic feet=1 cubic yard

GUNTER'S, OR SURVEYOR'S, CHAIN MEASURE

7.92 inches=1 link
100 links=1 chain=4 rods=66 feet
80 chains=1 survey mile=320 rods=5,280 feet

TROY WEIGHT

24 grains=1 pennyweight
20 pennyweights=1 ounce troy=480 grains
12 ounces troy=1 pound troy=240 pennyweights=5,760 grains

DRY MEASURE

2 pints=1 quart=67.2006 cubic inches
8 quarts=1 peck=537.605 cubic inches=16 pints
4 pecks=1 bushel=2,150.42 cubic inches=32 quarts

AVOIRDUPOIS WEIGHT

$27\,^{11}\!/_{32}$ grains=1 dram
16 drams=1 ounce=437 ½ grains
16 ounces=1 pound = 256 drams=7,000 grains
100 pounds=1 hundredweight
20 hundredweights=1 ton=2,000 pounds

WATER WEIGHTS

(at 20 degrees Celsius)

1 cubic inch=0.0360 pound
12 cubic inches=0.433 pound
1 cubic foot=62.4 pounds
1 cubic foot=7.48052 U.S. gallons
1.8 cubic feet=112.0 pounds
35.96 cubic feet=2240.0 pounds
1 U.S. gallon=8.33 pounds
13.45 U.S. gallons=112.0 pounds
269.0 U.S. gallons=2240.0 pounds
(metric weights of water at 4 degrees Celsius)
1 cubic centimeter=1 gram
1 liter=1 kilogram
1 cubic meter=1 metric ton

Order is heaven's first law.

—Alexander Pope, *An Essay on Man*

CHAPTER SIX

RELIGION

ANGELS

HIERARCHY

(There are various hierarchies for angels. This is the most-agreed-upon order, compiled by Gregory the Great, 6th c AD)

**Nine Orders of Angels
in Three Hierarchies**

(in descending rank of importance)

First hierarchy:
  Seraphim (highest angels of love, light, and fire)
  Cherubim (one who prays or intercedes)
  Thrones (in charge of justice)
Second hierarchy:
  Dominations/Dominions (regulate angel duties)
  Principalities (protectors of religion)
  Powers (impose order on heavenly pathways)
Third hierarchy:
  Virtues (work miracles on earth)
  Archangels (minister and make propitiation for people's sins)
  Angels (guardians of men and nations; messengers between God and man)

ZODIAC AND ASSOCIATED ANGELS

Capricorn:	Hanael
Aquarius:	Gabriel
Pisces:	Barchiel
Aries:	Hachidiel
Taurus:	Asmodel
Gemini:	Ambriel
Cancer:	Muriel
Leo:	Verchiel
Virgo:	Hamaliel
Libra:	Uriel
Scorpio:	Barbiel
Sagittarius:	Adnachiel

BIBLE

BOOKS OF THE BIBLE

Old Testament

Law (Pentateuch, Torah)
  Genesis
  Exodus
  Leviticus
  Numbers
  Deuteronomy
Prophets (Former)
  Joshua
  Judges
  Samuel 1, Samuel 2
  Kings 1, Kings 2

"Hierarchy of Angels"

Hans-Werner Hegemann, *Der Engel in der deutschen Kunst.* (14th century)

BIBLE
Books of the Bible
(cont.)

Prophets (Latter)
Isaiah
Jeremiah
Ezekiel

*(next twelve are sometimes considered
Book of Twelve Prophets)*

Hosea
Joel
Amos
Obadiah
Jonah
Micah
Nahum
Habakkuk
Zephaniah
Haggai
Zechariah
Malachi
Writings
Psalms
Proverbs
Job
Song of Songs (Solomon)
Ruth
Lamentations
Ecclesiastes
Esther
Daniel
Ezra
Nehemiah
Chronicles 1, Chronicles 2

New Testament

Gospels
Matthew
Mark
Luke
John

Acts of the Apostles
Epistles
Romans
Corinthians 1, Corinthians 2
Galatians
Ephesians
Philippians

Colossians
Thessalonians 1, Thessalonians 2
Timothy 1, Timothy 2
Titus
Philemon
Letter to the Hebrews
7 General or 'Catholic' Letters
James
Peter 1, Peter 2
John 1, John 2, John 3
Jude
Book of Revelation (or the
Apocalypse)

Apocrypha *(canonical only in
Catholicism)*
Baruch
Additions to the Book of Daniel
Book of Ecclesiasticus by Sirach
Additions to the Book of Esther
Books of Esdras
Letter of Jeremiah
Book of Judith
Books of the Maccabees
Book of Tobit (Tobias)
Wisdom of Solomon

BOOKS OF THE BIBLE—TYPES

The Historical Books

Joshua
Judges
Ruth
1 Samuel
2 Samuel
1 Kings
2 Kings
1 Chronicles
2 Chronicles
Ezra
Nehemiah
Tobit (Apocrypha)
Judith (Apocrypha)
Esther
1 Maccabees (Apocrypha)
2 Maccabees (Apocrypha)

The Poetical or Wisdom Books

Job
Psalms
Proverbs
Ecclesiastes
Song of Solomon (Songs)
Wisdom (Apocrypha)
Sirach (Apocrypha)

The Prophetical Books

Isaiah
Jeremiah
Lamentations
Baruch (Apocrypha)
Ezekiel
Daniel
Hosea
Joel
Amos
Obadiah
Jonah
Micah
Nahum
Habakkuk
Zephaniah
Haggai
Zechariah
Malachi

ENGLISH BIBLE— VERSIONS AND EDITIONS

(This listing includes the most well-known translations and revisions.)

John Wyckliffe (based on Latin Vulgate), 1382
William Tyndale (New Testament), 1525–26
Miles Coverdale, 1535
Thomas Matthew (aka John Rogers), 1537
Archbishop Cranmer's Great Bible, 1539
Geneva Bible, 1560
Bishops' Bible, 1568

Douay Bible, 1582/1609
Roman Catholic Authorized, 1609/10
King James's Version/Authorized Version, 1611
Revised Version, 1881/1885
American Standard Version, 1901
Revised Standard Version, 1946–52
New English Bible, 1961–70
New American Standard Bible, 1963–71
Good News Bible, 1966–76
Jerusalem Bible, 1966
New American Bible, 1970
The Living Bible, 1971
New International Version, 1978
Revised King James Version, 1982
New Revised Standard Version, 1989
The Revised English Bible, 1989

BIBLE

LISTS FROM THE BIBLE

Covenants

First Covenant: God's promise to Noah that there would never be another flood to cover the earth. (Genesis 9:9)
Second Covenant: God's promise to Israel that he would forgive their sins, fulfilled (in Christian doctrine) in the coming of Jesus. (Jeremiah 31:31–34, Hebrews 8:8–13)

Days of Creation
(Genesis 1:1–31; 2:1–3)

In the beginning God created the heavens and the earth.
1. On the first day, He created light and dark, Day and Night.
2. On the second day, He made the firmament, dividing the waters. The firmament He called Heaven.
3. On the third day, He made the Earth, and the Seas, and grasses, herbs, and trees upon the earth.

4. On the fourth day, He made the stars and the sun and the moon.
5. On the fifth day, God created the creatures of the sea and the air, the fish and the fowl.
6. On the sixth day, God created the living creatures of the land and created man.
7. On the seventh day, He rested.

Four Horsemen of the Apocalypse

(Revelation 6:2–8)

War
Famine
Pestilence
Death

Gifts of the Holy Spirit

(in I Corinthians 12:4–11)

1. the utterance of wisdom
2. the utterance of knowledge
3. faith
4. gifts of healing
5. the working of miracles
6. prophecy
7. the ability to distinguish between spirits
8. speaking in different kinds of tongues
9. interpretation of tongues

Plagues of Egypt

(Lord set ten plagues upon Egyptians after Pharaoh refused Moses' plea to free the Hebrews from slavery; Exodus 7–11)

1. blood
2. frogs
3. lice
4. flies
5. murrain, by which all cattle of Egypt were killed
6. boils
7. hail
8. locusts

9. darkness
10. slaying of the firstborn of Egypt

Plagues Mnemonic

Retaliating **F**or **L**ong **F**rustration
Moses **B**adgered **H**ostile **L**eader
Demanding **F**reedom

river turned to blood
frogs
lice
flies
murrain (dire pestilence)
boils
hail
locusts
darkness
first-born killed

Seven Joys of Mary

1. The Annunciation, when the Angel Gabriel announced that she would be with child (Luke 1:26–38)
2. The Visitation, the visit of the Virgin Mary to her cousin Elizabeth, who was also with child (Luke 1:39–56)
3. The Nativity, or the birth of Christ
4. The Adoration of the Magi, when the Three Wise Men arrived bearing gifts for the King of the Jews (Matthew 2:11)
5. The Presentation in the Temple (Luke 2:25–39)
6. The Finding of the Lost Child Jesus in the temple where he had been astonishing the elders with his learning (Luke 2:42–51)
7. The Assumption, when the Virgin Mary arose bodily into Heaven

Seven Sorrows of Mary

1. The Prophecy at the Temple, made by Simeon (Luke 2:25–59)
2. The Flight into Egypt to escape Herod's slaughter of the children

of Bethlehem (Matthew 2:13–21)
3. Jesus Lost in the Temple, when he was missing from his parents for three days (Luke 2:25–93)
4. The Betrayal by Judas Iscariot (Luke 22:1–53)
5. The Crucifixion
6. The taking down from the Cross (Mark 15:42–47)
7. The Ascension, when Christ ascended into Heaven (Luke 24: 50–53)

Ten Commandments
(Revised Standard Version: Exodus, Chapter 20)

1. I am the Lord your God, who brought you out of the land of Egypt, out of the house of bondage. You shall have no other gods before me.
2. You shall not make for yourself a graven image, or any likeness of anything that is in heaven above, or that is in the earth beneath, or that is in the water under the earth; you shall not bow down to them or serve them; for I the Lord your God am a jealous God, visiting the iniquity of the father upon the children to the third and fourth generation of those who hate me, but showing steadfast love to thousands of those who love me and keep my commandments.
3. You shall not take the name of the Lord your God in vain; for the Lord will not hold him guiltless who takes his name in vain.
4. Remember the sabbath day, to keep it holy. Six days you shall labor, and do all your work; but the seventh day is a sabbath to the Lord your God; in it you shall not do any work, you, or your son, or your daughter, your manservant, or your maidservant, or your cattle, or the sojourner who is within your gates; for in the six days the Lord made heaven and earth, the sea, and all that is in them, and rested the seventh day; therefore the Lord blessed the sabbath day and hallowed it.
5. Honor your father and your mother, that your days may be long in the land which the Lord your God gives you.
6. You shall not kill.
7. You shall not commit adultery.
8. You shall not steal.
9. You shall not bear false witness against your neighbor.
10. You shall not covet your neighbor's house; you shall not covet your neighbor's wife, or his manservant, or his maidservant, or his ox, or his ass, or anything that is your neighbor's.

BUDDHISM

CALENDAR
(begins in April)

Citta
Vesakha
Jettha
Asalha
Savana
Potthapada
Assayuia
Kattika
Maggasira
Phussa
Magha
Phagguna

DHARMA

(doctrines or teachings of Buddha)

Four Noble Truths:
Life is full of suffering.
Suffering is caused by attachment, greed, or desire.
Suffering ends when we see the impermanence of everything.
There is a path to peace and contentment, the eightfold noble path.

Eightfold Noble Path:
Right understanding (seeing the world as it really is)
Right intentions (kindness and compassion)
Right speech (not lying, criticizing, hurting with words)
Right action (not harming, not stealing, not overindulging)
Right livelihood (earning a living by not harming others)
Right effort (attempting to do meritorious things)
Right mindfulness (being aware and alert)
Right concentration (meditation and avoidance of excess)

FIVE HINDRANCES

1. seeking worldly advantage
2. desiring to hurt others
3. slackness of mind
4. worry
5. uncertainty of mind

FIVE MORAL PRECEPTS

1. not taking life, including animals
2. no stealing
3. no wrong sexual relations
4. no wrong use of speech (lying, malicious gossip)
5. moderation or abstinence from alcohol and drugs

FOUR SIGNS

(The four encounters with suffering and impermanence experienced by Siddhartha, the Buddha)

old age
sickness
death
austerity

SACRED TEXTS

(The Pali Canon Tripitaka (Three Baskets))

Vinaya Pitaka, discipline or rules of conduct
Sutta Pitaka, doctrine or teachings of the Buddha
Abhidhamma Pitaka, higher teachings or philosophy

SCHOOLS & SECTS

Theravada
Mahayana
  Madhyamika
  Yogacara
  Avatamsaka
  Pure Land
  Dhyana/Zen
Hinayana
  Abhidharma-Kosa
  Dharmaguptaka
  Dharma-Laksana
  Insight Meditation
  Lokottaravada
  Mantra
  Sammatiya
  Sarvastivada
  Satyasiddhi
  Sukhavati
  Tibetan
  Vinaya

THREE JEWELS

(also called Threefold Refuge)

belief in the Buddha
belief in the Dharma, the Buddha's
 teachings
belief in the Sangha, the religious
 community of the Buddha

CHRISTIANITY

Anglican / Episcopalian Churches

Church of England Organization

two provinces: Canterbury and York

monarch (official head of church)
Archbishop of Canterbury (the
 Primate of All England)
General Synod (church parliament
 made up of bishops, clergy, and lay
 people)
dioceses (governed by bishops)
parishes (governed by clergy)

Episcopal Church Liturgical Calendar

Ash Wednesday
First Sunday in Lent
Passion/Palm Sunday
Good Friday
Easter Day
Ascension Day
The Day of Pentecost
Trinity Sunday
First Sunday of Advent
 (November/December)

BEATITUDES OF JESUS

(Matthew 5: 3–12, Jesus's Sermon on the Mount)

1. Blessed are the poor in spirit, for theirs is the kingdom of heaven.
2. Blessed are those who mourn, for they shall be comforted.
3. Blessed are the meek, for they shall inherit the earth.

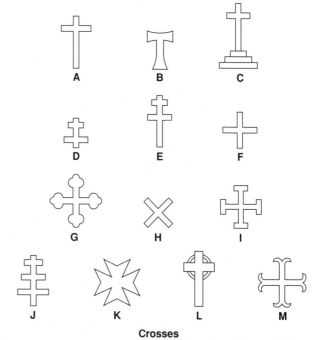

Crosses
A. Latin cross; **B.** Tau cross or St. Anthony's cross; **C.** Cross of Calvary;
D. Cross of Lorraine; **E.** Patriarchal cross; **F.** Greek cross; **G.** Botonée;
H. St. Andrew's cross; **I.** Cross potent; **J.** Papal cross; **K.** Maltese cross;
L. Celtic cross; **M.** Moline

4. Blessed are those who hunger and thirst after righteousness, for they shall be satisfied.
5. Blessed are the merciful, for they shall obtain mercy.
6. Blessed are the pure in heart, for they shall see God.
7. Blessed are the peacemakers, for they shall be called sons of God.
8. Blessed are those who are persecuted for righteousness' sake, for theirs is the kingdom of heaven.
9. Blessed are you when men shall revile you and persecute you and utter all kinds of evil against you falsely on my account. Rejoice and be glad, for your reward is great in heaven, for so men persecuted the prophets who were before you.

CALVINISM

Five Tenets of Calvin

(Institutes of the Christian Religion, 1536)

1. Transcendence of God
2. Total depravity of natural man
3. Predestination of particular election (God chose some for salvation)
4. Sole authority of the scriptures and the Holy Spirit
5. Community must enforce the discipline of the church

otherwise worded as:

1. God as majesty
2. Christ as prophet, priest, and king
3. Holy Spirit as giver of faith
4. Bible as the final authority
5. Church as the holy people of god

CANONICAL HOURS

(Psalms 119: 164, the seven hours for daily psalms of praise for God's righteous ordinances)

Matins (or Mattins) with lauds: midnight or 2 a.m., but often at sunrise
Prime: first hour of the day or 6 a.m.
Tierce: third hour after sunrise
Sext: sixth hour of the day or noon
Nones: ninth hour after sunrise
Vespers: late afternoon or in evening
Complin (or Compline): just before bedtime

CHRISTIAN CHURCH HISTORY

Early Church

after the Schism (1054) became:

Eastern Orthodox, Western Catholic (or Church of Rome) (which, after the Reformation, became the Roman Catholic Church)

Western Catholic
  Roman Catholic
  Church of England/Anglican
    (broke from Rome in 1534)
  Protestant Reformation
    Presbyterian/Calvinist
    Lutheran
    Congregational
    Baptist
    Methodist
    Salvation Army
    other Protestant denominations
Eastern Orthodox, including
  Greek Orthodox
  Russian Orthodox
  Coptic
  Syrian American

CHURCHES OF ASIA

(listed in Revelation 1:11)

Ephesus
Smyrna
Pergamum
Thyatira
Sardis
Philadelphia
Laodicea

DANTE (ALIGHIERI)

Dante's Levels of Hell

(from The Inferno)

Portal: entranceway
Acheron: river separating world from underworld
Circle 1/Limbo: home of unbaptized
Circle 2: home of "carnal sinners"
Circle 3: home of the gluttonous
Circle 4: home of the prodigal and avaricious
Circle 5/Styx: home of the wrathful
Dis: walled city containing the remainder of Hell
  a. Circle 6: heretics

b. Circle 7
  i. Phlegethon: those who were violent to their neighbors
  ii. those who were violent to themselves
  iii. those who were violent to nature and God
c. Abyss
d. Circle 8 / Malebolge: has 10 deeper bastions
  i. Bolgia: panderers and seducers
  ii. flatterers
  iii. buyers/sellers of pardons and powers (simoniacs)
  iv. fortunetellers
  v. grafters
  vi. hypocrites
  vii. robbers
  viii. evil counselors
  ix. scandalmongers
  x. iars
e. Circle 9 / Cocytus: a frozen lake
  i. pit of Giants
  ii. traitors
    a. traitors to family
    b. traitors to country
    c. traitors to guests
    d. traitors to employers or masters (including Judas Iscariot; Brutus and Cassius, assassins of Julius Caesar)
f. center of the earth, home of Lucifer, Hell's monarch

(Vergil and Dante emerge through a tunnel into the opposite hemisphere, which is covered with water, to approach the island of the mountain of Purgatory.)

Dante's Mystic Three

(from The Divine Comedy, journey to:)

Hell (Inferno)
Purgatory (Purgatorio)
Earthly Paradise (Paradiso)
(then on to God)

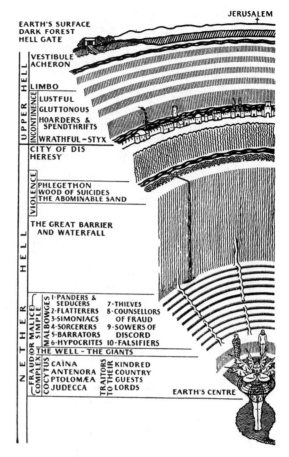

Dante's Levels of Hell (by C.W. Scott-Giles, 1949)

ORTHODOX CHRISTIANITY

Calendar

January 1: St. Basil's Day; Circumcision of the Lord
January 6: Epiphany
February 2: Hypapante (Christ's meeting with Simeon)
March 25: Annunciation
March: Orthodox Sunday
March or April: Palm Sunday
March or April: Easter
April or May: Ascension Day
May: Pentecost

July 17: St. Marina's Day
August 6: Transfiguration
August 15: Assumption
September 8: Nativity of Blessed
Virgin
September 14: Exaltation of Holy Cross
October 26: St. Demetrius' Day
November 21: Presentation of
Blessed Virgin Mary in Temple
November 30: St. Andrew's Day
December 25: Christmas Day

Church Branches

Antiochian Orthodox
Brotherhood of the Holy Sepulchre
Coptic Church
Cyprus Orthodox Church
Greek Orthodox Church
Orthodox-Catholic Church
Orthodox Church in America
Orthodox Church of Bulgaria
Orthodox Church of Czechoslovakia
Orthodox Church of Finland
Orthodox Church of Poland
Orthodox Church of Romania
Orthodox Church of Serbia
Orthodox Church of Turkey
(Constantinople)
Orthodox Church of Yugoslavia
Russian Orthodox Church

Greek Orthodox Movable Ecclesiastical Calendar

Triodion (January or February)
Saturday of Souls
Meat Fare
Second Saturday of Souls
Lent (February or March)
St. Theodore, Third Saturday of Souls
Sunday of Orthodoxy
Saturday of Lazarus
Palm Sunday
Holy (Good) Friday
Orthodox Easter (March or April)
Ascension
Saturday of Souls

Pentecost
All Saints Day (June)

Historical Hierarchy of Orthodox Churches

autocephalous (governed by its own patriarch or head bishop) churches:
Constantinople
Alexandria (Egypt)
Damascus (Syria)
Jerusalem
Russia
Republic of Georgia
Serbia
Romania
Bulgaria

nonpatriarchcal churches in order of precedence:
Cyprus
Athens
Tirana (Albania)
Poland
Czech Republic
Slovakia
America

Orthodox Christian Hierarchy

Synod (bishops in an ecclesiastical
territory, presided over by an
archbishop or metropolitan; also
archbishops and metropolitans
may form a synod, headed by
patriarch)
Council (presbyters)
Patriarch (leading bishop in a great
region or national church)
Archbishop (chief bishop)
Metropolitans (bishop of a chief city)
Bishop (leader of diocese, a church
for a region)
Presbyter (leader of parish, a local
congregation)
Deacon
Subdeacon
Reader
Acolyte

PROTESTANTISM

Branches

(largest memberships)

Anglican Communion
Baptist
Congregational
Episcopal
Evangelical
Fundamentalist
Lutheran
Mennonite
Methodist
Moravian
Pentecostal
Presbyterian
Quaker

Protestant Movements

Lutheran
Calvinist (Reformed)
Anglican
Anabaptist
Congregational (Separatist)
Baptist
Methodist

Governmental Structures:

Episcopal (e.g. Anglican, Episcopal,
    Lutheran; have bishop)
Presbyterian (Calvinist; have
    presbyter or elder, an elected
    representative of a congregation)
Congregational (e.g. Baptist,
    Congregational, Lutheran;
    congregation is highest authority)

Presbyterian Hierarchy

presbyters (or elders): manage
    spiritual conduct of church
deacons and trustees: handle
    temporal affairs
courts (highest to lowest) composed
    of clerical and lay presbyters:
general assembly (presided over by
    moderator)

synod
presbytery or colloquy
court of the congregation or session

ROMAN CATHOLIC CHURCH

Calendar

*(Easter falls on the first Sunday following
the first full moon after the vernal
equinox, and ranges from
March 22 to April 25)*

January 1: Solemnity of Mary, Mother
    of God
January 6: Epiphany
Febuary or March: Ash Wednesday
March 19: St Joseph's Day
March 25: The Annunciation
March or April: Palm Sunday
March or April: Holy Week
March or April: Easter
April or May: Ascension Day
April or May: Pentecost
May or June: Trinity Sunday
May or June: Corpus Christi
June 29: St. Peter and St. Paul
August 6: Transfiguration
August 15: Assumption of Blessed
    Virgin Mary
September 8: Nativity of the Virgin
November 1: All Saint's Day
December 8: Immaculate Conception
December 25: Christmas Day

Hierarchy and Organization

Supreme Pontiff / Pope (elected by
    College of Cardinals)
College of Cardinals
    Cardinal (appointed by Pope,
        normally from among bishops)
Archbishop (bishop of highest rank,
    heading archdiocese or
    province)
archdiocese/province/metropolitan
    see (province of "suffragan"
    dioceses)

Bishop (high-ranking cleric, heading
diocese)
diocese (territory of large number
of parishes)
chancery/curia (assist bishop: lay
vicar general, officialis,
chancellor, consultors, synodal
examiners, promotor of justice,
defender of the bond)
Monsignor (honorary title)
Parish Priest or Pastor (cleric of
second grade, just below a
bishop)
Deacon (cleric just below a priest)
parish (community)
Abbot (superior of a monastery)
abbey/abbey nullius

Roman Catholic Administration

Pope
Synod of Bishops (elected
representatives from the
episcopate)
National and Regional Conferences
of Bishops
College of Cardinals
Roman Curia (complex of
congregations, offices,
tribunals, and secretariates
through which the pope directs
the church's central
government)
Cardinal vicar general of Rome
Chamberlain
Major Penitentiary
Congregation
cardinal prefect
secretary
undersecretary
papal appointees
7 bishops assigned from various
countries
lesser officials and consultors
Council of the Laity
Papal Commission for Promoting
Justice and Peace

The Sacred Congregations
Sacred Congregation for the
Teaching of the Faith
Sacred Congregation for the
Oriental Churches
Sacred Congregation for Bishops
Sacred Congregation for the
Sacraments and for Divine
Worship
Sacred Congregation for the Causes
of Saints
Sacred Congregation for Religious
and Secular Institutes
Sacred Congregation for Catholic
Education
Secretariats
Papal Secretariat and the Papal
Council for the Church's Public
Affairs
Secretariat for Promoting Christian
Unity
Secretariat for Non-Christians
Secretariat for Non-Believers
The Sacred Tribunals
Supreme Tribunal of the Apostolic
Signature
Sacred Roman Rota
Sacred Apostolic Penitentiary
The Sacred Offices
Apostolic Chancery
Prefecture of the Holy See's
Economic Affairs
Apostolic Chamber/Administration
of the Patrimony of St. Peter
Prefecture of the Apostolic Palace
Central Statistics Office

Papal Succession

1. St. Peter (32–67)
2. St. Linus (67–76)
3. St. Anacletus (Cletus) (76–88)
4. St. Clement I (88–97)
5. St. Evaristus (97–105)
6. St. Alexander I (105–115)
7. St. Sixtus I (115–125)—also
called Xystus I

8. St. Telesphorus (125–136)
9. St. Hyginus (136–140)
10. St. Pius I (140–155)
11. St. Anicetus (155–166)
12. St. Soter (166–175)
13. St. Eleutherius (175–189)
14. St. Victor I (189–199)
15. St. Zephyrinus (199–217)
16. St. Callistus I (217–22)
17. St. Urban I (222–30)
18. St. Pontain (230–35)
19. St. Anterus (235–36)
20. St. Fabian (236–50)
21. St. Cornelius (251–53)
22. St. Lucius I (253–54)
23. St. Stephen I (254–257)
24. St. Sixtus II (257–258)
25. St. Dionysius (260–268)
26. St. Felix I (269–274)
27. St. Eutychian (275–283)
28. St. Caius (283–296)—also called Gaius
29. St. Marcellinus (296–304)
30. St. Marcellus I (308–309)
31. St. Eusebius (April-August 309 or 310)
32. St. Miltiades (311–14)
33. St. Sylvester I (314–35)
34. St. Marcus (January-October 336)
35. St. Julius I (337–52)
36. Liberius (352–66)
37. St. Damasus I (366–83)
38. St. Siricius (384–99)
39. St. Anastasius I (399–401)
40. St. Innocent I (401–17)
41. St. Zosimus (417–18)
42. St. Boniface I (418–22)
43. St. Celestine I (422–32)
44. St. Sixtus III (432–40)
45. St. Leo I (the Great) (440–61)
46. St. Hilarius (461–68)
47. St. Simplicius (468–83)
48. St. Felix III (II) (483–92)
49. St. Gelasius I (492–96)
50. Anastasius II (496–98)
51. St. Symmachus (498–514)
52. St. Hormisdas (514–23)
53. St. John I (523–26)
54. St. Felix IV (III) (526–30)
55. Boniface II (530–32)
56. John II (533–35)
57. St. Agapetus I (535–36)—also called Agapitus I
58. St. Silverius (536–37)
59. Vigilius (537–55)
60. Pelagius I (556–61)
61. John III (561–74)
62. Benedict I (575–79)
63. Pelagius II (579–90)
64. St. Gregory I (the Great) (590–604)
65. Sabinian (604–606)
66. Boniface III (February-November 607)
67. St. Boniface IV (608–15)
68. St. Deusdedit (Adeodatus I) (615–18)
69. Boniface V (619–25)
70. Honorius I (625–38)
71. Severinus (May-August 640)
72. John IV (640–42)
73. Theodore I (642–49)
74. St. Martin I (649–55)
75. St. Eugene I (655–57)
76. St. Vitalian (657–72)
77. Adeodatus (II) (672–76)
78. Donus (676–78)
79. St. Agatho (678–81)
80. St. Leo II (682–83)
81. St. Benedict II (684–85)
82. John V (685–86)
83. Conon (686–87)
84. St. Sergius I (687–701)
85. John VI (701–05)
86. John VII (705–07)
87. Sisinnius (January-February 708)
88. Constantine (708–15)
89. St. Gregory II (715–31)
90. St. Gregory III (731–41)
91. St. Zachary (741–52)

92. Stephen II (March 752)
93. Stephen III (752–57)
94. St. Paul I (757–67)
95. Stephen IV (767–72)
96. Adrian I (772–95)
97. St. Leo III (795–816)
98. Stephen V (816–17)
99. St. Paschal I (817–24)
100. Eugene II (824–27)
101. Valentine (August-September 827)
102. Gregory IV (827–44)
103. Sergius II (844–47)
104. St. Leo IV (847–55)
105. Benedict III (855–58)
106. St. Nicholas I (the Great) (858–67)
107. Adrian II (867–72)
108. John VIII (872–82)
109. Marinus I (882–84)
110. St. Adrian III (884–85)
111. Stephen VI (885–91)
112. Formosus (891–96)
113. Boniface VI (April 896)
114. Stephen VII (896–97)
115. Romanus (August-November 897)
116. Theodore II (November-December 897)
117. John IX (898–900)
118. Benedict IV (900–03)
119. Leo V (July-December 903)
120. Sergius III (904–11)
121. Anastasius III (911–13)
122. Lando (913–14)
123. John X (914–28)
124. Leo VI (May-December 928)
125. Stephen VIII (929–31)
126. John XI (931–35)
127. Leo VII (936–39)
128. Stephen IX (939–42)
129. Marinus II (942–46)
130. Agapetus II (946–55)
131. John XII (955–63)
132. Leo VIII (963–64)
133. Benedict V (May-June 964)

134. John XIII (965–72)
135. Benedict VI (973–74)
136. Benedict VII (974–83)
137. John XIV (983–84)
138. John XV (985–96)
139. Gregory V (996–99)
140. Sylvester II (999–1003)
141. John XVII (June-December 1003)
142. John XVIII (1003–09)
143. Sergius IV (1009–12)
144. Benedict VIII (1012–24)
145. John XIX (1024–32)
146. Benedict IX (1032–45)
147. Sylvester III (January-March 1045)
148. Benedict IX (April-May 1045)
149. Gregory VI (1045–46)
150. Clement II (1046–47)
151. Benedict IX (1047–48)
152. Damasus II (July-August 1048)
153. St. Leo IX (1049–54)
154. Victor II (1055–57)
155. Stephen X (1057–58)
156. Nicholas II (1058–61)
157. Alexander II (1061–73)
158. St. Gregory VII (1073–85)
159. Victor III (1086–87)
160. Urban II (1088–99)
161. Paschal II (1099–1118)
162. Gelasius II (1118–19)
163. Callistus II (1119–24)
164. Honorius II (1124–30)
165. Innocent II (1130–43)
166. Celestine II (1143–44)
167. Lucius II (1144–45)
168. Eugene III (1145–53)
169. Anastasius IV (1153–54)
170. Adrian IV (1154–59)
171. Alexander III (1159–81)
172. Lucius III (1181–85)
173. Urban III (1185–87)
174. Gregory VIII (1187)
175. Clement III (1187–91)
176. Celestine III (1191–98)
177. Innocent III (1198–1216)

178. Honorius III (1216–27)
179. Gregory IX (1227–41)
180. Celestine IV (October-November 1241)
181. Innocent IV (1243–54)
182. Alexander IV (1254–61)
183. Urban IV (1261–64)
184. Clement IV (1265–68)
185. Blessed Gregory X (1271–76)
186. Blessed Innocent V (January-June 1276)
187. Adrian V (July-August 1276)
188. John XXI (1276–77)
189. Nicholas III (1277–80)
190. Martin IV (1281–85)
191. Honorius IV (1285–87)
192. Nicholas IV (1288–92)
193. St. Celestine V (July-December 1294)
194. Boniface VIII (1294–1303)
195. Blessed Benedict XI (1303–04)
196. Clement V (1305–14)
197. John XXII (1316–34)
198. Benedict XII (1334–42)
199. Clement VI (1342–52)
200. Innocent VI (1352–62)
201. Blessed Urban V (1362–70)
202. Gregory XI (1370–78)
203. Urban VI (1378–89)
204. Boniface IX (1389–1404)
205. Innocent VII (1406–06)
206. Gregory XII (1406–15)
207. Martin V (1417–31)
208. Eugene IV (1431–47)
209. Nicholas V (1447–55)
210. Callistus III (1445–58)
211. Pius II (1458–64)
212. Paul II (1464–71)
213. Sixtus IV (1471–84)
214. Innocent VIII (1484–92)
215. Alexander VI (1492–1503)
216. Pius III (September-October 1503)
217. Julius II (1503–13)
218. Leo X (1513–21)
219. Adrian VI (1522–23)
220. Clement VII (1523–34)
221. Paul III (1534–49)

222. Julius III (1550–55)
223. Marcellus II (April 1555)
224. Paul IV (1555–59)
225. Pius IV (1559–65)
226. St. Pius V (1566–72)
227. Gregory XIII (1572–85)
228. Sixtus V (1585–90)
229. Urban VII (September 1590)
230. Gregory XIV (1590–91)
231. Innocent IX (October-November 1591)
232. Clement VIII (1592–1605)
233. Leo XI (April 1605)
234. Paul V (1605–21)
235. Gregory XV (1621–23)
236. Urban VIII (1623–44)
237. Innocent X (1644–55)
238. Alexander VII (1655–67)
239. Clement IX (1667–69)
240. Clement X (1670–76)
241. Blessed Innocent XI (1676–89)
242. Alexander VIII (1689–91)
243. Innocent XII (1691–1700)
244. Clement XI (1700–21)
245. Innocent XIII (1721–24)
246. Benedict XIII (1724–30)
247. Clement XII (1730–40)
248. Benedict XIV (1740–58)
249. Clement XIII (1758–69)
250. Clement XIV (1769–74)
251. Pius VI (1775–99)
252. Pius VII (1800–23)
253. Leo XII (1823–29)
254. Pius VIII (1829–30)
255. Gregory XVI (1831–46)
256. Blessed Pius IX (1846–78)
257. Leo XIII (1878–1903)
258. St. Pius X (1903–14)
259. Benedict XV (1914–22)
260. Pius XI (1922–39)
261. Pius XII (1939–58)
262. Blessed John XXIII (1958–63)
263. Paul VI (1963–78)
264. John Paul I (August-September 1978)
265. John Paul II (1978–   )

CHURCH OF JESUS CHRIST AND LATTER-DAY SAINTS (MORMONS)

Church Hierarchy

First Presidency: President and two counselors
Council of the Twelve Apostles
Patriarch
First Quorum of the Seventy
Presiding Bishopric: three members
Stakes: collection of several wards
Wards: 400–600 members each

SEVEN HOLY SACRAMENTS

1. Baptism
2. Reconciliation (Penance)
3. Eucharist (Holy Communion)
4. Confirmation
5. Holy Matrimony
6. Holy Orders
7. Anointing of the Sick (also Extreme Unction or Last Rites)

SEVEN DEADLY/CAPITAL SINS

1. pride
2. covetousness
3. lust
4. anger
5. gluttony
6. envy
7. sloth

SEVEN WORKS OF MERCY

(Matthew 25:35–45, seven corporal works)

feed the hungry
give drink to the thirsty
harbor the stranger
clothe the naked
tend the sick
minister to prisoners
bury the dead

Or:

(seven spiritual works)

convert the sinner
instruct the ignorant
counsel the doubtful
comfort the sorrowing
bear wrongs patiently
forgive injuries
pray for the living and the dead

STATIONS OF THE CROSS

(typical arrangement)

1. Pilate's condemnation/ sentencing of Jesus
2. Christ receives his Cross
3. Christ falls to the ground first time
4. Christ meets His mother
5. Simon of Cyrene takes the cross
6. Veronica wipes Christ's face
7. Christ falls a second time
8. Christ tells the women of Jerusalem not to weep for him
9. Christ falls a third time
10. Christ is stripped of clothing
11. Christ is nailed to the cross
12. Christ dies on the cross
13. Christ's body is taken down from the cross and placed in arms of his mother
14. Christ's body is entombed

THREE WISE MEN

The Magi
Melchior, with gold
Gaspar/Caspar, with frankincense
Balthazar, with myrrh

TRINITY

God
Father
Son
Holy Spirit

TWELVE DISCIPLES

Peter, Saint Peter (brother of Andrew)
Andrew, Saint Andrew (brother of Peter)
James (son of Zebedee, brother of John)
John, Saint John (the Apostle; brother of James)
Philip
Bartholomew
Thomas
Matthew, Saint Matthew
James of Alphaeus
Simon the Cananaean (in Matthew and Mark) or Simon Zelotes (in Luke and the Acts)
Judas Iscariot (not an apostle)
In the Bible books Matthew and Mark, Thaddaeus is the 12th disciple, while in Luke and the Acts it is Judas of James.
Matthias succeeded to the place of the betrayer Judas Iscariot.

WEDDING RITUAL

Processional

best man and bridegroom
ushers
flower girl
bridesmaids
maid and matron of honor
bride with father
pages carrying bride's train

Recessional

ushers and bridesmaids (paired off)
flower girl
maid or matron of honor and best man
bride and groom

CONFUCIANISM

CONFUCIAN TEXTS

four books:

Lun Yu: The Analects, sayings of Confucius
Chung Yung: The Doctrine of the Mean
Ta Hsueh: The Great Learning
Meng Tzu, by Mencius

five classics:

Shu Ching, The Book of History
Shih Ching, The Book of Odes, Poems, and Songs
I Ching, The Book of Changes
Ch'un Ch'iu, The Book of history of Lu State
Li Ching, The Book of Rites

FIVE CARDINAL VIRTUES

Jen, benevolence
Yi, duty
Li, manners
Chih, wisdom
Hsin, faithfulness

GREEK AND ROMAN MYTHOLOGY

Twelve Olympian Gods

Zeus (overlord, god of sky; Roman Jupiter)
Hera (goddess of sky; Roman Juno)
Poseidon (god of sea and earthquakes: Roman Neptune)
Demeter (goddess of harvest; Roman Ceres)
Apollo (god of prophecy, music, medicine; no Roman equivalent)
Artemis (goddess of charity, childbirth, the young; Roman Diana)

GREEK AND ROMAN
MYTHOLOGY

Twelve Olympian
Gods (cont.)

Ares (god of war; Roman Mars)
Aphrodite (goddess of love, beauty;
  Roman Venus)
Hermes (god of trade, travelers;
  Roman Mercury)
Athene/Athena (goddess of

prudence, wise counsel; Roman
  Minerva)
Hephaestus (god of fire, metacraft;
  Roman Vulcan)
Hestia (goddess of fire; Roman Vesta)

Gods and Goddesses in Mythology

	Aztec	Babylonian	Celtic	Egyptian	Greek	Hindu	Mayan	Norse	Roman
Ruler	Tonacatecutli	An Anu Marduk	Dagda	Amon-Re	Zeus	Indra Vishnu Shiva	Hun-Ahpu	Odin	Jupiter (Jove)
Queen	Tonacacihuatl	Innini	Danu	Hathor Isis	Hera	Lakshmi Parvati (Kali)	Ixazaluoh	Frigg	Juno
Sun-Light	Tezcatlipoca	Babbar Shamash	Lug	Amon-Re Horus	Apollo	Surya Mitra Savitar	Hun-Ahpu Itzamna	Balder	Apollo
Moon	Meztli	Nanna Sin	Branwen	Thoth Hathor Isis	Artemis	Soma Yaruna	—	—	Diana
War	Huitzilopochtli	Enlil Marduk Adad	Morrigan Macha Taranis	Mont	Ares	Indra Skanda Rudra	Hurakan	Thor	Mars
Sea	Tlaloc	Enki Ea	Manannan	Osiris	Poseidon	Varuna Parjanya	Chac	Aegir Frey	Neptune
Fertility	Tzinteotl Coatlicue	Nanna Ishtar	Danu	Isis Osiris	Dionysus Demeter	Parvati	Itzamma	Frey	Ceres
Love	Tlazolteotl	Nanna Ishtar Tammuz	Branwen	Hathor	Aphrodite Eros	Kama Krishna	—	Freya Frigg	Venus Cupid
Hell	Michtlante-cutli	Ereshkigal	Bran Urien	Anubis Osiris	Hades (Dis)	Yama	Humahau	Hel	Pluto
Wisdom Knowledge	Quetzalcoatl	Nabu Ea	Lug Brigit Bran	Thoth Isis	Athena Apollo	Rudra Sarasvati	Itzamna Kukulcan	Odin Bragi Mimir	Minerva
Creativity	Quetzalcoatl	Ea	Goibniu Lug	Ptah	Athena	—	Ixazaluoh	Volund Frigg	Vulcan Minerva

Source: Encyclopedia Americana, 1992.

HINDUISM

AIMS OF LIFE

(categorization of the goals of human existence)

Dharma, right conduct
Artha, material gain
Kama, pleasure such as sexual love
Moksa, spiritual liberation

CALENDAR

Chaitra or Caitra (March/April)
Vaisakha
Jyestha or Jyaistha
Ashadha or Asadha
(Dvitiya Asadha, certain leap years)
Sravana
(Dvitiya Sravana, certain leap years)
Bhadrapada
Asvina
Karttika
Margasirsha or Margasirsa or
   Margasivsa
Pausa or Pansa
Magha
Phalguna (February/March)

FESTIVALS

April—Hindu/Sikh New Year
July—Monsoon Begins
August—Krishna's Birthday
September—remembering ancestors
   of Shradh
October—Durga Puja: celebration of
   goddesses
      Dashera: Rama's victory over
   Ravana
November—Divali: Festival of lights
January—Kumbha Mela: pilgrim fairs
February—Mahashivaratri: festival
   for Shiva
March—Holi: spring Harvest
   celebration

CASTE SYSTEM

twice-born castes (jatis):
Brahmins: priests and scholars
Kshatriyas: warriors and rulers
Vaisyas: skilled traders, merchants,
   farmers, minor officials

not twice-born castes:
Sudras: unskilled workers, peasants,
   laborers
Pariah/Harijans: outcasts,
   Untouchables, Children of God
(four varna are: Brahmins, Kshatriyas,
   Vaisyas, Sudras)

FOUR STAGES OF LIFE

(for twice-born)

1. student (Brahmacarin)
2. householder (Grhastha)
3. forest-dweller (Vanaprastha)
4. renouncer (Sannyasin)

FOUR WAYS TO GOD

Jnana Yoga, the way to God through
   knowledge
Bhakti Yoga, the way to God through
   love
Karma Yoga, the way to God through
   work
Raja Yoga, the way to God through
   psychological exercise

HINDU GODS

Gods of the Vedas

Indra—Thunder god, god of battle
Varuna—Guardian of order; divine
   overseer
Agni—god of fire
Surya—deity associated with the sun

Gods of Hinduism

Brahma—the creator
Vishnu—the preserver, has ten
  incarnations:
Matsya—the fish
Kurma—tortoise
Varaha—the boar
Barasunga—the man-lion
Vamana—the dwarf
Parasurama—Rama bearing the axe
Ramachandra—also Rama, who
  carries a bow and quiver of arrows
Krishna—god featured in the
  Bhagavadgita. Worshipped as a
  baby or as a flute-playing cowherd
Buddha—the exalted teacher from
  the 6th–5th century BCE
Kalki—"the one to come"
Shiva—god of destruction
Ganesh—elephant-headed god,
  worshipped as god of good luck
Hanuman—monkey warrior god,
  associated with Rama

Goddesses

Durga—omnipotent warrior, also
  known as Amba
Parvati—wife of Shiva
Kali—goddess associated with
  destruction
Lashmi—goddess of beauty, wealth
  and fortune, wife of Vishnu
Saraswati—goddess of learning, arts,
  and Music

HINDU CONCEPTIONS OF THE UNIVERSE

earth
middle space (atmosphere)
ether (sky)

Or:

men
semi-divine creatures
gods

Or:

territory of the demons (hell)
earth
heaven

HINDU SACRED TEXTS

Shruti: Revealed Scriptures

Vedas
Rig-Veda: songs for praising gods
  Samhitas, prayers and hymns,
    priestly commentaries
  Brahamanas, ritual theology,
    explanation, and priestly writings
  Aranyakas, forest meditations
  Upanishads, important teachings
    and works of philosophy
Sama-Veda: hymns and instructions
  for chanting
  Samhitas, prayers and hymns,
    priestly commentaries
  Brahamanas, ritual theology,
    explanation, and priestly writings
  Aranyakas, forest meditations
  Upanishads, important teachings
    and works of philosophy
Yajur-Veda: hymns and instructions
  for sacrifices
  Samhitas, prayers and hymns,
    priestly commentaries
  Brahamanas, ritual theology,
    explanation, and priestly writings
  Aranyakas, forest meditations
  Upanishads, important teachings
    and works of philosophy
Atharva-Veda: sayings, spells, and
  incantations
  Samhitas, prayers and hymns,
    priestly commentaries
  Brahamanas, ritual theology,
    explanation, and priestly writings
  Aranyakas, forest meditations
  Upanishads, important teachings
    and works of philosophy

Other writings: Puranas: legend and instruction,

Ramayana: epic adventures of Ramachandra and Sit
Mahabharata, including the Bhagavad-Gita: epic conflict between the Padavas and the Kavavas; in Bhagavad-Gita, the god Krishna and Pandava warrior Arjuna have a philosophical dialogue
The Manu Smriti: "Code of Manu," religions and social law

ISLAM

Classification of Actions
obligatory (fard)
meritorious or recommended (mandub)
indifferent, bringing neither reward nor punishment (mubah)
reprehensible, not punishable but disapproved (makruh)
forbidden (haram)

ISLAMIC CALENDAR (LUNAR BASED; MOVABLE IN REFERENCE TO GREGORIAN CALENDAR)

Muharram)
Safar or Saphar
Rabi I or Rabia I
Rabi II or Rabia II
Jumad I or Jomada I or Jumada I
Jumad II or Jomada II or Jumada II
Rajab
Sha'ban or Shaaban or Shaban
Ramadan (month of fasting)
Shawwal
Dhul-Quada or Dulkaada or Dhu al-Qadah
Dhul-Hijjah or Dulheggia or Dhu al-Hiijah

FIVE PILLARS OF ISLAM

1. Profession of faith to Allah and Muhammad as his prophet
2. Prayer—5 times a day, at designated times, facing Mecca
3. Zakat—almsgiving; giving a proportion of one's wealth to the needy
4. Fasting—between dawn and dusk during Ramadan
5. The Hajj—pilgrimage to Mecca once in one's lifetime
(Jihad sometimes regarded as another pillar of faith, described as duty of waging "holy wars" to spread Islam)

PRAYER TIMES

1. dawn prayer, from first light until sunrise
2. noon prayer, from sun's zenith

HINDUISM
ISLAM

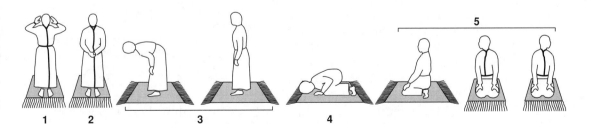

Muslim Prayer Sequence
1. Niya; **2.** Fatihah; **3.** Ruku; **4.** Sujud; **5.** Jalsah

until an object's shadow equals its height plus the length of whatever shadow was cast at the zenith
3. afternoon prayer, between end of preceding and sunset
4. sunset prayer, immediately after sunset till darkness
5. nighttime prayer, from end of twilight just before dawn

ISLAMIC SACRED TEXTS

The Koran/Qur'an: revealed to Muhammad by Allah through angel Gabriel
   Zabur, Psalms of David (Dawud)
   Tawrat, Torah of Moses (Musa)
   Injil, Gospel of Jesus (Isa)
   Suhufi Ibrahim, Scrolls of Abraham
The Hadith: what Muhammad said and did
The Sunnah: rules and regulations of Muslim life

ISLAMIC SECTS

Sunnite: traditional (largest group)
Shi'ite: emphasize sacrifice and martyrdom (largest minority)
Baha'ism: no sacraments, clergy, or formal organization
Wahhabis: puritanical, stressing the simplicity of early Islam
Ismailite: allegiance to Ismail, the successor of the sixth Imam
Sufism: Muslim mystics
Black Muslims: American movement, also called Nation of Islam
(other sects, schools, branches: Alawite, Bohra, Deoband, Donme, Druze, Ithna Ashariyah, Kharijite, Mahdist, Maturidiyah, Mutazilah, Rafidah, Yazidi)

JUDAISM

BRANCHES

Biblical Judaism

Essenes: awaited the "End of Days"
Karaites: rejected rabbinic Oral Law
Pharisees: separated from ritual impurity and defilement
Rechabites: emphasized faithfulness and self-discipline
Sadducees: rejected resurrection and immortality of soul
Samaritans: emphasized unique God, Moses as only prophet, sanctity of Torah (Pentateuch)

Modern Judaism

Conservative Judaism: adapts traditional beliefs and practices to contemporary knowledge and culture
Hasidism: strict observance of laws; follows charismatic leader, tzaddik or rebbe
Kabbalism: Jewish mysticism
Orthodox Judaism: keeps traditional beliefs and ways of life (halakhah), as in Torah and Talmud
Reconstructionist Judaism: articulates left-wing rationalism
Reform Judaism: emphasizes moral and ethical teachings rather than ritual and tradition
Zionism: national movement for Jewish homeland in Israel

JEWISH CALENDAR
(beginning around mid-September on the Gregorian calendar)

Tishri (September/October)
Cheshvan or Heshvan
Kislev
Teveth or Tebet

Shevat or Shebat
Adar
(Veadar, 13th month in 3rd, 6th, 8th,
    11th, 14th, 17th year of a 19-year
    cycle)
Nisan
Iyar
Sivan
Tammuz
Av or Ab
Elul (August/September)

JEWISH HOLY DAYS, FESTIVALS, AND FASTS

Rosh Hashanah (New Year)
Fast of Gedalya
Yom Kippur (Day of Atonement)
Sukkot (Feast of Tabernacles)
Shmini Atzeret (Eighth Day of Sukkot)
Simhat Torah (Ninth Day of Sukkot)
Chanukah (Feast of Lights)
Fast of the 10th of Tevet
Tu Bishevat (New Year of Trees; Jewish
    Arbor Day)
Ta'anit Esther (Fast of Esther)
Purim
Passover
Lag Omer
Shavuot (Pentecost)
Fast of the 17th Day of Tammuz
Fast of the 9th Day of Av

QUESTIONS ASKED AT SEDER

*(the Four Questions, asked by youngest
child at Passover meal)*

1. Why is this night different from all
   other nights?
2. On all other nights, we eat all kinds
   of herbs, why on this night do we
   eat only bitter herbs?
3. On all other nights, we do not dip
   our food into condiments at all,
   why on this night do we dip it
   twice?

4. On all other nights, we eat sitting
   upright, why on this night do we
   recline?

JEWISH SACRED TEXTS

Hebrew Bible or Tanakh
    Torah or Pentateuch (The Law):
        Genesis, Exodus, Leviticus,
        Numbers, Deuteronomy
    Nevi'im (The Prophets): Joshua,
        Judges, 1 Samuel, 2 Samuel, 1
        Kings, 2 Kings, and the later
        prophets Isaiah, Jeremiah,
        Ezekiel, and the Book of the
        Twelve (minor prophets)
        including Hosea, Joel, Amos,
        Obadiah, Jonah, Micah,
        Nahum, Habakkuk, Zephaniah,
        Haggai, Zechariah, and
        Malachi
    Ketubim (The Writings): Psalms,
        Proverbs, Job, Song of Songs,
        Ruth, Lamentations,
        Ecclesiastes, Esther, Daniel,
        Ezra, Nehemiah, 1 Chronicles,
        2 Chronicles
Talmud
    Mishnah: the Oral Law, as passed
        down from Moses to the
        prophets and rabbis;
        interpretations and
        commentaries by rabbis and
        teachers (tanaim) from 1st c. BC –
        2d c. CE (divided into 6 orders)
    Six Orders (62 tractates)
    Zeraim ("seeds"; agriculture)
    Moed ("seasons"; festivals)
    Nashim ("women"; marital laws)
    Nezikim ("damages"; civil and
        criminal laws)
    Kodashim ("holy things"; temple
        services)
    Tohorot ("ritual purity")
    Gemara: commentaries and an
        elaboration of the Mishnah text

by rabbis and teachers
(amoraim) from 3d-5th cent. CE

Midrash: sermons and popular
interpretation of the Bible

Tosephta: supplement to the
Mishnah

Zohar: fundamental kabbalistic
work

SYNAGOGUE ORGANIZATION

Rabbi
Cantor
Gabbai (rituals official)
Shammash (beadle or sexton)
President, Vice President(s)
Executive Board
Men's Club
Sisterhood (or Ladies' Auxiliary)
Congregants

THIRTEEN PRINCIPLES OF JEWISH FAITH

(by philosopher Moses Maimonides)

1. that God exists
2. that God is One alone
3. that God has no corporeal presence
4. that God is outside the scope of time
5. that God alone is to be worshipped
6. that God informs his prophets
7. that Moses was the greatest of the prophets
8. that the Torah is the work of God
9. that the Torah cannot change
10. that God apprehends the thoughts and acts of all people
11. that those who do good will receive their reward, and those who do evil will receive retribution
12. that the Messiah will come
13. that there will be a bodily

resurrection of the dead, although
only the soul may be eternal

THIRTEEN ARTICLES OF FAITH

("Ehad Mi Yodea" song)

1. Thirteen are the attributes of God
2. Twelve are the tribes of Israel
3. Eleven were the stars in Joseph's dream
4. Ten commandments were given on Sinai
5. Nine is the number of the holidays
6. Eight are the days to the service of the covenant
7. Seven days are there in a week
8. Six sections the Mishnah has
9. Five books there are in the Torah
10. Four is the number of the matriarchs
11. Three, the number of the patriarchs
12. Two are the tables of the commandments
13. One is our God, in heaven and on earth

TREE OF LIFE—THE CABALA

(Jewish mystic knowledge; mastering its 10 spheres, one can achieve greatness)

(roots to top)

Malkhuth: physical body and health
Yesod: personality
Hod: logic and reason
Netsah: needs, passions, and senses
Tifereth/Rahamin: energy or life force
Geburah/Pachad/Din: our destructive nature
Hesed/Gedulah: love and mercy
Binah: soul
Hokhmah: creativity
Kether: ultimate unity of all aspects of human nature

The Ten Sefirot from a Cabalistic work by Moses Cordovero (1522–1570)

Twelve Tribes of Israel

The 12 tribes were descended from the 12 sons of Jacob, who was renamed Israel:

1. Reuben
2. Simeon
3. Judah (Levi, not counted as it has holy duties)
4. Issachar
5. Zebulun
6. Dan
7. Napthali
8. Gad
9. Asher
10. Benjamin

Joseph's sons:

11. Manasseh
12. Ephraim

Wedding Ritual

Processional

rabbi (walks down aisle if wedding is not held in temple or synagogue)
ushers
best man
bridegroom in between parents
bridesmaids
maid or matron of honor
flower girl
bride in between parents
pages carrying bride's train

Recessional

rabbi
ushers and bridesmaids
flower girl
maid or matron of honor and best man
groom's parents
bride's parents
bride and groom

SATAN

Satanic Hierarchy

Satan or the Devil: Lucifer

First Group:
Beelzebub (sins of pride)
Leviathan (sins against faith)
Asmodeus (sins of luxuriousness and wantonness)
Balberith (homicides, quarrels, and blasphemy)
Astaroth (idleness, sloth)
Verrine (impatience)
Gressil (impurity, uncleanness)
Sonneillon (hatred)

Second Group:
Carreau (hard-heartedness)
Carnivean (obscenity)
Ocillet (temptation to break vow of poverty)
Rosier (abandoning god for the flesh)
Verrier (disobedience)

Third Group:
Belias (arrogance)
Olivier (mercilessness)
Iuvart (inactive)

DEMONS WHO SERVE DEVILS

Fire Devils (live in upper air)
Aerial Devils (inhabit atmosphere)
Terrestrial Devils (inhabit woods, fields, forests)
Aqueous Devils (inhabit bodies of water and waterways)
Subterranean Devils (inhabit caves and mountains)
Heliophobic Devils (appear only at night)

SIKHISM

Calendar
Magh (January/February)
Phalgan
Chait
Vaisakh
Jaith
Har
Sawan
Bhadro
Asun
Katik
Magar
Poh (January)

FIVE "Ks" OF SIKHISM

1. Kesa (hair must be uncut and in turban)
2. Kangha (comb for keeping hair clean)
3. Kacch (shorts worn under clothes)
4. Kirpan (sabre)
5. Kara (bracelet of steel worn on right arm)

HIERARCHY IN SIKHISM

gurus
priests (any baptized Sikh can act as one)

also:

non-Jats: erstwhile Brahmans, Ksatriyas, and Vaisyas
Jats: agricultural tribes
Mazahabis: untouchables

SIKH RELIGIOUS STRUCTURE

Threefold service:
Tan/physical: useful work
Man/mental: study of Adi Granth, share religion
Dhan/material: 10% of earnings given to charity

Five "Khands": realms or levels of spiritual reality:
Dharam Khand: level of seeking moral duty
Gian Khand: level of wisdom and knowledge
Saram Khand: level of effort
Karam Khand: level of fulfillment
Sach Khand: level of truth, permanent union with God

SACRED TEXTS

Adi Granth, most sacred book
Dasam Granth, second holy book
The Vars, heroic ballads
The Rahatnamas, codes of conduct and traditions

TAOISM

TAO TRINITY

Tao entered into creation in three stages:
1. The Celestial Venerable of the Mysterious Origin
2. The August Ruler of the Tao
3. The August Old Ruler, Lao-tzu was held to be an incarnation of this god.

VOODOO

Classifications
Batuque (Brazil)
Condomble (Brazil)
Macumba (Brazil)
Santeria (Cuba)
Shango (Trinidad)
Vodu (Haiti)

PRIESTLY HIERARCHY

loa (saints)
hungan (priest)
mambo (priestess)

WITCHCRAFT & WIZARDRY (WICCA)

GRADES OF WITCHES

(highest to lowest)

High Priestess/High Priest: leader of a
   coven, group of 13 witches
Witch Queen/Magus: high-ranking
   member of coven
Priestess/Priest: has mastered basics
   and is initiated into a coven
Witch: one permitted to study
   witchcraft

ORDERS AND GRADES OF WIZARDS

(least to most powerful)

Outer Order:
Neophyte
Zelator
Theoricus
Practicus
Philosophus

Second Order:
Adeptus Minor
Adeptus Major
Adeptus Exemptus

Third Order:
Magister
Magus
Ipsissimus

STAGES OF A SEANCE

1. Clearing: emptying of the mind
2. Slowing: relaxing the body
3. Withdrawing: soul of medium
   retreats
4. Phasing: spirit communicates
   through the medium's body
5. Dephasing: spirit departs
6. Restoring: medium is back to
   normal

WORLD RELIGIONS

RELIGIONS WITH LARGEST FOLLOWINGS

Baha'ism
Buddhism
   Theravada
   Mahayana
   Tibetan
Christianity
   Anglican
      Church of England, etc.
   Baptist
      Southern Baptist Convention
      National Baptist Convention, etc.
   Church of Christ
   Congregationalist
   Lutheran
      United Churches
      United Lutheran Protestant
      Evangelical Lutheran
      Lutheran Church-Missouri
         Synod, etc.
   Methodist
      United Methodist, etc.
   Orthodox
      Russian Orthodox

TAOISM
WITCHCRAFT &
   WIZARDRY
WORLD RELIGIONS

Ethiopian Orthodox
Romanian Orthodox
Greek Orthodox, etc.
Pentecostal
Presbyterian
Roman Catholic
Unitarian
United Churches
   United Church of Christ, etc.
Christian Scientists
Confucianism
Hinduism
   Vishnu
   Shiva
   Shakti
Islam
   Sunni
   Shi'ah
   Sufi
   Ismaili
Jainism
   Digambara
   Swetabara
Jehovah's Witnesses
Judaism
Mormons
Scientology
Seventh-Day Adventists
Shintoism
Sikhism

Society of Friends/Quakers
Spiritualism
Taoism
Unification Church
Zoroastrianism

WORLD RELIGIONS BY ADHERENTS

(approximate)

Christains (all denominations)
   2,000,000,000
Muslims 1,300,000,000
Hindus 900,000,000
Buddhists 350,000,000
Chinese folk religionists 225,000,000
Sikhs 23,000,000
Yorubas 20,000,000
Juches 19,000,000
Spiritists 14,000,000
Jews 14,000,000
Baha'is 6,000,000
Jains 4,000,000
Shintoists 4,000,000
Caodaists 3,000,000
Tenrikoists 2,400,000

One tries to find in events an old-fashioned divine governance—an order of things that rewards, punishes, educates, and betters ...

—Friedrich Nietzche, *The Will to Power*

CHAPTER SEVEN

HISTORY

AGES & ERAS

BIBLICAL AGES

First Age: creation to Deluge,
4004–2349 BC

Second Age: to the coming of
Abraham into Canaan, 2348–
1922 BC

Third Age: to the Exodus from Egypt,
1921–1491 BC

Fourth Age: to the founding of
Solomon's Temple, 1490–1014 BC

Fifth Age: to the capture of Jerusalem,
1014–588 BC

Sixth Age: to the birth of Christ, 588–
4 BC

Seventh Age: to the present time,
4 BC-

HISTORIC AGES AND ERAS

(approximately)

Stone Age: 570 million years ago–
3000 BC
Palaeolithic stage/Early Stone Age
Mesolithic stage/Middle Stone Age
Neolithic stage/New Stone Age
Early civilizations: 5000 BC
Bronze Age: 3000–1200 BC
(Dark Ages in Greece: 1100–700 BC)
Iron Age: 1100–1000 CE
Roman Empire: 500 BC–476 CE
Early Middle Ages: 476–1000 CE
Middle Ages: (Medieval Period)
476–1450
Renaissance: 1450–1750
Exploration: 1490–1911
Reformation: 1500–1600
Colonization and invention:
1600–1700
Revolution and independence:
1700–1815
Industrial Revolution:1750–1900
Warring World: 1900–46
Cold War: 1947–1991

HESIOD'S AGES

("Works and Days" c. 800–850 BC)

Age of Gold and the Immortals: ease
and peace, before Zeus, when
Cronus ruled; age of innocence and
joy

Age of Silver: humans become less
noble, Zeus ruled; age of
unpleasantness

Age of Bronze/Brazen Age: age of
warring with bronze

Age of Epic Heroes/Heroic Age:
Trojan War and surrounding period

Age of Iron and Dread Sorrow: age of
corruption, warfare, and
unhappiness; no rest from labor

AUSTRALIA

PRIME MINISTERS

1901–1903	Edmund Barton
1903–1904	Alfred Deakin
1904	John Christian Watson
1904–1905	George Houstoun Reid
1905–1908	Alfred Deakin
1908–1909	Andrew Fisher
1909–1910	Alfred Deakin
1910–1913	Andrew Fisher
1913–1914	Joseph Cook
1914–1915	Andrew Fisher
1915–1923	William Morris Hughes
1917–1923	William Morris Hughes
1923–1929	Stanley Melbourne Bruce, Viscount Bruce of Melbourne
1929–1932	James Henry Scullin
1932–1939	Joseph Aloysius Lyons
1939	Earle Christian Grafton Page
1939–1941	Robert Gordon Menzies
1941	Arthur William Fadden
1941–1945	John Joseph Curtin
1945	Francis Michael Forde

1945–1949	Joseph Benedict Chifley
1949–1966	Robert Gordon Menzies
1966–1967	Harold Edward Holt
1967–1968	John McEwen
1968–1971	John Grey Gorton
1971–1972	William McMahon
1972–1975	Gough Whitlam
1975–1983	John Malcolm Fraser
1983–1991	Robert James Lee Hawke
1991–1996	Paul Keating
1996–	John Howard

AUSTRIA

MARGRAVE OF AUSTRIA

House of Babenburg

976–994	Leopold I
994–1018	Heinrich I
1018–1055	Adalbert
1055–1075	Ernest
1075–1096	Leopold II
1096–1136	Leopold III
1136–1141	Leopold IV
1141–1156	Heinrich II Jasomirgott

DUKE OF AUSTRIA

House of Babenburg

1156–1177	Henry II Jasomirgott
1177–1194	Leopold V
1194–1198	Friedrich I
1198–1230	Leopold VI
1230–1246	Friedrich II
1246–1251	No duke
1251–1276	Ottokar (II of Bohemia)

House of Habsburg

1276–1291	Rudolf I
1282–1298	Albrecht (Albert) I Joint ruler to 1290
1282–1290	Rudolf II Joint ruler
1298–1358	Albrecht II Joint ruler to 1339
1298–1339	Otto Joint ruler
1298–1326	Leopold I Joint ruler
1298–1330	Friedrich II Joint ruler
1298–1307	Rudolf III Joint ruler
1365–1395	Albrecht III Joint ruler to 1379
1365–1379	Leopold III Joint ruler
1358–1365	Rudolf IV
1395–1404	Albrecht IV
1404–1439	Albrecht V
1439–1457	Ladislas 'Posthumus'
1457–1493	Friedrich V (Frederick III, Holy Roman Emperor)
1493–1804	As Holy Roman Emperor

AUSTRIAN EMPIRE

Monarchs—House of Habsburg

1804–1835	Franz I (Francis II, Holy Roman Emperor)
1835–1848	Ferdinand I
1848–1867	Franz Josef (Francis Joseph) I

AUSTRO-HUNGARIAN EMPIRE

Emperors—House of Habsburg

1867–1916	Franz Josef (Francis Joseph) I
1916–1918	Karl (Charles)

REPUBLIC OF AUSTRIA

Presidents

1918–1920	Karl Satz
1920–1928	Michael Hainisch
1928–1938	Wilhelm Miklas
1938–1945	German rule
1945–1950	Karl Renner
1950–1957	Theodor Korner
1957–1965	Adolf Scharf
1965–1974	Franz Jonas
1974–1986	Rudolf Kirchslager
1986–1992	Kurt Waldheim
1992–	Thomas Klestil

BRAZIL

EMPERORS

House of Braganca

1822–1831 Pedro I (IV of Portugal)
1831–1889 Pedro II

PRESIDENTS

1889–1891 Manoel Deodoro da Fonseca
1891–1894 Floriano Peixoto
1894–1898 Prudente Jose de Morais Barros
1898–1902 Manuel Ferraz de Campos Sales
1902–1906 Francisco de Paula Rodrigues Alves
1906–1909 Alfonso Pena
1909–1910 Nilo Pecanha
1910–1914 Hermes Rodrigues da Fonseca
1914–1918 Venceslau Bras Pereira Gomes
1918–1919 Francisco de Paula Rodrigues Alves
1919–1922 Epitacio Pessoa
1922–1926 Artur da Silva Bernardes
1926–1930 Washington Luis Pereira de Sousa
1930–1945 Getulio Dornelles Vargas
1945–1951 Eurico Gaspar Dutra
1951–1954 Getulio Dornelles Vargas
1954–1955 Joao Cafe Filho
1955 Carlos Coimbra da Luz
1955–1956 Nereu de Oliveira Ramos
1956–1961 Juscelino Kubitschek de Oliveira
1961 Janio da Silva Quadros
1961–1963 Joao Belchior Marques Goulart
1963 Pascoal Ranieri Mazilli
1963–1964 Joao Belchior Marques Goulart
1964 Pascoal Ranieri Mazilli
1964–1967 Humberto de Alencar Castelo Branco
1967–1969 Artur da Costa e Silva
1969–1974 Emilio Garrastazu Medici
1974–1979 Ernesto Geisel
1979–1985 Joao Baptista de Oliveira Figueiredo
1985–1990 Jose Sarney Costa
1990–1992 Fernando Collor de Mello
1992–1995 Itamar Franco
1995– Fernando Henrique Cardoso

BRAZIL
BYZANTIUM

BYZANTIUM

EMPERORS

395–408 Arcadius
408–450 Theodosius II
450–457 Marcianus
457–474 Leo I
474 Leo II
474–491 Zeno
475–476 Basiliscus Joint Emperor
491–518 Anastasius I
518–527 Justin I
527–565 Justinian I
565–578 Justin II
578–582 Tiberius II
582–602 Maurice
602–610 Phocas
610–641 Heraclius
641 Constantine III
641 Heracleonas Joint Emperor
641–648 (Flavius Heraclius) Constans II
668–685 Constantine IV Pogonatus
685–695 Justinian II
695–698 Leontius
698–705 Tiberius III Apsimar
705–711 Justinian II (restored)
711–713 Philippicus
713–715 Anastasius II
715–717 Theodosius III
717–741 Leo III Isauricus

741–775	Constantine V Copronymus
775–780	Leo IV
780–789	Constantine VI
797–802	Irene
802–811	Nicephorus I
811	Stauracius
811–813	Michael I
813–820	Leo V 'the Armenian'
820–829	Michael II
829–842	Theophilus
842–867	Michael III
867–886	Basil I 'the Macedonian'
886–912	Leo VI
912–959	Constantine VII Porphyrogenitus Joint Emperor to 913 and 920–944
912–913	Alexander Joint Emperor
920–944	Romanus I Lecapenus Regent and Joint Emperor
959–963	Romanus II
963–969	Nicephorus II Phocas
969–976	John I Tzimisces
976–1028	Constantine VIII
976–1025	Basil II Bulgaroctonus Joint Emperor
1028–1050	Zoe Joint Empress
1028–1034	Romanus III Argyrus Joint Emperor
1034–1041	Michael IV 'the Paphlagonian' Joint Emperor
1041–1042	Michael V Calaphates Joint Emperor
1042–1055	Constantine IX Monomachus Joint Emperor
1042–1056	Theodora Joint Empress until 1055
1056–1057	Michael VI Stratioticus
1057–1059	Isaac I Comnenus
1059–1067	Constantine X Ducas
1068–1071	Romanus IV Diogenes
1071–1078	Michael VII Ducas
1078–1081	Nicephorus III Botaneiates

COMNENIAN EMPERORS

1081–1118	Alexius I Comnenus
1118–1143	John II Comnenus
1143–1180	Manuel I
1180–1183	Alexius II
1183–1185	Andronicus I Comnenus
1185–1195	Isaac II Angelus
1195–1203	Alexius III
1203–1204	Isaac II Angelus (restored)
1203–1204	Alexius IV Joint Emperor
1204	Alexius V Ducas

LATIN EMPERORS

1204–1205	Baldwin I
1205–1216	Henry
1216–1217	Peter of Courtenay
1217–1219	Yolande
1219–1228	Robert
1228–1261	Baldwin II

EMPERORS AT NICEA

1204–1222	Theodore I Lascaris
1222–1254	John III Varatzes
1254–1258	Theodore II
1258–1261	John IV Joint Emperor from 1259
1259–1261	Michael VIII Palaeologus Regent and Joint Emperor

PALAEOLOGI EMPERORS AT BYZANTIUM

1261–1282	Michael VIII Palaeologus
1282–1328	Andronicus II Palaeologus Joint Emperor 1295–1320
1295–1320	Michael IX Joint Emperor
1328–1341	Andronicus III Palaeologus
1341–1391	John V Joint Emperor 1347–1354 and from 1376

1347–1354	John VI Cantacuzene Regent and Joint Emperor
1376–1379	Andronicus IV Joint Emperor
1390	John VII Joint Emperor
1391–1425	Manuel II Joint Emperor
1399–1402	John VII Joint Emperor
1425–1448	John VIII
1448–1453	Constantine XI

CELTIC SOCIAL STRUCTURE

TRIBE

King

Chieftain: head of a village; often elected from ranks of nobles or warriors

Archdruid: one in charge of each Druid class

Druids: priests, religious teachers, judges, civil administrators

three classes, assisted by female prophets or sorcerers:

prophets

bards

priests

Nobles: major landowners and merchants

Warriors: highly regarded cavalrymen and charioteers

Commoners

Metal-working smiths: very important to farming and war

Bards: interpreted and applied local historical records

Free peasants: small landowners

Semi-free peasants: laborers bound to a noble but having possessions

Retainers: servants who lived with nobles

Slaves: prisoners of war who were sold or sacrificed

CHINA

ARTISTIC DYNASTIES

Time between fall of T'ang Dynasty (CE 618–907, a period of great literary and poetic works and introduction of Buddhism) and founding of Sung Dynasty (CE 960–1279, one of China's golden ages of ceramics, painting, Confucianism)

1. Later Liang, 907 CE
2. Later T'ang, 923
3. Later Chin, 936
4. Later Han, 947
5. Later Chou, 951 (first complete printing of Confucian classics, 953)

DYNASTIES

(also pertains to art as pottery and porcelain are dated by dynasty/emperor)

T'ang Kingdom (legendary), 3rd millennium BC

Yu Kingdom (Xia) (legendary), 3rd millennium BC

Hsia Dynasty, c. 1994–1523 BC

Shang (Yin) Dynasty, c. 1523–1028 BC

Chou Dynasty (Zhou), c.1027–256 BC

Ch'in Dynasty (Qin), 221–206 BC

Han Dynasty, 206 BC-220 CE

Three Kingdoms (Shu, Wei, Wu), 220–265

Chin (Tsin) Dynasty, 265–420

Southern Dynasties (Liu Sung, Ch'i, Liang, Ch'en), 420–589

Northern Dynasties (Later Wei, Eastern Wei, Western Wei, Northern Ch'i, Northern Chou), 386–581

Sui Dynasty, 581–618

T'ang Dynasty, 618–907

Five Dynasties (Later Liang, Later T'ang, Later Chin, Later Han, Later Chou), 907–960

Ten Kingdoms (Wu, Southern T'ang, Southern P'ing, Ch'u, Earlier Shu, Later Shu, Wu-yueh, Min, Southern Han, Northern Han), 902–979
Sung Dynasty (Song), 960–1279
Yuan Dynasty (Mongol), 1271–1368
Ming Dynasty, 1368–1644
Ch'ing Dynasty (Manchu), 1644–1912
Republic of China, 1912–1949
People's Republic of China, 1949-

CHINESE FEUDAL SYSTEM

(during time of Chou dynasty)

ruler of a state (5 grades determined by strength of state)
feudal lords (served in the ruler's court as ministers; 2–3 grades determined by lord-vassal relationship)
shih/gentlemen/knights (served at the households of the feudal lords)
commoners/peasants
slaves

CHINESE SAGES

(order of in terms of respect)

1. science
2. medicine
3. astrology
4. politics
5. physical fitness
6. military skill
7. sports
8. music
9. military strategy

CIVILIZATIONS & CULTURES

EARLIEST CIVILIZATIONS OF MAN

1. Egyptian, before 4000 BC
2. Sumeric or Sumerian, before 3500 BC
3. Indic, before 3000 BC
4. Chinese, before 2000 BC
5. Minoan, before 2000 BC
6. Hittite, 2000 BC
7. Mayan, after 2000 BC
8. Babylonian, c. 1500 BC
9. Hellenic, c. 1300 BC
10. Syriac, c. 1200 BC
11. Eskimo, c. 1100 BC
12. Spartan, c. 900 BC
13. Polynesian, c. 500 BC
14. Andean, c. 100 BC
15. Khmer, c. 100 CE
16. Far Eastern (main), 589 CE
17. Far Eastern (Japan and Korea), 645 CE
18. Western, c. 675 CE
19. Orthodox Christian (main), c. 680 CE
20. Hindu, c. 810 CE
21. Orthodox Christian (Russia), 950 CE
22. Arabic, c. 975 CE
23. Mexican, c. 1075 CE
24. Ottoman, c. 1310 CE

COLOMBIA

GRAN COLOMBIA—PRESIDENTS

1819–1830	Simon Bolivar
1830	Joaquin Mosquero
1830–1831	Rafael Urdaneta
1831	Domingo Caycedo
1831–1832	Jose Maria Obando

NEW GRANADA

1832	Jose Ignacio de Marquez
1832–1837	Francisco de Paula Santander
1837–1841	Jose Ignacio de Marquez
1841–1845	Pedro Alantara Herran
1845–1849	Tomás de Mosquera
1849–1853	Jose Hilario Lopez
1853–1854	Jose Maria Obando

1854	Jose Maria Melo
1854	Tomas Herrera
1854–1855	Jose de Obaldia
1855–1857	Manuel Maria Mallarino
1857–1861	Mariano Ospina Rodriguez
1861–1863	Tomás de Mosquera

UNITED STATES OF COLOMBIA

1863–1864	Tomás de Mosquera
1864–1866	Manuel Murillo Toro
1866–1867	Tomás de Mosquera
1867–1870	Santos Gutierrez
1870–1872	Eustorgio Salgar
1872–1874	Manuel Murillo Toro
1874–1876	Santiago Perez
1876–1878	Aquileo Parra
1878–1880	Julian Trujillo

REPUBLIC OF COLOMBIA

1880–1882	Rafael Nuñez
1882	Francisco Javier Zaldua
1882	Climaco Calderon
1882–1884	Jose Eusebio Otalora
1884–1886	Rafael Nuñez
1886–1887	Jose Maria Campo Serrano
1887–1894	Rafael Nuñez
1894–1896	Miguel Antonio Caro
1896	Guillermo Quintero Calderon
1896–1898	Miguel Antonio Caro
1898–1900	Manuel Antonio Sanclemente
1900–1904	Jose Manuel Marroquin
1904–1909	Rafael Reyes
1909–1910	Ramon Gonzalez Valencia
1910–1914	Carlos Restrepo
1914–1918	Jose Vicente Concha
1918–1921	Marco Fidel Suarez
1921–1922	Jorge Holguin
1922–1926	Pedro Nel Ospina
1926–1930	Miguel Abadia Mendez
1930–1934	Enrique Olaya Herrera

1934–1938	Alfonso Lopez
1938–1942	Eduardo Santos
1942–1945	Alfonso Lopez
1945–1946	Alberto Lleras Camargo
1946–1950	Mariano Ospina Perez
1950–1953	Laureano Gomez
1953–1957	Gustavo Rojas Pinilla
1957	*Military junta*
1958–1962	Alberto Lleras Camargo
1962–1966	Guillermo Leon Valencia
1966–1970	Carlos Lleras Restrepo
1970–1974	Misael Pastrana Borrero
1974–1978	Alfonso Lopez Michelsen
1978–1982	Julio Cesar Turbay Ayala
1982–1986	Belisario Betancur
1986–1990	Virgilio Barco Vargas
1990–1994	Cesar Gaviria Trujillo
1994–1998	Ernesto Samper Pizano
1998–	Andrés Pastrana Arango

CUBA

PRESIDENTS

1902–1906	Tomas Estrada Palma
1906–1909	U.S. rule
1909–1913	Jose Miguel Gomez
1913–1921	Mario Garcia Menocal
1921–1925	Alfredo Zayas y Alfonso
1925–1933	Gerardo Machado y Morales
1933	Carlos Manuel de Cespedes
1933–1934	Ramon Grau San Martin
1934–1935	Carlos Mendieta
1935–1936	Jose A Barnet y Vinagres
1936	Miguel Mariano Gomez y Arias
1936–1940	Federico Laredo Bru
1940–1944	Fulgencio Batista
1944–1948	Ramon Grau San Martin
1948–1952	Carlos Prio Socarras
1952–1959	Fulgencio Batista
1959	Manuel Urrutia
1959–1976	Osvaldo Dorticos Torrado
1976–	Fidel Castro Ruz

PRIME MINISTER

1959–   Fidel Castro Ruz, Prime Minister and First Secretary

CYPRUS

MONARCH-KINGDOM OF CYPRUS

Lusignan Dynasty

1192–1194	Guy of Lusignan
1194–1205	Amalric
1205–1218	Hugh I
1218–1253	Henry I
1253–1267	Hugh II
1267–1284	Hugh III
1284–1285	John I
1285–1324	Henry II
1324–1359	Hugh IV
1359–1369	Peter I
1369–1382	Peter II
1382–1398	James I
1398–1432	Janus
1432–1458	John II
1458–1464	Charlotte Joint ruler
1458–1464	Louis Joint ruler
1460–1473	James II Rival King until 1464
1473–1474	James III
1473–1489	Caterina Cornaro Regent and Joint ruler until 1474
1489–1571	Venetian rule
1571–1914	Turkish rule
1914–1960	British rule

PRESIDENTS

1960–1977	Archbishop Makarios III (Mihail Christodoulou Mouskos)
1977–1988	Spyros Kyprianou
1988–1993	Georgios Vassiliou
1993–	Clafos Clerides

CZECH REPUBLIC

DUKE OF BOHEMIA

House of Premysl

873–895	Borzhivoi I
895–921	Vratislav I Joint ruler to 912
895–912	Spitihnev I Joint ruler
921–929	Vaclav I (St. Wenceslas)
929–967	Boleslav I
967–999	Boleslav II
999–1002	Boleslav III
1002–1003	Vladivoi
1003	Boleslav III (restored)
1003–1012	Jaromir
1012–1034	Odalrich
1034–1055	Bretislav I
1055–1061	Spitihnev I
1061–1092	Vratislav I King from 1086
1092	Conrad
1092–1100	Bretislav II
1100–1107	Borzhivoi II
1107–1109	Svatopluk
1109–1117	Vladislav I
1117–1120	Borzhivoi II (restored)
1120–1125	Vladislav I (restored)
1125–1140	Sobeslav I
1140–1173	Vladislav II
1173–1179	Sobeslav II
1179–1189	Frederick
1189–1191	Conrad-Otto
1191–1192	Václav II
1192–1193	Premysl Otakar I
1193–1197	Bretislav-Henry
1197	Vladislav III
1197–1198	Premysl Otakar (restored)

KINGS OF BOHEMIA

House of Premysl

1198–1230	Premysl Otakar I
1230–1253	Václav I
1253–1278	Premysl Otakar II

1278–1305 Václav II
1305–1306 Václav III

LATER KINGS

1306–1307 Rudolf (III of Austria)
1307–1310 Henry of Carinthia
1310–1346 John 'the Blind' (of
Luxembourg)
1346–1378 Charles (IV) Holy Roman
Emperor
1378–1419 Václav IV (Wenceslas)
Holy Roman Emperor
1419–1437 Sigismund Holy Roman
Emperor
1437–1440 Albert Holy Roman
Emperor
1440–1457 Ladislaus Posthumus (V
of Hungary)
1457–1471 George of Podebrady
1471–1516 Vladislav Jagiellon
1516–1526 Louis King Lajos II of
Hungary
1526–1918 Part of Austria

PRESIDENT—STATE OF CZECHOSLOVAKIA

1918–1935 Tomas Garrigue Masaryk
1935–1938 Edvard Benes
1938–1939 Emil Hacha
1939–1945 Emil Hacha
1941–1945 Edvard Benes
Government in exile
1945–1948 Edvard Benes
1948–1953 Klement Gottwald
1953–1957 Antonin Zapotocky
1957–1968 Antonin Novotny
1968–1975 Ludvik Svoboda
1975–1989 Gustav Husak
1989–1992 Václav Havel

PRESIDENT—CZECH REPUBLIC

1993– Václav Havel

PRIME MINISTERS

1918–1919 Karel Kramar
1919–1920 Vlastimil Tusar
1920–1921 Jan Cerny
1921–1922 Edvard Benes
1922–1926 Antonin Svehla
1926 Jan Cerny
1926–1929 Antonin Svehla
1929–1932 Frantisek Udrzal
1932–1935 Jan Malypetr
1935–1938 Milan Hodza
1938 Jan Syrovy
1938–1939 Rudolf Beran
1940–1945 Jan Sramek in exile
1945–1946 Zdenek Fierlinger
1946–1948 Klement Gottwald
1948–1953 Antonin Zapotocky
1953–1963 Viliam Siroky
1963–1968 Josef Lenart
1968–1970 Oldrich Cernik
1970–1988 Lubomir Strougal
1988–1989 Ladislav Adamec
1989–1992 Marian Calfa
1992–1993 Jan Strasky
1993–1977 Václav Klaus
1997–1998 Josef Tosovský
1998– Milos Zeman

FIRST SECRETARY

1948–1952 Rudolf Slansky
1953–1968 Antonin Novotny
1968–1969 Alexander Dubcek
1969–1987 Gustav Husak
1987–1989 Milos Jakes
1989 Karel Urbanek
1989–1992 Ladislav Adamec

DENMARK

MONARCHS—KINDOM OF DENMARK

House of Gorm

c. 900–c. 950 Gorm 'The Old'

c. 950–985	Harald I Gormsson 'Blue-Tooth'
985–1014	Svein I Haraldsson 'Fork-Beard'
1014–1019	Harald II
1019–1035	Knut Sveinsson (Canute)
1035–1042	Hardaknut Knutsson
1042–1047	as Norway
1047–1076	Svein II Estridsson
1076–1080	Harald III Hen
1080–1086	Knut IV 'the Holy'
1086–1095	Olaf IV
1095–1103	Erik I Ejegod
1104–1134	Niels
1134–1137	Erik II Emune
1137–1147	Erik III
1147–1157	Svein III, rival king
1147–1157	Knut V, rival king
1157–1182	Valdemar I 'the Great'
1182–1202	Knut VI
1202–1241	Valdemar II
1241–1250	Erik IV
1250–1252	Abel
1252–1259	Kristofer I
1259–1286	Erik V
1286–1320	Erik VI
1320–1332	Kristofer II
1340–1375	Valdemar III Atterdag
1375–1387	Olaf V (Olaf IV of Norway from 1380)
1387–1397	Margrethe I (Margareta) (queen of Norway from 1387, Sweden from 1389)

MONARCHS—KALMAR UNION

House of Gorm

1397–1412	Margrethe (Margareta) (queen of Norway and Sweden)
1412–1439	Erik VII (of Pomerania) (Erik III of Norway and XIII of Sweden)
1439–1448	Kristofer III (of Bavaria) (Kristofer I of Norway and Sweden)

House of Oldenburg

1448–1481	Kristian I (king of Norway, king of Sweden 1457–64, 1465–67, 1470–81)
1481–1513	Hans (king of Norway, king Johan II of Sweden)
1513–1523	Kristian II (king of Norway, king of Sweden to 1521)

MONARCHS OF DENMARK AND GERMANY

House of Oldenburg

1523–1534	Frederik I
1534–1559	Kristian III
1559–1588	Frederik II
1588–1648	Kristian IV
1648–1670	Frederik III
1670–1699	Kristian V
1699–1730	Frederik IV
1730–1746	Kristian VI
1746–1766	Frederik V
1766–1808	Kristian VII
1808–1814	Frederik VI

MONARCHS—KINGDOM OF DENMARK

House of Oldenburg

1814–1839	Frederik VI
1839–1848	Kristian VIII
1848–1863	Frederik VII
1863–1906	Kristian IX
1906–1912	Frederik VIII
1912–1947	Kristian X
1947–1972	Frederik (Frederick) IX
1972–	Margrethe II

EGYPT'S DYNASTIES

Dynasties 1–2, Protodynastic/Early Dynastic (also estimated at 3110–2665 BC)
I. 3110–2884 BC (Menes, major ruler)
II. 2884–2780 BC

Dynasties 3–6, Old Kingdom (also estimated at 2664–2180 BC)

   III. 2780–2680 BC (Snefru, major ruler)

   IV. 2680–2565 BC (Khufu (Cheops), Khafre, Menkaure, major rulers)

   V. 2565–2420 BC

   VI. 2420–2258 BC (Pepi I, II, major rulers)

Dynasties 7–11, First Intermediate (also estimated at 2180–2052 BC)

   VII, VIII. 2258–2225 BC

   IX, X. 2225–2134 BC

   XI. 2134–c.2000 BC (Mentuhotep II, major ruler)

Dynasty 12, Middle Kingdom (also estimated at 2052–1786 BC)

   XII. 2000–1786 BC (Amenemhet I, II, III, IV, Sesostris I, II, major rulers)

Dynasties 13–17, Second Intermediate (also estimated at 1785–1554 BC)

   XIII-XVII. 1786–1570 BC (Hyksos, major ruler)

Dynasties 18–20, New Kingdom (also estimated at 1554–1075 BC)

   XVIII. 1579–c.1342 BC (Amenhotep I, Thutmose I, II, III, IV, Akhenaton, Tutankhamun, major rulers)

   XIX. c. 1342–1200 BC (Ramses I, II, major rulers)

   XX. 1200–1085 BC (Ramses III, major ruler)

Dynasties 21–25, Late, 1075–664 BC

   XXI. 1085–945 BC

   XXII. 945–745 BC (Sheshonk I)

   XXIII. 745–718 BC

   XXIV. 718–712 BC

   XXV. 712–663 BC (Taharka, major ruler)

Dynasty 26, Saite

   XXVI. 663–525 BC (Necho, major ruler)

Dynasty 27, First Persian

   XXVII. 525–405 BC (Achaemenids of Persia, Darius II, major rulers)

Dynasties 28–30, Last Egyptian Kingdom (also estimated at 404–341 BC)

   XXVIII, XXIX, XXX. 405–322 BC (Nekhtnebf I, major ruler)

Dynasty 31, Second Persian, 341–332 BC

EGYPTIAN GOVERNMENTAL ORGANIZATION

Pharaoh

Vizier of Upper Egypt (at Thebes)—all official positions duplicated for Upper and Lower Egypt

Vizier of Lower Egypt (at Memphis)

Departments of Treasury, the Granaries, Royal Works, Cattle, and Foreign Affairs

Governors (rural districts) with staffs of officials, messengers, and scribes

Mayors (towns) with staffs of officials, messengers, and scribes

POLITICAL HIERARCHY

(There were 2000 titles— these being the most important.)

Pharaoh: king of Egypt and incarnation of Ra, the sun god

Crown Prince: heir to the throne

Princes: younger or adopted children

Superintendent of all the Works of the King: recorded, organized, and carried out pharaoh's edicts

Viziers: philosophers, sages, or scholars who advised pharaoh

Keepers/Directors: aides to viziers

Priests: oversaw education, archives, science, workplaces, and rites

Nomarchs: provincial rulers

General of the Braves of the King: led the best soldiers

Generals and Captains: led axemen,

spearsmen, archers, reserves

Grandees: noblemen who were friends of the royal household; highest were those allowed to kiss the feet of the pharaoh

Steward of the Harem: responsible for pharaoh's wives

Overseers: responsible for specific duties within the pharaoh's household or the kingdom's civic projects

Scribes and Artists: recordkeepers of the lives of pharaohs, priests, and noblemen

FRANCE

MONARCHS— KINGDOM OF THE FRANKS

House of Charlemagne

768–814 Charlemagne
814–840 Louis I 'the Pious'
840–843 Civil war

MONARCHS— KINGDOM OF THE WEST FRANKS

House of Charlemagne

843–877 Charles I 'the Bald'
877–879 Louis II 'the Stammerer'
879–884 Carloman Joint ruler to 882
879–882 Louis III Joint ruler

MONARCHS—KINGDOM OF FRANCE

House of Charlemagne

884–887 Charles II 'the Fat'

House of Charlemagne (Restored)

893–922 Charles III 'the Simple' Rival king until 898

House of Capet

888–898 Eudes

House of Capet (Restored)

922–923 Robert I
923–936 Raoul

House of Charlemagne (Restored)

936–954 Louis IV 'd'Outre-Mer'
954–986 Lothaire
986–987 Louis V 'le Faineant'

DUKES OF NORMANDY

911–932   Ganger-Hrolf (Rollo)
932–942   William I
942–996   Richard I
996–1027 Richard II
1027–1028 Richard III
1028–1035 Robert I
1035–1087 William II (I of England) 'the Conqueror'
1087–1106 Robert Curthose
1106–1135 Henry I (King of England)
1135–1144 Civil war
1144–1150 Geoffrey of Anjou
1150–1204 Henry II (King of England)
1204–   Part of France

House of Capet (Restored)

987–996   Hugh Capet
996–1031 Robert II
1031–1060 Henri I
1060–1108 Philippe I
1108–1137 Louis VI 'the Fat'
1137–1180 Louis VII
1180–1223 Philippe II (Philippe-Auguste)
1223–1226 Louis VIII 'the Lion'
1226–1270 Louis IX (St Louis)
1270–1285 Philippe III 'the Bold'
1285–1314 Philippe IV 'the Fair'
1314–1316 Louis X 'the Quarrelsome'
1316   Jean I

1316–1322 Philippe V 'the Tall'
1322–1328 Charles IV 'the Fair'

House of Valois

1328–1350 Philippe VI
1350–1364 Jean II 'the Good'
1364–1380 Charles V 'the Wise'
1380–1422 Charles VI 'the Foolish'
1422–1461 Charles VII
1461–1483 Louis XI
1483–1498 Charles VIII 'the Affable'

House of Valois/Orléans

1498–1515 Louis XII

House of Valois/Angoulême

1515–1547 François I
1547–1559 Henri II
1559–1560 François II
1560–1574 Charles IX
1574–1589 Henri III

Dukes of Lorraine

1697–1729 Leopold
1729–1736 Francis III (I, Holy Roman Emperor)
1736–1766 Stanislas Leszczynski

House of Bourbon

1589–1610 Henri IV (of Navarre)
1610–1643 Louis XIII
1643–1715 Louis XIV
1715–1774 Louis XV
1774–1793 Louis XVI
1793–1795 Louis XVII (not crowned)

REVOLUTIONARY GOVERNMENT

First Republic

1792–1795 National Convention
1795–1799 Directory
1799–1804 Consulate (Napoléon Bonaparte, First Consul)

MONARCHS—FRENCH EMPIRE

First Empire

1804–1814 Napoléon I
1815 Napoléon II (not crowned)

MONARCHS—KINGDOM OF FRANCE

House of Bourbon (Restored)

1814–1824 Louis XIII
1824–1830 Charles X

House of Orléans

1830–1848 Louis-Philippe

PRESIDENTS

Second Republic

1848–1851 Charles Louis Napoléon Bonaparte

MONARCHS—FRENCH EMPIRE

Second Empire

1852–1870 Napoléon III (Charles Louis Napoleon Bonaparte)

PRESIDENTS

Third Republic

1870–1871 Commune
1871–1873 Louis Adolphe Thiers
1873–1879 Marie Edmé de Mac-Mahon
1879–1887 Jules Grévy
1887–1894 Sadi Carnot
1894–1895 Jean Pierre Paul Casimir-Périer
1895–1899 Francois Félix Faure
1899–1906 Emile Loubet

1906–1913	Armand Fallières
1913–1920	Raymond Poincaré
1920	Paul Deschanel
1920–1924	Alexandre Millerand
1924–1931	Gaston Doumergue
1931–1932	Paul Doumer
1932–1940	Albert Lebrun
1940–1945	German rule
1945–1947	*No President*

Fourth Republic

1947–1954	Vincent Auriol
1954–1958	René Coty

Fifth Republic

1958–1969	Charles de Gaulle
1969–1974	Georges Pompidou
1974–1981	Valéry Giscard d'Estaing
1981–1995	Francois Mitterrand
1995–	Jacques Chirac

PRIME MINISTERS

1815	Charles-Maurice, Prince de Talleyrand-Périgord
1815–1818	Armand-Emmanuel Vignerot-Duplessis, Duc de Richelieu
1818–1819	Jean Joseph, Marquis Dessolle
1819–1820	Elie, Comte Decazes
1820–1821	Armand Vignerot-Duplessis, Duc de Richelieu
1821–1829	Guillaume-Aubin, Comte de Villele
1829–1830	Auguste, Prince de Polignac
1830–1831	Jacques Lafitte
1831–1832	Casimir Périer
1832–1834	Nicolas Soult
1834	Etienne, Comte Gérard
1834	Napoléon Joseph Maret, Duc de Bassano
1834–1835	Etienne Mortier, Duc de Tréviso
1835–1836	Achille, Duc de Broglie

1836	Adolphe Thiers
1836–1839	Louis, Comte Mole
1839–1840	Nicolas Soult
1840	Adolphe Thiers
1840–1847	Nicolas Soult
1847–1848	Francois Guyzot
1848	Jacques Charles Dupont de L'Eure
1848	Louis-Eugène Cavaignac
1848–1849	Odilon Barrot
1849–1870	No Prime Minister
1870–1871	Jules Favre
1871–1873	Jules Dufaure
1873–1874	Albert, Duc de Broglie
1874–1875	Ernest Louis Courtot de Cissey
1875–1876	Louis Buffet
1876	Jules Dufaure
1876–1877	Jules Simon
1877	Albert, Duc de Broglie
1877	Gaétan de Grimaudet de Rochebouet
1877–1879	Jules Dufaure
1879	William H. Waddington
1879–1880	Louis de Freycinet
1880–1881	Jules Ferry
1881–1882	Léon Gambetta
1882	Louis de Freycinet
1882–1883	Eugène Duclerc
1883	Armand Fallières
1883–1885	Jules Ferry
1885–1886	Henri Brisson
1886	Louis de Freycinet
1886–1887	René Goblet
1887	Maurice Rouvier
1887–1888	Pierre Tirard
1888–1889	Charles Floquet
1889–1890	Pierre Tirard
1890–1892	Louis de Freycinet
1892	Emile Loubet
1892–1893	Alexandre Ribot
1893	Charles Dupuy
1893–1894	Jean Casimir-Périer
1894–1895	Charles Dupuy
1895	Alexandre Ribot
1895–1896	Leon Bourgeois
1896–1898	Jules Meline

1898	Henri Brisson
1898–1899	Charles Dupuy
1899–1902	Pierre Waldeck-Rousseau
1902–1905	Emile Combes
1905–1906	Maurice Rouvier
1906	Jean Sarrien
1906–1909	Georges Clémenceau
1909–1911	Aristide Briand
1911	Ernest Monis
1911–1912	Joseph Caillaux
1912–1913	Raymond Poincaré
1913	Aristide Briand
1913	Jean Louis Barthou
1913–1914	Gaston Boumergue
1914	Alexandre Ribot
1914–1915	René Viviani
1915–1917	Aristide Briand
1917	Alexandre Ribot
1917	Paul Painlevé
1917–1920	Georges Clémenceau
1920	Alexandre Millerand
1920–1921	Georges Leygues
1921–1922	Aristide Briand
1922–1924	Raymond Poincaré
1924	Frédéric Francois-Marsal
1924–1925	Edouard Herriot
1925	Paul Painlevé
1925–1926	Aristide Briand
1926	Edouard Herriot
1926–1929	Raymond Poincaré
1929	Aristide Briand
1929–1930	André Tardieu
1930	Camille Chautemps
1930	André Tardieu
1930–1931	Théodore Steeg
1931–1932	Pierre Laval
1932	André Tardieu
1932	Edouard Herriot
1932–1933	Joseph Paul-Boncour
1933	Edouard Daladier
1933	Albert Sarrault
1933–1934	Camille Chautemps
1934	Edouard Daladier
1934	Gaston Doumergue
1934–1935	Pierre Etienne Flandin
1935	Fernand Bouisson
1935–1936	Pierre Laval
1936	Albert Sarrault
1936–1937	Léon Blum
1937–1938	Camille Chautemps
1938	Léon Blum
1938–1940	Edouard Daladier
1940	Paul Reynaud
1940–1944	Philippe Pétain
1944–1946	Charles de Gaulle
1946	Félix Gouin
1946	Georges Bidault
1946–1947	Léon Blum
1947	Paul Ramadier
1947–1948	Robert Schuman
1948	André Marie
1948	Robert Schuman
1948–1949	Henri Queuille
1949–1950	Georges Bidault
1950	Henri Queuille
1950–1951	René Pleven
1951	Henri Queuille
1951–1952	René Pleven
1952	Edgar Faure
1952–1953	Antoine Pinay
1953	René Mayer
1953–1954	Joseph Laniel
1954–1955	Pierre Mendès-France
1955–1956	Edgar Faure
1956–1957	Guy Alcide Mollet
1957	Maurice Bourges-Maunoury
1957–1958	Félix Gaillard
1958	Pierre Pflimin
1958–1959	Charles de Gaulle
1959–1962	Michel Debré
1962–1968	Georges Pompidou
1968–1969	Maurice Couve de Murville
1969–1972	Jacques Chaban Delmas
1972–1974	Pierre Mesmer
1974–1976	Jacques René Chirac
1976–1981	Raymond Barre
1981–1984	Pierre Mauroy
1984–1986	Laurent Fabius
1986–1988	Jacques René Chirac
1988–1991	Michel Rocard
1991–1992	Edith Cresson
1992–1993	Pierre Beregovoy

1993–1995	Edouard Balladur
1995–1997	Alain Juppé
1997–	Lionel Jospin

EMPIRES

First Empire: in France under Napoléon Bonaparte from 1804–1814
Second Empire:France under Napoléon III from 1852–1870

FRENCH NOBILITY

Duc, Duchesse
Prince, Princesse
Marquis, Marquise
Comte, Comtesse
Vicomte, Vicomtesse
Baron, Baronne

FRENCH REPUBLICS

1. First Republic, 1792–1804, the result of the French Revolution
2. Second Republic, 1848–1852, deposition of Louis-Philippe, to 1852's Second Empire
3. Third Republic, 1870–1940, fall of Napoléon III till German occupation of World War II
4. Fourth Republic, 1946–1958
5. Fifth Republic, since 1958 presidency of Charles de Gaulle

GERMANY

ELECTOR OF BRANDENBURG

House of Hohenzollern

1415–1440	Friedrich I (of Nuremberg)
1440–1471	Friedrich II
1471–1486	Albrecht (Albert III) Achilles
1486–1499	Johann Cicero

1499–1535	Joachim I
1535–1571	Joachim II
1571–1598	Johann Georg
1598–1608	Joachim Friedrich
1608–1620	Johann Sigismund
1620–1640	Georg Wilhelm
1640–1688	Friedrich Wilhelm (Frederick William) 'the Great Elector'
1688–1701	Friedrich III

KINGS OF PRUSSIA

House of Hohenzollern

1701–1713	Friedrich I (III of Brandenburg)
1713–1740	Friedrich Wilhelm I
1740–1786	Friedrich (Frederick) II 'the Great'
1786–1797	Friedrich Wilhelm (Frederick William) II
1797–1840	Friedrich Wilhelm (Frederick William) III
1840–1861	Friedrich Wilhelm (Frederick William) IV
1861–1871	Wilhelm I

KAISERS—GERMAN EMPIRE

House of Hohenzollern

1871–1888	Wilhelm I
1888	Friedrich (Frederick) (III of Prussia)
1888–1918	Wilhelm II

Chancellors

1871–1890	Otto von Bismarck
1890–1894	Georg Leo, Graf von Caprivi
1894–1900	Chlodwic, Prince von Hohenlohe-Schillingfurst
1900–1909	Bernhard Heinrich, Prince von Bulow

1909–1917 Theobald von Bethmann Hollweg
1917–1918 Georg von Herfling
1918 Prince Max of Baden

WEIMAR REPUBLIC

Heads of State (Chancellors)

1918 Friedrich Ebert
1919–1920 Philipp Scheidemann
1920 Hermann Muller
1920–1921 Konstantin Fehrenbach
1921–1922 Karl Joseph Wirth
1922–1923 Wilhelm Cuno
1923 Gustav Stresemann
1923–1925 Wilhelm Marx
1925–1926 Hans Luther
1926–1928 Wilhelm Marx
1928–1929 Herman Muller
1929–1932 Heinrich Bruning
1932–1933 Franz von Papen
1933– Adolf Hitler (ended Weimar Republic, established Nazi regime)

GERMAN FEDERAL REPUBLIC

(to 1990 West Germany)

Presidents

1949–1959 Theodor Heuss
1959–1969 Heinrich Lubke
1969–1974 Gustav Heinemann
1974–1979 Walter Scheel
1979–1984 Karl Carstens
1984–1994 Richard von Weizsäcker
1994– Roman Herzog

Chancellors

1949–1963 Konrad Adenauer
1963–1966 Ludwig Erhard
1966–1969 Kurt Georg Kiesinger
1969–1974 Willy Brandt
1974–1982 Helmut Schmidt
1982–1998 Helmut Kohl
1998– Gerhard Schröder

GERMAN DEMOCRATIC REPUBLIC

(East Germany)

Presidents

1949–1960 Wilhelm Pieck

Chairman of the Council of State

1960–1973 Walter Ulbricht
1973–1976 Willi Stoph
1976–1989 Erich Honecker
1989 Egon Krenz
1989–1990 Gregor Gysi General Secretary as Chairman

Premiers

1949–1964 Otto Grotewohl
1964–1973 Willi Stoph
1973–1976 Horst Sindermann
1976–1989 Willi Stoph
1989–1990 Hans Modrow
1990–1990 Lothar de Maiziere

NOBILITY

Herzog, Herzogin
Furst, Furstin
Prinz, Prinzessin
Markgraf, Markgrafin
Pfalzgraf, Pfalzgrafin
Landgraf, Landgrafin
Graf, Grafin
Baron, Baronin
Freiherr, Freiherrin
Freier, Freierin

GERMAN REICHS

1. Holy Roman Empire, ninth century to 1806
2. German Empire, 1815–1918
3. Nazi regime (Third Reich), 1933–1945

GREAT BRITAIN AND UNITED KINGDOM

PEERAGE

Duke or Duchess (your grace)

Marquess or Marchioness (my lord,
my lady or madam)

Earl or Countess (my lord, my lady or
madam)

Viscount or Viscountess (my lord, my
lady or madam)

Baron or Baroness (my lord, my lady
or madam)

Life Baron or Life Baroness (my lord,
my lady)

TITLES OF NOBILITY

Life Peerages (honorary; non-
hereditary)

Lord or Lady (my lord, my lady)

Knight or Dame (Sir, Lady)

Baronetcy (hereditary; non-peerage)

Baronet or Baronetess (my lord, my
lady)

HERALDIC COAT OF ARMS

**Marks of Cadency (for order of birth
for sons)**

eldest/first cadet: label (horizontal
band with three or more downward
"pieces")

second cadet: crescent with upward-
pointing cusps

third cadet: mullet (five-pointed star)

fourth cadet: martlet/swallow

fifth cadet: amulet/ring

sixth cadet: fleur-de-lis

seventh cadet: five hearts in a rose
atop a mullet

eighth cadet: cross moline

ninth cadet: double quatrefoil

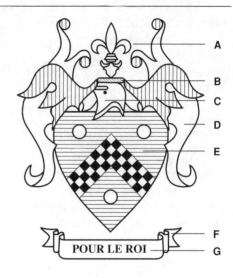

Coat of Arms
A. Crest; **B.** Torse; **C.** Helmet; **D.** Mantling;
E. Escutcheon; **F.** Scroll; **G.** Motto

BRITISH ROYAL HOUSE MNEMONIC

No **P**lan **L**ike **Y**ours **T**o **S**tudy
History **W**isely

Normandy, 1066–1154

Plantagenet, 1154–1399

Lancaster, 1399–1471

York, 1461–1485

Tudor, 1485–1603

Stuart, 1603–1714

Hanover, 1714–1901

Windsor, 1902–

BRITISH MONARCHS POEM

Willy, Willy, Harry, Ste, (for Stephen)
Harry, Dick, John, Harry three,
One, Two, Three Neds, Richard two,
Henry Four, Five, Six—then who?
Edward Four, Five, Dick the Bad,

Harries twain and Ned the Lad,
Mary, Bessie, James the Vain,
Charlie, Charlie, James again.
William and Mary, Anna Gloria,
Four Georges, William and Victoria.
Ned Seventh ruled till 1910,
When George the Fifth came in, and
  then
Ned went when Mrs. Simpson
  beckoned,
Leaving George and Liz the Second.

ENGLISH RULERS AND MONARCHS

Saxons

802–839	Egbert
839–858	Ethelwulf
858–860	Ethelbald
860–865?	Ethelbert
865?–871	Ethelred I
871–899	Alfred the Great
899–924	Edward the Elder
924–939	Athelstan
939–946	Edmund I
946–955	Edred
955–959	Edwig
959–975	Edgar
975–978?	Edward the Martyr
978?–1016	Ethelred II
1016	Edmund II

Danes

1016–1035	Canute
1035–1040	Harold I
1040–1042	Hardecanute

Saxons

1042–1066	Edward the Confessor
1066	Harold II

Normans

1066–1087	William I
1087–1100	William II
1100–1135	Henry I
1135–1154	Stephen

Plantagenet Family

1154–1189	Henry II
1189–1199	Richard I
1199–1216	John
1216–1272	Henry III
1272–1307	Edward I
1307–1327	Edward II
1327–1377	Edward III
1377–1399	Richard II

House of Lancaster

1399–1413	Henry IV
1413–1422	Henry V
1422–1461	Henry VI

House of York

1461–1470	Edward IV

House of Lancaster

1470–1471	Henry VI

House of York

1471–1483	Edward IV
1483	Edward V
1483–1485	Richard III

House of Tudor

1485–1509	Henry VII
1509–1547	Henry VIII
1547–1553	Edward VI
1553	Grey, Lady Jane
1553–1558	Mary I
1558–1603	Elizabeth I

House of Stuart

1603–1625	James I
1625–1649	Charles I

Commonwealth

1649–1653	Long Parliament

Protectorate

1653–1658	Oliver Cromwell
1658–1659	Richard Cromwell

House of Stuart

1660–1685   Charles II
1685–1688   James II
1689–1694   Mary II
1689–1702   William III
1702–1714   Anne

BRITISH MONARCHS

House of Stuart

1702–1714   Anne

House of Hanover

1714–1727   George I
1727–1760   George II
1760–1820   George III
1820–1830   George IV
1830–1837   William IV
1837–1901   Victoria

House of Saxe-Coburg-Gotha

1901–1910   Edward VII
1910–1917   George V

House of Windsor

1917–1936   George V
      1936   Edward VIII
1936–1952   George VI
1952–   Elizabeth II

SIX WIVES OF HENRY THE EIGHTH

Catherine of Aragon
Anne Boleyn
Jane Seymour
Anne of Cleves
Catherine Howard
Catherine Parr

TRIANGLE TRADE

(1500–1800)

1. ships left England with guns and cloth
2. ships exchanged goods for slaves on west coast of Africa
3. ships took slaves to Caribbean and the Americas, exchanging for sugar, tobacco, rum, molasses, etc.
4. ships return to England, sell goods for profit

PRIME MINISTERS

1721–1742   Robert Walpole, Earl of Orford (Whig)
1742–1743   Spencer Compton, Earl of Wilmington (Whig)
1743–1754   Henry Pelham (Whig)
1754–1756   Thomas Pelham (Holles), Duke of Newcastle (Whig)
1756–1757   William Cavendish, 1st Duke of Devonshire (Whig)
1757–1762   Thomas Pelham (Holles), Duke of Newcastle (Whig)
1762–1763   John Stuart, 3rd Earl of Bute (Tory)
1763–1765   George Grenville (Whig)
1765–1766   Charles Watson Wentworth, 2nd Marquis of Rockingham (Whig)
1766–1767   William Pitt, 1st Earl of Chatham (Whig)
1767–1770   Augustus Henry Fitzroy, 3rd Duke of Grafton (Whig)
1770–1782   Frederick North, 8th Lord North (Tory)
      1782   Charles Watson Wentworth, 2ng Marquis of Rockingham (Whig)
1782–1783   William Petty, 2nd Earl of Shelburne (Whig)
      1783   William Henry Cavendish, Duke of Portland Coal
1783–1801   William Pitt (Tory)
1801–1804   Henry Addington, 1st Viscount Sidmouth (Tory)
1804–1806   William Pitt (Tory)
1806–1807   William Wyndham Grenville, 1st Baron Grenville (Whig)

1807–1809	William Henry Cavendish, Duke of Portland Coal
1809–1812	Spencer Perceval (Tory)
1812–1827	Robert Banks Jenkinson, 2nd Earl of Liverpool (Tory)
1827	George Canning (Tory)
1827–1828	Frederick John Robinson, 1st Earl of Ripon (Tory)
1828–1830	Arthur Wellesley, 1st Duke of Wellington (Tory)
1830–1834	Charles Grey, 2nd Earl Grey (Whig)
1834	William Lamb, 2nd Viscount Melbourne (Whig)
1834–1835	Robert Peel (Con)
1835–1841	William Lamb, 2nd Viscont Melbourne (Whig)
1841–1846	Robert Peel (Con)
1846–1852	Lord John Russell, 1st Earl Russell (Lib)
1852	Edward Geoffrey Smith Stanley, 14th Earl of Derby (Con)
1852–1855	George Hamilton-Gordon, 4th Earl of Aberdeen Peelite
1855–1858	Henry John Temple, 3rd Viscount Palmerston (Lib)
1858–1859	Edward Geoffrey Smith Stanley, 14th Earl of Derby (Con)
1859–1865	Henry John Temple, 3rd Viscount Palmerston (Lib)
1865–1866	Lord John Russell, 1st Earl Russell (Lib)
1866–1868	Edward Geoffrey Smith Stanley, 14th Earl of Derby (Con)
1868	Benjamin Disraeli, 1st Earl of Beaconsfield (Con)
1868–1874	William Ewart Gladstone (Lib)
1874–1880	Benjamin Disraeli, 1st Earl of Beaconsfield (Con)
1880–1885	William Ewart Gladstone (Lib)
1885–1886	Robert Arthur James Gascoyne-Cecil, 5th Marquis of Salisbury (Con)
1886	William Ewart Gladstone (Lib)
1886–1892	Robert Arthur James Gascoyne-Cecil, 5th Marquis of Salisbury (Con)
1892–1894	William Ewart Gladstone (Lib)
1894–1895	Archibald Philip Primrose, 5th Earl of Rosebery (Lib)
1895–1902	Robert Arthur James Gascoyne-Cecil, 5th Marquis of Salisbury (Con)
1902–1905	Arthur James Balfour, 1st Earl of Balfour (Con)
1905–1908	Henry Campbell-Bannerman (Lib)
1908–1915	Herbert Henry Asquith, 1st Earl of Oxford and Asquith (Lib)
1915–1916	Herbert Henry Asquith, 1st Earl of Oxford and Asquith (Coal)
1916–1922	David Lloyd-George, 1st Earl Lloyd-George of Dwyfor (Coal)
1922–1923	Andrew Bonar Law (Con)
1923–1924	Stanley Baldwin, 1st Earl Baldwin of Bewdley (Con)
1924	James Ramsay MacDonald (Lab)
1924–1929	Stanley Baldwin, 1st Earl Baldwin of Bewdley (Con)
1929–1931	James Ramsay MacDonald (Lab)
1931–1935	James Ramsay MacDonald (Nat)

1935–1937	Stanley Baldwin, 1st Earl Baldwin of Bewdley (Nat)
1937–1940	(Arthur) Neville Chamberlain (Nat)
1940–1945	Winston Leonard Spencer Churchill (Coal)
1945–1951	Clement Richard Atlee, 1st Earl Attlee (Lab)
1951–1955	Winston Leonard Spencer Churchill (Con)
1955–1957	(Robert) Anthony Eden, 1st Earl of Avon (Con)
1957–1963	(Maurice) Harold Macmillan, 1st Earl of Stockton (Con)
1963–1964	Alexander Frederick (Alec) Douglas-Home, Baron Home of the Hirsel (Con)
1964–1970	(James) Harold Wilson, Baron Wilson (Lab)
1970–1974	Edward Richard George Heath (Con)
1974–1976	(James) Harold Wilson, Baron Wilson (Lab)
1976–1979	(Leonard) James Callaghan, Baron Callaghan (Lab)
1979–1990	Margaret Hilda Thatcher, Baroness Thatcher (Con)
1990–1997	John Major (Con)
1997–	Tony Blair (Lab)

GREECE

ANCIENT ATHENIAN ARMY

strategoi/commanders (10 total, one Athenian from each of the Athenian tribes and elected by the Assembly)

phyle/regiment (group of soldiers provided by each of the ten tribes)

cavalry (group of soldiers provided by each of the ten tribes)

hipparchs/commanders (two men who each controlled five squadrons)

phalanx (long block of soldiers, usually 8 ranks deep)

hoplites (armed foot soldiers)

ephebes (young men of 18+ doing two years' military training)

psiloi (auxiliary soldiers, including archers and stone slingers)

ekdromoi ("runners out" who would run out of the phalanx to chase the enemy)

SEVEN SAGES OF GREECE

Solon of Athens
Thales of Miletus
Pittacus of Mitylene
Bias of Priene in Caria
Chilon of Sparta
Cleobulus, tyrant of Lindus in Rhodes
Periander, tyrant of Corinth

ATHENIAN SOCIAL STRUCTURE

(women took social status from male relations and were not permitted to take part in public life)

free people

citizens (free men born to Athenian parents who could take part in politics)

metics (free men born outside Athens; could never become citizens)

slaves

SPARTA

Spartan Political and Social Structure

hereditary kings (one each from two separate families; leaders of the army and also holding religious duties)

Gerousia (council of kings and 28 elected elders who directed much of Spartan policy)

Ephors (five elected officials of the apella who had wide judicial and administrative powers, supervised the training and discipline of the citizens, and controlled the helots with the help of the secret police/ crypteia)

Apella (assembly of all adult male citizens over 30 men of Spartan birth; served in army and could vote)

Spartiatai (governing class, rulers, and soldiers descended from the Dorians)

Perioeci (free men allowed to trade and serve in the army but who had no political rights)

Helots (descendants of Sparta's original inhabitants, who were made serfs bound to the land and had to farm it for their masters)

GOVERNMENTS

First Republic—President

1829–1831	Ioannis Kapodistrias

Monarchs—Kingdom of Greece

1832–1862	Otho (Otto of Wittelsbach)
1863–1913	Georgios (George) I
1913–1917	Konstantinos (Constantine) I
1917–1920	Alexandros (Alexander)
1920–1922	Konstantinos (Constantine) I (restored)
1922–1923	Georgios (George) II
1923–1924	Pavlos Koundouriotis

Second Republic—Presidents

1924–1926	Pavlos Koundouriotis
1926	Theodoros Pangalos
1926–1929	Pavlos Koundouriotis
1929–1935	Alexandros T Zaimis

Monarchs—Kingdom of Greece

1935	Georgios Kondylis
1935–1947	Georgios (George) II
1947–1964	Pavlos (Paul) I
1964–1967	Konstantinos (Constantine) II
1967–1973	Military junta
1973	Georgios Papadopoulos

Third Republic—Presidents

1973	Georgios Papadopoulos
1973–1974	Phaedon Gizikis
1974–1975	Michael Stasinopoulos
1975–1980	Konstantinos Tsatsos
1980–1985	Konstantinos Karamanlis
1985–1990	Christos Sartzetaki
1990–1995	Konstantinos Karamanlis
1995–	Kostis Stephanopoulos

Prime Ministers

(Since 1940)

1936–1941	Yanni Metaxas
1941	Alexandros Koryzis
1941	Georgios (George) II Chairman of Ministers
1941	German occupation (Emmanuel Tsouderos)
1941–1942	Georgios Tsolakoglou
1942–1943	Konstantinos Logothetopoulos
1943–1944	Ioannis Rallis
1945	Nikolaos Plastiras
1945	Petros Voulgaris
1945	Damaskinos, Archbishop of Athens
1945	Panagiotis Kanellopoulos
1945–1946	Themistocles Sophoulis
1946	Panagiotis Politzas
1946–1947	Konstantinos Tsaldaris
1947	Dimitrios Maximos
1947	Konstantinos Tsaldaris
1947–1949	Themistocles Sophoulis

1949–1950 Alexandros Diomedes
1950 Ioannis Theotokis
1950 Sophocles Venizelos
1950 Nikolaos Plastiras
1950–1951 Sophocles Venizelos
1951 Nikolaos Plastiras
1952 Dimitrios Kiusopoulos
1952–1955 Alexandros Papagos
1955 Stephanos C. Stefanopoulos
1955–1958 Konstantinos Karamanlis
1958 Konstantinos Georgakopoulos
1958–1961 Konstantinos Karamanlis
1961 Konstantinos Dovas
1961–1963 Konstantinos Karamanlis
1963 Panagiotis Pipinellis
1963 Stylianos Mavromichalis
1963 Georgios Papandreou
1963–1964 Ioannis Paraskevopoulos
1964–1965 Georgios Papandreou
1965 Georgios Athanasiadis-Novas
1965 Elias Tsirimokos
1965–1966 Stephanos C. Stefanopoulos
1966–1967 Ioannis Paraskevopoulos
1967 Panagiotis Kanellopoulos
1967–1974 Military junta
1967 Konstantinos Kollias
1967–1973 Georgios Papadopoulos
1973 Spyridon Markezinis
1973–1974 Adamantios Androutsopoulos
1974–1980 Konstantinos Karamanlis
1980–1981 Georgios Rallis
1981–1989 Andreas Georgios Papandreou
1989 Tzannis Tzannetakis
1989–1990 Xenofon Zolotas
1990–1993 Konstantinos Mitsotakis
1993–1995 Andreas Georgios Papandreou
1995– Kostas Simitis

HISTORICAL STUDIES

INVESTIGATION & RESEARCH DISCIPLINES

anthropology
archaeology
bibliography
chronology
dendrochronology (tree rings)
diplomatics (old official documents)
epigraphy (ancient inscriptions)
genealogy
geography
heraldry
historical geography
historiography (historical literature)
iconography (study of subject matter and its meaning in visual arts)
iconology (study of symbols, images and their contextual significance)
paleography (ancient writing)
papyrology (papyrus manuscripts)
radiometric dating (determining age of organic materials based on radioactive elements)
sigillography (study of seals)

HUNGARY

MONARCHS

Arpad Dynasty

1000–1038 Istvan (St Stephen) I
1038–1041 Peter Orseolo
1041–1044 Samuel Aba
1044–1046 Peter Orseolo (restored)
1046–1060 Andras I
1060–1063 Bela I
1063–1074 Salomon
1074–1077 Geza I
1077–1095 Ladislas I
1095–1116 Kalman
1116–1131 Istvan II
1131–1141 Bela II

1141–1162 Geza II
1161–1172 Istvan III
1162–1163 Ladislas II (rival king)
1163–1165 Istvan IV (rival king)
1172–1196 Bela III
1196–1204 Emeric
1204–1205 Ladislas III
1205–1235 Andras II
1235–1270 Bela IV
1270–1272 Istvan V
1272–1290 Ladislas IV
1290–1301 Andras III

Later Kings

1301–1305 Vaclav (III of Bohemia)
1308–1342 Charles Robert of Anjou
1342–1382 Lajos I 'the Great' (King
           Louis of Poland from
           1370)
1382–1395 Mary (joint ruler from
           1387)
1387–1439 (as Holy Roman Emperor)
1440–1444 Vladislav Jagiellon (VI of
           Poland)
1444–1457 Ladislas V
1458–1490 Mattias I Corvinus
1490–1526 (as Bohemia)
1526–1866 (Austrian rule)
1866–1916 Franz Josef (Francis
           Joseph) I (dual
           monarchy)
1916–1918 Karoly IV (Charles)

INDIA

CASTE SYSTEM

1. Brahmans: priests
2. Kshatriyas: royals or warriors
3. Vaisyas: merchants or
   professionals
4. Sudras: workers
5. Untouchables: beggars or diseased

EARLY EMPERORS

Maurya Dynasty

c. 320–c. 300 BC   Chandragupta
                   Maurya
c. 300–c. 273 BC   Bindusara
c. 273–c. 232 BC   Ashoka Vardhana
c. 232–c. 225 BC   Kunala West
c. 232–c. 225 BC   Dasaratha East
c. 225 BC–?   Samprati
                   Salisuka
                   Devadharma
?–c. 194 BC   Satamdhanu
c.194–c. 187 BC   Brihadratha

Sunga Dynasty

c. 187–c. 151 BC   Pushyamitra Sunga
c. 151–c. 143 BC   Agnimitra
c. 143–c. 133 BC   Vasujyeshtha
c. 133 BC–   ?   Vasumitra
              ?   Andhraka
              ?   Pulindaka
              ?   Ghosha
              ?   Vajramitra
?–c. 85 BC   Bhagavata
c. 85–c. 75 BC   Devabhumi

Kanva Dynasty

c. 75–c. 66 BC   Vasudeva
c. 66–c. 52 BC   Bhumimitra
c. 52–c. 40 BC   Narayana
c. 40–c. 30 BC   Susarman

IRAN

KINGDOM OF PERSIA

House of Achaemenes

c. 700–675 BC   Hakhamanish
                (Achaemenes)
c. 675–640 BC   Chishpish (Teispes)
c. 640–600 BC   Kurush (Cyrus) I
c. 600–559 BC   Kambujiya
                (Cambyses) I

559–530 BC	Kurush (Cyrus) II 'the Great'
530–522 BC	Kambujiya (Cambyses) II
522 BC	Badiya-Gaumata (Smerdis)
522–486 BC	Darayavahush (Darius) I 'the Great'
486–465 BC	Khshayarsha (Xerxes) I
465–424 BC	Artakhshassa (Artaxerxes) I Longimanus
424–423 BC	Khshayarsha II
423–404 BC	Darayavahush (Darius) II Ochus
404–359 BC	Artakhshassa (Artaxerxes) II Mnemon
359–338 BC	Artakhshassa (Artaxerxes) III Ochus
338–336 BC	Arsha
336–330 BC	Darayavahush (Darius) III Codomannus
330–329 BC	Artakhshassa IV (Bessus) (Bactria)

SHAHS

Qajar Dynasty

1779–1797	Agha Muhammad
1797–1834	Fath Ali
1834–1848	Muhammad
1848–1896	Nasir-ud-Din
1896–1907	Mazaffar-ud-Din
1907–1909	Mohammed Ali
1909–1925	Ahmad Mirza

Pahlavi Dynasty

1925–1941	Mohammed Reza Khan
1941–1979	Mohammed Reza Pahlavi

REPUBLIC

Leaders of Islamic Revolution (Wali Faqih)

1979–1989	Ruhollah Khomeini
1989–	Sayed Ali Khamenei

Presidents

1980–1981	Abolhassan Bani-Sadr
1981	Mohammed Ali Rajai
1981–1989	Sayed Ali Khamenei
1989–	Ali Akbar Hashemi Rafsanjani

IRELAND

HIGH KINGS OF TARA

died c.450	Niall Noigiallach Nath I
450–463	Loeguire
463–482	Ailill Molt (of Connaught)
482–507	Lugaid
507–534	Muirchertach mac Erc (of Ailech)
534–544	Tuathal Maelgarb
544–565	Diarmaid mac Cerrbel (of Meath)
565–566	Forrgus (of Ailech)
566	Domhall Ilchegach (of Ailech)
566–569	Ainmuire mac Setnae
569–572	Baetan mac Muirchertach (of Ailech)
572	Eochaid (of Ailech)
572–586	Baetan mac Ninnid
586–598	Aed mac Ainmuire
598–604	Aed Slaine (of Brega)
604	Colman Rimid (of Ailech)
604–612	Aed Allan mac Domhall (of Ailech)
612–615	Mael Cobo
615–628	Suibne Menn (of Ailech)
628–642	Domhall mac Aed
642–654	Conall Cael
654–658	Cellach

658–665	Diarmaid mac Aed (of Brega)
665	Blathmac mac Aed (of Brega)
665–671	Sechnussach (of Brega)
671–675	Cenn Faelad (of Brega)
675–695	Finsnechta Fledach (of Brega)
695–703	Loingsech
703–710	Congal Cennmagair
710–722	Fergal (of Ailech)
722–724	Fogartach
724–728	Cinaed (of Brega)
728–743	Aed Allan mac Fergal (of Ailech)
743	Flaithbertach, deposed
743–763	Domhall Midi (of Meath)
763–778	Niall Frossach (of Ailech)
778–797	Donnchad Midi (of Meath)
797–819	Aed Oirnide (of Ailech)
819–833	Conchobar (of Meath)
833–846	Niall Caille (of Ailech)
846–862	Mael Sechnaill I (of Meath)
862–879	Aed Findliath (of Ailech)
879–916	Flann Sinna (of Meath)
916–919	Niall Glundub (of Ailech)
919–944	Donnchad Donn (of Meath)
944–956	Congalach Cnoba (of Brega)
956–980	Domhall Ua Niall (of Ailech)
980–997	Mael Sechnaill II (of Meath)
997–1014	Brian Boroimhe (Brian Boru) (of Munster)
1014–1022	Mael Sechnaill II (of Meath) (restored)
1022–1072	No High King
1072–1086	Tairrdelbach Ua Briain (Turlough O'Brien) (of Munster)
1086–1114	Muirchertach Ua Briain (Murtough O'Brien) (of Munster) Rival king from 1090
1090–1121	Domhall Ua Lochlainn (Donnell O'Loughlin) (of Ailech) Rival king
1118–1156	Tairrdelbach Ua Conchobar (Turlough O'Connor) (of Connaught) Rival king to 1121 and from 1150
1150–1166	Muirchertach mac Lochlainn (Murtough MacLoughlin) (of Ailech) Rival king to 1156
1166–1186	Ruaidri Ua Conchobar (Rory O'Connor) (of Connaught)

GOVERNOR—GENERAL

1922–1927	Timothy Michael Healy
1927–1932	James McNeill
1932–1936	Donald Buckley

PRESIDENTS

1938–1945	Douglas Hyde
1945–1959	Sean Thomas O'Kelly (Sean Tomas O Ceallaigh)
1959–1973	Eamon de Valera
1973–1974	Erskine Hamilton Childers
1974–1976	Carroll Daly
1976–1990	Patrick J. Hillery
1990–1997	Mary Robinson
1997–	Mary McAleese

PRIME MINISTERS

1919–1921	Eamon de Valera
1922	Arthur Griffiths
1922–1932	William Thomas Cosgrave
1932–1948	Eamon de Valera
1948–1951	John Aloysius Costello
1951–1954	Eamon de Valera
1954–1957	John Aloysius Costello

1957–1959	Eamon de Valera
1959–1966	Sean Lemass
1966–1973	John (Jack) Lynch
1973–1977	Liam Cosgrave
1977–1979	John (Jack) Lynch
1979–1982	Charles James Haughey
1982–1987	Garrett FitzGerald
1987–1992	Charles James Haughey
1992–1995	Albert Reynolds
1995–1997	John Bruton
1997–	Bertie Ahern

ISRAEL

KINGDOM

Kings

975–960 BC	David
961–933 BC	Solomon

(in 933 Palestine divided into two states: Israel in the north, Judah in the south)

Kings of Israel:

933–912 BC	Jeroboam
912–911 BC	Nadab
911–888 BC	Baasha
888–887 BC	Elah
887 BC	Zimri
887–886 BC	Omri
876–853 BC	Ahab
853 BC	Ahazia
853–843 BC	Jehoram
843–816 BC	Jehu
816–800 BC	Jehoahaz
800–785 BC	Jehoash
785–745 BC	Jeroboam II
744 BC	Zechariah
743 BC	Shallum
743–736 BC	Menahem
736–735 BC	Pekahiah
735–730 BC	Pekah
730–721 BC	Hoshea

Kings of Judah:

933–917 BC	Rehoboam
917–915 BC	Abijam
915–875 BC	Asa
875–851 BC	Jehoshaphat
851–844 BC	Jehoram
844–843 BC	Ahaziah
843–837 BC	Athaliah
837–798 BC	Joash
798–780 BC	Amaziah
780–740 BC	Azariah
740–735 BC	Jotham
735–720 BC	Ahaz
720–692 BC	Hezekiah
692–638 BC	Manasseh
638–637 BC	Amon
637–608 BC	Josiah
608 BC	Jehoahaz
608–598 BC	Jehoiakim
598–597 BC	Jehoiachin
597–586 BC	Zedekiah

STATE

Prime Ministers

1948–1953	David Ben-Gurion
1953–1955	Moshe Sharett
1955–1963	David Ben-Gurion
1963–1969	Levi Eshkol
1969–1974	Golda Meir
1974–1977	Yitzhak Rabin
1977–1983	Menachem Begin
1983–1984	Yitzhak Shamir
1984–1986	Shimon Peres
1986–1992	Yitzhak Shamir
1992–1995	Yitzhak Rabin
1995–1996	Shimon Peres
1996–1999	Benjamin Netanyahu
1999–2001	Ehud Barak
2001–	Ariel Sharon

ITALY

ITALIAN REPUBLIC

Presidents

1946–1948	Enrico de Nicola
1948–1955	Luigi Einaudi
1955–1962	Giovanni Gronchi
1962–1964	Antonio Segni
1964–1971	Giuseppe Saragat
1971–1978	Giovanni Leone

1978–1985 Alessandro Pertini
1985–1992 Francesco Cossiga
1992–1999 Oscar Luigi Scalfaro
1999– Carlo Azeglio Ciampi

PRIME MINISTERS

1861 Count Camillo Benso di Cavour
1861–1862 Bettino, Baron Ricasoli
1862 Urbano Rattazzi
1862–1863 Luigi Carlo Farini
1863–1864 Marco Minghetti
1864–1866 Alfonso Ferrero, Marquis de la Marmora
1866–1867 Bettino, Baron Ricasoli
1867 Urbano Rattazzi
1867–1869 Luigi Federcio Menabrea
1869–1873 Giovanni Lanza
1873–1876 Marco Minghetti
1876–1878 Agostino Depretis
1878 Benedetto Cairoli
1878–1879 Agostino Depretis
1879–1881 Benedetto Cairoli
1881–1887 Agostino Depretis
1887–1891 Francesco Crispi
1891–1892 Antonio di Rudini
1892–1893 Giovanni Giolitti
1893–1896 Francesco Crispi
1896–1898 Antonio di Rudini
1898–1900 Luigi Pelloux
1900–1901 Giuseppe Saracco
1901–1903 Giuseppe Zanardelli
1903–1905 Giovanni Giolitti
1905–1906 Alessandro Fortis
1906 Baron Sydney Sonnino
1906–1909 Giovanni Giolitti
1909–1910 Baron Sydney Sonnino
1910–1911 Luigi Luzzatti
1911–1914 Giovanni Giolitti
1914–1916 Antonio Salandra
1916–1917 Paolo Boselli
1917–1919 Vittorio Emmanuele Orlando
1919–1920 Francesco Saverio Nitti
1920–1921 Giovanni Giolitti
1921–1922 Ivanoe Bonomi
1922 Luigi Facta

1922–1943 Benito Mussolini
1943–1944 Pietro Badoglio
1944–1945 Ivanoe Bonomi
1945 Ferrucio Parri
1945–1953 Alcide de Gasperi
1953–1954 Giuseppe Pella
1954 Amintore Fanfani
1954–1955 Mario Scelba
1955–1957 Antonio Segni
1957–1958 Adone Zoli
1958–1959 Amintore Fanfani
1959–1960 Antonio Segni
1960 Fernando Tambroni
1960–1963 Amintore Fanfani
1963 Giovanni Leone
1963–1968 Aldo Moro
1968 Giovanni Leone
1968–1970 Mariano Rumor
1970–1972 Emilio Colombo
1972–1974 Giulio Andreotti
1974–1976 Aldo Moro
1976–1978 Giulio Andreotti
1979–1980 Francisco Cossiga
1980–1981 Arnaldo Forlani
1981–1982 Giovanni Spadolini
1982–1983 Amintore Fanfani
1983–1987 Bettino Craxi
1987 Amintore Fanfani
1987–1988 Giovanni Goria
1988–1989 Ciriaco de Mita
1989–1992 Giulio Andreotti
1992–1993 Giuliano Amato
1993–1994 Carlo Azeglio Campi
1994 Silvio Berlusconi
1995–1996 Lamberto Dini
1996–1998 Romano Prodi
1998–2000 Massimo D'Alema
2000–2001 Giuliano Amato
2001– Silvio Berlusconi

NOBILITY

Duca, Duchesa
Principe, Principessa
Marchese, Marchesa
Conte, Contessa
Visconte, Viscontessa
Barone, Baronessa

JAPAN

EMPERORS

(Traditional dates for early reigns are estimates)

c. 40–c. 10 BC

	Traditional Date(T.D.)	
	660–658 BC	Jimmu

c. 10 BC–c. 20 CE

	T.D. 581–549 BC	Suizei
c. 20–c. 50,	T.D. 549–510 BC	Annei
c. 50–c. 80,	T.D. 510–475 BC	Itoku
c. 80–c. 110,	T.D. 475–392 BC	Kosho
c. 110–c. 140,	T.D. 392–290 BC	Koan
c. 140–c. 170,	T.D. 290–214 BC	Korei
c. 170–c. 200,	T.D. 214–157 BC	Kogen
c. 200–c. 230,	T.D. 157–97 BC	Kaika
c. 230–c. 259,	T.D. 97–29 BC	Sujin
c. 259–c. 291,	T.D. 29 BC–71 CE	Suinin
c. 291–c. 323,	T.D. 71–131	Keiko
c. 323–c. 356,	T.D. 131–192	Seimu
c. 356–c. 363,	T.D. 192–201	Chuai
c. 363–c. 380,	T.D. 201–270	Jingo
c. 380–c. 395,	T.D. 270–313	Ojin
c. 395–c. 428,	T.D. 313–400	Nintoku
c. 428–c. 433,	T.D. 400–406	Richu
c. 433–c. 438,	T.D. 406–412	Hanzei
c. 438–c. 455,	T.D. 412–454	Inkyo
c. 455–c. 457,	T.D. 454–457	Anko
c. 457–c. 490,	T.D. 457–480	Yuryaku
c. 490–c. 495,	T.D. 480–485	Seinei
c. 495–c. 498,	T.D. 485–488	Kenso
c. 498–c. 504,	T.D. 488–499	Ninken
c. 504–c. 510,	T.D. 499–507	Muretsu
c. 510–c. 534,	T.D. 507–534	Keitai
534–536		Ankan
536–540		Senka
540–572		Kimmei
572–586		Bidatsu
586–588		Yomei
588–593		Sujun
593–629		Suiko
629–642		Jomei
642–645		Kogyoku
645–655		Kotoku

655–662	Saimei (Kogyoku restored)
662–672	Tenchi
672–673	Kobun
673–686	Temmu
686–697	Jito
697–708	Mommu
708–715	Gemmyo
715–724	Gensho
724–749	Shomu
749–759	Koken
759–765	Junnin
765–770	Shotoku (Koken restored)
770–782	Konin
782–806	Kwammu
806–810	Heijo
810–824	Saga
824–834	Junna
834–851	Nimmyo
851–859	Montoku
859–877	Seiwa
877–885	Yozei
885–889	Koko
889–898	Uda
898–931	Daigo
931–947	Shujaku
947–968	Murakami
968–970	Reizei
970–985	Enyu
985–987	Kazan
987–1012	Ichijo
1012–1017	Sanjo
1017–1037	Go-Ichijo
1037–1047	Go-Shujaku
1047–1069	Go-Reizei
1069–1073	Go-Sanjo
1073–1087	Shirakawa
1087–1108	Horikawa
1108–1124	Toba
1124–1142	Sutoku
1142–1156	Konoe
1156–1159	Go-Shirakawa
1159–1166	Nijo
1166–1169	Rokujo
1169–1181	Takakura

1181–1184	Antoku
1184–1199	Go-Toba
1199–1211	Tsuchi-Mikado
1211–1221	Juntoku
1221–1222	Chukyo
1222–1233	Go-Horikawa
1233–1243	Shijo
1243–1247	Go-Saga
1247–1260	Go-Fukakusa
1260–1275	Kameyama
1275–1288	Go-Uda
1288–1299	Fushima
1299–1302	Go-Fushima
1302–1308	Go-Nijo
1308–1319	Hanazono
1319–1331	Go-Daigo
1331–1333	Kogen
1333–1339	Go-Daigo (restored) South only from 1336
1336–1349	Komyo North
1339–1368	Go-Murakami South
1349–1352	Suko North
1352–1372	Go-Kogen North
1368–1373	Chokei South
1372–1384	Go-Enyu North
1373–1392	Go-Kameyama South
1384–1413	Go-Komatu North only until 1392
1413–1429	Shoko
1429–1465	Go-Hanazono
1465–1501	Go-Tsuchi-Mikado
1501–1527	Go-Kashiwabara
1527–1558	Go-Nara
1558–1587	Ogimachi
1587–1612	Go-Yozei
1612–1630	Go-Mizu-no-o
1630–1644	Myosho
1644–1655	Go-Komyo
1655–1663	Go-Saiin
1663–1687	Reigen
1687–1710	Higashiyama
1710–1736	Naka-no-Mikado
1736–1748	Sakuramachi
1748–1763	Momozono
1763–1771	Go-Sakuramachi
1771–1780	Go-Momozono
1780–1817	Kokaku

1817–1847	Ninko
1847–1867	Komei
1867–1912	Meiji (Mutsuhito)
1912–1926	Taisho (Yoshihito)
1926–1989	Showa (Hirohito)
1989–	Heisei (Akihito)

MINAMOTO SHOGUNS

1192–1199	Yoritomo Minamoto
1199–1203	Yori-ie Minamoto
1203–1219	Sanemoto Minamoto

FUJIWARA SHOGUNS

1220–1244	Yoritsune Fujiwara
1244–1251	Yoritsugu Fujiwara

IMPERIAL SHOGUNS

1251–1266	Munetaka
1266–1289	Koreyasu
1289–1308	Hisakira
1308–1333	Morikune

ASHIKAGA SHOGUNS

1338–1358	Takauji Ashikaga
1358–1367	Yoshiaki Ashikaga
1367–1395	Yoshimitsu Ashikaga
1395–1423	Yoshimochi Ashikaga
1423–1428	Yoshikazu Ashikaga
1428–1441	Yoshinori Ashikaga
1441–1443	Yoshikatsu Ashikaga
1443–1474	Yoshimasa Ashikaga
1474–1490	Yoshihisa Ashikaga
1490–1493	Yoshitane Ashikaga
1493–1508	Yoshizume Ashikaga
1508–1521	Yoshitsane Ashikaga (Yoshitane restored)
1521–1545	Yoshiharu Ashikaga
1545–1565	Yoshiteru Ashikaga
1565–1568	Yoshihide Ashikaga
1568–1573	Yoshiaki Ashikaga

TOKUGAWA SHOGUNS

1603–1605 Ieyasu Tokugawa
1605–1623 Hidetada Tokugawa
1623–1651 Iemitsu Tokugawa
1651–1680 Ietsuna Tokugawa
1680–1709 Tsunayoshi Tokugawa
1709–1713 Ienobu Tokugawa
1713–1716 Ietsugu Tokugawa
1716–1745 Yoshimune Tokugawa
1745–1761 Ieshige Tokugawa
1761–1787 Ieharu Tokugawa
1787–1838 Ienari Tokugawa
1838–1853 Ieyoshi Tokugawa
1853–1858 Iesada Tokugawa
1858–1866 Iemochi Tokugawa
1866–1867 Yoshinobu Tokugawa

PRIME MINISTERS

1885–1888 Hirobumi Ito
1888–1889 Kiyotaka Kuroda
1889–1891 Aritomo Yamagata
1891–1892 Masayoshi Matsukata
1892–1896 Hirobumi Ito
1896–1898 Masayoshi Matsukata
1898 Hirobumi Ito
1898 Shigenbu Okuma
1898–1900 Aritomo Yamagata
1900–1901 Hirobumi Ito
1901–1906 Taro Katsura
1906–1908 Kimmochi Saionji
1908–1911 Taro Katsura
1911–1912 Kimmochi Saionji
1912–1913 Taro Katsura
1913–1914 Gonnohyoe Yamamoto
1914–1916 Shigenobu Okuma
1916–1918 Masatake Terauchi
1918–1921 Takashi Hara
1921–1922 Korekiyo Takahashi
1922–1923 Tomosaburo Kato
1923–1924 Gonnohyoe Yamamoto
1924 Keigo Kiyoura
1924–1926 Takaaki Kato
1926–1927 Reijiro Wakatsuki
1927–1929 Giichi Tanaka
1929–1931 Osachi Hamaguchi

1931 Reijiro Wakatsuki
1931–1932 Tsuyoshi Inukai
1932–1934 Makoto Saito
1934–1936 Keisuke Okada
1936–1937 Koki Hirota
1937 Senjuro Hayashi
1937–1939 Fumimaro Konoe
1939 Kiichiro Hiranuma
1939–1940 Nobuyuki Abe
1940 Mitsumasa Yonai
1940–1941 Fumimaro Konoe
1941–1944 Hideki Tojo
1944–1945 Kuniaki Koiso
1945 Kantaro Suzuki
1945 Naruhiko Higashikuni
1945–1946 Kijuro Shidehara
1946–1947 Shigeru Yoshida
1947–1948 Tetsu Katayama
1948 Hitoshi Ashida
1948–1954 Shigeru Yoshida
1954–1956 Ichiro Hatoyama
1956–1957 Tanzan Ishibashi
1957–1960 Nobusuke Kishi
1960–1964 Hayato Ikeda
1964–1972 Eisaku Sato
1972–1974 Kakuei Tanaka
1974–1976 Takeo Miki
1976–1978 Takeo Fukuda
1978–1980 Masayoshi Ohira
1980–1982 Zenko Suzuki
1982–1987 Yasuhiro Nakasone
1987–1989 Noburu Takeshita
1989 Sasuke Uno
1989–1991 Toshiki Kaifu
1991–1993 Kiichi Miyazama
1993–1994 Morihiro Hosokawa
1995–1996 Tomiichi Murayama
1996–1998 Ryutaro Hashimoto
1998–2000 Keizo Obuchi
2000– Yoshiro Mori

HISTORICAL PERIODS

Yamato, c. 300–592 AD, conquest of
the Yamato plain
Asuka, 592–710, accession of the
Empress Suiko

Nara, 710–794, completion of the
  Heijo; capital moves to Nagaoka
Heian, 794–1192, completion of
  Heian (Kyoto)
  Fujiwara, 858–1160, Fujiwara-no-
  Yoshifusa becomes regent
  Taira, 1160–1185, Taira-no-
  Kiyomori assumes control
Kamakura, 1192–1333, Yoritomo
  becomes shogun
Namboku, 1334–1392, restoration of
  Emperor Godaigo
Ashikaga, 1338–1573, Ashikaga
  Takauji becomes shogun
  Muromachi, 1392–1573, unification
  of Southern and Northern Courts
  Sengoku, 1467–1600, beginning of
  Onin war
Momoyama, 1573–1603, Nobunaga
  deposes last Ashikaga shogun
Edo, 1603–1867, Ieyasu becomes
  shogun
Meiji, 1868–1912, Emperor Mutsuhito
Taisho, 1912–1926, Emperor Yoshihito
Showa, 1926–1989, Emperor Hirohito
Heisei, 1989– , Emperor Akihito

MEDIEVAL EUROPE

FEUDAL SYSTEM

(manorial system)

King (all land ultimately held by him)
Vassals/Nobles (held land from the
  king and in turn leased it to lesser
  nobles, etc)
Lesser Nobles
Dukes
Counts
Knights (mounted warriors who were
  granted a fief to support
  themselves and their entourage)
Squire
Seigneur or Suzerain (lord of the
  manor)

Villeins and Serfs (held land from the
  lord of the manor, surrendered
  their freedom and were bound to
  the fief, worked for the lord, paid
  rent and dues to him)
Free peasants or freemen (lived on
  fief and paid rent and dues to the
  lord)

English Feudal System

King (leased land, known as fief)
Lords or Overlords (tenants in chief)
Vassals (or Tenants) (took oath of
    loyalty and pledge of military
    service on request)
  Mesne (intermediate tenants)
  In demesne (tenants who actually
    managed the property)
Knights (owing service to overlord)
  Squire: age 14 to approx. 21, in
    training, first becoming:
    Shieldbearer or Ecuyer or
    Armiger or Bannerbearer
  or
    Damoiseau or Lordling or Varlet
    or Valet (attendants)
  Page (age 7–13, in training)
Stewards (managed secondary
    manors)
Priests
Scholars
Townsmen (merchants and
    craftsmen)
Servants (owned by nobility and
    wealthy merchants)
Serfs (peasants who worked the land
    for the lords)

MEXICO

GOVERNORS

Emperor

1822–1823 Agustin de Iturbide

MEXICO

Presidents

1824–1829	Guadelupe Victoria
1829	Vicente Guerrero
1829	Jose Maria de Bocanegra
1829–1830	Triumvirate (Lucas Alaman, Luis Quintanar, Pedro Velez)
1830–1832	Anastasio Bustamente
1832	Melchor Muzquiz
1832–1833	Manuel Gomez Pedraza
1833	Valentin Gomez Farias
1833–1835	Antonio Lopez de Santa Anna
1835–1836	Miguel Barragan
1836–1837	Jose Justo Corro
1837–1839	Anastasio Bustamente
1839	Antonio Lopez de Santa Anna
1839	Nicolas Bravo
1839–1841	Anastasio Bustamente
1841	Javier Echeverria
1841–1842	Antonio Lopez de Santa Anna
1842–1843	Nicolas Bravo
1843	Antonio Lopez de Santa Anna
1843–1844	Valentin Canalizo
1844	Antonio Lopez de Santa Anna
1844–1846	Jose Joaquin de Herrera
1846	Mariano Paredes y Arrillaga
1846	Nicolas Bravo
1846	Mariano Salas
1846–1847	Valentin Gomez Farias
1847	Antonio Lopez de Santa Anna
1847	Pedro Maria Anaya
1847	Antonio Lopez de Santa Anna
1847–1848	Manuel de la Pena y Pena
1848–1851	Jose Joaquin de Herrera
1851–1853	Mariano Arista
1853	Juan Bautista Ceballos
1853	Manuel Maria Lombardini
1853–1855	Antonio Lopez de Santa Anna
1855	Martin Carrera
1855	Romulo Diaz de la Vega
1855	Juan Alvarez
1855–1858	Ignacio Comonfort
1858–1864	Benito Pablo Juarez
1858	Felix Zuloaga Rival President
1858–1859	Manuel Robles Pezuala Rival President
1859–1860	Mariano Salas Rival Acting President
1860	Miguel Miramon Rival President
1860	Jose Ignacio Pavon Rival President
1860	Miguel Miramon Rival Acting President

Emperor

| 1864–1867 | Maximilian of Habsburg |

Presidents

1867–1872	Benito Pablo Juarez
1872–1876	Sebastian Lerdo de Tejada (Jose de la Cruz) Porfirio Diaz
1876–1877	Juan N. Mendez
1876–1877	Jose Maria Iglesias Rival President
1877–1880	(Jose de la Cruz) Porfirio Diaz
1880–1884	Manuel Gonzalez
1884–1911	(Jose de la Cruz) Porfirio Diaz
1911	Francisco Leon de la Barra
1911–1913	Francisco I Madero
1913–1914	Victoriano Huerta
1914	Francisco Carvajal
1914	Venustiano Carranza
1914–1915	Eulalio Gutierrez
1915	Roque Gonzalez Garza
1915	Francisco Lagos Chazaro
1917–1920	Venustiano Carranza
1920	Adolfo de la Huerta

1920–1924 Alvaro Obregon
1924–1928 Plutarco Elias Calles
1928–1930 Emilio Portes Gil
1930–1932 Pascual Ortiz Rubio
1932–1934 Abelardo L. Rodriguez
1934–1940 Lazaro Cardenas
1940–1946 Manuel Avila Camacho
1946–1952 Miguel Aleman
1952–1958 Adolfo Ruiz Cortines
1958–1964 Adolfo Lopez Mateos
1964–1970 Gustavo Diaz Ordaz
1970–1976 Luis Echeverria
1976–1982 Jose Lopez Portillo
1982–1988 Miguel de la Madrid Hurtado
1988–1993 Carlos Salinas de Gortari
1993–2000 Ernesto Zedillo
2000– Vicente Fox Quesada

NETHERLANDS

STADTHOLDER OF THE NETHERLANDS

House of Orange

1572–1584 Willem (William) I 'the Silent' of Nassau
1584–1625 Maurice
1625–1647 Frederik Henrik
1647–1650 Willem II
1650–1672 (no stadtholder)
1672–1702 Willem (William) III (king of England and Scotland from 1689)
1702–1747 (no stadtholder)
1747–1751 Willem IV (Charles Henry Friso)
1751–1795 Willem V
1795–1806 (Batavian Republic)

MONARCHS— KINGDOM OF HOLLAND

House of Bonaparte

1806–1810 Lodewijk (Louis Bonaparte)

1810–1813 (French rule)

MONARCHS— KINGDOM OF THE NETHERLANDS

House of Orange (Restored)

1813–1840 Willem I
1840–1849 Willem II
1849–1890 Willem III
1890–1948 Wilhelmina (Queen Emma, regent to 1898)
1948–1980 Juliana
1980– Beatrix

NORWAY

MONARCHS—YNGLING DYNASTY

c. 870–c. 940 Harald I Halfdanarson 'Fine/Fairhair'
c. 940–c. 945 Erik Haraldsson 'Bloodaxe'
c. 945–c. 960 Haakon I Haraldsson 'the Good'
c. 960–c. 970 Harald II Eriksson 'Greycloak'
c. 970–c. 995 Haakon, Jarl of Lade
c. 995–1000 Olaf I Tryggvason
1000–1015 Erik, Jarl of Lade
1015–1028 Olaf II Haraldsson (St. Olaf)
1028–1035 Svein Knutsson
1035–1047 Magnus I Olafsson 'the Good'
1047–1066 Harald III Sigurdsson 'Hardrada' (the Ruthless)
1066–1093 Olaf III Haraldsson 'the Peaceful' (joint ruler to 1069)
1066–1069 Magnus II (joint ruler)
1093–1103 Magnus III Olafsson 'Barelegs'
1103–1130 Sigurd I Magnusson 'the Crusader' (joint ruler to 1122)

1103–1115	Olaf Magnusson (joint ruler)
1103–1122	Eystein I Magnusson (joint ruler)
1130–1135	Magnus IV 'the Blind' (joint ruler)
1130–1136	Harald IV Gille (joint ruler to 1135)
1136–1161	Inge I (joint ruler to 1157)
1136–1155	Sigurd II (joint ruler)
1142–1157	Eystein II (joint ruler)
1161–1162	Haakon II
1162–1184	Magnus V Erlingsson
1184–1202	Sverrir Sigurdsson
1202–1204	Haakon III
1204	Gutorm Sigurdsson
1204–1217	Inge II Baardsson
1217–1263	Haakon IV Haakonsson 'the Old'
1263–1280	Magnus VI Haakonsson 'the Law-Reformer'
1280–1299	Erik II
1299–1319	Haakon V
1319–1343	(as Sweden)
1343–1380	Haakon VI
1130–1136	Harald IV Gille (joint ruler)

DANISH KINGS

1380–1387	Olaf IV (V of Denmark)
1387–1397	Margrethe I (Margareta)
1397–1814	(as Denmark)
1814–1905	(as Sweden)

HOUSE OF OLDENBURG

1905–1957	Haakon VII
1957–1991	Olaf V
1991–	Harald V

PRE-COLUMBIAN CIVILIZATIONS

AZTEC CASTES AND CLASSES

castes (a number of social classes within these three, according to wealth, occupation, and political office)

pipiltin (plural of pilli)
   nobles by birth and members of the royal lineage
   priestly and bureaucratic class (administration of the empire)
   warriors earning this rank
maceualtin: commoners
   (commoners who had captured four enemy warriors were promoted to rank of tlalmaitl; certain occupations accorded higher prestige than others—merchants (pochteca), lapidarians, goldsmiths, featherworkers and all urban occupations had higher status than rural farming
mayeques: slaves / serfs attached to rural estates
   pawns (indentured servants who could buy their freedom)
   slaves

AZTEC POLITICAL SYSTEM

Emperor
State (approximately 50–60 square miles)
   tlatoani (head of state)
   staff of professional administrators (including calpixque, or tax collectors)
Calpulli/barrio/ward (a number of households organized into an internally complex group—physical, territorial, and socially organized unit; unit of political

administration within the
state and also a military
regiment)
Chief
Council of heads of households;
served the tlatoani (military
service)
Territorial subdivisions/barrios
pequeños ("little wards")
Nuclear family

tax collector-governor
garrison

AZTEC RULERS

King of Tenochtitlan

1372–1391	Acamapichtli
1391–1415	Huitzilihuitl
1415–1426	Chimalpopoca
1426–1440	Itzcoatl
1440–1468	Moctezuma I Ilhuicamina
1468–1481	Axayacatl
1481–1486	Tizoc
1486–1502	Ahuitzotl
1502–1520	Moctezuma II Xocoyotzin
1520	Cuitlahuac
1520–1521	Cuauhtemoc
1521–1821	Spanish rule

RULERS OF TEXOCO

c. 1300–c. 1357	Quinatzin
c. 1357–c. 1409	Techotlala
c. 1409–1418	Ixlilxochitl
1418–1426	Tezozomoc
1426–1428	Maxtla
1431–1472	Nezahualcoyotl
1472–1515	Nezahualpilli
1515–1520	Cacma
1520–1521	Coanacochtzin

ORGANIZATION OF THE PROVINCES:

state
  provinces
    capital

INCAN CIVILIZATION

Political (organized by tens; for every
10,000 people there were 1,331
officials)

emperor (absolute power) of
Tahuantinsuyu ("Land of the
Four Quarters")
court of administrators and
advisors
Four Quarters (subdivided into
complex tributary systems;
waranga = 1,000 tributaries)
apos (governor rulers of the Four
Quarters, each with 10 districts;
resided in Cuzco)
curacas (local leaders who resided
in provinces and made up the
bulk of the administrative class)
homokorakas (district governors who
ruled 10,000 people each)
mallcu (headman of a large village
who ruled 10 foremen)
pacha-koraka (foreman/straw boss
who ruled 10 groups of workers)
ayulla (extended family landholding)
puric (able-bodied, tax-paying
Indian)

Social

emperor
royal family/rulers
upper aristocracy/nobles
imperial administrators
petty nobility
commoners (farm laborers, some
artisans)
special group of craftspeople and
servants

INCA SOCIAL HIERARCHIES

cacique (head of community
    comprised of a group of ayllu)
ayllu (Inca community, localized
    group which traced descent
    patrilineally)
    upper
    lower

*also, an age-grade system of 12
ranks, in which persons passed from
one social status to another according
to age*

*also, land for each ayllu divided
into three unequal parts: largest part
for farming, other two for cult of the
sun and one for the state*

MAYAN CIVILIZATION

(in Formative Period)

king (all-powerful)
two-class system
    elite priestly class of stargazers,
    calendar keepers, rulers
    (representatives of ruling
    dynasty), nobles, priests, and
    warriors)
    large class of peasantry who
    worked in the fields and
    supported the elite with labor
    and produce (artists, artisans,
    traders; peasants, slaves, bearers,
    laborers)

PRE-COLUMBIAN TIME PERIODS

Pre-Classic and Classic periods
    Early hunters to 6500 BC
    Beginning of agriculture, 6500 BC
    Early Formative Period, 1500–900
      BC
    Middle Formative Period, 900–300
      BC
    Late Formative Period, 300 BC- CE

    100
Early Classic Period, 100–600
Late Classic non-Maya Meso-
    America, 600–900
Late Classic lowlands Maya,
    600–900
Post-Classic Period, 900–1519

ROMANS—ANCIENT

SOCIAL ORDERS

Patricians (descended from early
    landowners and political leaders)
Equites/businessmen (qualified for
    this class by property holding)
Plebeians/commoners (poor farmers
    and traders)
Capite censi/Proletarii (citizens who
    were free, but poor and not allowed
    to vote)
Slave (could become a Proletarii)

OCCUPANTS OF ROMAN TERRITORY:

cives=Roman citizens
peregrini=foreigners
provincials=people who lived outside
    Rome itself but within Roman
    territory; did not have full rights of
    Romans
slaves=owned by other people; no
    freedom or rights

ROMAN ARMY

Ranks

Imperator or General (leader of an
    army of several legions)
Legate (aide to general)
Tribune (commander of one legion)
Company Officer (2 to a maniple)
Centurion (leader or officer of a
    century or maniple)
    Senior

Junior
Contubernalis (cadet)
Aquilifer (finest soldier in legion)
Imaginifer (bearer of image of the
    emperor)
Signifer (standard-bearer)
Legionary or Trooper (common
    infantryman or cavalry)
Sagitarii (archer)
Cornicen (trumpeter)
Auxiliary (reservist)
Calo (non-combatant servant)

Battle Line, rear to front

velites: youthful novices
triarii: older men with light infantry
principes: seasoned veterans
hastati: men with some battle
    experience

ROMAN REPUBLIC CLASS SYSTEM

populus Romanus: free inhabitants
    with voting privileges in the
    Comitia or Assembly
Latins: belonged to cities having the
    "Latin franchise", the cities of
    Latium that were conquered; fairly
    easy to gain full Roman citizenship
Italians or socii: inhabitants of allied
    and dependent states; no share in
    political affairs

ROMAN REPUBLIC STRUCTURE

Legislative branch:

Senate (300 men chosen from ex-
    magistrates by the censors)
Concilium Plebis (people's assembly)

Magistrates:

2 consuls (elected annually from
    candidates proposed by the
    Senate to the comitia centuriata
    [law-passing assembly]; presided
    over Senate and were supreme
    commanders in war)
2–8 praetors (judges/administrators
    of law)
    praetor urbanus (worked in Rome)
    praetor peregrinus (worked
        abroad)
4 quaestors (in charge of finances)
2 censors (supervised contracts,
    public morals)
aediles (responsible for streets,
    temples, public works, grain
    supply, public games)
prefects (leader of a decury, a group
    of 10 lictors)
lictors (civil servants who preceded
    the consuls and praetors, clearing
    the way and carrying fasces, the
    symbol of office)
10 tribunes (advocates for the
    plebeians, with veto power over
    magistrates and laws)

KINGS

753–716 BC	Romulus
716–672 BC	Numa Pompilius
672–640 BC	Tullus Hostilius
640–616 BC	Ancus Marcius
616–578 BC	Lucius Tarquinius Priscus
578–534 BC	Servius Tullius
534–509 BC	Lucius Tarquinius Superbus

(Republic, 509–30 BC)

EMPERORS

30 BC–14 AD	Augustus (Gaius Julius Caesar Octavianus)
14–37	Tiberius (Tiberius Julius Caesar Augustus)
37–41	Caligula (Gaius Julius Caesar Germanicus)
41–54	Claudius I (Tiberius

Claudius Nero
Germanicus)

54–68 Nero (Lucius
Domitius
Ahenobarbus)

68–69 (Servius Sulcipius)
Galba

69 (Marcus Salvius) Otho

69 (Aulus) Vitellius

69–79 Vespasian (Titus
Flavius Vespasianus)

79–81 Titus (Flavius Sabinus
Vespasianus)

81–96 Domitian (Titus
Flavius Domitianus)

96–98 (Marcus Cocceius)
Nerva

98–117 Trajan (Marcus Ulpius
Trajanus)

117–138 Hadrian (Publius
Aelius Hadrianus)

138–161 (Titus Aurelius
Fulvus) Antoninus
Pius

161–180 Marcus Aurelius
(Verus)

161–169 (Lucius Aurelius)
Verus Joint Emperor

180–192 (Marcus Aurelius
Antoninus)
Commodus

193 (Publius Helvius)
Pertinax

193 (Marcus) Didius
Julianus

193–211 (Lucius Septimius)
Severus

193–194 Gaius Pescennius
Niger Rival Emperor

193–197 Decimus Clodius
Albinus Rival
Emperor

211–217 (Marcus Aurelius
Antoninus) Caracalla

211–212 Publius Septimius
Antoninus Geta Joint

Emperor

217–218 (Marcus Opellius)
Macrinus

218–222 Heliogabalus (Varius
Avitus Bassianus)

222–235 (Marcus Aurelius)
Alexander Severus

235–238 (Gaius Julius)
Maximinus

238 Gordian I (Marcus
Antonius Gordianus)

238 Gordian II (Marcus
Antonius Gordianus)
Joint Emperor

238 (Marcus Clodius)
Pupienus

238 (Decimus Caelius)
Balbinus

238–244 Gordian III (Marcus
Antonius Gordianus
Pius)

244–249 Philip the Arab
(Marcus Julius
Philippus Arabs)

249–251 (Gaius Messius
Quintus Trajanus)
Decius

251–253 (Gaius Vibius
Trebonianus) Gallus
Joint Emperor

251–253 (Gaius Vibius)
Volusianus Joint
Emperor

253 (Marcus Aemilius)
Aemilianus

253–260 Valerian (Publius
Licinius Valerianus)
Joint Emperor

253–268 (Publius Licinius)
Gallienus Joint
Emperor

260–269 (Marcus Latinius)
Postumus Emperor in
Gaul

260–261 (Titus Fulvius)
Macrianus Rival

Emperor

260–261 Titus Fulvius Quietus Rival Emperor

268–270 (Marcus Aurelius) Claudius II Gothicus

269 Lucius Aelianus Emperor in Gaul

269 Marcus Aurelius Marius Emperor in Gaul

269–270 (Marcus Piavonius) Victorinus Emperor in Gaul

270 (Marcus Aurelius) Quintillus

270–275 Aurelian (Lucius Domitius Aurelianus)

270–274 (Gaius Pius) Tetricus I Emperor in Gaul

274 (Gaius Pius) Tetricus II Emperor in Gaul

275–276 (Marcus Claudius) Tacitus

276 (Marcus Annius) Florianus

276–282 (Marcus Aurelius) Probus

282–283 (Marcus Aurelius) Carus

283–285 (Marcus Aurelius) Carinus Joint Emperor until 284

283–284 (Marcus Aurelius) Numerianus Joint Emperor

284–305 Diocletian (Gaius Aurelius Diocletianus) Joint Emperor (East)

286–305 Maximian (Marcus Aurelius Maximianus) Joint Emperor (West)

286–293 (Marcus Aurelius) Carausius Emperor in Britain

293–296 Allectus Emperor in Britain

305–306 (Marcus Flavius) Constantius Chlorus Joint Emperor (West)

305–311 (Gaius) Galerius (Valerius Maximianus) Joint Emperor (East)

306–308 Maximian (Marcus Aurelius Maximianus) (restored as Rival Emperor-West)

306–312 (Marcus Aurelius) Maxentius Rival Emperor (West)

306–337 Constantine I 'the Great' (Flavius Valerius Aurelius Constantinus) Joint Emperor (West) until 324

307–324 (Gaius Flavius Valerius) Licinius Joint Emperor (East)

308–313 (Galerius Valerius) Maximianus Daia Joint Emperor (East)

337–340 Constantine II (Flavius Valerius Claudius Constantinus) Joint Emperor

337–350 (Flavius Valerius Julius) Constans I Joint Emperor (West)

337–361 (Flavius Valerius Julius) Constantius II Joint Emperor (East) until 350 and from 360

350–353 (Flavius Magnus) Magnentius Rival Emperor

360–363 Julian 'the Apostate' (Flavius Claudius Julianus) Joint Emperor until 361

363–364	Jovian (Flavius Claudius Jovianus)
364–375	Valentinian I (Flavius Valentinianus) Joint Emperor (West)
364–378	(Flavius) Valens Joint Emperor (East)
367–383	Gratian (Augustus Gratianus) Joint Emperor (West)
375–392	Valentinian II (Flavius Valentinianus) Joint Emperor (West)
379–395	(Flavius) Theodosius I 'the Great' Joint Emperor (East)
383–388	Magnus (Clemens) Maximus Joint Emperor (West)
392–394	Eugenius Joint Emperor (West)

Western Empire

395–423	(Flavius) Honorius
407–411	Constantine III (Flavius Claudius Constantinus) Joint Emperor
421	(Flavius) Constantius III Joint Emperor
423–425	Johannes
425–455	Valentinian III (Flavius Placidius Valentinianus)
455	(Flavius Ancius) Petronius Maximus
455–456	(Flavius Maecilius Eparchius) Avitus
457–461	(Julius Valerius) Majorianus
461–465	(Libius Severianus) Severus
467–472	(Procopius) Anthemius
472	(Anicius) Olybrius
473–474	(Flavius) Glycerius
474–475	Julius Nepos
475–476	(Flavius Momyllus) Romulus Augustus

ROMAN TRIUMVIRATES

First Triumvirate, 60 BC

(informal understanding)

Julius Caesar
Marcus Licinius Crassus
Pompey

Second Triumvirate, 43 BC

(absolute, dictatorial authority)

Marcus Aemilius Lepidus
Mark Antony
Octavian (Octavius, later Augustus)

RUSSIA

ARMY RANKS OF SOVIET UNION

Officers

Generalissimo of the Soviet Union
Marshal of the Soviet Union
Chief Marshal
Marshal
General of the Army
Colonel General
Lieutenant General
Major General
Colonel
Lieutenant Colonel
Major
Captain
Senior Lieutenant
Lieutenant
Junior Lieutenant

Enlisted personnel

Praporshchik
Glav Starshina
Starshina

Senior Sergeant
Sergeant
Corporal
Private

COMMUNIST PARTY OF THE SOVIET UNION (CPSU)

General Secretary (highest office)
Secretariat
Politburo (chosen by Central
    Committee)
Central Committee (elected by
    Congress)
All-Union Congress (supreme
    policymaking body)
committees:
    republic
    regional
    district
    city
    rural
cells (primary party organizations)

POLITICAL ORGANIZATION OF SOVIET UNION

(Soviets dissolved in 1993 and reorganized as smaller dumas / assemblies)

Supreme Soviet
peasants' soviets
    central executive committee
soldiers' soviets
    central executive committee
workers' soviets
    central executive committee

GRAND DUKES OF MOSCOW

House of Riurik

1283–1303	Daniel
1303–1325	Yuri
1325–1341	Ivan I Kalita
1341–1353	Semeon

1353–1359	Ivan II
1359–1389	Dmitri I Donskoy
1389–1425	Vasily I
1425–1462	Vasily II
1462–1472	Ivan III 'the Great'

RULERS

House of Riurk

1472–1505	Ivan III 'the Great'
1505–1533	Vasily III
1533–1547	Ivan IV 'the Terrible'

TSARS

House of Riurik

1547–1584	Ivan IV 'the Terrible'
1584–1598	Fedor I
1598–1605	Boris Godunov
1605	Fedor II
1605–1606	Dmitri II (The 'false Dmitri')
1606–1610	Vasily IV Shuisky
1610–1613	Civil war

House of Romanov

1613–1645	Mikhail (Michael Romanov)
1645–1676	Alexei I Mihailovitch
1676–1682	Fedor III
1682–1725	Peter I 'the Great' Joint ruler to 1696
1682–1696	Ivan V Joint ruler
1725–1727	Catherine I
1727–1730	Peter II
1730–1740	Anna Ivovna
1740–1741	Ivan VI
1741–1762	Elizabeth Petrovna
1762	Peter III
1762–1796	Catherine II 'the Great'
1796–1801	Paul
1801–1825	Alexander I
1825–1855	Nicholas I
1855–1881	Alexander II 'the Liberator'

1881–1894	Alexander III
1894–1917	Nicholas II

PRESIDENTS

1917	Lev Borisovich Kamenev
1917–1919	Yakov Mikhailovich Sverlov
1919–1946	Mikhail Ivanovich Kalinin
1946–1953	Nikolai Mikhailovich Shvernik
1953–1960	Klimenti Efremovich Voroshilov
1960–1964	Leonid Ilyich Brezhnev
1964–1965	Anastas Ivanovich Mikoyan
1965–1977	Nikolai Viktorovich Podgorny
1977–1982	Leonid Ilyich Brezhnev
1982–1983	Vasily Vasiliyevich Kuznetsov
1983–1984	Yuri Vladimirovich Andropov
1984	Vasily Vasiliyevich Kuznetsov
1984–1985	Konstantin Ustinovich Chernenko
1985	Vasily Vasiliyevich Kuznetsov
1985–1988	Andrei Andreevich Gromyko
1988–1990	Mikhail Sergeevich Gorbachev

EXECUTIVE PRESIDENT

1990–1991	Mikhail Sergeevich Gorbachev

RUSSIAN FEDERATION

Presidents

1991–1999	Boris Yeltsin
1999–	Vladimir Putin

Prime Ministers

1991–1992	Yegor Gaidar
1992–1998	Victor Chernomyrdin
1998–1999	Yugeny Primakov
1999–1999	Sergey Stephashin
1999–2000	Vladimir Putin
2000–	Mikhail Kasynov

SPAIN

NOBILITY

Duque, Duquesa
Principe, Principesa
Marques, Marquesa
Conde, Condesa
Visconde, Viscondesa
Baron, Baronesa

SPANISH MONARCHS

1516–1556	Charles I (Holy Roman Emperor)
1556–1598	Phillip II
1598–1621	Phillip III
1621–1665	Philip IV
1665–1700	Charles II
1700–1724	Philip V
1724	Louis I
1724–1746	Philip V
1746–1759	Ferdinand VI
1759–1788	Charles III
1788–1808	Charles IV
1808	Ferdinand VII
1808–1813	Joseph Bonaparte
1814–1833	Ferdinand VII
1833–1868	Isabella II
1870–1873	Amadeo
1875–1885	Alfonso XII
1886–1931	Alfonso XIII
1975–	Juan Carlos I

TURKEY

OTTOMAN EMPIRE

Sultans

1299–1326	Osman I

1326–1359	Orkhan
1359–1389	Murad I
1389–1403	Bayezit I
1403–1421	Mehmet I Rival sultan to 1413
1403–1410	Suleyman I Rival sultan
1410–1413	Musa Rival sultan
1421–1444	Murad II
1444–1446	Mehmet II 'the Conqueror'
1446–1451	Murad II (restored)
1451–1481	Mehmet II 'the Conqueror' (restored)
1481–1512	Bayezit II
1512–1520	Selim I 'the Grim'
1520–1566	Suleyman II 'the Magnificent'
1566–1574	Selim II
1574–1595	Murad III
1595–1603	Mehmet III
1603–1617	Ahmet I
1617–1618	Mustafa I
1618–1622	Osman II
1622–1623	Mustafa I (restored)
1623–1640	Murad IV
1640–1648	Ibrahim
1648–1687	Mehmet IV
1687–1691	Suleyman III
1691–1695	Ahmet II
1695–1703	Mustafa II
1703–1730	Ahmet III
1730–1754	Mahmut I
1754–1757	Osman III
1757–1774	Mustafa III
1774–1789	Abd-ul-Hamid I
1789–1807	Selim III
1807–1808	Mustafa IV
1808–1839	Mahmut II
1839–1861	Abd-ul-Medjid
1861–1876	Abdul-Aziz
1876	Murad V
1876–1909	Abd-ul-Hamid II
1909–1918	Mehmet V Resat
1918–1922	Mehmet VI Vahideddin

REPUBLIC OF TURKEY

Presidents

1923–1938	Mustafa Kemal Ataturk
1938–1950	Ismet Paza Inonu
1950–1960	Celal Bayar
1961–1966	Cemal Gursel
1966–1973	Cevdet Sunay
1973–1980	Fahri S. Koruturk
1982–1989	Kenan Evren
1989–1993	Turgut Ozal
1993–2000	Suleyman Demirel
2000–	Ahmet Necdet Sezer

UNITED NATIONS

SECRETARY GENERALS

1946–1953	Trygve Halvdan Lie (Norway)
1953–1961	Dag Hjalmar Agne Carl Hammarskjold (Sweden)
1962–1971	U Thant (Burma)
1971–1981	Kurt Waldheim (Austria)
1982–1992	Javier Perez de Cuellar (Peru)
1992–1997	Boutros Boutros Ghali (Egypt)
1997–	Kofi Annan (Ghana)

UNITED STATES

CIVIL WAR NAVY RANKS

Union:

Rear Admiral (no equivalent in Confederacy)
Commodore
Captain
Commander
Lieutenant Commander (no equivalent in Confederacy)
Lieutenant
Master
Ensign

Confederacy:

Flag Officer
Captain
Commander
Lieutenant
Master
Passed Midshipman

CONTINENTAL (REGULAR) ARMY OF REVOLUTIONARY WAR

(Before the Continental Congress in 1778, each state prescribed its own organizational table and, although there were similarities, each was different.)

Artillery

Commander in Chief
General
Major General
Brigadier General
Quartermaster General
Adjutant General
Deputy Adjutant General
Colonel
Lieutenant Colonel
Major
Captain
Captain Lieutenant
First Lieutenant
Second Lieutenant
Ensign
Sergeant Major
Sergeant
Corporal
Drum Major
Fife Major
Drummer/Fifer
(also Chaplain, Adjutant, Regimental Quartermaster, Surgeon, Surgeon's Mate, Quartermaster's Sergeant, Paymaster)
(also Commissary, Clerk, Conductor, Bombardier, Gunner, Matross, Cadet, Bandsman)

(Artillery Artificers [artillery shop]: carpenters, blacksmiths, wheelwrights, tinners, turners, harness makers, coopers, nailers, farriers)

CAVALRY

Regiment:

Colonel
Lieutenant colonel
Major
Adjutant
 chaplain
 quartermaster
 surgeon
 surgeon's mate
 ridingmaster
 paymaster
 riding master
 trumpet major
 saddler
 sergeant major
 supernumeraries

troop members:

Captain
Lieutenant
Cornet (carried colors for cavalry)
Quartermaster sergeant
Orderly or Drill sergeant
Trumpeter
Farrier (blacksmith)
Corporal
Dragoon (mounted infantryman with short musket)
Private
Armorer (upkeep of small arms, ammunition)

ROOSEVELT'S FOUR FREEDOMS

(State of the Union, 1941, President Franklin D. Roosevelt)

1. freedom of speech and expression

2. freedom of the individual to worship God in his own way
3. freedom from want
4. freedom from fear

STATES

Admission of 13 Original States
(ratification of the Constitution)

1. Delaware (12-7-1787)
2. Pennsylvania (12-12-1787)
3. New Jersey (12-18-1787)
4. Georgia (1-2-1788)
5. Connecticut (1-9-1788)
6. Massachusetts (2-6-1788)
7. Maryland (4-28-1788)
8. South Carolina (5-23-1788)
9. New Hampshire (6-21-1788)
10. Virginia (6-25-1788)
11. New York (7-26-1788)
12. North Carolina (11-21-1789)
13. Rhode Island (5-29-1790)

Admission of States to Union
(admission date/readmission after Civil War)

1. Delaware (1787)
2. Pennsylvania (1787)
3. New Jersey (1787)
4. Georgia (1788/1868,1870)
5. Connecticut (1788)
6. Massachusetts (1788)
7. Maryland (1788)
8. South Carolina (1788/1868)
9. New Hampshire (1788)
10. Virginia (1788/1870)
11. New York (1788)
12. North Carolina (1789/1868)
13. Rhode Island (1790)
14. Vermont (1791)
15. Kentucky (1792)
16. Tennessee (1796)
17. Ohio (1803)
18. Louisiana (1812/1868)
19. Indiana (1816)
20. Mississippi (1817/1870)
21. Illinois (1818)
22. Alabama (1819/1868)
23. Maine (1820)
24. Missouri (1821)
25. Arkansas (1836/1868)
26. Michigan (1837)
27. Florida (1845/1868)
28. Texas (1845/1870)
29. Iowa (1846)
30. Wisconsin (1848)
31. California (1850)
32. Minnesota (1858)
33. Oregon (1859)
34. Kansas (1861)
35. West Virginia (1863)
36. Nevada (1864)
37. Nebraska (1867)
38. Colorado (1876)
39. North Dakota (1889)
40. South Dakota (1889)
41. Montana (1889)
42. Washington (1889)
43. Idaho (1890)
44. Wyoming (1890)
45. Utah (1896)
46. Oklahoma (1907)
47. New Mexico (1912)
48. Arizona (1912)
49. Alaska (1959)
50. Hawaii (1959)

CIVIL WAR—SECESSION OF STATES

1. South Carolina (12-20-1860)
2. Mississippi (1-9-1861)
3. Florida (1-10-1861)
4. Alabama (1-11-1861)
5. Georgia (1-19-1861)
6. Louisiana (1-26-1861)
7. Texas (2-1-1861)
8. Virginia (4-17-1861)
9. Arkansas (5-6-1861)
10. North Carolina (5-20-1861)
11. Tennessee (6-8-1861)

RECONSTRUCTION— READMISSION OF STATES

1. Tennessee (7-24-1866)
2. Arkansas (6-22-1868)
3. Alabama (6-25-1868)
4. Florida (6-25-1868)
5. Georgia (6-25-1868, 7-15-1870)
6. Louisiana (6-25-1868)
7. North Carolina (6-25-1868)
8. South Carolina (6-25-1868)
9. Virginia (1-26-1870)
10. Mississippi (2-23-1870)
11. Texas (3-30-1870)

U.S. TERRITORIAL EXPANSION

Louisiana Purchase, 1803
Florida Territory, 1819
Texas, 1845
Oregon Territory, 1846
Cession from Mexico, 1848
Gadsden purchase (southern
    Arizona, New Mexico), 1853
Alaska, 1867
Hawaii, 1898
Puerto Rico, 1898
Guam, 1898
Philippine Islands, 1898
American Samoa, 1899
Panama Canal Zone, 1904 (returned
    to Panama by treaty of 1979)
Virgin Islands, 1916

UNDERGROUND RAILROAD

Hierarchy

1. President, supervised all operations
2. Stationmaster, homeowner ("depot") who provided food and shelter
3. Conductor, person who led the way
4. Passenger ("freight"), escaped slave

PRESIDENTS

President	Party	Served
G. Washington	N	1789–1797
J. Adams	F	1797–1801
T. Jefferson	D/R	1801–1809
J. Madison	D/R	1809–1817
J. Monroe	D/R	1817–1825
J.Q. Adams	D/R	1825–1829
A. Jackson	D	1829–1837
M. Van Buren	D	1837–1841
W. H. Harrison	W	1841
J. Tyler	W	1841–1845
J. K. Polk	D	1845–1849
Z. Taylor	W	1849–1850
M. Fillmore	W	1850–1853
F. Pierce	D	1853–1857
J. Buchanan	D	1857–1861
A. Lincoln	R	1861–1865
A. Johnson	D	1865–1869
U. S. Grant	R	1869–1877
R. B. Hayes	R	1877–1881
J. A. Garfield	R	1881
C. A. Arthur	R	1881–1885
G. Cleveland	D	1885–1889
B. Harrison	R	1889–1893
G. Cleveland	D	1893–1897
W. McKinley	R	1897–1901
T. Roosevelt	R	1901–1909
W. H. Taft	R	1909–1913
W. Wilson	D	1913–1921
W. G. Harding	R	1921–1923
C. Coolidge	R	1923–1929
H. C. Hoover	R	1929–1933
F. D. Roosevelt	D	1933–1945
H. S. Truman	D	1945–1953
D. D. Eisenhower	R	1953–1961
J. F. Kennedy	D	1961–1963
L. B. Johnson	D	1963–1969
R. M. Nixon	R	1969–1974
G. R. Ford	R	1974–1977
J. E. Carter, Jr.	D	1977–1981
R. W. Reagan	R	1981–1989
G. H. W. Bush	R	1989–1993
W. J. Clinton	D	1993–2001
G.W. Bush	R	2001–

*N = none; F = Federalist; D/R = Democratic-Republican;
W = Whig; D = Democrat; R = Republican

VIKINGS

SOCIAL HIERARCHY

King, rules a realm divided into fylkir or shires

Hirdmen: king's bodyguards who were military leaders in wartime

Chieftain: leader of a fylkir

Jarl: tax collector

Hersir: agent for the jarl

Bondi: property owners

Leysingi: freedmen who were former thralls,—but worked for owner who freed them; had some legal and political rights

Thralls/slaves: mainly foreign captives or debtors

VIKING POLITICAL SYSTEM

Althing: legislative assembly with sole legal and judicial authority (all freedmen of fixed domicile or representatives of the different cantons)

king: elected by the Althing; also religious chief

chieftains: elected by the Althing

specialized artisans: smiths, soldiers, merchants, carpenters, professional people

freedmen: owners of the land they cultivated (also called jarls)

slaves (thralls): born serfs, captured in war, or freedmen deprived of legal rights

There is no structural organization of society which can bring about the coming of the Kingdom of God on earth, since all systems can be perverted by the selfishness of man.

—William Temple, *The Malvern Manifesto*

CHAPTER EIGHT

SOCIETY & SOCIAL INSTITUTIONS

AWARDS

NOBEL PRIZE CATEGORIES

(consisting of a medal and cash award)

Physics
Chemistry
Physiology-Medicine
Literature
Peace
Economics

PULITZER PRIZES

($1,000 American dollars for each award)

Journalism

1. Disinterested and meritorious service rendered by a U.S. reporter
2. Distinguished example of local reporting, written under deadline pressure
3. Distinguished example of local reporting judged not by deadline pressure, but by resourcefulness and initiative of reporter
4. Distinguished example of reporting on national affairs
5. Distinguished example of reporting on international affairs
6. Distinguished editorial writing
7. Distinguished example of a cartoonist's work
8. Outstanding example of news photography

Literature

1. Distinguished fiction book, preferably dealing with American life
2. American play, preferably dealing with American life
3. Distinguished book about history of the U.S.
4. Distinguished American biography or autobiography teaching

patriotic and unselfish services to the people
5. Distinguished volume of verse, published by an American author

Music

Distinguished musical composition in the form of chamber, orchestral, or choral music, or for an opera or ballet.

CASTES AND CLASSES

CAPITALIST CASTE SYSTEM

(Eugene Debs, 1912 Socialist Party candidate for U.S. President)

1. We Work for All, We Feed All: workers supporting everyone
2. We Eat for You: rich eating what workers produced
3. We Shoot at You: soldiers who defended the rich
4. We Foot You: clergy guaranteeing workers their reward in the next world
5. We Rule You: "kings" of labor and politics

GENERAL HIERARCHICAL CASTE SYSTEM

1. persons of holy descent
2. landowners and administrators
3. priests
4. craftsmen
5. agricultural tenants and laborers
6. herders
7. despised persons

CLASSES OF ALIENS IN U.S.

1. Illegal aliens: entered country secretly or by using false documents or who have ignored conditions of their visas.

2. Temporary visitors: admitted by visa for business or school; stay is limited and visas must be renewed.
3. Refugees: admitted after being forced to flee other countries' war or oppression
    Parole: temporary status with no set time limit
    Conditional Entrant: eligible for permanent resident status in two years
4. Permanent Resident Aliens: stay as long as they like; cannot vote or hold public office

SOCIOLOGICAL CLASSES

upper class: owners, managers, top public officials
middle class: nonmanual white-collar workers, owners of small businesses
working class: manual laborers
lower class/underclass: irregularly employed and rural poor

SOCIALIST STATE CLASSES

upper class: political elite and industrial managers
middle class: lower nonmanual workers
lower class: manual workers
lowest class: large farm population (collective and state workers)

SOCIAL CLASSES ACCORDING TO MARX

aristocratic class (superior through education, ability, wealth, or social prestige)
bourgeoisie (middle class, or in Marxist theory the property-owning class)
petite bourgeoisie (lower middle class, having least wealth and lowest social status)
proletariat (in Marxist theory, the class of industrial wage earners who do not possess capital or property and must labor to survive)

CLASSIFICATION OF NATIONS

First World nation: country or group of countries that is major force in international politics or finance
Second World nation: advanced and powerful but less prosperous
Third World nation: neither a major force in international politics or finance; many live at or below level of extreme poverty

SOCIAL ESTATES

first estate: clergy
second estate: nobility
third estate: the commoners, townsmen, or middle class of a country
fourth estate: the press; journalists
fifth estate: sometimes defined as the trade unions or scholars

FICTIONAL CLASSES

Brave New World's Hierarchies

(from Aldous Huxley's "Brave New World")

Political
    World Controllers: 10, picked from Resident Controllers
    Resident Controllers: rule nations
    Secretaries
        Second Secretaries

Governors
  Deputy Governors
Superintendents
  Assistant Superintendents
    Deputy Assistant
      Superintendents
Directors
  Assistant Directors
Chiefs
Managers
  (also, Chief Justices and Arch-
    Community-Songsters)
Social (each caste has "plus" and
    "minus" levels)
Alphas (gray): very clever/genius;
    highest is Alpha Double-Plus
Betas (mulberry): intelligent
Gammas (green): stupid; lowest is
    Gamma-Minus
Deltas (khaki): perform menial
    labor only
Epsilons (black): very stupid; lowest
    is Epsilon-Minus Semi-
    Moron
There are also Savages, who live in
    primitive areas outside cities.

Power Structure in *1984*

(from George Orwell's "1984")

1. Big Brother: all-powerful leader
2. Thought Police: all-seeing
   discipliners
3. Inner Party: 6 million members
   from the population of Oceania,
   the "brain of the state"
4. Outer Party: commoners
5. The Low or Proles: slave population of the equatorial regions

Utopia's Hierarchies

(Sir Thomas More's "Utopia")

Political

1. National lietalk/parliament: each
   town sends three representatives
2. Mayor: elected by Stywards from a

candidate from each of the town's
four quarters
3. Bencheater: senior district
   controller, elected by Stywards
4. Styward/District Controller:
   represents 30 households, has
   one-year term; 200 Stywards per
   town
5. Household: organized into groups
   of 30

Social

husband, head of Household
wife
children
  students
  laborers
  slaves
    free people from other countries
    condemned prisoners from other
      countries
    native-born Utopians who
      squandered the offerings of
      Utopia

FAMILY

COUSINS

first cousin: child of a person's uncle
  or aunt
second cousin: child of a first cousin
  of one of a person's parents

also

cross-cousin: cousin who is the child
  of either one's mother's brother or
  one's father's sister
parallel/ortho-cousin: cousin who is
  the child of either one's mother's
  sister or of one's father's brother

GOVERNMENT

British Commonwealth of Nations

The following recognize the British monarch as their sovereign

Antigua and Barbuda
Australia
Bahamas
Bangladesh
Barbados
Belize
Canada
Grenada
Jamaica
Mauritius
New Zealand
Papua New Guinea
St Kitts and Nevis
St Lucia
St Vincent and the Grenadines
Solomon Islands
Tuvalu
United Kingdom

The following recognize the British monarch as symbolic head

Botswana
Brunei
Cyprus
Dominica
Gambia
Ghana
Guyana
India
Kenya
Kiribati
Lesotho
Malawi
Malaysia
Maldives
Malta
Naura
Nigeria
Pakistan
Seychelles
Sierra Leone
Singapore
Sri Lanka
Swaziland
Tanzania
Tonga
Trinidad and Tobago
Uganda
Vanuatu
Western Samoa
Zambia
Zimbabwe

Cadre System

(persons appointed to paid position in government or party system)

Five formal categories for cadre assessment:

1. virtue (character and political correctness)
2. ability
3. attention to duties
4. achievements
5. level of formal study

CHINESE GOVERNMENT

Communes

commune (average of 15,000 inhabitants; in the countryside)
production brigades (about 1,000 people)
production teams (20–60 households that farm the land and operate as a cooperative)
[After 1983, production teams no longer farm land as a unit. The fields are contracted out to single families.]

GOVERMENT LEVELS AND STRUCTURES

supranational political systems: empires, confederations, commonwealths

national political systems: nation-
state systems, federal state systems
urban governments
subnational political systems: tribal,
rural, regional community
governments

GOVERNMENTAL SYSTEMS

anarchy: rule by no one
autocracy or monarchy: rule by one
oligarchy or aristocracy: rule by a few
leaders
plutocracy: rule by the wealthy
ochlocracy: rule by a mob
democracy or polity: rule by the
people

POLITICAL IDEOLOGIES

anarchism
Communism
conservatism
Fascism
liberalism
Marxism
nationalism
socialism

Representative Democracy

legislature: deliberates on and passes
laws
judiciary: interprets laws, monitors
actions of executive and legislative
executive: carries out the law and
administers the country through
departments

RUSSIAN GOVERNMENT

Court System

Supreme Court
Supreme Courts of union republic
and regional courts
tribunals / people's courts

office of state prosecution
procurator-general
hierarchy of procurators:
union republics
autonomous republics
autonomous oblasts
(regions)
autonomous okrugs and
krays (provinces)
rural and urban rayons (rural
districts)

Government

Executive President (elected by
Congress of People's Deputies)
Supreme Soviet (elected by Congress
of People's Deputies)
Council of the Union
Council of Nationalities
Congress of People's Deputies (2250
total)
100, Communist
650, selected by official union,
youth, and professional groups
1500, from national and territorial
districts

U.S. GOVERNMENT

Census Divisions and Regions

West
Pacific: Alaska, Washington,
Oregon, California
Mountain: Montana, Idaho,
Wyoming, Nevada, Utah,
Colorado, Arizona, New Mexico
Midwest
West North Central: North Dakota,
South Dakota, Nebraska, Kansas,
Minnesota, Iowa, Missouri
East North Central: Wisconsin,
Illinois, Indiana, Michigan, Ohio
South
West South Central: Texas,
Oklahoma, Arkansas, Louisiana

East South Central: Mississippi, Alabama, Tennessee, Kentucky
South Atlantic: Florida, Georgia, South Carolina, North Carolina, West Virginia, Virginia, Washington DC, Maryland, Delaware
Northeast
Middle Atlantic: New York, Pennsylvania, New Jersey
New England: Maine, New Hampshire, Vermont, Massachusetts, Rhode Island, Connecticut

Central Intelligence Agency

Director of Central Intelligence
  Director Intelligence Community Staff
  National Intelligence Council
  General Counsel
  Inspector General
  Office of Legislative Liaison
Deputy Director of Central Intelligence
Executive Director
  Public Affairs
  Equal Employment Opportunity
  Personnel
  Comptroller
Deputy Directors (4) (direct 24 different offices)
  operations
  science and technology
  intelligence
  administration

Diplomatic Personnel Organization

(three classes of heads of mission)

1. ambassadors or nuncios (answering to heads of state and heads of missions equal in rank)
2. envoys, ministers, and internuncios (answering to heads of state)
3. charges d'affaires (answering to ministers of foreign affairs)

Embassy Staff:

ambassador or foreign minister
deputy secretary or secretary-general
under secretaries
  deputies
  assistant secretaries
departments attaches (examples):
administration
personnel
finances
economic affairs
legal advisor's office
archives

U.S. GOVERNMENT

Executive Branch:
President
Vice President
Cabinet
  Department of State
  Department of the Treasury
  Department of Defense
  Department of Justice
  Department of the Interior
  Department of Agriculture
  Department of Commerce
  Department of Labor
  Department of Health and Human Services
  Department of Housing and Urban Development
  Department of Transportation
  Department of Energy
  Department of Education
  Department of Veterans Affairs
Executive Office of the President
White House Office
Office of Management and Budget
Council of Economic Advisers
National Security Council
Office of the U.S. Trade Representative

Council on Environmental Quality
Office of Science and Technology
    Policy
Office of National Drug Control
    Policy
Office of Administration

Legislative Branch:
Congress: House and Senate
Architect of the Capitol
U.S. Botanic Garden
General Accounting Office
Government Printing Office
Library of Congress
Office of Technology Assessment
Congressional Budget Office

Judicial Branch:
Supreme Court
Courts of Appeals
District Courts
Territorial Courts
Court of International Trade
Court of Federal Claims
Court of Military Appeals
Tax Court
Court of Veterans Appeals
Administrative Office of the Courts
Federal Judicial Center
Sentencing Commission

Presidential Cabinet Hierarchy

Vice President
Secretary of State
(followed in rank by Deputy secretary,
    Under secretary, and Assistant
    secretary; the same in all other
    departments except Justice)
  Deputy secretary
  Under secretary
  Assistant secretary
Secretary of the Treasury
Secretary of Defense
Attorney General (Justice
    Department)
  Deputy Attorney General
  Associate Attorney General

Solicitor General
Legal Counsel
Pardon Attorney
Secretary of the Interior
Secretary of Agriculture
Secretary of Commerce
Secretary of Labor
Secretary of Health and Human
    Services
Secretary of Housing and Urban
    Development
Secretary of Transportation
Secretary of Energy
Secretary of Education
Secretary of Veterans' Affairs
Vice President
Speaker of the House of
    Representatives
President Pro Tempore of the Senate
Secretary of State
Secretary of the Treasury
Secretary of Defense
Attorney General
Secretary of the Interior
Secretary of Agriculture
Secretary of Commerce
Secretary of Labor
Secretary of Health and Human
    Services
Secretary of Housing and Urban
    Development
Secretary of Transportation
Secretary of Energy
Secretary of Education
Secretary of Veterans' Affairs

Social Security Number System

001–003, New Hampshire
004–007, Maine
008–009, Vermont
010–034, Massachusetts
035–039, Rhode Island
040–049, Connecticut
050–134, New York
135–158, New Jersey

GOVERNMENT
U.S. Government
(cont.)

159–211, Pennsylvania
212–220, Maryland
221–222, Delaware
223–231, Virginia
232–236, West Virginia
232, 237–246, North Carolina
247–251, South Carolina
252–260, Georgia
261–267, 589–595, Florida
268–302, Ohio
303–317, Indiana
318–361, Illinois
362–386, Michigan
387–399, Wisconsin
400–407, Kentucky
408–415, Tennessee
416–424, Alabama
425–428, 587–588, Mississippi
429–432, Arkansas
433–439, Louisiana
440–448, Oklahoma
449–467, Texas
468–477, Minnesota
478–485, Iowa
486–500, Missouri
501–502, North Dakota
503–504, South Dakota
505–508, Nebraska
509–515, Kansas
516–517, Montana
518–519, Idaho
520, Wyoming
521–524, Colorado
525–585, New Mexico
526–527, 600–601, Arizona
528–529, Utah
530, Nevada
531–539, Washington
540–544, Oregon
545–573, 602–626, California
574, Alaska
575–576, Hawaii
577–579, District of Columbia
580, Virgin Islands
580–584, 596–599, Puerto Rico
586, Guam, American Samoa,
Philippine Islands

State Government Organization
(example: Indiana)

governor
lieutenant governor
secretary of state
attorney general
treasurer (some states have
comptroller)
auditor
general assembly: senate and house

U.K. GOVERNMENT

Constitutional Monarchy

Monarch (King or Queen)
Parliament (each house has a speaker
and leader, and a leader of the
Opposition)
House of Lords (upper house: 750
hereditary peers and peeresses,
20 Lords of Appeal, 370 life peers;
2 archbishops, 24 bishops of
Church of England—all non-
elected)
House of Commons (lower house:
651 elected members serving 5
years)
Prime Minister (head of government)
Cabinet Ministries
Agriculture, Fisheries, and Food
(headed by Minister of
Agriculture)
Defence (Secretary of State)
Education (Secretary of State)
Employment (Secretary of State)
Environment (Secretary of State)
Foreign and Commonwealth
Affairs (Foreign Secretary)
Health (Secretary of State)
Home Office (Home Secretary)
National Heritage (Secretary of
State)
Northern Ireland (Secretary of
State)
Public Service and Science

(Minister of Public Service and Science)
Scottish Office (Secretary of State)
Social Security (Secretary of State)
Trade and Industry (Secretary of State and President of the Board of Trade)
Transport (Secretary of State)
Treasury (Chancellor of the Exchequer)
Welsh Office (Secretary of State)
Duchy of Lancaster
Law Officers
Privy Council Office

U.S. LEGAL HOLIDAYS—ANNUAL

New Year's Day	January 1
Martin Luther King Day	third Monday of January
President's Day	third Monday in February
Memorial Day	last Monday in May
Independence Day	July 4
Labor Day	first Monday of September
Columbus Day	second Monday in October
Veteran's Day	November 11
Thanksgiving Day	fourth or last Thursday of November
Christmas	December 25

HOSPITALS

CLINICAL DEPARTMENTS

(Yale-New Haven Hospital)

Anesthesiology
Child Psychiatry
Dentistry
Dermatology (skin)
Diagnostic Imaging
Internal Medicine
  AIDS
  Cardiovascular
  Digestive Diseases
  Endocrinology (glands and hormones)
  General medicine
  Geriatrics (old age)
  Hematology (blood)
  Immunology (immune system)
  Infectious diseases
  Medical oncology (tumors)
  Nephrology (kidneys)
  Occupational medicine
  Pulmonary and critical care
  Rheumatology (muscles, tendons, joints)
  Tropical medicine
Laboratory Medicine
Neurology (nervous system)
Obstetrics & Gynecology (pregnancy & women)
Ophthalmology (eyes)
Orthopedics (skeletal system)
Pathology (disease)
Pediatrics
  Anesthesiology/pain service
  Adolescent medicine
  Pediatric cardiology
  Pediatric critical care and applied physiology
  Pediatric endocrinology and metabolism
  Pediatric Gastroenterology/hepatology (digestion and stomach/liver)
  General pediatrics
  Pediatric hematology/oncology
  Pediatric infectious diseases
  Pediatric nephrology
  Pediatric neurology
  Perinatology (time near birth)
  Pediatric rehabilitation
  Pediatric respiratory medicine
  Pediatric surgery
Psychiatry
Surgery
  Cardiothoracic
  Emergency medicine
  Gastroenterology
  General
  Neuro
  Oncology
  Otolaryngology
  Pediatric

GOVERNMENT
HOSPITALS

229 ■

Plastic
Trauma
Transplantation
Vascular
Urology
Therapeutic Radiology
Emergency Department
Primary Care Center
Specialty Clinics and Centers

HOSPITAL STRUCTURE

Administrative Structure

Governing Board/Board of
   Trustees/Board of Directors
Executive
   head/administrator/medical
   director
   Housekeeping
   Food services
   Plant operation
   Nursing
   Medical records
   Laboratory
   Pharmacy
   Blood bank
   Accounting

Hospital Divisions

medical staff
nursing staff
social services
education and research
medical records
support staff and volunteers

TYPES OF HOSPITALS

General hospitals (examples):
   medical, surgical, obstetric,
   pediatric, psychiatric,
   rehabilitation, outpatient, clinics,
   emergency wards, extended care
   services, home care services
Special hospitals (examples):
   children's, maternity,
eye/ear/nose/throat, cancer,
mental

TREATMENT SEQUENCE
*(for patient information when
entering hospital)*

diagnosis
condition
vital signs
ambulation
nursing orders
diet
intake and output
symptomatic drugs
specific drugs
examinations
laboratory

LAW

CRIME CLASSIFICATIONS

Felony: serious offense
Misdemeanor: less serious offense

or:

Crimes against person: rape, armed
   robbery, predatory crime
Crimes against property: burglary,
   arson, larceny; involve no threat to
   a victim

also:

Crimes committed by government:
   wiretapping
White collar crime: embezzlement
Victimless crime: drug addiction,
   prostitution
Organized crime: mob activities

also:

(Marshall B. Clinard & Richard Quinney)

1. violent person crime, eg murder,
   assault, forcible rape, child
   molestation

2. occasional property crime, eg shoplifting, check forgery, vandalism, auto theft
3. occupational crime, eg white-collar crime
4. political crime, eg treason, sedition, espionage, sabotage, military draft violation, war collaboration, criminal protest
5. public order crime, eg drunkenness, vagrancy, nonforced sex offenses, gambling, drug addiction ("crimes without victims")
6. conventional crime, eg robbery, larceny, burglary, youth gang crime
7. organized crime, eg racketeering, commercialized vice, drug traffic, illegal gambling
8. professional crime, eg confidence games, forgery, counterfeiting, pickpocketing

---

FBI HIERARCHY

Headquarters:

Director
Deputy Director
Associate Deputy Directors
  Administration
  Investigation
Assistant Directors
  Records Management
  Identification Division
  Administration Services
  Technical Services
  Training
  Intelligence
  Criminal Investigative Division
  Laboratory Division
Section Chiefs
Unit Chiefs
Supervisory Special Agents

Field offices: LAW

Special Agent in Charge
Assistant Special Agent in Charge
Supervisory Special Agents
Special Agents
(Some cities have an Assistant Director and Deputy Assistant in field offices.)

INTERNATIONAL LAW— WORLD COURT SYSTEM

(in order of precedence)

1. treaties between nations
2. international custom
3. existing national laws
4. previous international decisions
5. previous national decisions
6. testimony of experts from a variety of nations

LEGAL AND RELIGIOUS MILESTONES

5/6: compulsory schooling begins
  8: Age of Reason, age of first possible offense
12: Mormon males can become deacons
12: girl may consent to common law matrimony (but state law prevails)
13: Bar/Bat Mitzvah, Jewish boy/girls's ceremony at age of religious responsibility
14: boy may consent to common law matrimony (but state law prevails)
14: Age of Discretion, can be legally prosecuted for offense
16: Age of Consent (can legally marry); minimum school-leaving age; driver's license (many states)
18: males in U.S. eligible for military draft (when in effect)

LAW

Legal and Religious
Milestones (cont.)

18: age one may legally engage in sexual intercourse

18: age one may sign a contract

20: Mormon males can become elders

21: former coming of age; can adopt a child

22: Roman Catholic males can become deacons

24: Roman Catholic and Anglican males can become priests

25: minimum age to become a U.S. Representative

30: Roman Catholic and Anglican males can become bishops

30: minimum age to become a U. S. Senator

35: minimum age to become U.S. President

55: compulsory retirement age in armed forces

62: earliest age for Social Security pension benefits

65: age of retirement; maximum age for jury duty; Medicare benefits begin

70: driving license must be renewed

75: Roman Catholic bishops must retire

MIRANDA WARNING

1. You have the right to remain silent and refuse to answer any questions.
2. Anything you say may be used against you in a court of law.
3. As we discuss this matter, you have a right to stop answering my questions at any time you desire.
4. You have a right to a lawyer before speaking to me, to remain silent until you can talk to him/her, and to have him/her present when you are being questioned.
5. If you want a lawyer but cannot afford one, one will be provided to you without cost.
6. Do you understand each of these rights I have explained to you?
7. Now that I have advised you of your rights, are you willing to answer my questions without an attorney present?

quick version:

You have the right to remain silent, anything you say may be used against you as evidence, and you have the right to the counsel of an attorney.

NINE POINTS OF THE LAW

ideal requirements of a successful legal case or trial:

1. a good deal of money
2. a good deal of patience
3. a good cause
4. a good lawyer
5. a good counsel
6. a good witness
7. a good jury
8. a good judge
9. good luck

INFORMATION RADIOED IN BY POLICE MNEMONIC

CYMBOL

color
year
make
body style
occupants
license plate number

SEARCH WARRANT EXCEPTIONS MNEMONIC

COP IS ME

Consent
Open view
Public place
Incidental to a lawful arrest
Stop and frisk a suspicious person
Mobil premises
Emergency

STRUCTURE OF THE LAW

Public (state, community interest)

constitutional
administrative
criminal
international

Private (actions of individuals
toward each other)

property
contract and business
delict/tort (misdemeanor/wrongful
act)
corporation
inheritance
family

U.S. COURT SYSTEM

(In the U.S., there are two systems, at federal and state level.)

U.S. Supreme Court
U.S. Courts of Appeals
  U.S. special courts
  Federal circuit court of appeals
  claims court
  court of military appeals
U.S. District Courts
state supreme courts
state appellate courts
state district courts (divorce, murder)

county courts (state/county traffic,
  contract collections)
municipal courts (dog bite, local
  traffic)
justices of the peace

U.S. LAWS

Hierarchy
(in order of precedence)

1. Constitution
2. U.S. laws and treaties
3. state constitutions
4. state laws
5. local laws (county, township; city,
   town, village)

PUBLIC LAW BRANCHES

Laws concerning authority and
  power of the state
Laws concerning relations among
  sovereign states
Laws concerning acts viewed as crimes
Laws promoting public welfare
Laws concerning taxation
Laws of judicial procedure
Private Law Branches
Civil procedure law
Family Law
Law of property
Law of torts
Laws concerning economic
  transactions

LINGUISTICS

BRANCHES

Historical linguistics (how language
  changes over time)
Structural linguistics (nature and
  structure of language as
  systems of units)

phonology (distribution and patterns of speech sounds)

morphology (the forms language can take)

syntax (natural rules or patterns that govern how sentences are formed)

semantics (how languages structure and present meaning)

Language classification

Psycholinguistics (relationship between language and users' psychological processes)

Sociolinguistics (interactions of language and society)

Related fields

anthropological linguistics (relationship between language and culture)

applied linguistics (linguistic theory applied in teaching, psychology, lexicography, etc.)

computational linguistics (applications of computers in processing and analyzing language)

dialect geography (mapping of geography)

dialectology (mapping of dialects)

epigraphy (study of inscriptions)

grammatology (study and science of systems of graphic script)

graphemics (study of alphabets)

metagraphemics (study of change in alphabets)

subgraphemics (study of pseudo-alphabets)

linguistic geography (regional variations of speech forms)

mathematical linguistics (applications of mathematical models and procedures to linguistic studies)

neurolinguistics (neurological processes underlying development and use of language)

paleography (interpretation of ancient written documents)

philosophy of language (exploration of the general nature and status of language)

social dialectology (relationship of dialects to society)

stylistics (use of elements of language style in particular contexts, as metaphor)

WRITING SYSTEMS

1. picture word: communication by means of drawings of objects involved
2. symbol: a simplification of the picture word
3. ideograph: stylized picture used as a symbol for an idea/concept
4. hieroglyph: pictures to represent things, names, and words
5. hieratic script: hieroglyphic pictures in abbreviated versions
6. alphabet: hieratic forms adapted by the Greeks to a system of symbol-to-soung correspondence. The Romans modified Greek forms and developed the capitals of our alphabet. (Alcuin, a scholar in Charlemagne's empire, developed the small letters, called Carolingian minuscules.)

WRITING SYSTEMS—NUMBER OF CHARACTERS USED

Chinese, 40–50,000 ideographic characters

Japanese, 18,000 ideographic characters

Khmer/Cambodian, 74 alphabetic characters

Sanskrit, 48

Cyrillic, 33
Russian, 33
Persian, 32
Turkish, 29
Spanish, 29
Arabic, 28
German, 27
English, 26
French, 26
Roman , 23
Greek, 24
Hebrew, 22
Early Latin, 21
Italian, 21
Hawaiian, 12
Rotokas, 11 (Solomon Islands)

WRITING SYSTEMS' STRUCTURE
linguistic structure

meaning-based:
text
topic
speech act
word (logographic writing)
morpheme (logographic writing)

sound-based:
syllable (syllabic writing)
segment (consonantal writing)
phoneme (alphabetic writing)
phone (phonetic alphabet)
feature (featural writing system)

LANGUAGES OF THE WORLD

Dutch Language Development

Old Dutch (400–1100)
Middle Dutch (1100–1550)
Modern Dutch (1550-present)

English Language Development

Old English or Anglo-Saxon (449- AD 1100)
Middle English (1100–1500)

Modern English (1500-present)

German Language Development

High German (500- AD 700)
Old High German (700–1100)
Middle High German (1100–1500)
Modern German (1500-present)

Classification

African languages
  Afro-Asiatic
  Khoisian
  Niger-Congo
  Nilo-Saharan
Altaic languages
  Manchu-Tungus
  Mongol languages (Manchu, Mongol, Samoyed, etc.)
  Turko-Tataric languages (Turkish, Uzbek, etc.)
American Indian languages
  North America (Apache, Iroquois, Sioux, etc.)
  Central America (Maya, Aztec, Zapotec, etc.)
  South America (Peruvian, Quechua, etc.)
Austro-Asiatic languages
  Mon-Khmer (Mon, Vietnamese, Khmer)
  Munda
  Nicobarese
Austronesian languages
Bantu languages
  languages of the interior of Africa
    Negro tongues (Hausa, Wolof, etc.)
    Clicking languages (Hottentots, etc.)
Caucasian languages (Georgian, etc.)
Chinese languages
Dravidian languages (Telugu, Tamil, Kannada, Malayalam, etc.)
Hamitic-Semitic languages
  Hamitic
  Semitic

Indo-European
  Albanian
  Anatolian
  Armenian
  Balto-Slavic/Slavonic languages
    Russian
    Polish
    Czech, Moravian, Slovak
    Serbo-Croatian
    Slovene
    Bulgarian
    Albanian
    Lithuanian
  Indo-Iranian languages
    Indic: Sanskrit, Bengali, Kafir,
      Hindi, etc.
    Iranian: Persian, Kurdish, Afghan,
      etc.
  Celtic languages
    Irish
    Gaelic
    Welsh
    Cornish
  Romance languages
    French
    Provencal
    Walloon
    Spanish
    Portuguese
    Italian
    Romanian
  Germanic languages
    English
    German
    Swedish
    Danish
    Norwegian
    Dutch
    Frisian
    Flemish
Indo-Pacific languages
Japanese-Korean languages

Malay-Polynesian languages
  Malay
  Melanesian, Polynesian, Maori
Sino-Tibetan languages
  Burmic languages
  Miao-Yao languages
  Sinitic languages
  Tibetic languages
Tai languages
Uralic languages
  Finnish/Estonian/Livonian/Lapp
    etc.
  Magyar/Hungarian
  Samoyedic
  Ugric
Unclassified and isolated languages
  Iberian
  Basque
  northern Asia and America
    (Eskimo, Aleutian)
  Sumerian
  Etruscan

PRINCIPAL NATIVE LANGUAGES OF THE WORLD

Mandarin	930 mil.
English	463 mil.
Hindi	400 mil.
Spanish	371 mil.
Russian	291 mil.
Arabic	214 mil.
Bengali	192 mil.
Portuguese	179 mil.
Malay-Indonesian	152 mil.
Japanese	126 mil.
French	124 mil.
German	120 mil.

INDO-EUROPEAN LANGUAGES

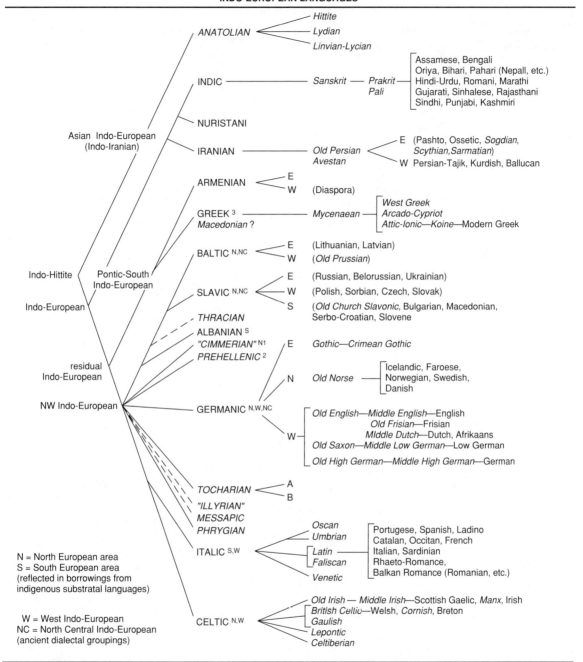

N = North European area
S = South European area
(reflected in borrowings from
indigenous substratal languages)

W = West Indo-European
NC = North Central Indo-European
(ancient dialectal groupings)

[1] hypothesized substratum language in proto-Baltic and Slavic area   [2] substratum language in Greek area (called by some "Pelasgian")

(The names of languages extinct as vernaculars have been italicized.)

FOREIGN ALPHABETS

ARABIC			GERMAN[1]		GREEK			HEBREW			RUSSIAN		
Letter	Name	Transliteration	Letter	Transliteration	Letter		Name	Transliteration	Letter	Name	Transliteration	Letter		Transliteration
ا	alif	ʼ[1], a	𝔄 ɑ	a	A α	alpha	a	א	aleph	- or ʼ	А а	a
ب	bā	b	𝔄̈ ɑ̈	ae, ä	B β	beta	b	ב	beth	b, bh, v	Б б	b
ت	tā	t	𝔅 b	b	Γ γ	gamma	g	ג	gimel	g, gh	В в	v
ث	thā	th	ℭ c	c	Δ δ	delta	d	ד	daleth	d, dh	Г г	g
ج	jim	j	𝔇 d	d							Д д	d
ح	ḥā	ḥ[2]	𝔈 e	e	E ε	epsilon	e	ה	he	h	Е е	e, ye
خ	khā	kh	𝔉 f	f	Z ζ	zeta	z	ו	vav	v, w	Ж ж	zh, ż
د	dāl	d	𝔊 g	g	H η	eta	e (or ē)	ז	zayin	z	З з	z
ذ	dhāl	dh	𝔥 h	h							И и	i
ر	rā	r	𝔍 i	i	Θ θ	theta	th	ח	cheth	ḥ	Й й	ĭ, y, j, i
ز	zā	z	𝔍 j	j	I ι	iota	i	ט	teth	ṭ			
س	sin	s	𝔎 k	k	K κ	kappa	k	י	yod	y, j, i	К к	k
ش	shin	sh	𝔏 l	l	Λ λ	lambda	l				Л л	l
ص	ṣād	ṣ	𝔐 m	m					כ ך[1]	kaph	k, kh	М м	m
ض	ḍād	ḍ	𝔑 n	n	M μ	mu	m	ל	lamed	l	Н н	n
ط	ṭā	ṭ	𝔬 o	o	N ν	nu	n				О о	o
ظ	ẓā	ẓ	𝔬̈ ö	oe, ö	Ξ ξ	xi	x	מ ם[1]	mem	m	П п	p
ع	ʼain	ʼ[3]	𝔭 p	p					נ ן[1]	nun	n	Р р	r
غ	ghain	gh	𝔮 q	q	O o	omicron	o				С с	s
ف	fā	f	𝔯 r	r	Π π	pi	p	ס	samekh	s	Т т	t
ق	qāf	q[4]	𝔰 ſ ß[2]	s	P ρ	rho	r	ע	ayin	ʼ	У у	u
ك	kāf	k	𝔱 t	t	Σ σ, ς[1]	sigma	s	פ ף[1]	pe	p, ph, f	Ф ф	f
ل	lām	l	𝔲 u	u	T τ	tau	t	צ ץ[1]	sadhe	ṣ	Х х	kh, x
م	mim	m	𝔲̈ ü	ue, ü	Y υ	upsilon	y	ק	koph	q	Ц ц	ts, c
ن	nūn	n	𝔳 v	v	Φ φ	phi	ph	ר	resh	r	Ч ч	ch, č
ه	hā	h	𝔴 w	w	X χ	chi	ch, kh	שׁ	shin	sh, š	Ш ш	sh, š
و	wāw	w, ū	𝔵 x	x	Ψ ψ	psi	ps	שׂ	sin	ś	Щ щ	shch, šč
ي	yā	y, ī	𝔶 y	y	Ω ω	omega	o (or ō)	ת	tav	t	Ъ ъ[1]	"
			𝔷 z	z								Ы ы	y, i
												Ь ь[2]	ʼ
												Э э	ė, eh, e
												Ю ю	yu, ju
												Я я	ya, ja

[1]Glottal stop.
[2]A voiceless pharyngeal fricative.
[3]A voiced pharyngeal fricative.
[4]A voiceless uvular stop.

[1]This type style, known as Fraktur or Gothic, was dropped in favor of conventional European type by government decree in 1941.
[2]At end of syllable.

[1]At end of word.

[1]At end of word.

[1]Represents the sound (y) between an unpalatalized consonant and a vowel.
[2]Indicates that the preceding consonant is palatalized, or represents (y) between a palatalized consonant and a vowel.

American Manual Alphabet

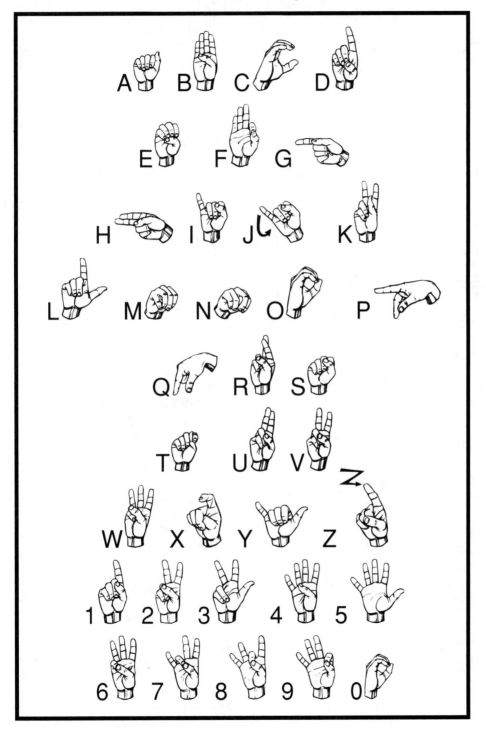

Capital sign	Comma
Semi-colon	
Period	Single quotation mark
Dash	
Exclamation point	Question mark

A 1	B 2	C 3	D 4	E 5
F 6	G 7	H 8	I 9	J 0
K	L	M	N	O
P	Q	R	S	T
U	V	W	X	Y
Z	Number sign			

(Source: American Foundation for the Blind)

Braille Alphabet

MILITARY

CANADIAN MILITARY

Army and Air Force Ranks

General
Lieutenant-General
Major-General
Brigadier-General
senior officers
   Colonel
   Lieutenant-Colonel
   Major
junior officers
   Captain
   Lieutenant
   Second Lieutenant

subordinate officer
   Officer Cadet
non-commissioned members
   Chief Warrant Officer
   Master Warrant Officer
   Warrant Officer
   Sergeant
   Master-Corporal/Senior Corporal
     of Section
   Corporal
   Private

Navy Ranks

Admiral
Vice-Admiral
Rear-Admiral
Commodore
senior officers
   Captain
   Commander
   Lieutenant-Commander
junior officers
   Lieutenant
   Sub-Lieutenant
   Acting Sub-Lieutenant
subordinate officer
   Officer Cadet/Midshipman
non-commissioned members
   Chief Petty Officer 1st class
   Chief Petty Officer 2nd class
   Petty Officer 1st class
   Petty Officer 2nd class
   Master Seaman/Senior Corporal of
     Section
   Leading Seaman
   Able Seaman

CHINESE ARMED FORCES

Army Ranks

Generalissimo
General of the Army
General
Lieutenant General
Major General

Colonel
Lieutenant Colonel
Major
Captain
First Lieutenant
Second Lieutenant
Warrant Officer
Chief Sergeant Major
Senior Sergeant Major
Sergeant Major
Master Sergeant
Sergeant First Class
Staff Sergeant
Sergeant
Corporal
Private First Class

FRENCH ARMED FORCES

Army Ranks

Officers:
Maréchal de France/Marshal of
   France
Général d'Armée
Général de Corps d'Armée
Général de Division
Général de Brigade/Brigadier General
Colonel
Lieutenant Colonel
Commandant
Capitaine
Lieutenant
Sous Lieutenant

Enlisted Personnel:
Adjutant-Chef
Adjutant
Sergent-major
Sergent
Caporal-chef
Caporal
Soldat, 1ère Classe
Soldat, 2ème Classe

ITALIAN ARMED FORCES

Army Ranks

Lieutenant General
Major General
Brigadier General
Colonel
Lieutenant Colonel
Major
Captain
First Lieutenant
Second Lieutenant
Aiutante di Battaglia/Superior
   Warrant Officer
Warrant Officer First Class
Warrant Officer Second Class
Warrant Officer Third Class
First Sergeant
Sergeant
First Corporal
Corporal

UK ARMED FORCES RANKS

Army

Field Marshal
General
Lieutenant-General
Major-General
Brigadier
Colonel
Lieutenant-Colonel
Major
Captain
Lieutenant
Second Lieutenant

Navy

Admiral of the Fleet
Admiral
Vice-Admiral
Rear-Admiral
Commodore
Captain
Commander

Lieutenant-Commander
Lieutenant
Sub-Lieutenant
Acting Sub-Lieutenant

Royal Air Force

Marshal of the RAF
Air Chief Marshal
Air Marshal
Air Vice-Marshal
Air Commodore
Group Captain
Wing Commander
Squadron Leader
Flight Lieutenant
Flying Officer
Pilot Officer

U.S. ARMED FORCES RANKS

U.S. Air Force Ranks (grade)

General of the Air Force (5-star, O8)
General (4-star, O8)
Lieutenant General (3-star, O8)
Major General (2-star O8)
Brigadier General (1-star, O7)
Colonel (O6)
Lieutenant Colonel (O5)
Major (O4)
Captain (O3)
First Lieutenant (O2)
Second Lieutenant (O1)
Chief Warrant Officer (W4)
Chief Warrant Officer (W3)
Chief Warrant Officer (W2)
Warrant Officer (W1)
Chief Master Sergeant (E9)
Senior Master Sergeant (E8)
Master Sergeant (E7)
Technical Sergeant (E6)
Staff Sergeant (E5)
Senior Airman (E4)
Airman First Class (E3)
Airman (E2)
Airman Basic (E1)

U.S. Air Force Groups

flight = 2 aircraft
squadron = 2 flights
group = 2 squadrons
wing = 2 groups
air division = 2 wings
air force = 2 air divisions
air command = all divisions and
    support units

U.S. Air Force Organization

Air Combat Command
    8th Air Force
    1st Air Force
    9th Air Force
    12th Air Force
Air Force Intelligence Command
Air Force Materiel Command
Air Mobility Command
    21st Air Force
    15th Air Force
    22nd Air Force
Air Force Space Command
Air Force Special Operations
    Command
Pacific Air Forces
    5th Air Force
    7th Air Force
    11th Air Force
    13th Air Force
U.S. Air Forces, Europe
    3rd Air Force
    16th Air Force
    17th Air Force

U.S. Army Organization

Forces Command
    First U.S. Army
    Second U.S. Army
    Third U.S. Army
    Fifth U.S. Army
    Sixth U.S. Army
    I Corps
    III Corps (Phantom Corps)
        1st Infantry (The Big Red One)

4th Infantry (The Ivy Division)
1st Cavalry
2nd Armored
13th Corps support command
XVIII Airborne Corps
  1st Cavalry
  7th Infantry
  10th Mountain (Climb to Glory)
  24th Infantry (Victory)
  82nd Airborne (All American)
  101st Airborne (Screaming Eagles)
XVIII airborne corps artillery
  1st Corps Support Command
National Training Center
U.S. Army Europe (7th Army)
  V Corps
  3rd Infantry (Marne)
  1st Armored (Old Ironsides)
  32nd Air Defense Command
  3rd Corps Support Command
  21st Theater Army Area Command
  Seventh Army Training Command
  Seventh Army Medical Command
U.S. Army Pacific
  U.S. Army, Japan, IX Corps
  6th Infantry
  25th Infantry (Tropic Lightning)
Eighth Army
  2nd Infantry (Indianhead)
U.S. Army South
National Guard
  28th Infantry (Keystone)
  29th Infantry (Blue and Grey)
  34th Infantry
  35th Infantry (Santa Fe)
  38th Infantry (Cyclone)
  40th Infantry (Sunshine)
  42nd Infantry (Rainbow)
  49th Armored (Lone Star)

U.S. Army Ranks

Commissioned Officers (grade):
General of the Army (5-star, O8)
General (4-star, O8)
Lieutenant General (3-star, O8)
Major General (2-star, O8)
Brigadier General (1-star, O7)
Colonel (O6)
Lieutenant Colonel (O5)
Major (O4)
Captain (O3)
First Lieutenant (O2)
Second Lieutenant (O3)
Chief Warrant Officer (W4)
Chief Warrant Officer (W3)
Chief Warrant Officer (W2)
Warrant Officer (W1)

Noncommissioned Officers (grade):
Sergeant Major/Specialist 9 (E-9)
First/Master Sergeant/Specialist 8 (E-8)
Sergeant First Class/Specialist 7 (E-7)
Staff Sergeant/Specialist 6 (E-6)
Sergeant/Specialist 5 (E-5)

Enlisted ranks (grade):
Corporal/Specialist 4 (E-4)
Private First Class (E-3)
Private (E-2)
Private (E-1)

U.S. Army Groups

unit = 2 soldiers
squad = 5–10 soldiers (commander is sergeant)
platoon = 4 squads or 30–50 people (lieutenant)
company = 2 platoons or 100–200 people (captain)
battalion = 2–5 companies or 500–1000 people (lieutenant colonel)
group = 2 battalions
brigade = 2 groups or 2000–4000 people (colonel)
division = 3 brigades or 10,000–17,000 people (major general)
corps = 2 divisions
field army = 2 corps

U.S. Draft Classification

1-A (available to serve)

1-A-M (medical or other specialist)

1-A-O (conscientious objector; noncombatant service)

1-C (present member of armed forces)

1-H (exempt from induction for other reasons than below)

1-O (conscientious objector; nonmilitary service)

1-W (conscientious objector; no service)

2-A-M (medical or other specialist; deferred for community obligations)

2-D (theological student; deferred)

2-M (medical student; deferred)

3-A (sole supporter of others; deferred)

4-A (already served in military)

4-B (public servant; deferred)

4-C (alien)

4-D (clergy)

4-F (unqualified, often due to medical problem)

4-G (only used in wartime)

4-W (conscientious objector who already served in nonmilitary capacity)

U.S. Marine Corps Ranks (grade)

General (4-star, O8)

Lieutenant General (3-star, O8)

Major General (2-star, O8)

Brigadier General (1-star, O7)

Colonel (O6)

Lieutenant Colonel (O5)

Major (O4)

Captain (O3)

First Lieutenant (O2)

Second Lieutenant (O1)

Chief Warrant Officer (W4)

Chief Warrant Officer (W3)

Chief Warrant Officer (W2)

Warrant Officer (W1)

Sergeant Major/Master Gunnery Sergeant (E9)

First/Master Sergeant (E8)

Gunnery Sergeant (E7)

Staff Sergeant (E6)

Sergeant (E5)

Corporal (E4)

Lance Corporal (E3)

Private First Class (E2)

Private (E1)

U.S. Marine Corps Organization

Fleet Marine Force, Atlantic

Fleet Marine Force, Pacific

Marine Corps Combat Development Command

I Marine Expeditionary Force

II Marine Expeditionary Force

III Marine Expeditionary Force

Marine Corps Air Ground Combat Center

U.S. Gun Salute by Degrees

50 = July 4th at noon

21 = arrival and departure of President, former President, or President-elect OR a foreign leader or royalty

19 = arrival and departure of Vice President, Speaker of the House, cabinet members, Senate president pro tempore, chief justice, or state governor; OR U.S. or foreign ambassador, prime minister, premier; OR secretary of a military branch, chairman of the Joint Chiefs of Staff, and some other military people

17 = arrival and departure of general, admirals, assistant secretaries of military branches; OR arrival of a chairman of a congressional committee

15 = arrival of American or visiting

foreign envoys or ministers; OR for
lieutenant general or vice admiral
13 = arrival of rear admiral (upper
half) or resident ministers
11 = arrival of brigadier general or
rear admiral (lower half) OR for
American charges d'affaires,
foreign counterparts, and consuls
general

U.S. Navy and Coast Guard Ranks (grade)

Officers:
Fleet Admiral (5-star, O8)
Admiral (4-star, O8)
Vice Admiral (3-star, O8)
Rear Admiral (upper half, 2-star, O81)
Rear Admiral (lower half, 1-star, O7;
    formerly Commodore)
Captain (O6)
Commander (O5)
Lieutenant Commander (O4)
Lieutenant (O3)
Lieutenant Junior Grade (O2)
Ensign (O1)
Chief Warrant Officers (W4)
Chief Warrant Officers (W3)
Chief Warrant Officers (W2)
Warrant Officer (W1)

Enlisted Personnel:
Master Chief Petty Officer (E9)
Senior Chief Petty Officer (E8)
Chief Petty Officer (E7)
Petty Officer First Class (E6)
Petty Officer Second Class (E5)
Petty Officer Third Class (E4)
Seaman (E3)
Seaman Apprentice (E2)
Seaman Recruit (E1)

U.S. Navy Groups

division = 4 ships
squadron = 2 divisions
fleet = 2 squadrons

U.S. Navy Operating Forces Organization

Pacific Fleet
    Third Fleet
    Seventh Fleet
Atlantic Fleet
    Second Fleet
U.S. Naval Forces Europe
    Sixth Fleet
Military Sealift Command
Naval Reserve Force
Mine Warfare Command
Operational and Test Evaluation
    Force
Naval Forces Southern Command
Naval Forces Central Command
    Middle East Force
Naval Special Warfare Command

U.S. Navy Organization

Office of the Undersecretary
Office of the Assistant Secretary
    (material)
Office of the Assistant Secretary
    (research & development)
Office of the Assistant Secretary
    (personnel & reserves)
Executive Offices of the Secretary
Office of the Chief of Naval
    Operations
Headquarters United States Marine
    Corps
United States Coast Guard (in
    wartime)
Bureau of Medicine and Surgery
Bureau of Naval Personnel
Bureau of Naval Weapons
Bureau of Ships
Bureau of Supplies and Accounts
Bureau of Yards and Docks

U.S. Reserves Ranks

(Air Force, Army, Navy)

Drilling Reserves, paid
    Category A

MILITARY
  U.S. Armed Forces
    Ranks (cont.)
NATIVE AMERICANS

Category B
Drilling Reserves, unpaid
  Category D
Inactive Reserves, unpaid/no training
  Category H

NATIVE AMERICANS

NORTH AMERICAN TRIBES

Native American Tribes—
North America

(According to Encyclopedia Americana, 1991)

Middle America
Maya
Olmec
Zapotec
Toltec
Aztec
Southwest
Taos
Santa Clara
San Ildefonso
Santo Domingo
Isleta
Acoma
Zuni
Hopi
Pima
Papago
Yuman
Navajo
Wasapai
Havasupai
Apache
The Eastern Woodlands
Natchez
Taensa
Choctaw
Chickasaw
Creek
Shawnee
Cherokee

Seminole
Yuchi
Catawva
Tuscarora
Powhatan Confederacy
Delaware
Iroquois
Huron
Algonkin
Fox
Sauk
Winnebago
Menomini
Ojibwa
The Plains
Blackfoot
Crow
Arapaho
Cheyenne
Comanche
Wichita
Pawnee
Omaha
Iowa
Dakota (or Sioux)
Mandan
Hidatsa
Assiniboin
Gros Ventre
The Great Basin
Paiute
Shoshoni
Bannock
California
Wintum
Pomo
Maidu
Miwok
Yokuts
The Plateau
Nez Perce
Umatilla
Flathead
Kutenai
Shuswap
Thompson

The Subarctic
Cree
Chpewyan
Beaver
Slave
Kaska
Kutchin
The Northwest Coast
Tlingit
Haida
Tsimshian
Bella Coola
Kwaikiutl
Nootka
Coast Salish
Chinook
Yurok
The Arctic
Aleut
Alaskan Eskimo
Canadian and Greenland Eskimo

POLITICAL STRUCTURE

Chief/Headman/Sachem: strongest
and/or wisest man
  Peace Chief: liaison between tribes
  Warrior Chief/Tree Chief:
    responsible for non-political
    activities
Shaman/Medicine Man: communed
  with supernatural spirits
Functionary: person chosen to
  oversee specific tasks in a tribe
Tribesman/Tribeswoman: general
  member of tribe, including
  braves
Adoptee: prisoner or slave who
  becamc member of tribe to
  replace dead Indian
Slave: people claimed through wars
  with other tribes

SOCIAL STRUCTURE

Nation/Group: by common
  occupation, location, and by
  language
Tribe/Village/Band: small
  settlements
  chiefs (at least two: civil chief in
    charge of affairs within tribe and
    a war chief to lead war parties
    against enemies)
  tribal council
Clan: related persons who shared a
  common ancestor and family
  responsibilities (extended family
  of 100 or more members)
  clan chief
  council (men only, though women
    often helped choose council)
Moiety/Half: family within the clans
  who competed or was assigned
  specific duties
Family: grandparents, parents, and
  their children
Fireside: (Iroquois only) mother and
  her children

also:

alliance of villages
alliance council (representatives from
  each village)
village
village council (representatives from
  each family)
chief (presiding officer and liaison for
  village or clan)

ORGANIZATIONS

ALCOHOLICS ANONYMOUS

Twelve Steps
  1. We admitted we were powerless
    over alcohol—that our lives had
    become unmanageable.

ORGANIZATIONS

Alcoolics Anonymous
(cont.)

2. Came to believe that a Power greater than ourselves could restore us to sanity.

3. Made a decision to turn our will and our lives over to the care of God as we understood Him.

4. Made a searching and fearless moral inventory of ourselves.

5. Admitted to God, to ourselves, and to another human being the exact nature of our wrongs.

6. We're entirely ready to have God remove all these defects of character.

7. Humbly asked Him to remove our shortcomings.

8. Made a list of all persons we had harmed, and become willing to make amends with all of them.

9. Made direct amends to such people whenever possible, except when to do so would injure them or harm others.

10. Continued to take personal inventory and when we were wrong promptly admitted it.

11. Sought through prayer and meditation to improve our conscious contact with God as we understood Him, praying only for knowledge of His will for us and the power to carry that out.

12. Having had a spiritual awakening as the result of these Steps, we tried to carry this message to alcoholics, and to practice these principles in all our affairs.

BOY SCOUTS & GIRL SCOUTS

Boy Scouts of America Rankings

Tiger Cub	grade 1	
Cub Scout	grades 2–5	group = pack or den
Arrow of Light		
Webelos		
Bear		
Wolf		
Bobcat		
Boy Scout	grades 6–8	group = troop
Eagle		
Life		
Star		
First Class		
Second Class		
Tenderfoot		
Explorer	grades 9–12, up to age 21	group = post or ship

Girl Scouts of the U.S. of America Rankings

Daisy	age 4–5
Brownie	age 6–8
Junior	age 9–11
Cadette	age 12–14
Senior	age 14–17

FREEMASONRY

Freemasonry Hierarchy

(secret brotherhood, from lowest to highest)

York Rite

Lodge
1. Entered Apprentice
2. Fellow Craftsman
3. Master Mason

Chapter
4. Mark Master
5. Past Master
6. Most Excellent Master
7. Royal Arch Mason

Council
8. Royal Master
9. Select Master
10. Super Excellent Master

Commandery
11. Red Cross Knight
12. Knight Templar
13. Knight of Malta

Scottish Rite

Lodge
1. Entered Apprentice
2. Fellow Craftsman
3. Master Mason

Lodge of Perfection
4. Secret Master
5. Perfect Master
6. Intimate Secretary
7. Provost and Judge
8. Intendant of the Building
9. Master Elect of Nine
10. Master Elect of Fifteen
11. Sublime Master Elected
12. Grand Master Architect
13. Master of the Ninth Arch
14. Grand Elect Mason

Councils of Princes of Jerusalem
15. Knight of the East or Sword
16. Prince of Jerusalem

Chapters of Rose Croix
17. Knight of the East and West
18. Knight of the Rose Croix de H.R.D.M.

Consistories of Sublime Princes of the Royal Secret
19. Grand Pontiff
20. Master Ad Vitam
21. Patriarch Noachite
22. Prince of Libanus
23. Chief of the Tabernacle
24. Prince of the Tabernacle
25. Knight of the Brazen Serpent
26. Prince of Mercy
27. Commander of the Temple
28. Knight of the Sun
29. Knight of St. Andrew
30. Grand Elect Knight, K.H., or Knight of the White and Black Eagle
31. Grand Inspector Inquisitor Commander
32. Sublime Prince of the Royal Secret
33. Sovereign Grand Inspector-General of the 33rd and Last Degree

LIBRARY

Library System

Acquisitions
Cataloguing
Circulation
  Borrower registration
  Checkouts
    Regular Checkouts
    Reserve Checkouts
    Special Checkouts
  Check-ins
  Overdue Books
Reference

MAFIA

Hierarchy (Cosa Nostra)

Commission (heads of most powerful families)
Don or Capo di Tutti Capi or Boss (authority only challenged by commission)
Bougata or Underboss (equivalent to vice president or deputy director)
Consigliere (counselor or adviser)
Caporegime (captain or lieutenant, under the underboss, a go-between for the workers and the don)
Soldier/Button Man (often in charge of one of the family's legal operations)

SALVATION ARMY

Structure

General (runs international
   headquarters)
High Council
   commissioners (run territorial
      headquarters)
divisional headquarters
corps command

officers:
chief officer (national commander)
commissioner
lieutenant commissioner
colonel
lieutenant colonel
brigadier
major
captain
lieutenant
cadet

noncommissioned:
corps sergeant major
color sergeant

PSYCHOLOGY

BRANCHES

Applied Psychology
   clinical psychology
   consumer psychology
   counseling psychology
   engineering psychology
   environmental psychology
   industrial/organizational
      psychology
   personnel psychology
   psychiatry
Experimental/Basic Psychology
   child psychology
   cognitive psychology
   comparative psychology
   developmental psychology
   educational psychology
   personality psychology
   physiological psychology
   quantitative/psychometric
      psychology
   social psychology

DRUNKENNESS STAGES

verbose
grandiose
amicose
bellicose
morose
stuporous
comatose

FREUD, SIGMUND (1856–1939)

Division of the Psyche

conscious (aware of oneself and one's
   environment, able to perceive and
   react to objects and events)
preconscious (all contents of the
   mind not immediately at a
   conscious level, but which can
   readily be brought into
   consciousness)
unconscious (the part of the mind
   not readily accessible to conscious
   awareness, but that may manifest
   its existence in symptom
   formation, in dreams, and under
   influence of drugs)

Structural Categorization

ego (desires countered by defense
   mechanisms; essential core that
   balances the other two)
id (primitive illogical urges;
   animalistic part of psyche)
superego (guilt-causing aggressive
   elements; conscience that governs
   our standards of conduct)

GOALS OF PSYCHOLOGY

prediction
application
control
explanation
description

JUNG, CARL

Personality Types

attitude types:
extroverted (outward-looking)
introverted (inward-looking)

which are then grouped according to which psychological functions are the most developed:
feeling
intuition
sensation
thinking

LEVELS OF CONSCIOUSNESS

(ascending order)

1. ordinary wakefulness: body relaxed and mind stilled
2. deep rest or personal awareness
3. cosmic consciousness: a sense of illumination beyond self and time
4. God consciousness: sense of inseparability of creator and creation
5. consciousness transcended in a unity with the whole, or oneness

MASLOW'S HIERARCHY OF NEEDS

(five sets of basic needs, in order of basic to less necessary)

1. Physiological—hunger, thirst, sex, etc.
2. Safety—protection against danger, threat, deprivation, etc.
3. Social—belonging, association, acceptance by others, giving and receiving friendship and love
4. Ego—self-esteem (self-confidence, independence, achievement, competence, knowledge) and personal reputation (status, recognition, appreciation, respect)
5. Self-fulfillment—realizing one's own potential, continued self-development, creativity

PHASES OF A MEMORY

learning (experiencing or perceiving event, registering or recording a description in memory)
retention (when the person is not thinking about that event)
retrieval (a memory is remembered and utilized in guiding performance)
also:
short-term memory system (contents of awareness to which one has immediate access)
long-term memory system (everything else in memory that typically can be retrieved, but more slowly)

PHOBIA CLASSIFICATION

Animal and Plant Phobias

animals: zoophobia
bacteria: bacteriophobia, microphobia
bees: apiphobia, melissophobia
birds: ornithophobia
cats: ailurophobia, gatophobia
chickens: alektorophobia
dogs: cynophobia
feathers: pteronophobia
fish: ichthyophobia
flowers: anthophobia

PSYCHOLOGY
Phobia Classification.
(cont.)

fur: doraphobia
horses: hippophobia
insects: entomophobia
leaves: phyllophobia
lice: pediculophobia
mice: musophobia
microbes: bacilliphobia
parasites: parasitophobia
reptiles: batrachophobia
snakes: ophidiophobia, ophiophobia
spiders: arachnophobia
trees: dendrophobia
wasps: spheksophobia
worms: helminthophobia

Environmental Phobias

auroral lights: auroraphobia
clouds: nephophobia
dampness, moisture: hygrophobia
flood: antlophobia
fog: homichlophobia
ice, frost: cryophobia
lakes: limnophobia
lightning: astraphobia
meteors: meteorophobia
precipices: cremnophobia
rain: ombrophobia
rivers: potamophobia
sea: thalassophobia
snow: chionophobia
stars: siderophobia
sun: heliophobia
thunder: brontophobia,
  keraunophobia
water: hydrophobia
wind: ancraophobia

Food and Drink Phobias

drink, alcohol: potophobia
drinking: dipsophobia
eating: phagophobia
food: sitophobia
meat: carnophobia

Health and Anatomical Phobias

beards: pogonophobia
blood: haematophobia

cancer: cancerophobia,
  carcinophobia
childbirth: tocophobia
cholera: cholerophobia
death, corpse: necrophobia,
  thanatophobia
deformity: dysmorphophobia
disease: nosophobia, pathophobia
drugs: pharmacophobia
eyes: ommatophobia
faeces: coprophobia
germs: spermophobia
hair: chaetophobia
heart conditions: cardiophobia
heredity: patroiophobia
illness: nosemaphobia
infection: mysophobia
inoculations, injections:
  trypanophobia
insanity: lyssophobia, maniaphobia
knees: genuphobia
leprosy: leprophobia
mind: psychophobia
physical love: erotophobia
poison: toxiphobia
pregnancy: maieusiophobia
semen: spermatophobia
sex: genophobia
sexual intercourse: coitophobia
skin: dermatophobia
skin disease: dermatosiophobia
soiling: rypophobia
surgical operations: ergasiophobia
syphilis: syphilophobia
teeth: odontophobia
tuberculosis: phthisiophobia
venereal disease: cypridophobia
vomiting: emetophobia
wounds, injury: traumatophobia

Inanimate Object Phobias

books: bibliophobia
crystals, glass: crystallophobia
glass: nelophobia
machinery: mechanophobia
metals: metallophobia

mirrors: eisoptrophobia
missiles: ballistophobia
money: chrometophobia
needles: belonophobia
pins: enetephobia
points: aichurophobia
slime: blennophobia, myxophobia
string: linonophobia

Miscellaneous Phobias

certain names: onomatophobia
darkness: nyctophobia
dawn: eosophobia
daylight: phengophobia
depth: bathophobia
dirt: mysophobia
disorder: ataxiophobia
draughts: anemophobia
dreams: oneirophobia
duration: chronophobia
dust: amathophobia, koniphobia
electricity: electrophobia
everything: pantophobia
failure: kakorraphiaphobia
fall of man-made satellites:
    keraunothnetophobia
fears: phobophobia
fire: pyrophobia
flashes: selaphobia
flogging: mastigophobia
freedom: eleutherophobia
ghosts: phasmophobia
graves: taphophobia
gravity: barophobia
ideas: ideophobia
imperfection: atelophobia
jealousy: zelophobia
justice: dikephobia
marriage: gamophobia
monsters, monstrosities:
    teratophobia
music: musicophobia
names: nomatophobia
narrowness: anginaphobia
neglect of duty: paralipophobia
new things: neophobia

night, darkness: achluophobia
novelty: cainophobia
nudity: gymnophobia
number 13: triskaidekaphobia,
    terdekaphobia
one thing: monophobia
poverty: peniaphobia
punishment: poinephobia
responsibility: hypegiaphobia
ridicule: katagelophobia
ruin: atephobia
rust: iophobia
shock: hormephobia
stealing: kleptophobia
stillness: eremophobia
strong light: photophobia
void: kenophobia
weakness: asthenophobia
words: logophobia
work: ergophobia
writing: graphophobia
Phobias concerning Groups
black people: negrophobia
children: paediphobia
human beings: anthropophobia
men: androphobia
robbers: harpaxophobia
women: gynophobia
young girls: parthenophobia

Phobias concerning Religion

churches: ecclesiaphobia
demons: demonophobia
God: theophobia
heaven: ouranophobia
hell: hadephobia, stygiophobia
sacred things: hierophobia
Satan: Satanophobia
sinning: peccatophobia

Sensory Phobias

being cold: frigophobia
being dirty: automysophobia
being scratched: amychophobia
being touched: haphephobia

PSYCHOLOGY
Phobia Classification.
(cont.)

blushing: ereuthophobia, eyrythrophobia
cold: cheimatophobia
colour: chromatophobia, chromophobia, psychrophobia
fatigue: kopophobia, ponophobia
heat: thermophobia
itching: acarophobia, scabiophobia
noise: phonophobia
odours: osmophobia
odours (body): osphresiophobia
pain: algophobia, odynophobia
pleasure: hedonophobia
sleep: hypnophobia
smell: olfactophobia
smothering, choking: pnigerophobia
sound: akousticophobia
speaking: halophobia
speaking aloud: phonophobia
speech: lalophobia
sourness: acerophobia
stings: cnidophobia
stooping: kyphophobia
taste: geumatophobia
thinking: phronemophobia
touch: haptophobia
touching: haphephobia, thixophobia
trembling: tremophobia

Situation Phobias

being alone: monophobia, autophobia
being beaten: rhabdophobia
being bound: merinthophobia
being buried alive: taphophobia
being looked at: scopophobia
crowds: demophobia, ochlophobia
enclosed spaces: claustrophobia
going to bed: clinophobia
heights: acrophobia, altophobia
high places: hypsophobia
home: domatophobia, oikophobia
home surroundings: ecophobia
infinity: apeirophobia
passing high objects: batophobia
places: topophobia
open spaces: agoraphobia

school: scholionophobia
shadows: sciophobia
sitting idle: thaasophobia
standing: stasophobia
standing upright: stasiphobia
solitude: eremitophobia, eremophobia

Travel Phobias

bridge: gephyrophobia
crossing streets: dromophobia
flying, the air: aerophobia
motion: kinesophobia, kinetophobia
sea swell: cymophobia
speed: tachophobia
travel: hodophobia
traveling by train: siderodromophobia
vehicles: amaxophobia, ochophobia
walking: basiphobia

STATES OF FEELING
(agitated to unaware)

Beta-Theta state: disturbed and negative; feeling of unhappiness
Beta state: subject to anger, excitement, tension
Alpha-Beta state: wakeful, calm, creative, perceptive; sensitive, investigative, intellectual thoughts
Alpha state: feeling of transcendence; alert, calm, elated; sense of insight
Alpha-Theta state: inner stillness; decreased self-awareness; pleasant feeling of freedom
Theta state: dreamlike trance; no self-awareness

STATES OF MIND / MOODS
(Personality and Ability Testing Inc.'s eight key mood states it measures)

1. anxiety
2. stress
3. depression

4. regression
5. fatigue
6. guilt
7. extraversion
8. arousal

SCHOOLS

COLLEGE DEGREES

Associate (2 years)
Bachelor's (4 years)
Master's (2–6 years)
Doctorate (3–8 years)

COLLEGE GRADUATING HONORARY TITLES

cum laude, with honor
magna cum laude, with great honor
summa cum laude, with highest
   honor

PUBLIC SCHOOL SYSTEM

(example from U.S. Census)

central office administration
superintendent
deputy/associate superintendent
assistant superintendent
finance and business administrator
instructional services administrator
public relations/information
   administrator
staff personnel services administrator
subject area supervisors
school building administration
      (elementary, junior high/middle,
      senior high)
   principals
   assistant principals
   classroom teachers
auxiliary professional personnel
   counselors
   librarians
   school nurses

secretarial/clerical personnel
   central office
      secretaries/stenographers
   central office accounting/payroll
      clerks
   central office clerk-typists
   school building
      secretaries/stenographers
   school building library clerks
other support personnel
   teacher aides (instructional,
      noninstructional)
   custodians
   cafeteria workers
   bus drivers

SOCIAL STUDIES

BRANCHES

Anthropology

Cultural Anthropology
   Archaeology (study of remains of
         past cultures and
         civilizations)
      historic archaeology
         (reconstruction of sites
         supplemented by written
         sources)
      prehistoric archaeology (cultures
         with no written languages)
      protohistoric archaeology (some
         documentation)
   Ethnography (study of individual
         cultures)
   Ethnology (study of historical and
         structural views of human
         cultures)
      comparative ethnology
         folklore, mythology,
         musicology, etc.
      economic anthropology
         (economic analyses of
         cultures)
      ethnopsychology or cultural

PSYCHOLOGY
SCHOOLS

psychology (psychological features within cultures)

social anthropology (social features of cultures)

Linguistic anthropology (study of languages of cultures and civilizations)

Paleoanthropology (study of fossils to trace physical characteristics)

Physical Anthropology (study of man as biological species)

Anthropometry (measurement of body parts)

Genetics and growth studies

Human evolution

Primatology (study of primate behavior and societies)

Economics

Business administration

Consumer economics

Economic geography

Economic theory

Finance

accounting

banking and financial services

public finance

International economics

Investment

securities

stock market

Labor economics

Taxation

Geography

Cartography (mapping)

Human geography:

cultural and social geography (cultural and social values, tools, and organization)

economic geography (how people satisfy their needs and make a living)

historical geography (evolution of present patterns)

linguistic geography (language characteristics)

medical geography (health and diseases, malnutrition, health-care facilities)

political geography (political organization)

population geography (distribution of population in relation to certain characteristics)

social geography (social characteristics)

urban geography (concentration in cities and metropolitan areas)

Physical geography:

biogeography (distribution and ecology of plants and animals)

ecology (science of relationships between organisms and environment)

phytogeography (concerning plants)

zoogeography (concerning animals)

climatology and meteorology (study of state of atmosphere)

geomorphology (study of the forms and processes of land's surface)

hydrography and oceanography (study of earth's waters)

paleogeography (study and interpretation of ancient written documents)

resource management and environmental studies

soil geography (study of distribution and types of soil)

Regional geography (associations within regions of all or some of the above elements)

History

Events

Historiography (historical research and presentation)

People, civilizations, and institutions

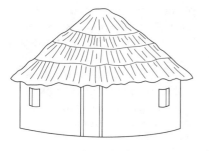

Hut (many cultures)

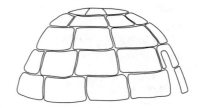

Igloo (Eskimo)

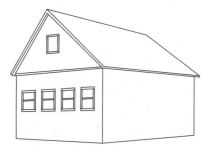

Izba (rural Russia)

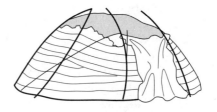

Pile dwelling (many cultures)

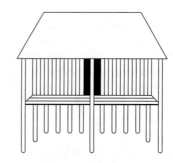

Wigwam (Native American)

Tepee (Native American)

Yurt (Mongol)

Native Houses

Philosophy of history
Linguistics
Psychology
Sociology
Applied sociology / social work /
    social service
Behaviorism
Biological sociology
Ethnic and racial relations
Marriage and the family
Mass communication and public
    opinion
Population growth
Social concerns
    correctional services / penology
    criminology and delinquency
    demography
    poverty
    welfare
Social gerontology
Social inequality and stratification
Social organization and
    disorganization
Social psychology
Sociology of art
Sociology of education
Sociology of family
Sociology of government/military
Sociology of industry
Sociology of language
Sociology of law
Sociology of medicine
Sociology of politics
Sociology of sex or gender differences
Sociology of religion

UNITED NATIONS

ORGANIZATION

1. General Assembly: discussion
   body (each member nation may
   send up to 5 representatives)
2. Security Council: monitors world
   peace (5 permanent members,
   with veto power: US, Russia, UK,
   France, China; 10 nonpermanent
   members)
3. Economic and Social Council:
   works on economic, social,
   cultural, and humanitarian
   problems (e.g. one of its agencies
   is UNICEF)
4. Trusteeship Council: prepares
   members for self-government and
   independence; handles trust
   territories—colonies that have
   been placed under the care of a
   country by the UN.
5. International Court of
   Justice/World Court: settles
   international legal problems (15
   judges elected for 9-yr terms by
   General Assembly and Security
   Council)
6. Secretariat (Secretary-General):
   political responsibility to carry out
   U.N. Charter's aims
       Executive Office of the
           Secretary-General
       Under-Secretary for General
           Assembly Affairs
       Offices of the Under-Secretaries
           for Special Political Affairs
       Office of Legal Affairs
       Office of the Controller
       Office of Personnel
   also:
       Political and Security Council
           Affairs
       Department of Economic and
           Social Affairs
       Department of Trusteeship and
           Information from Non-Self
           Governing Territories
       Office of Public Information
       Office of Conference Services
       Office of General Services
       U.N. Office at Geneva

BASIC RIGHTS OF ALL CHILDREN

1. To enjoy the rights listed regardless of race, color, religion or nationality.
2. To be able to grow in a healthy, normal way, free and dignified. Children should be specially protected and should be given special opportunities to grow.
3. To name and nationality.
4. To social security. This includes a decent place to live, good food, health care, and opportunities to play.
5. To special treatment, schooling and care if handicapped.
6. To love and understanding. Children should be raised so that they feel secure and loved and live with their parents, if possible.
7. To free schooling and an equal opportunity to become everything they can be.
8. To prompt protection and relief in times of disaster.
9. To protection against all kinds of neglect, cruelty, and abuse from others.
10. To protection from any kind of unfair treatment because of race or religion.

UNITED NATIONS

In a hierarchy, every employee tends to rise to his level of incompetence.

—Laurence Johnston Peter, *The Peter Principle*

CHAPTER NINE

BUSINESS & ECONOMICS

ACCOUNTING, BUDGETING AND PLANNING

Accounting Areas

financial or general accounting

cost accounting

managerial/management accounting (broad functional decision-making)

auditing

systems (design and installation)

taxes

budgeting

management services (administrative and specialized services)

ACCOUNTING TYPES

private or industrial accounting (confined to a single firm)

public accounting (offered to general public)

government accounting

fiduciary accounting (keeping of records by a trustee or administrator)

national income accounting (estimates gross national product, etc.)

integrated data processing (electronic collection, analysis, information-giving)

BUSINESS BUDGETS

A master budget coordinates and summarizes all subbudgets of a firm. Subbudgets cover particular segments or activities of a firm. Appropriations budgets usually show maximum amounts that may be used for particular projects.

Budget types

operating budgets (items involved in regular operation of firm)

programmed budgets (expenses subject to management's discretion, such as research and development or advertising)

capital budgets (proposed outlays for land, plant, equipment, furniture, fixtures)

fixed/static/forecast budgets (developed for only one level of activity)

variable budgets (figures developed to fit various levels of activity)

by duration:

short-term budgets (usu. a year long)
continuous/rolling budgets (current month and following 11 instead of calendar or fiscal year)
long-term budgets (5–20 years long)

BUSINESS PLAN

cover sheet

table of contents

executive summary

present situation

objectives

management and organization

product and service description

equipment and facilities

market analysis

financial projections

appendices

PERSONAL OR HOUSEHOLD BUDGET

Income

Salaries (total in household)

Bonuses, tips

Investments (interest, dividends, capital gains, real estate income)

TOTAL INCOME

ACCOUNTING,
BUDGETING AND
PLANNING
Personal or
Household Budget
(cont.)

Expenses

FIXED EXPENSES
Housing (rent or mortgage payments)
Food
Transportation
Utilities (gas, electric, water, telephone)
Taxes (federal, state, and local income;
local property tax; Social Security)
Interest payments (car, bank loan,
credit card, other loans)
Principal payments (amounts of
borrowed principal repaid)
Insurance (health, life, property)
Education (tuition, supplies, room
and board)
Personal expenses
Contributions

VARIABLE EXPENSES
Clothing
Entertainment
Vacations and recreation
Furniture, appliances, and home
improvements
Health and beauty
Savings (general or specific for future
purchases or objectives)
Miscellaneous
TOTAL EXPENSES

AMOUNT AVAILABLE FOR
INVESTING
(total income minus total expenses)

INCREASES

Debit	Credit
Assets	Liabilities
Expenses	Net worth
	Income

DECREASES

Debit	Credit
Liabilities	Assets
Net worth	Expenses
Income	

Accounting Debits and Credits

PERSONAL NET WORTH
(checklist to calculate current net worth)

Assets
Cash on hand and liquid assets:
Checking and savings
accounts
Cash value of life insurance
U.S. savings bonds
Equity in pension funds
Money market funds
Brokerage funds
Trusts
Debts owed you
Other
TOTAL
Personal holdings:
Car(s) (current value)
Home(s)
Boat(s)
Major appliances
Jewelry, furs, etc.
Antiques and collectibles
Art
Other
TOTAL
Investments:
Common stocks
Preferred stocks
Corporate and municipal
bonds
Mutual funds
Certificates of deposit
Business investments
Real estate investments
IRAs
Other
TOTAL
TOTAL ASSETS

Liabilities
Bills due
Revolving charge and bank-card
debts
Taxes due
Outstanding mortgage principal

Outstanding loans (bank,
    insurance, etc.)
Stock margin accounts payable
Other debts
TOTAL LIABILITIES

NET WORTH (Assets minus
    Liabilities)

BANKING

Numbers on a Check

(along bottom of bank check)
1. bank's Federal Reserve District
2. bank's individual ID number
3. check digit (used in a computer
   calculation to determine whether
   other digits are correct)
4. bank branch number
5. account number
6. check number

**(upper right-hand corner
of bank check)**
1. bank's American Banking
   Association number—bank's
   individual ID number
2. (under the line) bank's Federal
   Reserve District

**(after check has been cashed/cancelled,
bottom right of bank check)**
1. the amount of money you wrote
   the check for

BUSINESS MEETINGS

ORDER OF BUSINESS
(Robert's Rules of Order)

1. reading the minutes of the
   previous meeting (and their
   approval)
2. reports of standing committees

FORM OF A PERSONALIZED CHECK

Key to numerals

1. Serial number of personal check
2. Area bank uses to sort and record
   checks
3. Check routing numbers
4. Anybank's routing code (used by employers
   for direct deposits)
5. Customer's account number
6. Space where monetary exchange between
   banks is coded

3. reports of select committees
4. unfinished business
5. new business

BUSINESS STUDIES

BRANCHES

Advertising
General business practice
Goods production
Labor and labor unions
Management
Manufacturing
Marketing
Merchandising
Real estate
Services
Trade

COMMUNICATIONS & MEDIA

INDUSTRY CLASSIFICATION

advertising agencies
book publishing
business information services
cable television: cable system
   operators, cable network
   companies
computer networks and systems
filmed entertainment
interactive digital media
magazine publishing: consumer
   magazines, business & professional
   magazines
miscellaneous communications:
   satellites
newspaper publishing
photography
recorded image and sound
telephone and telegraph
television and radio broadcasting: TV
   networks, TV and radio stations

NEWSPAPERS

Editorial Sequence

1. news received
2. story assessed by city editor
3. city editor informs news editor
4. reporter assigned
5. photographer assigned by picture
   editor (as appropriate)
6. reporter covers event,
   photographer may assist
7. news editor decides story's
   placement in paper
8. staff writer may assist with
   research and writing
9. reporter files story
10. photographer prepares prints
11. page is laid out by make-up
   editor
12. copy reader at copy desk checks
   reporter's story, writes headline,
   marks copy for compositor
13. news editor reviews story and
   sends to the composing room
14. managing editor and chief
   editors review the day and decide
   what to include in the next
   edition

Six Questions asked by Reporters

who
what
where
when
how
why

ADVERTISING MEDIA

Print
direct mail: promotional advertising
   mailed to homes and businesses
magazines: consumer, business and
   professional
newspapers: local, national, business
Yellow Pages: national, local

Broadcast

radio: network, local, spot

television: network, cable network, syndication time; national spot, local spot

Electronic

electronic mail

Internet and World Wide Web (home pages, electronic catalogs)

Transit

outdoor advertising/billboard

Other

cinema

fringe media: hot-air balloons, parking meters, supermarket carts, milk bottles, window displays

point-of-purchase/sale promotion

special sales

CORPORATIONS

MANAGEMENT STRUCTURE

(e.g., Ford Motor Company)

Chairman of the Board

Board of Directors (represents interest of stockholders)

Chief Executive Officer

President

Chief Financial Officer

Division Organization (in each division)

Product Development
    Group Vice President

Marketing and Sales
    Group Vice President

Manufacturing
    Group Vice President

Production Purchasing
    Group Vice President

Executive and Non-Production
        Purchasing
    Group Vice President

Quality/Process
    Leadership/Employee
    Relations/Consumer
    Affairs/Finance
  Group Vice President

Senior Managers

Middle Managers

Lower Managers

ECONOMICS

BRANCHES OF STUDY

Business administration

Consumer economics

Economic geography

Economic theory

Finance
    accounting
    banking and financial services
    public finance

International economics

Investment
    securities
    stock market

Labor economics

Taxation

BUSINESS CYCLE

(alternating periods of business prosperity and repression)

1. Prosperity: industry picks up, more labor and capital are employed, higher wages, interest rates rise; large volume of business

2. Overextension and speculation: expansion tightens credit and raises interest rates, prices rise, profiteering sets in, credit becomes inflated, costs rise more than selling prices and speculation makes prices higher than warranted

3. Crisis: collapse of a period of prosperity and high profits

4. Emergency liquidation: goods placed on the market for whatever they will bring
5. Depression: prices low, curtailment of production, widespread unemployment, reduction or elimination of profits
6. Readjustment: irregular and uneven price movements after bottom reached; sharp competition, lower production costs, elimination of the inefficient
7. Recuperation or revival: deflation completed, bank reserves high, interest rates low

ECONOMIC SYSTEMS

1. Market economy or private enterprise (forces of supply and demand at work; ownership and control of companies by private individuals and not by the state)
2. Command economy (centrally planned/state economy)
3. Mixed economy (state-provided goods and services AND private enterprise)

Types of economics

Macroeconomics: how the economy as a whole works
Microeconomics: how scarce resources are allocated to meet needs of consumers

EUROPEAN ECONOMIC COMMUNITY

Member Nations

established on November 1, 1993, when the Maastricht Treaty was ratified by the following 12 nations:

Belgium
Denmark
France
Germany
Great Britain
Greece
Ireland
Italy
Luxembourg
Netherlands
Portugal
Spain

EMPLOYEES

BENEFITS

(example for private business)

paid benefits
  holidays
  lunch time
  military leave
  personal leave
  rest time / coffee breaks
  sick leave
  vacations
  worker's compensation
  unemployment compensation
unpaid benefits
  maternity leave
  paternity leave
  family leave
  funeral leave
  jury duty leave
insurance plans
  accident/sickness
  dental care
  life insurance
  long-term disability
  medical care
  short-term disability
retirement and savings plans
  401-K
  defined benefit pension
  defined contribution
  IRA
  Keogh plan
additional benefits
  child care

early retirement
eldercare
employee assistance programs
    (EAP)
flexible benefits plans
golden parachute
long-term care insurance
nonproduction bonuses, cash
parking
recreation facilities
reimbursement accounts
relocation allowance
severance pay
travel accident insurance
tuition assistance
wellness programs

FACTORY

CAR FACTORY STRUCTURE

management
designer/engineer: plans assemblies,
    systems, and processes
machine operator: works machines
    that fabricate and assemble parts
supervisor: oversees assembly-line
    workers
assembly-line worker: works with a
    team to assemble systems and
    assemblies
quality tester: checks finished parts
    and assemblies to ensure specified
    form, fit, and finish
driver: transports new cars to their
    destinations (car dealers)

CAR MANUFACTURING SEQUENCE

steel is cut and stamped
steel is welded by robots for car body
body is painted by robots
inside work is completed
body lowered onto engine and
    chassis
doors and windows added
final assembly, exterior
car is washed and polished
car is tested
car is shipped

GOLD

KARAT RANKS

*(karat is 1/24 part, or 4.1667 percent, of the
whole; thus, 16-karat gold is 16 parts gold
and 8 parts alloying metal)*

24k = 100% pure, fine gold
22k = 91.75%
18k = 75%
14k = 58.5%
12k = 50%
10k = 42%
 9k = 37.8% (not legally gold)
 8k = 33.75% (not legally gold)

INDUSTRIES

CHEMICAL PROCESS INDUSTRIES

adhesives industry
dyes industry
explosives industry
heavy chemical industries
synthetic fiber industry
paints and varnishes industry
papermaking industry
pharmaceutical industry
plastics and resins industry
rubber industry
soaps and detergents industry
cosmetics industry

EXTRACTION AND PROCESSING INDUSTRIES

coal
industrial metals industries
    chromium and manganese

copper, nickel, and cobalt
extractive metallurgy
iron
light metals
low-melting metals
mineral processing
mining
ore deposits
physical metallurgy
precious metals
refractory metals
steel
uranium
petroleum and natural gas

MANUFACTURING INDUSTRIES

aerospace industry
appliances
automotive industry
clothing and footwear industry
computers
electronics
floor coverings
food processing
furniture industry
printing
ship design and construction

NONFARM INDUSTRY CLASSIFICATION

(U.S. Census)

Goods-producing
 mining
 construction
 manufacturing
 nondurable manufacturing
Service-producing
 transportation
 wholesale trade
 retail trade
 finance, insurance, real estate
 services
  hotels and other lodging
  personal services

business services
auto repair, services, and garages
miscellaneous repair shops
motion pictures
amusement and recreation
 services
health services
legal services
educational services
social services
engineering, management, and
 consulting services
accounting, auditing, and
 bookkeeping services
research and testing services
management and public
 relations services
government

TEXTILE INDUSTRIES

development of textiles and
 textile industry
production of fabric
production of yarn
textile consumption
textile finishing processes

TECHNOLOGY INDUSTRY CLASSIFICATION

Level I: industries whose proportion
 of research and development
 employment is at least 50 percent
 higher than the average of all
 industries surveyed (e.g. drugs,
 communications equipment)
Level II: industries whose proportion
 of R & D employment is at least
 equal to the average of all
 industries surveyed, but less than
 50 percent higher than the average
 (e.g. pulp mills, engines and
 turbines)

INSURANCE

CLASSIFICATION

(by risks covered)
personal
property
liability
malpractice

(by perils covered)
accident
sickness
old age
fire
flood
storm
riot and civil commotion
crime

(by losses covered)
expense reimbursement
income replacement
replacement value

(by property covered)
dwellings
buildings
contents
money
vehicles

EXAMPLES OF INSURANCE

Compulsory Insurance
  Government
    personal risks: civil service
      retirement systems
    property risks: Federal Deposit
      Insurance Corporation
    liability risks: Federal Employees'
      Compensation Act
  Private
    personal risks: temporary
      nonoccupational disability
      insurance
    liability risks: automobile
      insurance

Voluntary Insurance
  Government
    personal risks: Veterans
      Administration
    property risks: Federal Housing
      Administration
  Private
    personal risks: life insurance
    property risks: income
      replacement
    liability risks: liability insurance
      on car, home, business

INSURANCE TYPES

Fire insurance
  standard provisions
  indirect losses
Marine insurance
  ocean marine insurance
  inland marine insurance
Property and liability insurance
  disability insurance
  homeowner's insurance
  motor-vehicle insurance
  liability insurance
  theft insurance
  aviation insurance
  workers' compensation insurance
  credit insurance
  title insurance
  unemployment insurance
  miscellaneous insurance
Suretyship
  fidelity bonds
  surety bonds
Life and health insurance
  life insurance
  private health insurance
Group insurance
  group life insurance
  group health insurance
  group dental insurance
  group vision insurance
  group annuities
Government-sponsored and/or

government-administered health insurance

Medicare

Medicaid

INVESTMENT

INVESTMENT OPTIONS

Direct investments
certificates of deposit
commodities
common stock
corporate bonds
futures
government bonds
  assessment bonds
  general obligation bonds
  revenue bonds
money market funds
mutual funds
preferred stock
real estate
securities
Institutional investments
investment clubs
life insurance
pension funds
savings institutions

MUTUAL FUNDS

Eight Types

Aggressive Growth Funds—buy low and sell high

Growth Funds—similar to the above, but don't usually trade stock options or borrow money to trade with

Growth-Income Funds—invest in utilities, Dow Industrials, and other seasoned stocks

Income Funds—focus on dividend income

International Funds—hold primarily foreign securities

Asset Allocation Funds—focus on stocks, bonds, gold, real estate, and money markets

Precious Metal Funds—investment in gold, silver, and platinum

Bond Funds—invest in corporate and government bonds

MARKETING

MARKET TYPES

markets for labor and services
markets for manufactured goods
markets for money and capital
markets for primary commodities

PRODUCT LIFE CYCLE

market research
product development
introduction
market growth
market maturity
sales decline

SALES & MARKETING GOALS

A: attention, get the attention of the consumer

I: interest, develop consumer's interest

D: desire, create a desire for the product

A: action, stimulate a course of action by the consumer

MONEY—U.S.

COIN DENOMINATIONS

$1, President Dwight Eisenhower (silver dollar)

$1, Susan B. Anthony (discontinued)

$ 0.50, President John F. Kennedy

$ 0.25, President George Washington

$ 0.10, President Franklin D.
Roosevelt

$ 0.05, President Thomas Jefferson

$ 0.01, President Abraham Lincoln

F6, Atlanta
G7, Chicago
H8, St. Louis
I9, Minneapolis
J10, Kansas City
K11, Dallas
L12, San Francisco

PAPER DENOMINATIONS

(discontinued in 1969)

$100,000 note, President Woodrow
Wilson (back is ornate 100,000)

$10,000, Treasury Secretary Salmon P.
Chase (1861–64) (back is ornate
10,000)

$5,000, President James Madison
(back is ornate 5000)

$1,000, President Grover Cleveland
(back is ornate 1000)

$500, President William McKinley
(back is ornate 500)

(currently in circulation)

$100, Benjamin Franklin (back is
Independence Hall)

$50, President Ulysses S. Grant (back
is US Capitol)

$20, President Andrew Jackson (back
is White House)

$10, Alexander Hamilton (back is
US Treasury Building)

$ 5, President Abraham Lincoln (back
is Lincoln Memorial)

$ 2, President Thomas Jefferson (back
is "The Signing of the Declaration
of Independence")

$ 1, President George Washington
(back is "One" and obverse/reverse
of Great Seal)

Paper Denominations by Federal Reserve Branch

A1, Boston
B2, New York
C3, Philadelphia
D4, Cleveland
E5, Richmond

SAVINGS BONDS

$50, George Washington
$75, John Adams
$100, Thomas Jefferson
$200, James Madison
$500, Alexander Hamilton
$1,000, Benjamin Franklin
$5,000, Paul Revere
$10,000, J. Wilson

TREASURY BILLS

$1,000, H. McCulloch
$5,000, J.G. Carlisle
$10,000, J. Sherman
$50,000, C. Glass
$100,000, A. Gallatin
$1,000,000, D. Wolcott

TREASURY BONDS

$50, Thomas Jefferson
$100, Andrew Jackson
$500, George Washington
$1,000, Abraham Lincoln
$5,000, James Monroe
$10,000, Grover Cleveland
$100,000, Ulysses S. Grant
$1,000,000, Theodore Roosevelt

TREASURY NOTES

$1,000, Abraham Lincoln
$5,000, James Monroe
$10,000, Grover Cleveland
$100,000, Ulysses S. Grant
$1,000,000, Theodore Roosevelt

$100,000,000, James Madison
$500,000,000, William McKinley

EXPENDITURES BY AMERICANS

27.7% federal taxes
15.6% housing & household
12.4% state/local taxes
10.4% medical care
09.6% food
08.8% Other
06.9% transportation
04.7% recreation
04.0% clothing

POSTAL SERVICE—U.S.

PATH OF A LETTER

(U.S. Postal Service)

letter deposited in mail box, picked up and taken to mail processing center (serves cities and areas of millions of people)

mechanized facility takes pouches of mail and puts them on culling belt

machines help postal clerks screen mail that is not letter-sized and it is put aside for manual handling

"machinable mail" is fed into equipment that faces each envelope (by sensing the corner where the stamp is)

stamps are automatically canceled and taken in trays to letter-sorting machines

machines operated by clerks key mail according to the first three digits of ZIP codes

the machine places the letter in the correct bin for the ZIP code

letter is put in nylon pouch and sent to the airport for distant destinations

in destination city, letter-sorting machine operator will again read ZIP code—looking at last two digits which represent local post office or branch

letter is handled by clerk familiar with streets served by each carrier

letter carrier organizes mail for his/her route

REAL ESTATE

LEASE CLASSIFICATION

1. residential lease (apartment, house)
2. commercial lease (office, store)
3. industrial lease (factory)
4. mining lease (for extracting oil, gas, minerals)
5. farm lease (agriculture)
6. limited use lease (sign, billboard)

RETAIL TRADE

CLASSIFICATION

(U.S. Census)

Building materials and garden supplies
  building materials, supply stores
  hardware stores
  retail nurseries and garden stores
  mobile home dealers
General merchandise stores
  department stores
  variety stores
  miscellaneous general merchandise stores
Food stores
  grocery stores
  meat and fish markets
  fruit and vegetable markets
  candy, nut, confectionery stores
  retail bakeries
Automotive dealers

new and used car dealers
used car dealers
auto and home supply stores
boat dealers
recreational vehicle dealers
motorcycle dealers
Gasoline service stations
Apparel and accessory stores
men's and boys' clothing stores
women's clothing stores
children's and infants' wear stores
family clothing stores
shoe stores
Furniture and home furnishings
stores
furniture stores
home furnishings stores
household appliance stores
radio, television, computer stores
computer and software stores
Eating and drinking places
eating places
restaurants and lunchrooms
refreshment places
drinking places
Drug stores and proprietary stores
Miscellaneous retail stores
liquor stores
used merchandise stores
sporting goods, bicycle shops
book stores
stationery stores
jewelry stores
hobby, toy, and game shops
camera, photo supply stores
gift, novelty, souvenir shops
sewing, needlework, and piece goods
catalog and mail-order houses
merchandising machine operators
direct selling establishments
fuel dealers
florists
optical goods stores

DEPARTMENT STORE ORGANIZATION

(These have many subdivisions within them. Managers of these five principal divisions are responsible to the general manager.)

Merchandising (buying and pricing of merchandise)
Sales Promotion (advertising, display, public relations, etc.)
Personnel (employment, training, and welfare of employees)
Operations (customer and selling services, deliveries; and receiving, marking, maintenance of merchandise)
Finance and Control (accounting, customer, credit, expense control, other financial and budgetary matters)

UNIVERSAL PRODUCT CODE (UPC / BAR CODE)

(digits, from left to right, see illustration p. 276)

a. Number System Character which identifies the product (for example: 0=national brands except the following, 2=variable weight (cheese, vegetables, meat), 3=drugs or health care, 4=discounted goods, 5=coupons)
b. product's manufacturer, number assigned by Uniform Code Council
c. product description by weight/size, color, other features
d. check digit (The other numbers, calculated in a certain way must total this number; any other number indicates a mistake.)

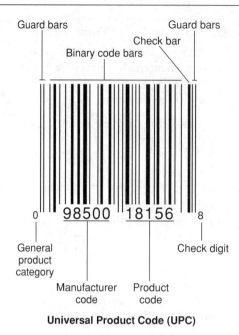

Universal Product Code (UPC)

Guard bars

Guard bars

Check bar

Binary code bars

0 98500 18156 8

General
product
category

Manufacturer
code

Product
code

Check digit

TAX SYSTEM OF U.S.

CLASSIFICATION

national government: personal and corporate income taxes; excise taxes; etc.

state government: income tax (most states), sales taxes (most states); excises on tobacco, motor vehicles, gasoline, alcoholic beverages, etc.

local government: property tax; income tax (some places)

FEDERAL TAX SYSTEM

Income tax
Estate and Gift tax
Self-Employment tax
Social Security tax (FICA):
  Old-age, survivors and disability insurance (OASDI)
  Hospital insurance (Medicare)

Unemployment compensation tax (FUTA)
Railroad retirement tax
Excise tax
  environmental taxes
  communications and air transportation taxes
  manufacturers' taxes
  tax on heavy trucks, trailers, and tractors
  ship passenger tax
  luxury items tax
  fuel tax
  wagering taxes
  export exemption certificate tax
  gas guzzler tax
  highway vehicle use tax
  alcohol tax
  tobacco tax
  firearms tax
  special fuels tax
  tax on motor vehicles sold at retail
  facilities and services tax
  documentary stamp taxes
  recreational equipment tax
  coal tax

STATE AND LOCAL TAX SYSTEM

Alcoholic beverages tax
Capital values and franchise tax (capital gains)
Cigarette tax
Gasoline tax
Income tax (most state; some local levels)
Inheritance, estate, and gift tax
Personal property tax
Pollution control tax
Property tax
Real estate tax
Sales and uses tax
Severance tax
Unemployment insurance tax

Tax Preparers

Tax attorneys
Certified public accountants
Enrolled agents
Seasonal tax preparers

Types

death and gift taxes
sales and excise taxes
social security and payroll taxes
tariffs and export taxes

taxes on corporation income and
  excess profits
taxes on personal income and capital
  gains
taxes on real and personal property

Things deprived suddenly of their putative meaning, the place assigned them in the ostensible order of things . . . make us laugh.

—Milan Kundera, *The Book of Laughter and Forgetting*

CHAPTER TEN

THE ARTS

ARCHITECTURE

BRANCHES OF ARCHITECTURE

(examples in parentheses)

agricultural (barns, silos, stables)

commercial and industrial (banks, factories, office buildings, refineries, stores)

domestic/residential (apartments, hotels, houses)

educational and public welfare (hospitals, prisons, schools, universities)

governmental (capitols, courthouses, post offices, city halls)

military (armories, forts)

outdoor (racetracks, golf courses, parks)

recreational (athletic facilities, auditoriums, libraries, museums, theaters)

religious and commemorative (churches, monuments, mosques, shrines, synagogues, tombs, temples)

ARCHITECTURAL STYLES

Classical
  Etruscan (750–100 BC)
  Greek (600–300 BC)
  Hellenistic (300–30 BC)
  Roman (300 BC-CE 365)
    Orders:
      Doric
      Ionic
      Corinthian
        Derived Orders:
          Tuscan
          Doric Roman
          Composite
Early Christian/European
  Early Christian (313-c.800)
  Byzantine (330–1453)
  Carolingian (c. 751–987)
  Romanesque (800–1270)
  Ottonian (919–1024)
  Cistercian (1098–1270)
  Gothic (1140–1534)
  Rayonnant (1194–1400)
  Flamboyant (1400–1500)
Early Christian/British
  Anglo-Saxon (650–11th century)
  Norman (1045–1180)
  Gothic (1140-c. 1630)
  Early English (c. 1175-c. 1250)
  Decorated Style (1290-c. 1375)
  Perpendicular (c. 1350-c. 1530)
Early Christian/Spanish and
          Portuguese
  Asturian (700–900)
  Visigothic (711–914)
  Mozarabic (800–1140)
  Mudejar (1110–1500)
  Manueline style (1450–1521)

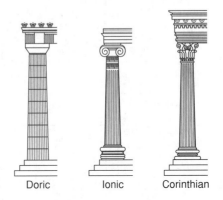

Doric   Ionic   Corinthian

Tuscan   Composite

Orders

ARCHITECTURE
  Architectural styles
  (cont.)

Renaissance
  English Tudor (1485–1558)
  English Elizabethan (1558-c. 1618)
  Mannerist (c. 1530-c. 1600)
17th Century
  Baroque (c. 1585-c. 1750)
  American Dutch Colonial
          (1614–1664)
  American English Colonial
          (1607–1776)
  Jacobean (c. 1618–1625)
18th Century
  Churrigueresque (c. 1680–1780)
  Federal (1790–1820s)
  Georgian (1714–1837)
  Jeffersonian (1790s–1830s)
  Neoclassical (1750s-1840s)

Barrel   Underpitch

Groin   Quadripartite   Sexpartite

Tierceron   Fan

Vaults

Basket handle

Equilateral

Gula

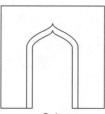
Horseshoe

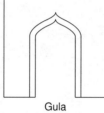
Lancet

Stilted

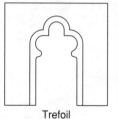
Trefoil

Tudor

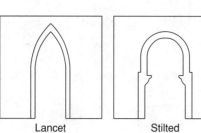
Arches

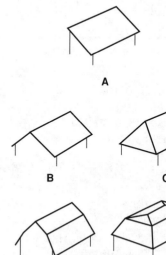
Roofs
A. Lean-to; **B.** Gable; **C.** Hip;
D. Gambrel; **E.** Mansard

Palladian (c. 1715–1770s)
Rococo (1720–1760)
19th Century
  Beaux Arts (c. 1865-c. 1913)
  Chicago School (1884–1909)
  Classical (1890s-c. 1943)
  Egyptian (latter 19th century)
  Empire (1800–1830s)
  Exotic (1830s-c. 1920s)
  Gothic (c. 1750-c. 1900)
  Greek (1798-c. 1860)
20th Century
  Art Deco (1920s-1930s)
  Art Nouveau (1880s-1914)
  Bauhaus (1919–1937)
  Expressionism (c. 1905–1933)
  Functionalism (1920s-1970s)
  International (1920s-)
  Post-Modernism (1970s-)
  Prairie style (c. 1900-c. 1920s)

Two major body positions

arabesque: weight of body on one leg,
  other leg extended backward with
  knee straight
attitude: similar to arabesque but
  knee of other leg is bent

STEPS

(examples in parentheses)

simple exercises: plié, battement
jumping or leaping steps: entrechat,
  jeté, assemblé, ballonné,
  changement de pieds, pas de chat,
  sauté

BALLET

STARTING POSITIONS

First position: heels touch (arms at
  sides, slightly curved downward)
Second position: feet apart 12 in
  (arms out and curved downward)
Third position: feet parallel, right heel
  in front of left (one arm curved
  downward at side, the other out
  and curved downward)
Fourth position: same with right heel
  outward 12 in (one arm curved
  downward and in front of the body,
  the other held above the head and
  curved toward the centerline)
Fifth position: feet parallel, right foot
  fully in front of left (both arms held
  above the head and curving toward
  the centerline)
closed positions: First, Third, Fifth
open positions: Second, Fourth

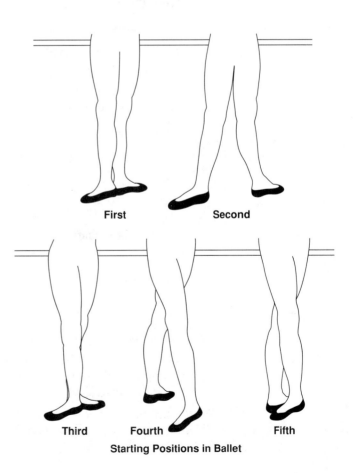

Starting Positions in Ballet

turning steps: pirouette, tour en l'air, chaîné, fouetté tour en l'air
traveling movements: chassé, glissade, pas de bourrée

BOOK PUBLISHING

BESTSELLER CATEGORIES

(from Publishers Weekly)

hardcover fiction
hardcover nonfiction
trade paperback
mass-market paperback
almanacs, atlases, and annuals

BOOK CLASSIFICATION

Copyright Page

(Library of Congress Cataloging-in-Publication Data)

author (last name, first name)
title of book and author (first name, last name)
subject(s) of book
International Standard Book Number (ISBN)
Library of Congress classification and classification number, year of publication
Dewey Decimal classification (optional)

International Standard Book Number (ISBN)

Ten-digit number assigned to every published book, identifying each work's national geographical or language grouping, its publisher, and each edition of a title.

For the US, the designated national standard book numbering agency is R.R. Bowker.

first digit: area of origin, 0 = English-speaking country
next two digits: publisher
next six digits: assigned to each edition of a title by publisher
last digit: check digit (computer-checked by calculation of preceding numbers to prevent errors)
For example, the ISBN of the hardcover edition of this book is 0-679-44478-5.

BOOK SIZES

(octavo formats)
$5\frac{1}{4} \times 8\frac{1}{2}$ inches
$5\frac{1}{2} \times 8\frac{1}{2}$
6×9
$6\frac{1}{8} \times 9\frac{1}{4}$
$6\frac{1}{2} \times 4\frac{1}{8}$
$7\frac{1}{4} \times 4\frac{7}{8}$
$8\frac{1}{2} \times 5\frac{1}{2}$

(quarto formats)
7×9
8×10
$8\frac{1}{4} \times 10\frac{7}{8}$
$8\frac{1}{2} \times 11$
$9\frac{3}{4} \times 7\frac{3}{8}$
$11 \times 8\frac{5}{8}$
double elephant folio, 25"+
atlas folio, 25"
elephant folio, 23"+
folio, 13"+
quarto, 11–13"
small quarto, 10"
octavo, 8–9"
small octavo, 7½–8"
duodecimo, 7"
sextodecimo, 6–7"
vigesimoquarto, 5–6"
trigesimosecundo, 4–5"
fortyeightmo, 4"
sixtyfourmo, 3"
miniature, 3"

BOOK TYPES

hardcover
trade paperback
mass market paperback
reference
children's
textbook
mail-order

COLORS

PRIMARY COLORS (IN MIXING)

red
blue
yellow

SECONDARY COLORS

green
orange
purple

TERTIARY COLORS

colors resulting from the mixing of
two secondary colors, e.g., brown,
olive, and orange-red

PRIMARY COLORS (ADDITIVE)

red
green
blue

FINE ARTS

*Nonutilitarian visual arts or arts
concerned with the creation of beauty:*

painting
sculpture
architecture
literature
music
dance

PAINTING AND SCULPTURE

Styles and Periods

Prehistoric art
　Paleolithic art (35,000–10,000 years
　　ago)
　Mesopotamian art (6000–539 BC)
Egyptian and Classical Art (3100 BC-
　CE 400)
　Egyptian art
　Ancient Greek-Hellenistic
　Roman art
Christianity and Early Middle Ages
　(100–1200)
　Early Christian art
　Migration period (150–1000)
　Byzantine art (330–1450)
　Carolingian art (800–870)
　Ottonian art (870–1050)
　Romanesque art (1050–1200)
　Islamic art (7th-17th centuries)
Middle Ages (1200–1450 AD)
　Gothic art
Early Renaissance to early 18th
　century (1300–1750)
　Renaissance (c. 1300–1545)
　Mannerism (c. 1520–1700)
　Baroque (c. 1600–1720)
Late 18th and early 19th century
　Rococo (c. 1735–1765)
　Neo-classicism (c. 1750–1850)
　Romanticism (c. 1780–1850)
　Realism (c. 1830–1880)
　Pre-Raphaelite (1848–1856)
Late 19th and early 20th century
　Art Nouveau (c. 1890–1915)
　Arts and Crafts Movement
　　(c. 1870–1900)
　Symbolism (c. 1880–1905)
　Impressionism (1874–1886)
　Pointillism (c. 1880–1915)
　Post-Impressionism (c. 1880–1910)
20th century
　Naive art
　Fauvism (c. 1905–1907)
　Die Brucke/The Bridge (c. 1905–1913)

Expressionism (c. 1905–1925)
Cubism (c. 1907–1923)
Futurism (c. 1909–1919)
School of Paris (c. 1910–1950)
Der Blaue Reiter (c. 1911–1914)
Dada (c. 1915–1923)
Bauhaus School (c. 1919–1933)
Surrealism (c. 1924)
Kinetic art (c. 1930)
Abstract Expressionism (c. 1940)
New York School (c. 1945–1960)
Op art (c. 1950)
Pop art (c. 1955)
Minimal art (c. 1960)

LITERATURE

ALLEGORICAL LITERATURE

*(four ways of interpreting allegorical
literature, esp. the Bible)*

allegorical (e.g. Jerusalem is the
Church)
anagogical/mystic (e.g. Jerusalem is
heaven)
historical or literal (e.g. Jerusalem is a
city in Palestine)
moral (e.g. Jerusalem is the believing
soul)

LITERARY GENRES

allegorical literature
children's literature
comedic literature
   farce
   jokes and anecdotes
   lampoon
   parody
   satire
dramatic literature
   melodrama
   religious drama and ritual
   tragedy
   tragicomedy

narrative fiction
   ballad, lay, and idyll
     Bildungsroman (education,
       development of protagonist)
     Entwicklungsroman
       (autobiographical, childhood
       to maturity)
   epic
     beast epic
     literary epic
     mock epic
     romantic epic
   fable, parable, and allegory
   fiction novel and tale
   novella
   roman à clef (historical novel
     disguised as fiction)
   romance
     Arthurian romance
     Gothic romance
     historical romance
     pastoral romance
     romance of adventure
     romance of chivalry
     romance of love
   saga
     king's sagas
     legendary sagas
   short story
nonfictional prose
   aphorism, epigram, adage, and
     maxim
   biographical and autobiographical
     literature
   dialogue
   doctrinal and religious literature
   essay
   historical literature
   journal article or monograph
   journalism
   letters
   literary criticism
   nonfiction novel and tale
   oration and speech
   philosophical literature
   polemical literature

(argumentation, controversy)
political literature
scientific literature
travel literature
poetry and lyric
  ballad
  elegy
  haiku
  hymn
  madrigal
  ode
  pastoral
  sonnet
primitive and folk literature
radio, motion-picture, and television
    scripts

ENGLISH LITERARY PERIODS

Periods

Old English period (450–1100)
  (alliterative verse, elegiac and
  heroic verse)
Early Middle English period
  (1100–1300) (didactic poetry, verse
  romance, lyric)
Late Middle English period
  (1300–1500) (courtly poetry)
Renaissance period (1400–1600)
  (including Elizabethan and early
  Stuart)
Restoration/Baroque period
  (1600–1700) (chroniclers, diarists,
  court wits)
18th Century (1700–1800) (political
  journalism, satire, psychological
  novel)
Romanticism (1800–1850)
Post Romanticism/Enlightenment/
  Victorian eras (1850–1900)
  (Victorian literature,
  Impressionism)
Modern English period (1900-
  present) (Edwardian, Realism,
  social focus in novels)

SHAKESPEARE'S PLAYS IN PUBLICATION ORDER

Titus Andronicus, 1594
Henry VI Part 2, 1594
The Taming of the Shrew, 1594
Henry VI Part 3, 1595
Romeo and Juliet, 1597
Richard II, 1597
Richard III, 1597
Henry VI Part I, 1598
Love's Labour's Lost, 1598
Henry IV Part 2, 1600
A Midsummer Night's Dream, 1600
The Merchant of Venice, 1600
Much Ado About Nothing, 1600
Henry V, 1600
Sir John Falstaff and the Merry Wives
  of Windsor, 1602
Hamlet, 1604
King Lear, 1608
Pericles, Prince of Tyre, 1609
Troilus and Cressida, 1609

posthumously published:

1622: Othello
1623: First Folio (36 plays), Henry IV
  Part I, The Two Gentlemen of
  Verona, The Comedy of Errors, King
  John, As You Like It, Julius Caesar,
  Twelfth Night, Measure for
  Measure, All's Well That Ends Well,
  Macbeth, Timon of Athens, Antony
  and Cleopatra, Coriolanus,
  Cymbeline, The Winter's Tale, The
  Tempest, Henry VIII

POETRY

Poetic Verse lengths

monometer, one foot
dimeter, two feet
trimeter, three feet
tetrameter, four feet
pentameter, five feet
hexameter, six feet

heptameter, seven feet
octameter, eight feet

Metrical Patterns

iamb (one short, one long in
    quantitative meter; one unstressed,
    one stressed in accentual meter)
trochee (one long, one short)
dactyl (one long, two short)
amphibrach (short, long, short)
amphimacer (long, short, long)
anapest (two short, one long)
spondee (two long)

MOTION PICTURES

ACADEMY AWARD CATEGORIES

Supporting Actor
Makeup
Supporting Actress
Art Direction
Sound Effects Editing
Live Action Short Film
Animated Short Film
Costume Design
Foreign Film
Sound
Scietific and Technical Awards
Documentary Awards
Cinematography Awards
Visual Effects
Original Score
Honorary Award
Writing Award
Actor
Original Song
Actress
Director
Picture

MOTION PICTURE CAST AND CREW
(from Warner Brothers' "Hamlet")

stars
featured players
additional cast (bit players, extras)
director
producer
screenwriter
executive producer
musical director/composer
editor
director of photography
production designer
costume designer
production controller
production supervisor
first assistant director
camera operator
sound mixer
casting director
voice coach
script supervisor
publicity coordinator
location manager
second assistant director
third assistant director
focus puller
loader
grip (shifts scenery)
camera trainee
boom swinger
sound maintenance person
production coordinator
producer's assistant
assistants to stars, director, producer
production runner
supervising art director
construction coordinator
set decorator
art director
production buyer
scenic artist
draftspeople
art department runner
wardrobe supervisor
assistant costume designer
wardrobe assistant
supervising makeup artist
makeup artists
makeup assistant
supervising hairdresser

hairdressers
stills photographer
publicity assistant
first assistant editor
second assistant editor
sound editor
dialogue editor
footsteps editor
music editor
assistant sound editor
re-recording mixer
production accountant
accounts assistant
cashier
stunt doubles
property master
property storeperson
chargehand standby prop person
standby prop person
chargehand dressing prop person
dressing prop
drapes master
gaffer (chief electrician)
chargehands
electricians
standbys
construction manager
construction storeperson
head of department painter
head of department carpenter
head of department plasterer
supervising carpenters
supervising plasterer
supervising rigger
chargehand stagehand
chargehand rigger
chargehand painter
chargehand carpenter
chargehand plasterer
chargehand plasterer laborer
sculptor/modeller
translator
medical officer
unit nurse
unit drivers
publicity
marketing consultants

orchestra
music engineer
music assistant
general music coordination
legal services
production lenders

MOTION PICTURE GENRES
(classification by style or subject matter)

3-D film
action film
adventure film
animated film
art film
biographical film
children's film
cinema vérité (realistic, improvised)
comedy
cops-and-robbers film
cult film
detective film
disaster film
documentary film
epic
erotic film
experimental or amateur film
fantasy film
film noir
foreign film
gangster film
historical film
horror film
melodrama
musical
mystery
police thriller/drama
psychological thriller
romantic comedy
science film
science-fiction film
silent comedy
slapstick
snuff film
social problem film
spectacle

sports film
spy film
thriller
war film
western

natural science
other
  children's
  sports

MOTION PICTURE RATINGS

*Code and Rating Administration
(Motion Picture Assn. of America)*

G=general audience; anyone admitted

PG=parental guidance; some material may not be suitable for children under 13

PG-13=parents strongly cautioned; some material may not be suitable for children under 13 (formerly called M, then GP)

R=persons under 17 admitted only if accompanied by a parent or adult guardian

NC-17=no one under 17 admitted (formerly called X)

NR=no rating

Note: The symbol XXX is unofficially used by motion-picture exhibitors for sexually explicit films.

MUSEUMS

SUBJECT AREAS

anthropology and culture
  natural history
  history
  religion
arts and antiquities
applied science and technology
  broadcasting and media
  computers
  crafts
  design
  film
  hobbies, toys, dolls

MUSIC

MUSICAL DYNAMICS

fortississimo: as loudly as possible (fff)
fortissimo: very loudly (ff)
forte: loudly (f)
mezzoforte: moderately loudly (mf)
mezzo: medium loudly (m)
mezzopiano: medium softly (mp)
piano: softly (p)
pianissimo: very softly (pp)
pianississimo: as softly as possible (ppp)

also:

crescendo: gradually louder
decrescendo: gradually softer
diminuendo: diminishing
transitions:
piu forte: louder (pf)
fortepiano: loud followed by soft (fp)

MUSICAL GENRES

primitive
folk
instrumental
  chamber
  concerto
  étude
  lieder
  march
  overture
  quartet
  rondo
  sonata
  suite
  symphony
  tance

choral music
  anthem
  cantata
  canticle
  chant
  chorale
  hymn
  Mass
  oratorio
  plainsong
  sequence
non-Western music
  Chinese music
  Indian music
  Vedic chant
theater music
  ballet
  musical
  opera
  operetta
jazz
  bebop
  Dixieland
  jazz-rock
  scat
  swing
popular
  alternative rock
  big band
  bluegrass
  blues
  boogie-woogie
  bossa nova
  calypso
  country and western
  electronic
  gospel
  heavy metal
  hip-hop
  honky-tonk
  pop
  punk rock
  ragtime
  rap
  reggae
  rhythm and blues

rock/rock and roll
salsa
soul
spiritual
zydeco

A HEAD

MUSICAL INSTRUMENT FAMILIES

Percussion instruments
  idiophones: cymbals, castanets,
      triangle, xylophone,
      glockenspiel, bells
  membranophones: side drum, bass
      drum, timpani, kazoo
Stringed instruments
  lutes: lute, guitar, violin
      violin family: violin, viola,
          violoncello or cello, double
          bass
  zithers
  lyres: Greek kithara, Welsh crwth
  harps
Keyboard instruments
  clavichord
  harpsichord
  piano
  organ
Wind instruments
  free aerophones: harmonica,
      melodeon
  flutes: recorder, flute
  reedpipes: clarinet, saxophone,
      oboe, bassoon
  lipped aerophones: horn, cornet,
      trumpet, trombone, tuba
Electronic instruments
  monophonic electrophone:
      trautonium
  polyphonic: synthesizers

MUSICAL INSTRUMENT TYPES

(Hornbostel and Sachs)

Idiophones
  struck: cymbals, triangle, castanets
  plucked: Jew's harp, elastic plaques

friction: scraper, rattle, musical
glasses
blown: blown sticks, Aolsklavier
Membranophones
struck: kettledrum, bass drum
plucked: Indian gopiyantra
friction: certain instruments of
Africa, Venezuela
singing/blown: kazoo
Chordophones
simple chordophones or zithers:
harpsichord, piano
composite chordophones: lutes,
guitar, violin, harps, lyres
Aerophones
free: harmonica, melodeon
wind instruments: trumpet, flute,
clarinet, oboe, recorder
Electrophones
monophonic: trautonium
polyphonic: synthesizers

MUSICAL NOTATION

breve=double whole note (Latin
brevis)
semibreve=whole note (Latin
semibrevis)
minim=half-note (Latin minima)
crotchet=quarter-note (Latin
semiminima)
quaver=eighth-note (Latin fusa)
semiquaver=sixteenth-note (Latin
semifusa)
demisemiquaver=thirty-second note
(Latin fusella)
hemidemisemiquaver=sixty-fourth
note (Latin fusellala)

MUSICAL RANGES (BY INSTRUMENT)

percussion

tuneable:
xylophone (3–4 octaves)
marimba (3)
vibraphone (3)
chimes/tubular bells (1½)
glockenspiel/metallophone (1–1½)
Caribbean steel drums (set of six)

rhythmic sound:
bass drum
snare drum, tambourine
cymbals, triangle
tam-tam, gong
tom-tom
bongo
block

string (by general range)

cello, violoncello (4 octaves)
viola (4)
violin (3)
double bass (3 octaves)
rebec (3)
viol da gamba (2)
zither (4 octaves)
sitar (3)
dulcimer (3)
autoharp (2)
harp (5½ octaves)
Welsh/Irish harp (3)
lyre (1)
banjo (3 octaves)
bouzouki (3)
guitar (3)
ukulele (2)
cittern (2)
lute (2)
mandolin (2)

keyboard (by general range)

church organ (8 octaves)
concert organ (8)
upright piano (7½)
Grand Piano (7½)
harpsichord (5)
spinet (4)
clavichord (3–4)
glockenspiel (3–4)

Musical Notes

NOTE SYMBOLS

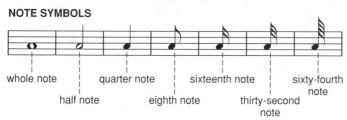

whole note   quarter note   sixteenth note   sixty-fourth note

half note   eighth note   thirty-second note

ORNAMENTS

appoggiatura   trill   turn   mordent

ACCIDENTALS

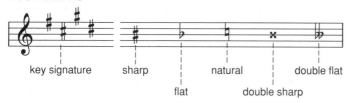

key signature   sharp   natural   double flat

flat   double sharp

REST SYMBOLS

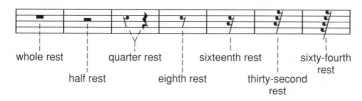

whole rest   quarter rest   sixteenth rest   sixty-fourth rest

half rest   eighth rest   thirty-second rest

CHORD   OTHER SIGNS

arpeggio   tie   accent mark   pause

MUSIC

Musical ranges (cont.)

woodwind (by general range)

double (contra-)bassoon (3 ½ octaves)
bassoon (3½)
clarinet (3 ¼)
bass clarinet (3 ¼)
piccolo (3)
flute (3)
alto flute (3)
oboe (2½)
baritone oboe (2½)
bass oboe (2½)
soprano saxophone (2½)
alto saxophone (2 ½)
melody saxophone (2 ½)
tenor saxophone (2 ½)
baritone saxophone (2 ½)
soprano recorder (2 ½)

MUSICAL TEMPOS

larghissimo: as slow as possible
largo: very slow and dignified, sustained
largamente: slow, broad
larghetto: diminutive of largo and slightly faster
grave: slow with solemnity
lento: slow
adagissimo: very slow, almost extremely slow
adagio: slow, at ease
adagietto: diminutive of adagio and slightly faster
andante: slow walking pace
andantino: steady walking pace
moderato: brisk walking pace
allegretto: with animation
allegramente: lightly, gaily
allegro: lively
vivace: fast
vivacissimo: very quick
presto: very fast
prestissimo: extremely fast
tempo changes:
accelerando: accelerating

poco a poco: little by little
stringendo: increasing speed and intensity
ritardando: retarding the tempo
morendo: dying away
tempo primo, a tempo: return to first tempo
l'istesso tempo: same tempo

NUMBER OF MUSICIANS

1 soloist
2 duet
3 trio
4 quartet
5 quintet
6 sextet
7 septet
8 octet
9 nonet

VOCAL RANGES

(highest to lowest)

Female

Soprano (highest female voice)
  Coloratura (high, flexible; ornamented)
  Lyric/Leggiero (medium, cantabile singing)
  Lyric spinto (full, bright)
  Lyric spogato/sfogato (high, reedy)
  Dramatic (largest soprano voice)
  Dramatic dugazon (powerful but sly)
  Dramatic falcon (with great flare)
Mezzo-Soprano (between soprano and alto)
Alto or Contralto (lowest female voice)
  Dramatic (largest and lowest female voice)

Male

Tenor (highest male voice)
  Leggiero/Lyric tenor (similar to lyric soprano)

Counter tenor (extremely high)
Trial (high and nasal)
Tenor di grazia (high and graceful)
Heldentenor (largest tenor voice,
Wagnerian)
Tenor di forza (more heroic)
Tenor robusto (full, vigorous)
Tenor spinto (high but dramatic)
Tenor buffo (low tenor; comic)
Baritone (medium and heavy)
Baritone-martin (high baritone)
Bass-baritone (between baritone
and bass)
Bass or Basso (lowest male voice)
Basso cantante (like lyric soprano)
Basso buffo (comic)
Basso profundo or Contra-basso
(deep, dark; lowest voice)

Vocal Ranges (by note)

soprano B3-C6
mezzo-soprano A3-A5 (exceptional:
B5)
contralto G3-G5
alto (E3-E5 (exceptional: F5)
tenor C3-B4 (exceptional: C5)

baritone F2-G4 (exceptional: A4)
bass E2-F4 (exceptional: G1)

SYMPHONY ORCHESTRA

Orchestra Instruments

String section:
violin
viola
violoncello
double bass

Woodwind section:
piccolo
flute
clarinet
bass clarinet
English horn
bassoon
oboe
contra bassoon

Brass section:
saxophone
cornet
trumpet
French horn

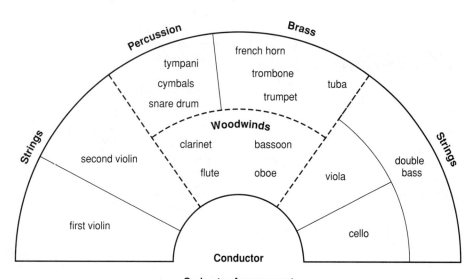

Orchestra Arrangement

trombone
tuba
bass tuba

Percussion section:
timpani
xylophone
snare drum
bass drum
bells
tom-tom
castanets
triangle
tambourine
cymbals
gong
chime
glockenspiel
piano

PERFORMING ARTS

AREAS

dance
  ballet
  folk dance
  jazz dance
  modern dance
  primitive dance
music
  classical music
  folk music
  jazz
  music for theater and motion
    pictures
  opera
  popular music
  primitive music
  rock music
motion pictures
theater
popular entertainment
  carnival and circus
  exposition and festival

parade and pageant
stage show
broadcasting
  radio
  television

PHOTOGRAPHY

FIELDS OF PHOTOGRAPHY

Aerophotography (aerial
  photography)
Astrophotography
Candid photography
Chromophotography
Chronophotography
Cinematography
Cinephotomicrography
Cystophotography
Heliophotography
Infrared photography
Macrophotography
Microphotography
Miniature photography
Phonophotography
Photogrammetry
Photomicrography
Photospectroheliography
Phototopography
Phototypography
Pyrophotography
Radiography
Radiophotography
Sculptography
Skiagraphy
Spectroheliography
Spectrophotography
Stroboscopic photography
Telephotography
Uranophotography
X-ray photography

THEATER

SEATING

orchestra seats: closest to stage
balcony
mezzanine: lower of two balconies
loge: front section of mezzanine

THEATER COMPANY

Theater general staff

executive producer
associate producer
general manager
public relations director
box office and subscription director
program advertising and group sales
  director
assistant to the executive producer
assistant to the general manager
assistant box office and subscription
  manager
bookkeeper
public relations associate
subscription associate
box office staff

Production staff:

resident stage manager
resident scenic designer
resident lighting designer
master carpenter
master electrician
flyperson
shop carpenter
props master
wardrobe supervisor
scenic artists
interns

house staff:

house manager
parking manager
concession manager
parking and concession staff
head usher
playhouse beautifier
house photographer
house doctor

STAGE PRODUCTION

producer
director
designer
lighting designer
technical director
production manager
stage manager
deputy stage manager
assistant stage managers
company manager
heads of departments (HODs)
dayperson
showperson
master carpenter
scenery handling staff
flyperson (flying scenery)
property master
props/property department staff
chief electrician
deputy chief electrician
assistant chief electrician
stage electricians
limes (follow-spot operators)
sound engineers
resident stage manager
wardrobe manager
wardrobe staff
stage doorperson
housekeeper

THEATRICAL GENRES

General theater
  comedy
  comedy of manners
  epic play
  experimental theater
  farce

melodrama
miracle play
morality play
mystery play
puppet theater
skit
tragedy
tragicomedy
Western theater
  commedia dell'arte (Italian stock-character comedy with masked actors)
  improvisation
  liturgical drama
  mime and pantomime
  musical and musical comedy
  opera and operetta
  passion play
Non-dramatic Western theater
  burlesque
  cabaret
  circus
  conjuring (magical arts)
  dance theater
  happening (improvised or spontaneous production)
  masque (allegorical court performance)
  minstrel show
  revue
  vaudeville
non-Western theater (two examples)
  Kabuki (Japanese singing, dancing drama)
  tamasha (Arabic entertainment)

VISUAL ARTS

architecture
  agricultural
  commercial and industrial
  domestic/residential
  educational and public welfare
  governmental
  military
  recreational

  religious and commemorative
  urban design
decorative arts and crafts
  basketry
  enamelwork
  floral decoration
  furniture and accessories
  glass design
  interior design
  lacquerwork
  metalwork
  mosaic
  pottery
  rugs, carpets, and tapestry
  stained glass
drawing
  animation
  caricature, cartoon, comic strip
  cartography and mapping
  drafting
  figures and still-life
  landscape
  nonrepresentational
  portrait
functional design
  body decoration
  clothing design
  coin and currency design
  household object design
  industrial design
  jewelry
  mechanical and electronic object design
  museum and gallery display
  plaything design
garden and landscape design
  private / residential
  public
graphic arts
  advertising art and design
  calligraphy
  printing arts
    bookbinding
    book cover design
    typography and layout
  sign and symbol design

painting
  cave
  landscape
  miniature
  mural
  portrait
  screen
  still-life
photography
  aerial
  astronomical
  holography
  landscape
  photojournalism

  portrait
  radiography
  still
  video camera recording
printmaking
  intaglio
  lithography and serigraphy
  relief or engraving
  woodcut
sculpture
  decorative
  nonrepresentational
  representational

I love all forms of taxonomy—lists, categories, compartments, containers, boundaries. When I went to the famous Amsterdam sex shops, I was struck mainly by the arrangement of movies and magazines into exceedingly minute subdivisions of pleasure and pain. I love doing errands, and what I especially love about doing errands is crossing things off my errand list. . . .

—David Shields, *Remote*

CHAPTER ELEVEN

DOMESTIC LIFE

BIRTHDAYS AND ANNIVERSARIES

ANNIVERSARY GIFTS

(traditional / modern)

1st: paper (plastic), cotton / clocks
2nd: cotton (calico), paper / china
3rd: leather / crystal, glass
4th: linen (silk, synthetics), iron / appliances, fruit/flowers
5th: wood / silverware
6th: iron, sugar / wood
7th: wool, (copper, brass) / desk sets
8th: bronze (electrical appliances) / linens, lace
9th: pottery (china), copper / leather
10th: tin (aluminum) / diamond
11th: steel / fashion jewelry
12th: silk (fine linen) / pearl, colored gems
13th: lace / textiles, furs
14th: ivory / gold jewelry
15th: crystal (glass) / watches
20th: china / platinum
25th: silver / sterling silver
30th: pearl / diamond
35th: coral (jade) / jade
40th: ruby (garnets) / ruby
45th: sapphire (tourmalines) / sapphire
50th: gold / gold
55th: emerald (turquoise) / emerald
60th: diamond (gold) / gold
70th: platinum

MODERN ANNIVERSARY GIFTS

(Jewelry Industry Council)

1st: gold jewelry
2nd: garnet
3rd: pearls
4th: blue topaz
5th: sapphire
6th: amethyst
7th: onyx
8th: tourmaline
9th: lapis
10th: diamond jewelry
11th: turquoise
12th: jade
13th: citrine
14th: opal
15th: ruby
16th: peridot
17th: watches
18th: cat's-eye
19th: aquamarine
20th: emerald
25th: silver jubilee
30th: pearl jubilee
35th: emerald
40th: ruby
45th: sapphire
50th: golden jubilee
60th: diamond jubilee

BIRTHDAY FLOWERS BY MONTH

January = carnation, snowdrop
February = violet, primrose
March = jonquil, violet
April = daisy, sweet pea
May = hawthorn, lily of the valley
June = rose, honeysuckle
July = larkspur, water lily
August = gladiolus, poppy
September = morning glory, aster
October = calendula, cosmos
November = chrysanthemum
December = narcissus, holly, poinsettia

BIRTHSTONES

(ancient/ modern)

January = garnet
February = amethyst
March = jasper / bloodstone or aquamarine

April = sapphire / diamond
May = agate / emerald
June = emerald / pearl, moonstone, or alexandrite
July = onyx / ruby
August = carnelian / sardonyx or peridot
September = chrysolite / sapphire
October = aquamarine / opal or tourmaline
November = topaz
December = ruby / turquoise or zircon

MOTHER GOOSE'S DAYS OF BIRTH

Monday, fair of face
Tuesday, full of grace
Wednesday, full of woe
Thursday, has far to go
Friday, loving and giving
Saturday, works hard for a living
Sunday, bonny and blithe, good and gay

Zodiac

ZODIAC

Qualities and Elements

Capricorn (Dec. 22–Jan. 19), Cardinal, Earth
Aquarius (Jan. 20–Feb. 18), Fixed, Air
Pisces (Feb. 19–Mar. 20), Mutable, Water
Aries (Mar. 21–Apr. 19), Cardinal, Fire
Taurus (Apr. 20–May 20), Fixed, Earth
Gemini (May 21–June 20), Mutable, Air
Cancer (June 21–July 22), Cardinal, Water
Leo (July 23–Aug. 22), Fixed, Fire
Virgo (Aug. 23–Sept. 22), Mutable, Earth
Libra (Sept. 23–Oct. 22), Cardinal, Air
Scorpio (Oct. 23–Nov. 21), Fixed, Water
Sagittarius (Nov. 22–Dec. 21), Mutable, Fire

CLOTHES

CLOTHING SIZES, INTERNATIONAL SYSTEM

Women's clothing

USA	UK	Europe
6	8	36
8	10	38
10	12	40
12	14	42
14	16	44
16	18	46
18	20	48
20	22	50

Women's coats

USA	UK	Europe
8	30	36
10	32	38
12	34	40
14	36	42

16	38	44
18	40	46
20	42	48

Women's shirts

USA	UK	Europe
30	32	38
32	34	40
34	36	42
36	38	44
38	40	46
40	42	48
42	44	50
44	46	52

Men's shirts (neck size)

USA	UK & Europe
12	31–31
12 ½	32
13	33
13 ½	34–35
14	36
14 ½	37
15	38
15 ½	39
16	40
16 ½	41
17	42
17 ½	43

Men's suits and overcoats

USA	UK & Europe
34	44
36	46
38	48
40	50
42	52
44	54
46	56
48	58

Children's clothing

USA	UK	Europe
2	16–18	40–45
4	20–22	50–55

6	24–26	60–65
7	28–30	70–75
8	32–34	80–85
9	36–38	90–95

Women's shoes

USA	UK	Europe
4	2	32–35
5	3	35–36
6	4	36–38
7	5	38–39
8	6	40
9	7	41–42
10	8	42–44
11	9	44–45

Men's shoes

USA	UK	Europe
7	6 ½	38–39
7 ½	7	40
8	7 ½	41
8 ½	8	42
9	8 ½	43
9 ½	9	43–44
10	9 ½	44
10 ½	10	44–45
11	10 ½	45
11 ½	11	45–46
12	11 ½	47
13	12	48

Men's socks

USA	UK & Europe
9	38–39
10	39–40
10 ½	40–41
11	41–42
11 ½	42–43

Children's shoes

USA	UK & Europe
0	15
1	17
2	18
3	19

Children's shoes (cont.)

USA	UK & Europe
4	20
4½	21
5	22
6	23
7	24
8	25
8½	26
9	27
10	28
11	29
12	30
12½	31
13	32

FABRIC CARE CODING SYSTEM

Method 1, machine wash warm

Method 2, machine wash warm, line dry

Method 3, machine wash warm, tumble dry, remove promptly

Method 4, machine wash warm delicate cycle, tumble dry low, use cool iron

Method 5, machine wash warm, do not dry clean

Method 6, hand wash separately, use cool iron

Method 7, dry clean only

Method 8, dry clean especially for pile fabrics

Method 9, wipe with damp cloth only

Method B, machine wash warm separately, remove white or light trim

Method C, machine wash warm, tumble dry, detergent only and no soap

Method E, machine wash cold separately, remove white or light trim

Method G, wash before wearing, wash and dry separately, do not dry clean, fabric fades

Method H, hand wash cold

Method J, machine wash warm, tumble dry, no strong detergents, bleach, fabric softener, or soap

Method K, dry clean only, may be wiped clean with damp cloth, do not iron

Method L, dry clean only, spot cleaning not recommended, do not iron

---

LUGGAGE SIZES

(largest to smallest)

steamer trunk
footlocker
pullman (25-inch to 34-inch)
wheeled wardrobe
garment bag
21-inch carry-on or flight bag or piggyback
duffle-extra large
duffle-large
duffle-medium
duffle-small
boarding bag
tote or satchel
beauty case or cosmetic case

COOKING, KITCHEN & DINING

KITCHEN TOOLS BY TYPE OF USE

Cutting

baller
chopper
cleaver
corer
cutter
grater
knive
mincer
peeler
scissor-shear

shredder
slicer
slicing machine

Pounding/Pressing/Pureeing

cracker
crusher
food mill
grinder
juicer
masher
mortar and pestle
pounder
press
ricer
rolling pin

Piercing

forks
needles
pick
pricker
skewer
tester

Handling and Spreading

beater
chopstick
ladle
lifter
paddle
pastry brush
scoop
sifter
skimmer
spatula
spoon
tong
turner

Separating and Mixing

beater
colander
dredger
homogenizer
mixer

processor
separator
shaker
sieve
sifter
spinner
strainer
whisk

Opening

corkscrew
opener

Measuring

cup
scale
spoon
thermometer

COOKWARE

stockpot (8–20 quarts)
saute pan (8–14 inches diameter)
omelet pan (8–10 inches)
skillet/frying pan (6–12 inches)
crepe pan (5–8 inches)
saucepot (4–8 quarts)
saucepan with cover (from 1 pint to 5
   quarts)
casserole (from 1 pint to 10 quarts)
dutch oven
gratin dish
baker (round, oval, or rectangular)
roasting pan
baking pan
cookie sheet
square cake pan
round cake pan
bundt cake pan
angel food cake pan
springform pan
charlotte mold
pie pan
bread pan/loaf pan
[bowl (from 1 1/2 to 6 1/2 quarts)]

SILVERWARE

(largest to smallest)

Knives
  dinner knife
  steak knife
  cheese knife
  fish knife
  dessert knife
  butter knife
Forks
  fondue fork
  dinner fork
  salad fork
  dessert fork
  fish fork
  oyster fork

Spoons
  tablespoon
  sundae spoon
  dessert spoon
  soup spoon
  teaspoon
  coffee spoon

NAPKINS

cocktail, 4 × 4 inches or less
luncheon, 6 × 6 inches or less
dinner, 7 × 7 inches or less

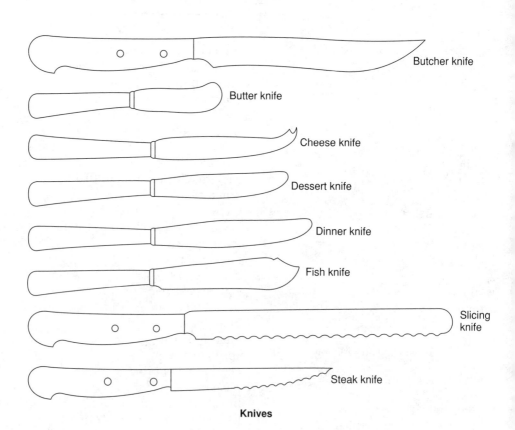

Butcher knife

Butter knife

Cheese knife

Dessert knife

Dinner knife

Fish knife

Slicing knife

Steak knife

Knives

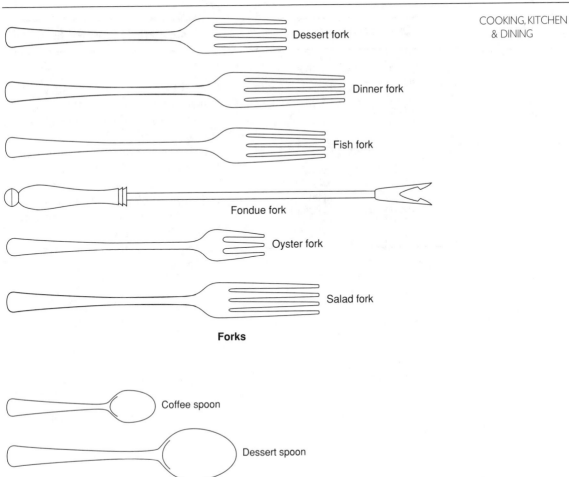

Dessert fork

Dinner fork

Fish fork

Fondue fork

Oyster fork

Salad fork

Forks

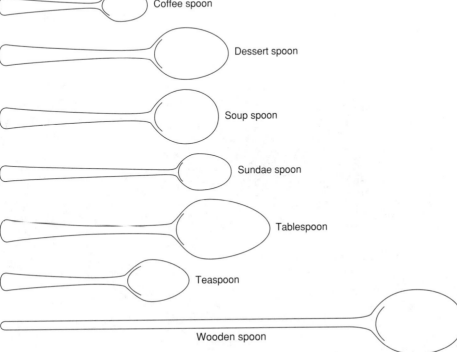

Coffee spoon

Dessert spoon

Soup spoon

Sundae spoon

Tablespoon

Teaspoon

Wooden spoon

Spoons

OVEN TEMPERATURES

175–225°F	warm
250–275	very slow
300–325	slow
350–375	moderate
400–425	hot
450–475	very hot

also

225–275°F	very cool
275–325	cool
325–375	moderate
375–425	moderately hot
425–475	hot
475+	very hot

COSMETIC SURGERY

TYPES

Face-lift (rhytidectomy)
Nose surgery (rhinoplasty)
Eyelid surgery (blepharoplasty)
Hair transplants
Breast augmentation (enlargement)
Breast reduction
Tummy tuck (abdominoplasty)
Injections (collagen, fat, or silicone)
Chemical peels and Dermabrasion
  (to remove scars)
Liposuction (suction-assisted
  lipectomy)

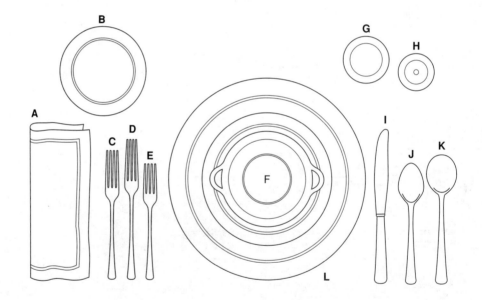

A. Napkin,
B. Salad plate,
C. Salad fork,
D. Dinner fork,
E. Dessert fork,
F. First-course bowl and liner plate

G. Water goblet,
H. Wine glass,
I. Dinner knife,
J. Teaspoon,
K. Soup spoon,
L. Dinner or service plate

Dinner Setup

FOODS & DRINKS

CAFFEINE CONTENT

(5 oz, unless noted otherwise)

decaffeinated coffee, 2–5 mg
tea, 40–100 mg
instant tea, 31 mg
hot chocolate, 2–10 mg
cola (12 oz), 45 mg

FIBER CONTENT OF FOODS

(gms of fiber per 100 gms)

44, wheat bran
27, all bran
16, prunes
12, lentils
11, corn flakes
8, peanuts
8, oatmeal
6, spaghetti
4, white flour
2, apple

FOOD CLASSES

1. cereals and cereal products
2. starchy roots
3. legumes (pulses)
4. other vegetables
5. fruits
6. nuts and seeds
7. sugars, syrups, sweets, and preserves
8. meat, including poultry, and meat products
9. seafood (fishes and shellfish)
10. eggs and roe
11. milk, cream, and cheese
12. fats and oils
13. herbs and spices
14. nonalcoholic, nondairy beverages
15. alcoholic beverages
16. dietary preparations
17. miscellaneous (e.g. salt, vinegar)

FOOD GRADES

(U.S. Department of Agriculture)

Beef, veal, lamb
  Prime
  Choice
  Good
Poultry
  Grade A
  Grade B
Fish
  Grade A
  Grade B
  Grade C
Pork
  Acceptable
  Unacceptable
Eggs and butter
  Grade AA
  Grade A
  Grade B
Fruits and vegetables, fresh*
  U.S. Fancy
  U.S. No. 1
  U.S. No. 2
Fruits and vegetables, canned; frozen juices; jams and jellies*
  Grade A
  Grade B
  Grade C
*These may vary for some specific products.

BEEF CUTS

Forequarters

chuck: blade steak and roast, shoulder steak and roast, pot roast cuts, chuck short ribs, stew beef, ground beef
rib: rib roasts, rib steak, rib eye steak and roast, Delmonico
short plate: short ribs, corned beef brisket, stew beef, ground beef
shank: cross cuts, stew beef

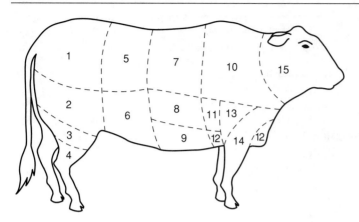

1. Rump
2. Round
3. Second-cut round
4. Hindshank
5. Loin
6. Flank
7. Ribs
8. Plate
9. Navel
10. Chuck
11. Cross ribs
12. Brisket
13. Shoulder clod
14. Foreshank
15. Neck

Cuts of Beef

Hindquarters

short loin: club steak (New York strip), T-bone, Porterhouse, tenderloin (filet mignon)

sirloin: pin bone steak, flat bone steak, wedge bone steak, tip steak and roast

rump: rump roast

round: top round and steak, bottom round and steak, eye of round, heel of round, cubed steak, ground beef, tip steak and roast

flank: flank steak, ground beef

EGG SIZE AND QUALITY

By weight:

jumbo: 30 oz per dozen
extra-large: 27 oz
large: 24 oz
medium: 21 oz
small: 18 oz
peewee: 15 oz

By quality:

AA
A
B

BASIC FOOD GROUPS IN HOME SCIENCE

1. vegetables and fruits (and their juices) [at least 4 servings per day recommended]
2. breads and cereals (foods based on whole grains or enriched flour or meal) [6–8 servings]
3. milk and milk products (milk, yogurt, cheese, ice milk, ice cream, and foods prepared with milk) [2–4 servings]
4. meats and meat alternates (meats, dry beans or peas, soybeans, lentils, eggs, nuts, seeds, peanut butter) [2 servings]
5. fats, sweets, and alcohol (fats, oils, mayonnaise and salad dressings, concentrated sweets, highly sugared beverages; unenriched, refined flour products, bacon, salt pork)

FOOD COMMODITIES

(U.S. Census classification)

Red meat
  beef
  veal
  lamb and mutton
  pork
Fish and shellfish
  fresh and frozen
  canned
  cured
Poultry products
  chicken
  turkey
Eggs

Dairy products
  fluid milk and cream
    beverage milks
      whole milk
      lowfat milk
      skim milk
      buttermilk
    yogurt
    cream
    sour cream
  condensed and evaporated milk
  cheese
  cottage cheese
  ice cream
  ice milk
Fats and oils
  butter
  margarine
  lard
  edible tallow
  shortening
  salad and cooking oils
  other edible fats and oils
Flour and cereal products
  wheat flour
  rye flour
  rice, milled
  corn products
  oat products
  barley products
Caloric sweeteners
  sugar
  corn sweeteners
  low-calorie sweeteners
Other
  cocoa beans
  coffee
  peanuts
  tree nuts

OLIVES

(by size)

Super Colossal (< 33 olives per pound)
Colossal (33–46)
Jumbo (47–60)
Extra Large (65–90; for a few varieties, 65–75)

Alsace glass   Bordeaux glass   Brandy snifter   Burgundy glass   Champagne flute   Cocktail glass

Highball glass   Liqueur glass   Old-fashioned glass   Port glass   Sparkling wine glass   Water goblet   White wine glass

Types of Glasses

Large (91–105)
Medium (106–127)
Small (128–140)

WINES

(by grape variety)

Reds

Cabernet
Gamay
Merlot
Nebbiolo
Pinot Noir
Sangiovese
Syrah
Zinfandel

Whites

Chardonnay
Chenin blanc
Gewürtztraminer
Riesling
Sauvignon Blanc
Scheuerbe

FRAGRANCES

Classification by fragrance concentration

Perfume	20–30%
Eau de Parfum	18–25%
Toilet Water	15–18%
Cologne	5–7%

JEWELS

DIAMONDS—FOUR C'S THAT DETERMINE VALUE

carat weight
color
clarity
cut

Baguette cut

Brilliant full cut

Cabochon cut

Eight cut

Emerald cut

French cut

Oval cut

Rose cut

Scissors cut

Step cut

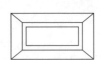

Table cut

Gemstone Cuts

LIGHTS

LIGHT BULB BASES

Mogul, 1^{19}⁄$_{32}$" diameter, high-wattage bulbs like outdoor security lights

Ad-Medium, 1^5⁄$_{32}$" diameter, sign bulbs

Medium/Edison, 1^1⁄$_{16}$" diameter, household bulbs

Intermediate, ⅝" diameter, refrigerators and appliances

Candelabra, ½", large Christmas tree lights

Min-can, ⁷⁄$_{16}$" diameter, special high-intensity lights

Miniature, ⅜" diameter, nightlights and small Christmas tree lights

Midget, smaller, signal lights

TYPES OF ARTIFICIAL LIGHTS

Incandescent
Tungsten-halogen
Fluorescent
High-intensity discharge (mercury vapor, sodium vapor, etc.)
Neon
Arc
LED (light-emitting diode)
Electroluminescent panels

LINENS

BLANKETS

crib (approximately 45" × 60")
stadium (50" × 60" to 54" × 72")
twin (60" × 90")
double (80" × 90")
queen (90" × 90" to 100" × 90")
king (108" × 90" to 108" × 100")

PILLOWS

standard (20" × 26")
queen (20" × 30" to 22" × 34")
king (20" × 36")

SHEETS / BED SIZES
(fitted)

crib (28" × 52")
twin (39" × 75"-76")
long twin (39" × 80")
full or double (54" × 75" to 54" × 76")
queen (60" × 80")
king (78" × 80" to 79" × 80")
California king (72" × 84")

TOWELS

wash cloth (12" × 12" to 14" × 14")
fingertip/guest towel (11" × 18" to 11" × 21")
hand towel (16" × 28" to 18" × 32")
bath towel (25" × 48" to 30" × 52")
bath sheet (35" × 60" to 40" × 75")

MATTRESSES

SIZES
(in inches)

Twin	38 × 75
Double or full	54 × 75
Queen	60 × 80
Eastern King	76 × 80
California King	72 × 84

PAINTS

TYPES
(degree of gloss or shine)

Flat
Satin or eggshell
Semigloss
Gloss

PAINTS
  Types (cont.)
PHOTOGRAPHY
TOOLS

(by base)

Latex
Acrylic
Alkyd
Oil

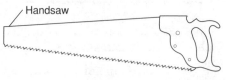

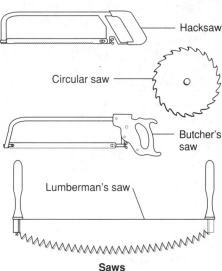

Handsaw

Hacksaw

Circular saw

Butcher's saw

Lumberman's saw

Saws

PHOTOGRAPHY

FILM SPEED RECOMMENDATIONS

(ISO [formerly ASA] numbers)

100 = sunny days or with flash
200 = all-purpose and with flash
400 = low-light conditions or with
    telephoto lens
1600 = very dim light (as in museums
    where no flash is allowed)

TOOLS

TOOLS BY TYPE

Cutting tools

axe
back saw
band saw
bench hook
bolt cutter
chain saw
coping saw
cutoff saw
die
folding saw
glass cutter
hack saw
hand saw
hatchet
jigsaw
keyhole saw
knive
log saw
miter box
one-man crosscut saw
pipe cutter

plane
portable circular saw
pruner
router
saber saw
scissor
scorp
scraper
scythe
shaver
shear
sickle
snip
spokeshave
table saw
tap
tile cutter
trimmer
tree saw
two-man crosscut saw
wire stripper

Chain Saw Classification

mini-saw (6–9 pounds)
light-duty (9–13 pounds)
medium-duty (13–18 pounds)
heavy-duty (over 18 pounds)

Holding/grasping & torsion tools

box wrench
clamps
crescent wrench
flat nosed pliers
holdfast
monkey wrench
needle-nosed pliers
open-end wrench
pipe wrench
pliers
socket wrench
vise
woodcarver's screw

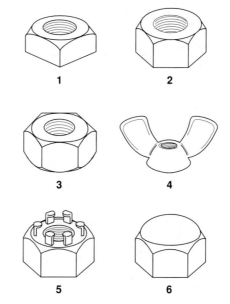

Nuts
1. Square nut; **2.** Hexagonal nut; **3.** Jam nut;
4. Wing nut; **5.** Castellated nut; **6.** Cap nut

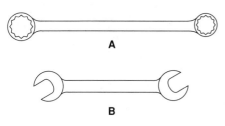
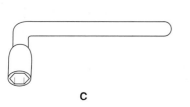
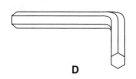

Wrenches
A. Box wrench; **B.** Open-end wrench;
C. Socket wrench; **D.** Allen wrench

Measuring/marking tools

caliper
chalk line
compass
gauge
level
plumb bob
rule
square
straight edge
tape measure

Boring/digging tools

adze
auger
awl
brace
chisel
digger
drill
driver

TOOLS

Tools by Type (cont.)

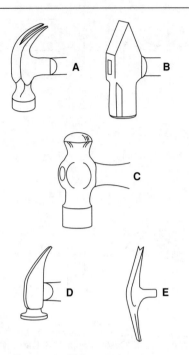

Hammers
A. Claw hammer; **B.** Engineer's hammer;
C. Ball-peen hammer; **D.** Shoemaker's hammer
E. Tack hammer

Grinding/sharpening tool

file
grinder
point and wheel
rasp
sander
sanding block
sharpener
stone

Striking/pushing/pulling tools

auger
crowbar
cultivator
flared-tip screwdriver
hammer
mallet
Phillips head screwdriver
pipe burring reamer

fork
gimlet
gouge
grubbing mattock
hoe
jig
mason's bolster
mattock
nail set
parting tool
pickax
point
press
punch
shovel
spade
taper reamer
tooler
trowel
wheel pricker

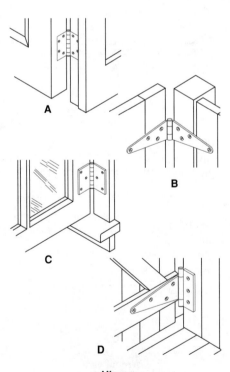

Hinges
A. Butt hinge; **B.** Strap hinge;
C. Blackflap hinge; **D.** T hinge

plunger
rake
riveter
screwdriver
spring tube bender

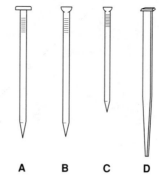

NAILS

Sizes

D Designation	Nail Length (inches)	Gauge (wire measure)
2	1	15
3	1¼	14
4	1½	12½
5	1¾	12½
6	2	11½
7	2¼	11½
8	2½	10¼
9	2½	10¼
10	3	9
12	3¼	9
16	3¼	8
20	4	6
30	4½	5
40	5	4
50	5½	3
60	6	2

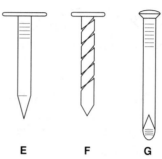

Types of Nails
A. Common nail; **B.** Finish nail;
C. Brad nail; **D.** Cut nail; **E.** Roofing nail;
F. Screw nail; **G.** Boat nail

SANDPAPER GRADES

500–600, super fine (finest grit available)
320–400, extra fine (smoothing paints, metal and glass polishing)
220–280, very fine (fine sanding of wood)
120–180, fine (general woodworking, smoothing joints, autobody finishing, prepaint finish for furniture)
60–100, medium (coarse sanding for wood, stripping wood floors and painted furniture, rough metal work and finishing)
30–50, coarse (de-rusting metals, stripping housepaint)
16–24, very coarse (removing rust, paint, etc.)

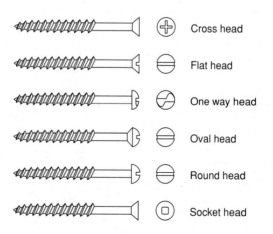

Cross head
Flat head
One way head
Oval head
Round head
Socket head

Types of Screws

TOOLS

knots

Bowline

Clove hitch

Cow hitch

Figure-eight knot

Fisherman's knot

Granny Knot

Heaving line knot

Overhand knot

Running bowline

Sheepshank

Square Knot

Knots

STEEL WOOL GRADES

#0000 or #4/0, super fine (polishing furniture finishes before applying top coat; cleaning windows)

#000 or #3/0, extra fine (removing rust from chrome; surface preparation between varnish coats)

#00, #2/0, fine (cleaning wood floors; polishing copper and brass)

#0, medium fine (cleaning metal before soldering; cleaning aluminum pots and pans)

#1, medium (preparing walls, wood for painting; removing rust from cast iron)

#2, medium coarse (rough cleaning jobs, as on masonry)

#3, coarse (removing paint and varnish)

#4, extra coarse (removing rust from metal and tile; engine cleaning; heavy-duty stripping of finishes)

...competition is the only form of organization which can afford a large measure of freedom to the individual.

—Frank Hyneman Knight, *Freedom and Reform*

CHAPTER TWELVE

SPORTS & RECREATION

AMERICAN SPORTS TEAMS

MAJOR LEAGUE BASEBALL

American League
  AL East
    Baltimore Orioles
    Boston Red Sox
    New York Yankees
    Tampa Bay Devil Rays
  AL Central
    Chicago White Sox
    Cleveland Indians
    Detroit Tigers
    Kansas City Royals
    Minnesota Twins
  AL West
    Anaheim Angles
    Oakland Athletics
    Seattle Mariners
    Texas Rangers
National League
  NL East
    Atlanta Braves
    Florida Marlins
    Montreal Expos
    New York Mets
    Philadelphia Phillies
  NL Central
    Chicago Cubs
    Cincinnati Reds
    Houston Astros
    Milwaukee Brewers
    Pittsburgh Pirates
    St. Louis Cardinals
  NL West
    Arizona Diamondbacks
    Colorado Rockies
    Los Angeles Dodgers
    San Diego Padres
    San Francisco Giants

MAJOR LEAGUE SOCCER

Eastern Division
  D.C. United
  MetroStars
  Miami Fusion
  New England Revolution
Central Division
  Chicago Fire
  Columbus Crew
  Dallas Burn
  Tampa Bay Mutiny
Western Division
  Colorado Rapids
  Kansas City Wizards
  Los Angeles Galaxy
  San Jose Earthquakes

NATIONAL BASKETBALL ASSOCIATION

Atlantic Division
  Boston Celtics
  Miami Heat
  New Jersey Nets
  New York Knicks
  Orlando Magic
  Philadelphia 76ers
  Washington Wizards
Central Division
  Atlanta Hawks
  Charlotte Hornets
  Chicago Bulls
  Cleveland Cavaliers
  Detroit Pistons
  Indiana Pacers
  Milwaukee Bucks
  Toronto Raptors
Midwest Division
  Dallas Mavericks
  Denver Nuggets
  Houston Rockets
  Minnesota Timberwolves
  San Antonio Spurs
  Utah Jazz
  Vancouver Grizzlies
Pacific Division
  Golden State Warriors
  Los Angeles Clippers
  Los Angeles Lakers
  Phoenix Suns
  Portland Trail Blazers
  Sacramento Kings
  Seattle SuperSonics

NATIONAL FOOTBALL LEAGUE

American Football Conference
AFC East
Buffalo Bills
Indianapolis Colts
Miami Dolphins
New England Patriots
New York Jets
AFC Central
Baltimore Ravens
Cincinnati Bengals
Cleveland Browns
Jacksonville Jaguars
Pittsburgh Steelers
Tennessee Titans
AFC West
Denver Broncos
Kansas City Chiefs
Oakland Raiders
San Diego Chargers
Seattle Seahawks
National Football Conference
NFC East
Arizona Cardinals
Dallas Cowboys
New York Giants
Philadelphia Eagles
Washington Redskins
NFC Central
Chicago Bears
Detroit Lions
Green Bay Packers
Minnesota Vikings
Tampa Bay Buccaneers
NFC West
Atlanta Falcons
Carolina Panthers
New Orleans Saints
St. Louis Rams
San Francisco 49ers

NATIONAL HOCKEY LEAGUE

Eastern Conference
Atlantic Division
New Jersey Devils
New York Islanders
New York Rangers
Philadelphia Flyers
Pittsburgh Penguins
Northeast Division
Boston Bruins
Buffalo Sabres
Montreal Canadiens
Ottawa Senators
Toronto Maple Leafs
Southeast Division
Atlanta Thrashers
Carolina Hurricanes
Florida Panthers
Tampa Bay Lightning
Washington Capitals
Western Conference
Central Division
Chicago Blackhawks
Columbus Blue Jackets
Detroit Red Wings
Nashville Predators
St. Louis Blues
Northwest Division
Calgary Flames
Colorado Avalanche
Edmonton Oilers
Minnesota Wild
Vancouver Canucks
Pacific Division
Mighty Ducks of Anaheim
Dallas Stars
Los Angeles Kings
Phoenix Coyotes
San Jose Sharks

ARCHERY

FIELD ARCHERY

Ring Points

black outer ring, 3 points
white inner ring, 4 points
black center spot, 5 points

TARGET ARCHERY

Ring Points

white outer ring, 1 point
white inner ring, 2 points
black ring, 3 points
black inner ring, 4 points
blue ring, 5 points
blue inner ring, 6 points
red ring, 7 points
red inner ring, 8 points
gold ring, 9 points
bull's-eye (gold inner ring), 10 points

© 1996 Joseph Chalupa
Peerless Blackline, Inc.

BASEBALL

BASEBALL POSITIONS BY NUMBER

1, pitcher
2, catcher
3, first base
4, second base

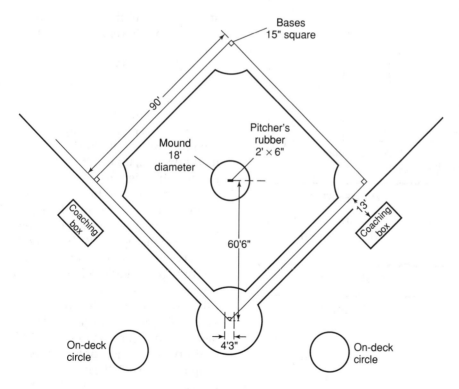

Baseball Diamond Dimensions

5, third base
6, shortstop
7, left field
8, center field
9, right field

BASKETBALL

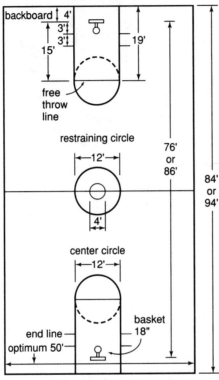

Basketball Court

Team Formation

forward   center   forward
    guard   guard

BOWLING

Pin Placement

7	8	9	10
	4	5	6
		2	3
		1	

BOXING

Weight Divisions

Amateur (Olympics)

junior (light) flyweight, up to 106 lb (48 kg)
flyweight, up to 112 lb (51 kg)
bantamweight, up to 119 lb (54 kg)
featherweight, up to 126 lb (57 kg)
lightweight, up to 132 lb (60 kg)
junior (light) welterweight or super lightweight, up to 140 lb (63.5 kg)
welterweight, up to 147 lb (67 kg)
junior (light) middleweight or super welterweight, up to 157 lb (71 kg)
middleweight, up to 165 lb (75 kg)
light heavyweight, up to 179 lb (81 kg)
heavyweight, up to 201 lb (91 kg)
super heavyweight, 201+ lb (91+ kg)

Professional

strawweight/minimum, up to 105 lb
junior (light) flyweight, up to 108 lb (49kg)
flyweight, up to 112 lb (51 kg)
junior bantamweight or super flyweight, up to 115 lb
bantamweight, up to 118 lb (53.5 kg)
junior featherweight or super bantamweight, up to 122 lb
featherweight, up to 126 lb (57 kg)
junior lightweight or super featherweight, up to 130 lb (59 kg)
lightweight, up to 135 lb (61.2 kg)
junior (light) welterweight or super lightweight, up to 140 lb (63.5 kg)
welterweight, up to 147 lb (66.5 kg)
junior (light) middleweight or super welterweight, up to 154 lb (70 kg)
middleweight, up to 160 lb (72.5 kg)
super middleweight, up to 168 lb
light heavyweight, up to 175 lb (79.4 kg)
cruiserweight or junior heavyweight, up to 195 lb (88.45 kg)
heavyweight, 195+ lb (88.45+ kg)

BILLIARDS

Various Billiard Setups

Continuous pool

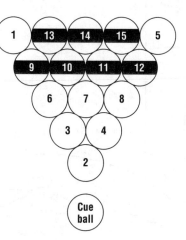

The #1 and #5 balls are the only balls that are placed in a specific spot. The other balls are randomly placed. The #1 ball is placed on the rackers's right corner, the #5 ball is placed on the racker's left corner.

Billiards/Pool

1. Yellow
2. Blue
3. Red
4. Purple
5. Orange
6. Green
7. Deep red
8. Black
9. White w/yellow stripe
10. White w/blue stripe
11. White w/red stripe
12. White w/purple stripe
13. White w/orange stripe
14. White w/green stripe
15. White w/deep red stripe

Eight Ball pool

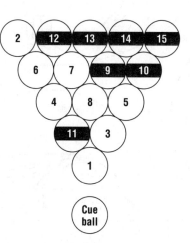

The #8 ball is placed in the center of the triangle, a stripe ball in one corner of the rack and a solid ball in the other corner. The remaining balls are placed randomly.

Snooker

Red ball worth 1 point.
Yellow ball worth 2 points.
Green ball worth 3 points.
Brown ball worth 4 points.
Blue ball worth 5 points.
Pink ball worth 6 points.
Black ball worth 7 points.

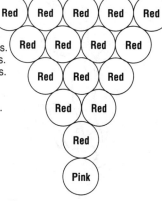

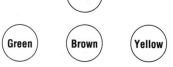

Bullfighting Stages
A. Paseo; **B.** Matador testing bull with *capote*; **C.** Banderilleros; **D.** Matador

BULLFIGHTING

BULLFIGHTERS AND STAGES

1. **paseo** (parade of matadors and assistants)
2. **banderilleros** (assistants on foot; taunt the bull)
3. **matador** (bullfighter; tests the bull's temperament)
4. **picadores** (assistants on horseback; thrust long lances at bull.
5. **banderilleros** (place brightly colored ribboned dart sticks (banderillas) in the bull's neck and back)
6. **matador** (comes in for the kill)

CARD GAMES

BRIDGE

Bidding Order

pass (no bid)

bid (offer to win a number of "odd tricks", tricks in excess of 6 (first 6 = "book")

double (increase the scoring value)

redouble (further increasing the scoring value of the trick)

Player Rankings

Sub-Master, under 100 rating points

Junior Master, 1–19 masters

Master, 20–49 masters

National Master, 50–99 masters

Senior Master, 100–199 masters

Advanced Senior Master, 200–299 masters, 20 or more of which must be red or gold

Life Master, 300 masters, 50 or more of which must be red or gold

Point Scale

1. rating point
2. master point = 100 rating points in a club game
3. black point = 100 rating points in sectional and regional play
4. red point = 100 rating points in national and North American competition
5. gold point = 100 rating points in a national victory

POKER

Chips (highest to lowest)

yellow or black: equal to 100 white chips

blue chips: equal to 10 or 20 white chips (agreed by table)

red chips: equal to 5 white chips

white chips: lowest value

Hands (highest to lowest)

1. Royal flush: ace, king, queen, jack, 10 of same suit
2. Straight flush: 5 cards of a suit in sequence (e.g., 7, 8, 9, 10, jack, all of spades)
3. Four-of-a-kind: 4 cards of the same rank (e.g., 5 of hearts, diamonds, spades, and clubs)
4. Full house: 3 of a kind (e.g., three aces) and a pair of another kind (e.g. two 10's)
5. Flush: 5 cards of the same suit, but not in sequence
6. Straight: 5 cards in sequence, regardless of suit
7. Three-of-a-kind: 3 cards of the same rank
8. Two pair: 2 cards of the same rank
9. one pair: 2 cards of the same rank
10. high card: highest-ranking card in a hand

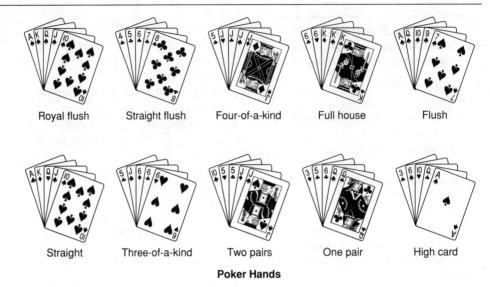

Royal flush   Straight flush   Four-of-a-kind   Full house   Flush

Straight   Three-of-a-kind   Two pairs   One pair   High card

Poker Hands

CHESS

PIECE RANKINGS

king
queen
rook (castle)
bishop
knight
pawn

FIGHTING POWER VALUES

king (can move in any direction, one
  square at a time)
queen = 9 (can move in any direction,
  any unobstructed distance)
rook = 5 (can move forward,
  backward, sideways for any
  unobstructed distance)
bishop = 3 (can move forward or
  backward diagonally for any
  unobstructed distance)
knight = 3 (can move two squares in
  any direction (not diagonally), then
  one square at a right angle)
pawn = 1 (can only move forward;

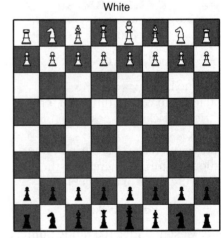

White

Black

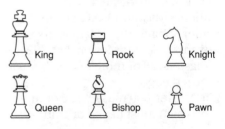

King   Rook   Knight

Queen   Bishop   Pawn

Chess Pieces and Board Setup

opening move one or two squares, succeeding moves only one square)
king (can move one square in any direction)

PLAYER RANKINGS

(by point value)

Class C, under 1600
Class B, 1600–1799
Class A, 1800–1999
Expert (Candidate Master), 2000–2199
Master (National Master), 2200–2399
Senior Master (International Master), 2400–2599
Grandmaster, 2600+

CIRCUS

CIRCUS EVENT

(The three rings present a rotation so the audience can see each act fully.)

1. advance agents make arrangements and promote the event
2. "flying squadron" trains arrive with cookhouse, horse tents, menagerie (wild animals), and calliope
3. "canvas train" and "lumber train" arrive bearing construction materials
4. performers arrive

CIRCUS ATTRACTIONS

acts of skill
aerial acts (high wire, tightrope, etc.)
clowns
equestrian acts
supporting attractions: music, menagerie, sideshow
tumbling and acrobatic acts
wild animal acts

COLLECTING

COIN COLLECTING

Conditions

fair: the coin can be barely identified
good: very worn, but the outline of the design is still visible
very good: design shows clearly, but detail is worn away
fine: shows signs of wear
very fine: shows slight wear
extra fine: almost perfect
uncirculated: mint condition, only marks caused by coins rubbing together
proof: mirrorlike finish and struck from polished dies, especially for collectors

DARTS

SCORING

bull's-eye (inner or double ring), 50 points

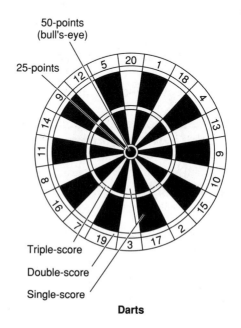

50-points (bull's-eye)

25-points

Triple-score

Double-score

Single-score

Darts

ring outside bull's-eye (single outer ring), 25 points
triple-score ring, points for the triangle it intersects are tripled
single-score ring
double-score ring, points for the triangle it intersects are doubled
no score outer ring

EQUESTRIAN SPORTS

HORSE GAITS

walk: four beats, each hitting ground separately—left hind, left fore, right hind, right fore
trot: two beats—left hind and right fore together, right hind and left fore together
canter: three beats—left hind, left fore and right hind together, then right fore
gallop: four beats—same as walk then all four come off the ground

THREE-DAY EVENT

first day: dressage
second day: endurance ride, cross-country race, and steeplechase
third day: jumping (through a ring)

TRIPLE CROWN RACING

Kentucky Derby (first Saturday in May)
Preakness Stakes
Belmont Stakes

FOOTBALL

SCORING

touchdown, 6 points
field goal, 3 points
safety, 2 points
two-point conversion, 2 points
point after touchdown (kick), 1 point

UNIFORM NUMBERS (TYPICAL)

backs = 10–49
centers = 50–59
guards = 60–69
tackles = 70–79
ends = 80–89

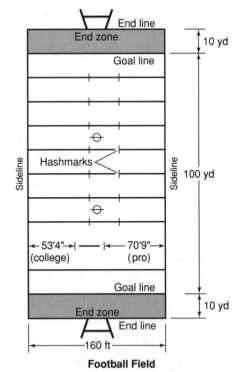

Football Field

Goal posts are 18'4" apart in professional football; 23'6" apart in college football.

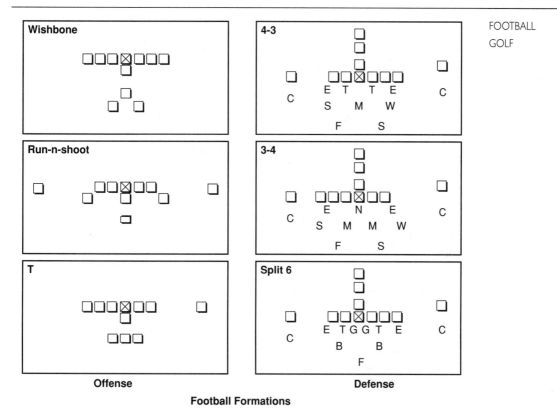

Offense Defense

Football Formations

GOLF

CLUBS BY DEGREE OF LOFT

Woods

1=11° (driver)
2=14° (brassie)
3=16° (spoon)
4=19° (baffy)
5=21° (no name)
6=23° (no name)

IRONS

1=17° (driving club or cleek)
2=20° (mid-iron)
3=23° (mid-mashie)
4=27° (mashie iron)

5=31° (mashie)
6=35° (spade mashie)
7=39° (mashie niblick)
8=43° (pitching niblick)
9=47° (niblick)
10=51° (pitching wedge)
11=56° (sand wedge)
putter for use on the green

SCORING

(USGA standards)

Par

Men
Par 3: up to 250 yards
Par 4: 251–470 yards
Par 5: 471 yards and over

Women

Par 3: up to 210 yards
Par 4: 211–400 yards
Par 5: 401–575 yards
Par 6: 576 yards and over

per hole

ace/hole-in-one: hole scored in one
  stroke
eagle: two strokes under par for a
  hole
birdie: one stroke under par on a hole
bogey: one stroke over par for a hole
double bogey: two strokes over par
  for a hole

ICE HOCKEY

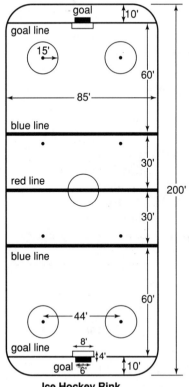

Ice Hockey Rink

MARTIAL ARTS

AIKIDO GRADES

(Japanese:)
Second-Sixth Kyu: white belt
First Kyu: brown belt

(outside Japan:)
First Kyo: yellow belt
Second Kyo: orange belt
Third Kyo: green belt
Fourth Kyo: blue belt
Fifth Kyo: brown belt

JUDO LEVELS OF PROFICIENCY

(two groups of "grades")

Kyu (pupil) Grades (lowest to highest)

absolute beginner: red belt
beginner (6th): white belt
5th: yellow belt
4th: orange belt
3rd: green belt
2nd: blue belt
1st: brown belt

Dan (degree) Grades (lowest to highest)

1st-5th: plain black belt
6th-8th: red-and-white belt
9th: red-and-black belt
10th: red belt (almost never conferred
  on anyone, except the founder of a
  style)

JUDO WEIGHT CATEGORIES

(class, weight for men, for women)

super lightweight, up to 132 lbs.
  (60kg), up to 106 lbs. (48 kg)
semi-lightweight, up to 143 lbs.
  (60–65 kg), up to 115 lbs. (48–52 kg)
lightweight, up to 157 lbs. (65–71 kg),
  up to 123 lbs. (52–56 kg)

semi-middleweight, up to 172 lbs. (71–78 kg), up to 134 (56–61 kg)

middleweight, up to 198 lbs. (78–86 kg), up to 146 (61–66 kg)

light-middleweight, up to 198 lbs. (86–95 kg), up to 159 lbs. (66–72 kg)

heavyweight, over 209 lbs. (95 kg), over 159 (72 kg)

KARATE PROMOTIONAL RANKINGS

(U.S. American Karate Federation, 18 reviews/promotions to next skill level; lowest to highest)

White Belt

Orange Belt = 12th Kyu, 11th Kyu (4 months training minimum)

Gold Belt = 10th Kyu, 9th Kyu (4 mos after Orange Belt)

Blue Belt = 8th Kyu, 7th Kyu (4 mos after Gold Belt)

Green Belt = 6th Kyu, 5th Kyu (4 mos after Blue Belt)

Purple Belt = 4B Kyu, 4A Kyu (4 mos after Green Belt)

Purple Belt = 3B Kyu, 3A Kyu (4 most after 4B Purple Belt)

Brown Belt = 2B Kyu, 2A Kyu (4 mos after 3B Purple Belt)

Brown Belt = 1B Kyu, 1A Kyu (4 mos after 2B Brown Belt)

Shodan Ho, 1st Dan, Probation (6 mos after 1B Brown Belt)

Black Belt, First Degree = Shodan (4 mos after Shodan-Ho)

Black Belt, Second Degree = Nidan (2 years after Shodan)

Black Belt, Third Degree = Sandan (3 yrs after Nidan)

Black Belt, Fourth Degree = Yodan (4 yrs after Sandan)

Black Belt, Fifth Degree = Godan (5 yrs after Yodan)

Black Belt, Sixth Degree = Ryokudan (6 yrs after Godan)

Black Belt, Seventh Degree = Shichidan (7 yrs after Ryokudan)

Black Belt, Eighth Degree = Hachidan (8 yrs after Shichidan)

Black Belt, Ninth Degree = Kudan (9 yrs after Hachidan)

Black Belt, Tenth Degree = Jodan (10 yrs after Kudan)

MARTIAL ARTS DAN GRADES

(These higher grades are conferred on those qualified to wear the black belt. Depending on the schools and techniques, there are between 5–12 Dan grades. In traditional martial arts, the Dan grades are:)

First Dan: student

Second Dan: disciple

Third Dan: confirmed disciple

Fourth Dan: expert

Fifth, Sixth Dan: spiritual expert

Seventh-Tenth Dan: expert becomes specialist (Ninth, Tenth Dan: master)

MARTIAL ARTS KYU GRADES

(These are the lower grades, below black belt. There are 9 in karate, 6 in judo and other disciplines.)

(Japanese Kyu grades, in ascending order:)

Sixth Kyu, white belt

Fifth Kyu, white belt

Fourth Kyu, white belt

Third Kyu, brown belt

Second Kyu, brown belt

First Kyu, brown belt

(outside Japan, in ascending order:)

white belt

yellow belt

orange belt

green belt

blue belt

brown belt

TYPES

aikido
judo
jujitsu
karate
kung fu
qi gong
tae kwon do
ta'i chi chu'an
wushu

TAE-KWON-DO GRADES

**(Keup/Kup/Kyu grades,
least to most experienced:)**
10th, white belt
9th, white with yellow bar
8th, yellow
7th, yellow with green bar
6th, green
5th, green with blue bar
4th, blue
3rd, blue with brown bar
2nd, brown
1st, brown with black bar

(Dan grades of black belt:)
1st Dan, student
2nd Dan: disciple
3rd Dan: accepted disciple
4th Dan: expert
5th Dan: expert
6th Dan: expert
7th, 8th Dan: expert
9th, 10th Dan: master

MONOPOLY™

BOARD REAL ESTATE

Boardwalk, $400
Park Place, $350
Pennsylvania Avenue, $320
North Carolina Avenue, $300
Pacific Avenue, $300
Marvin Gardens, $280
Ventnor Avenue, $260
Atlantic Avenue, $260
Illinois Avenue, $240
Indiana Avenue, $220
Kentucky Avenue, $220
New York Avenue, $200
Tennessee Avenue, $180
St. James Place, $180
Virginia Avenue, $160
States Avenue, $140
St. Charles Place, $140
Connecticut Avenue, $120
Vermont Avenue, $100
Oriental Avenue, $100
Baltic Avenue, $60
Mediterranean Avenue, $60

Utilities

Electric Company, $150
Water Works, $150

Railroads

B&O Railroad, $200
Pennsylvania Railroad, $200
Reading Railroad, $200
Short Line Railroad, $200

BOARD LAYOUT

In Order from Go

1. Go (collect $200)
2. Mediterranean Avenue
3. Community Chest
4. Baltic Avenue
5. Income tax, pay 10% or $200
6. Reading Railroad
7. Oriental Avenue
8. Chance
9. Vermont Avenue
10. Connecticut Avenue
11. In jail or just visiting
12. St. Charles Place
13. Electric Company
14. States Avenue
15. Virginia Avenue

16. Pennsylvania Railroad
17. St. James Place
18. Community Chest
19. Tennessee Avenue
20. New York Avenue
21. Free parking
22. Kentucky Avenue
23. Chance
24. Indiana Avenue
25. Illinois Avenue
26. B & O Railroad
27. Atlantic Avenue
28. Ventnor Avenue
29. Water Works
30. Marvin Gardens
31. Go to jail
32. Pacific Avenue
33. North Carolina Avenue
34. Community Chest
35. Pennsylvania Avenue
36. Short Line Railroad
37. Chance
38. Park Place
39. Luxury tax, pay $75
40. Boardwalk

MOTORCAR RACING

DRAG RACING

Dragsters elongated front-suspension with light front wheels and oversize rear tires, racing over a strip 440 yards (quarter mile) long.

RACING AND CIRCUIT CARS

Formula One, up to 3,000 cc unsupercharged, 1,500 cc supercharged, max. 12 cylinders
Formula Three, up to 2,000 cc, 4-cylinder
Formula Ford, production 1,600 cc Cortina/Opel engines
Formula Vee/Super Vee, production 1,300 cc/1,600 cc Volkswagen engines

Formula 5000, mass-production 5,000 cc engines
Indy Cars, up to 4,490 cc unsupercharged, 2,999 cc supercharged
Formula B/Formula Atlantic, single-seater, production 1,100–1,600 cc engines
Group One, series-production 4-seater sports touring cars
Group Two, limited-production 4-seater sports touring cars
Group Three, series-production 2-seater sports grand tourers.
Group Four, limited-production 2-seater sports grand tourers.
Group Five, long-distance open 2-seater sports cars.

RALLYING AND CROSS-COUNTRY RACING

Motor rallying, cars of groups 1–4 above
Hill-climb, classes according to the number and nature of entrants, as organized by the competition authority
Hill-trial, specially built light cars in three classes (750, production, and specials)
Rallycross, production sports and sedans only
Autocross, production sports and sedans, buggies, and specials (as organized in classes
Autotest/Slalom, production cars and specials

U.S. STOCK CAR RACING

Standard size, maximum engine capacity 7 liters (430 cubic inches), minimum wheelbase 119 inches (3.0226 meters); bodies as standard
Intermediate size, maximum engine

capacity 7 liters (430 cubic inches), wheelbase 115–119 inches (2.921–3.0226 meters)

MOTORCYCLE RACING

OFF-TRACK RACING

Moto-cross/Scrambles, classes defined by engine capacity (usually 125 cc, 250 cc, and 500 cc, sometimes sidecar races)
Trials riding, lightweight bikes
Grasstrack racing, less formal style of racing with speedway or special machines

TRACK-RACING

50cc, 125cc, 250cc, 350cc, 500cc, 750cc
Sidecar combination (500 cc and 750 cc)
Speedway, four-member teams
Ice track-racing, a sort of speedway on ice
Drag and sprint racing: drag machines have enlarged rear wheels for racing over a strip 440 yards (quarter mile) long

OLYMPIC GAMES

EVENTS

2000 Olympic Summer Games program (Sydney)

Archery

Men
  individual round (70m)
  team round (70m)
Women
  individual round (70m)
  team round (70m)

Badminton

Men
  singles
  doubles
Women
  singles
  doubles
Mixed
  mixed doubles

Baseball

Men
  8-team tournament

Basketball

Men
  12-team tournament
Women
  12-team tournament

Beach Volleyball

Men   24 pairs
Women   24 pairs

Boxing

Men
  light flyweight (up to 48 kg, 106 lbs.)
  flyweight (up to 51 kg, 112 lbs.)
  bantamweight (up to 54 kg, 119 lbs.)
  featherweight (up to 57 kg, 126 lbs.)
  lightweight (up to 60 kg, 132 lbs.)
  light welterweight (up to 63.5 kg, 140 lbs.)
  welterweight (up to 67 kg, 147 lbs.)
  light middleweight (up to 71 kg, 157 lbs.)
  middleweight (up to 75 kg, 165 lbs.)
  light heavyweight (up to 81 kg, 179 lbs.)
  heavyweight (up to 91 kg, 201 lbs.)
  super heavyweight (over 91 kg 201 lbs.)

Canoeing/Kayaking

Men
Flatwater
  C-1 500 meters
  C-1 1000 meters
  C-2 500 meters
  C-2 1000 meters
  K-1 500 meters
  K-1 1000 meters
  K-2 500 meters
  K-2 1000 meters
  K-4 1000 meters
Slalom
  C-1 (single)
  C-2 (double)
  K-1 (single)
Women
Flatwater
  K-1 500 meters
  K-2 500 meters
  K-4 500 meters
Slalom
  K-1 (single)

Cycling

Men
Track—
  1 km time trial
  individual sprint (3 laps)
  4,000-meter individual pursuit
  4,000-meter team pursuit
  points race
  Olympic sprint
  Madison
  Keirin
Road—
  individual time trial
  individual race
Mountain bike—
  cross-country
Women
Track—
  500-meter time trial
  individual sprint (3 laps)
  3,000-meter individual pursuit
  points race
Road—
  individual race (70 km)

individual time trial (70 km)
Mountain bike—
  cross-country

Diving

Men
  springboard (3 meters)
  platform (10 meters)
Women
  springboard (3 meters)
  platform (10 meters)

Equestrian

Mixed
  individual jumping
  team jumping
  individual dressage
  team dressage
  individual three-day event
  team three-day event

Fencing

Men
  individual foil
  team foil
  individual sabre
  team sabre
  individual epée
  team epée
Women
  individual foil
  team foil
  individual epée
  team epée

Field Hockey

Men
  12-team tournament
Women
  10-team tournament

Gymnastics

Men
Artistic—
  team competition
  individual all-around
  floor exercise

pommel horse
still rings
vault
parallel bars
horizontal bar
trampoline
Women
Artistic—
  team competition
  individual all-around
  vault
  uneven parallel bars
  balance beam
  floor exercise
  trampoline
Rhythmic—
  individual all-around
  team competition

Judo

Men
  up to 60 kg (132 lbs.)
  60 to 66 kg (145 lbs.)
  66 to 73 kg (161 lbs.)
  73 to 81 kg (179 lbs.)
  81 to 90 kg (198 lbs.)
  90 to 100 kg (220 lbs.)
  over 100 kg
Women
  up to 48 kg (106 lbs.)
  48 to 52 kg (115 lbs.)
  52 to 57 kg (126 lbs.)
  57 to 63 kg (139 lbs.)
  63 to 70 kg (154 lbs.)
  70 to 78 kg (172 lbs.)
  over 78 kg

Modern Pentathlon

Men
  individual competition (shooting,
    fencing, swimming, equestrian,
    cross-country running)
Women
  individual competition (shooting,
    fencing, swimming, equestrian,
    cross-country running)

Rowing

Men
  single sculls
  pair oars without coxswain
  double sculls without coxswain
  four oars without coxswain
  quadruple sculls without coxswain
  eight oars without coxswain
Lightweight
  double sculls without coxswain
  four oars without coxswain
Women
  single sculls
  pair oars without coxswain
  double sculls without coxswain
  quadruple sculls without coxswain
  eight oars without coxswain
Lightweight
  Double sculls without coxswain

Shooting

Men
  rapid-fire pistol, 25 meters
  free pistol, 50 meters
  air pistol, 10 meters
  running game target, 10 meters
  smallbore rifle three positions, 50
    meters
  smallbore rifle prone position, 50
    meters
  air rifle, 10 meters
  double trap
  trap
  skeet
Women
  air rifle, 10 meters
  smallbore rifle three positions, 50
    meters
  sport pistol, 25 meters
  air pistol, 10 meters
  double trap
  trap
  skeet

Soccer

Men
  16-team tournament

Women
  8-team tournament

Softball

Women
  8-team tournament

Swimming

Men
  50-meter freestyle
  100-meter freestyle
  200-meter freestyle
  400-meter freestyle
  1,500-meter freestyle
  100-meter backstroke
  200-meter backstroke
  100-meter breaststroke
  200-meter breaststroke
  100-meter butterfly
  200-meter butterfly
  200-meter individual medley
  400-meter individual medley
  4x100-meter freestyle relay
  4x200-meter freestyle relay
  4x100-meter medley relay
Women
  50-meter freestyle
  100-meter freestyle
  200-meter freestyle
  400-meter freestyle
  800-meter freestyle
  100-meter backstroke
  200-meter backstroke
  100-meter breaststroke
  200-meter breaststroke
  100-meter butterfly
  200-meter butterfly
  200-meter individual medley
  400-meter individual medley
  4x100-meter freestyle relay
  4x200-meter freestyle relay
  4x100-meter medley relay

Synchronized Swimming

Women
  Duet event
  Team event

Table Tennis

Men
  singles
  doubles
Women
  singles
  doubles

Taekwondo

Men
  under 58 kg (128 lbs.)
  under 68 kg (150 lbs.)
  under 80 kg (176 lbs.)
  over 80 kg
Women
  Under 49 kg (108 lbs.)
  Under 57 kg (126 lbs.)
  Under 67 kg (148 lbs.)
  Over 67 kg

Team Handball

Men
  12-team tournament
Women
  10-team tournament

Tennis

Men
  singles
  doubles
Women
  singles
  doubles

Track & Field

Men
  100 meters
  200 meters
  400 meters
  800 meters
  1,500 meters
  5,000 meters
  10,000 meters
  110-meter hurdles
  400-meter hurdles
  3,000-meter steeplechase

OLYMPIC GAMES
Events (cont.)

20 km walk
50 km walk
4x100-meter relay
4x400-meter relay
marathon
high jump
long jump
triple jump
pole vault
shot put
discus
javelin
hammer throw
decathlon (100 meters, long jump,
    shot put, high jump, 400 meters,
    110-meter hurdles, discus, pole
    vault, javelin, 1,500 meters)
Women
100 meters
200 meters
400 meters
800 meters
1,500 meters
5,000 meters
10,000 meters
20 km walk
100-meter hurdles
400-meter hurdles
4x100-meter relay
4x400-meter relay
marathon
high jump
long jump
hammer
pole vault
triple jump
shot put
discus
javelin
heptathlon (100-meter hurdles,
    high jump, shot put, 200 meters,
    long jump, javelin, 800 meters)

Triathlon

Men
1.5 km swim
40 km cycling
10 km running

Women
1.5 km swim
40 km cycling
10 km running

Volleyball

Men
12-team tournament
beach volleyball (24 pairs)
Women
12-team tournament
beach volleyball (16 pairs)

Water Polo

Men (12-team tournament)

Weightlifting

Men
up to 56 kg (123 lbs.)
up to 62 kg (137 lbs.)
up to 69 kg (152 lbs.)
up to 77 kg (170 lbs.)
up to 85 kg (187 lbs.)
up to 94 kg (207 lbs.)
up to 105 kg (231 lbs.)
over 105 kg
Women
up to 48 kg (106 lbs.)
up to 53 kg (117 lbs.)
up to 58 kg (128 lbs.)
up to 63 kg (139 lbs.)
up to 69 kg (152 lbs.)
up to 75 kg (165 lbs.)
over 75 kg

Wrestling

Men
Freestyle
up to 48 to 54 kg (119 lbs.)
up to 58 kg (128 lbs.)
up to 63 kg (139 lbs.)
up to 69 kg (152 lbs.)
up to 76 kg (168 lbs.)
up to 85 kg (187 lbs.)
up to 97 kg (214 lbs.)
97 to 130 kg (287 lbs.)

Greco-Roman
   48 to 54 kg (119 lbs.)
   up to 58 kg (128 lbs.)
   up to 63 kg (139 lbs.)
   up to 69 kg (152 lbs.)
   up to 76 kg (168 lbs.)
   up to 85 kg (187 lbs.)
   up to 97 kg (214 lbs.)
   97 to 130 kg (287 lbs.)

Yachting

Men
   470 class
   Mistral (boardsailing)
   Finn class (single-handed dinghy)
Women
   470 class
   Mistral (boardsailing)
   Europe class (single-handed
      dinghy)
Mixed
   Soling class
   Star Class
   Laser class
   Tornado class

2002 Olympic Winter Games program
(Salt Lake City, USA)

Biathlon (cross-country skiing and shooting)

Men
   10 km sprint
   20 km individual
   12.5 km pursuit
   4 × 7.5 km relay
Women
   7.5 km sprint
   15 km individual
   10 km pursuit
   4 × 7.5 km relay

Bobsled

Men
   two-man
   four-man
Women
   two-man

Curling

Men's tournament
Women's tournament

Figure Skating

Men's short program and free
   program
Women's short program and free
   program
Pairs short program and free program
Dance compulsory, dance original
   and dance free

Ice Hockey

Men's tournament
Women's tournament

Luge

Men
   single
   double (can be co-ed)
Women
   single

Skiing

Men
Alpine—
   downhill
   slalom
   giant slalom
   super giant
Freestyle—
   aerials
   moguls
Cross Country—
   10 km classical and 10 km free
      combined
   15 km classical
   30 km free
   50 km classical
   4x10 km relay
   1.5 km sprint
Jumping—
   normal hill (90 m)
   large hill (120 m)
   large hill team (120 m)

Nordic Combined—
  90 m individual jump and 15 km
    individual cross-country
  90 m team jumps and 4x5 km
    cross-country relay
  120 m jump and sprint 7.5 km
    cross-country
Women
Alpine—
  downhill
  slalom
  giant slalom
  super giant
Freestyle—
  aerials
  moguls
Cross Country—
  5 km classical and 5 km free
    combined
  10 km classical
  15 km free
  30 km classical
  4x5 km relay
  1.5 km sprint

Snowboarding

Men
  Halfpipe
  Parallel Giant Slalom
Women
  Halfpipe
  Parallel Giant Slalom

Speedskating

Men
Long track—
  500 meters
  1,000 meters
  1,500 meters
  5,000 meters
  10,000 meters
Short track—
  5000 meters
  1500 meters
  500 meters
  1,000 meters
  5,000-meter relay

Women
Long track—
  500 meters
  1,000 meters
  1,500 meters
  3,000 meters
  5,000 meters
Short track—
  1500 meters
  500 meters
  1,000 meters
  3,000-meter relay

SPECIAL OLYMPICS SPORTS

alpine skiing
aquatics
athletics
badminton
basketball
bowling
cycling
equestrian
figure skating
floor hockey
football (soccer)
golf
gymnastics
hockey
powerlifting
roller skating
softball
speed skating
table tennis
team handball
tennis
volleyball

OLYMPIC MEDALS

first: gold
second: silver
third: bronze

RUGBY

RUGBY LEAGUE POSITIONS

1 full back
2 right wing three-quarter
3 right center three-quarter
4 left center three-quarter
5 left wing three-quarter
6 stand-off half
7 scrum half
8 front row prop forward
9 hooker
10 front row forward
11 second row forward
12 second row forward
13 loose forward

RUGBY LEAGUE SCORING RANGE

try, 3 points
penalty goal, 2 points
conversion, 2 points
dropped goal, 1 point

RUGBY UNION POSITIONS

1 prop forward
2 hooker
3 prop forward
4 lock forward
5 lock forward
6 flank forward
7 flank forward
8 no. 8 forward
9 scrum half back
10 stand off or outside half back
11 left wing three-quarter back
12 left center three-quarter back
13 right center three-quarter back
14 right wing three-quarter back
15 full back

Rugby Union Scoring Range

try, 4 points
dropped goal, 3 points
penalty goal, 3 points
conversion, 2 points

SCRABBLE™

LETTER VALUES

By number of tiles
E = 12
A, I = 9
O = 8
N, R, T = 6
D, L, S, U = 4
G = 3
B, C, F, H, M, P, V, W, Y, blank = 2
J, K, Q, X, Z = 1

By letter value
Q, Z = 10
J, X = 8
K = 5
F, H, V, W, Y = 4
B, C, M, P = 3
D, G = 2
A, E, I, L, N, O, R, S, T, U = 1
blank = 0

SOCCER

(see illustration)

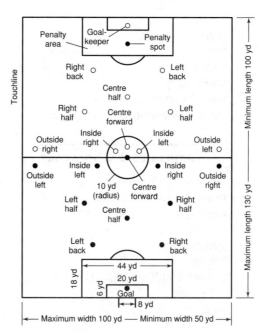

Soccer Field

SPORTS CLASSIFICATIONS

AIR SPORTS

aerial skiing
aerobatics
air racing
ballooning
gliding
hang gliding
helicopter flying
parasailing
skydiving & sport parachuting

ANIMAL SPORTS

bullfighting
camel racing
carriage driving
cockfighting
dogsled racing
dressage
fishing
greyhound racing
harness horse racing
horse racing
hunting
pigeon racing
polo
rodeo
show jumping
sled-dog racing
three-day event (equestrianism)

ATHLETICS & GYMNASTICS

aerobics & exercising
cross-country running
decathlon (contest of 10 track-and-
    field events)
gymnastics
hiking
marathon (26 mi. 385 yd. race) &
    jogging
mountaineering
orienteering

pentathlon (contest of 5 track-and-
    field events)
powerlifting
race walking
track and field
trampolining & tumbling
triathlon (contest of usu. swimming,
    bicycling, and distance running)
weightlifting

BALL & STICK SPORTS

bandy (game resembling ice hockey)
baseball
bowls
cricket
croquet
field hockey
golf
hurling
lacrosse
petanque
roller hockey
rounders (game resembling baseball)
shinty (game resembling field
    hockey)
softball
stickball

COMBAT SPORTS

aikido
boxing
fencing & swordplay
judo
karate
kendo (form of fencing)
kung fu
self-defense
sumo wrestling
tae-kwon-do (Korean martial art
    similar to karate)
wrestling

COURT SPORTS (NON-TEAM)

badminton
court handball

court tennis
jai alai
lawn tennis
paddleball
paddle tennis
pelota (game resembling jai alai)
platform tennis
racquetball
rugby fives (game resembling
   handball)
squash racquets
squash tennis
table tennis
tennis

TARGET SPORTS

archery
billiards
boccie/boules (game resembling
   lawn bowling)
bowling
candlepin bowling (bowling with
   smaller ball and straight-sided pins)
clay pigeon shooting
croquet
curling
darts
duckpin bowling (bowling with
   smaller ball and shorter tenpins)
golf
horseshoe pitching
lawn bowling
pistol shooting
pool
quoits
rifle & target shooting
shuffleboard
skeet shooting (form of trapshooting)
skydiving
snooker
trapshooting

TEAM SPORTS

baseball
basketball
Canadian football

canoe polo
cycle polo
cricket
football
Gaelic football
ice hockey
korfball (game resembling basketball)
netball (game resembling basketball)
polo
rugby
soccer
softball
speedball (game resembling soccer)
team handball
ultimate Frisbee
volleyball
polo

Number of Players on a Team

15, Rugby Union
13, Rugby League
12, lacrosse
11, football
11, soccer
11, cricket
10, softball
9, baseball
7, water polo
6, ice hockey
6, volleyball
5, basketball
4, curling
4, polo
2–4, bowling

WATER SPORTS

body surfing (riding waves without a
   surfboard)
canoeing
diving
fishing (fly fishing, trawling, etc.)
kayaking
motorboat racing
rowing & sculling
sailing

scuba diving
skin diving
snorkeling
surfing
swimming
synchronized swimming
water polo
water skiing
water ski jump
white-water canoeing & rafting
windsurfing (sailing on a surfboard)
yachting & sailing

WHEEL SPORTS

autocross/gymkhana (car racing on
    road course)
auto racing
bicycle racing
bicycle touring
drag racing
in-line skating/rollerblading
karting
motocross
motorcycle racing
mountain biking
off-road racing
rallying (long-distance race for sports
    cars)
roller skating
skateboarding
slalom / autotest (maneuverability
    auto race)
soap box derby
stock car racing

WINTER SPORTS

Alpine skiing (downhill skiing or
    competition)
biathlon (cross-country ski and rifle
    contest)
bobsledding
cross-country skiing
figure skating
ice boating
luge & tobogganing

mogul skiing (freestyle skiing down
    bumpy course)
Nordic skiing (cross-country skiing
    and ski jumping competition)
ski jumping
skibobbing (riding vehicle with two
    short skis)
skiing: downhill & slalom
snowboarding
snowmobiling
snowshoeing
speed skating
tobogganing

SWIMMING

DIVING CLASSIFICATION

*(more than 60 springboard dives are
grouped into five categories; 50+ tower
dives fall into six categories with an
additional class for armstand dives)*

Group I: the forward dives
Group II: the backward dives
Group III: the reverse dives
Group IV: the inward dives
    (cutaways)
Group V: the twisting dives
Group VI: armstand dives

MEDLEY ORDER

butterfly
backstroke
breaststroke
freestyle

TENNIS

GRAND SLAM TOURNAMENTS

Australian Open Championship
French Open Championship
Wimbledon
U.S. Open Championship

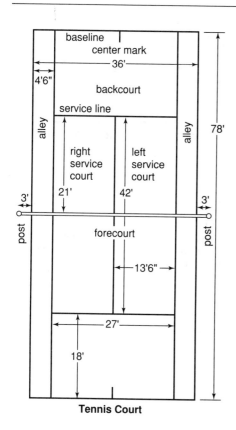

Tennis Court

20 kg = blue
15 kg = yellow (or green when there is no 50 kg)
10 kg = white
5 kg = white
2.5 kg = black
1.25 kg = chrome
0.5 kg = chrome
0.25 kg = chrome

WEIGHTLIFTING WEIGHT CLASSES

(Amateur Athletic Union)

Heavyweight	over 198¼ pounds
Middle-Heavyweight	181½–198¼
Light-Heavyweight	165–181¼
Middleweight	148½–165¼
Lightweight	132–148½
Featherweight	123¼–132
Bantamweight	under 123¼

SCORING

love=no score
15=first point
30=second point
40=third point
*-all (e.g. 40-all)=tied at * score
deuce=tie score on third point
advantage=one point won after deuce
game=fourth or winning point

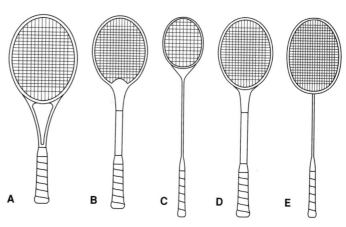

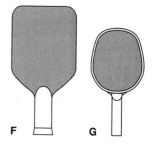

Rackets

A. Tennis; **B.** Court tennis; **C.** Squash;
D. Squash tennis; **E.** Badminton;
F. Paddle tennis; **G.** Table tennis

WEIGHTLIFTING

DISKS

50 kg = green
25 kg = red

WHITEWATER RAFTING

RIVER DIFFICULTY

(American Whitewater Affiliation)

Class I, Easy: fast-moving water with riffles and small waves

Class II, Novice: straightforward rapids with wide, clear channels

Class III, Intermediate: rapids with moderate, irregular waves which may be difficult to avoid

Class IV, Advanced: intense, powerful but predictable rapids requiring precise boat handling in turbulent water

Class V, Expert: extremely long, obstructed, or very violent rapids which explose paddler to above-average endangerment

Class VI, Extreme: exemplify extremes of difficulty, unpredictability, and danger; consequences of errors are very severe and rescue may be impossible

WRESTLING

SUMO RANKS

(highest to lowest); (wrestlers promoted if they win eight or more of the 15 bouts that make up one tournament)

Yokozumo, grand champion (cannot be demoted, but retire as soon as their performance starts to become unworthy of their rank)

Ozeki, champion (demoted if they record two successive makekoshi: eight or more losses)

Sekiwake, 3rd rank

Komusubi, 2nd rank

Maegashira, 1st rank

Juryo, 5th level

Maku-shita, 4th level

Sandanme, 3rd level

Jo-nidan, 2nd level

Jo-no-kuchi, 1st level

Mae-zumo, newcomer

WRESTLING WEIGHT CLASSES

(Amateur Athletic Union)

Heavyweight	over 191 pounds
Light-Heavyweight	174¼–191
Middleweight	160¾–174
Welterweight	147¾–160½
Lightweight	136¾–147½
Featherweight	125¾–136½
Bantamweight	114½–125¾
Flyweight	up to 114½

YACHTING CLASSES

(International yacht racing authorities recognize a large number of different classes; these are the customary classes for inshore yachting, as in the Olympic Games)

Tornado, plywood or fiberglass catamaran crewed by two; overall length 20 feet (6.096 meters);

Finn, fiberglass dinghy with a centerboard crewed by one; overall length 14 feet 9 inches (4.5 meters);

470, fiberglass dinghy with a centerboard crewed by two; overall length 15 feet 4¾ inches (4.7 meters);

Laser, fiberglass dinghy with a centerboard crewed by one; overall length 13 feet 10½ inches (4.23 meters);

Flying Dutchman, plywood or fiberglass dinghy with a centerboard crewed by two; overall length 19 feet 10 inches (6.04 meters);

Tempest, fiberglass keel yacht crewed
by two;
overall length 21 feet 11¾ inches (6.7
meters);
Soling, fiberglass keel yacht crewed
by three;
overall length 26 feet 9 inches (8.16
meters).

*(The customary classes for ocean or
offshore racing, involving larger boats
and a more numerous crew,
are according to overall length)*

Class V	21 feet to 22 feet 11 inches (6.4–7 meters).
Class IV	23 feet to 25 feet 5 inches (7.01–7.75 meters).
Class III	25 feet 6 inches to 28 feet 11 inches (7.77–8.8 meters).
Class II	29 feet to 32 feet 11 inches (8.84–10.03 meters).
Class I	33 feet to 70 feet (10.05–21.34 meters).

The human understanding is of its nature prone to suppose the existence of more order and regularity in the world than it finds.

—Francis Bacon, *Novum Organum*

CHAPTER THIRTEEN

GENERAL KNOWLEDGE & PHILOSOPHY

ANCIENT SCHEMES OF KNOWLEDGE

AGRIPPA, MARCUS (63–12 B.C.)

(Roman statesman, general, and engineer)

Tropes

Arguments Supporting Skeptical Suspension of Judgment)

1. Disagreement among philosophers concerning what, if anything, can be known.
2. Every proof requires premises which in turn must be proved.
3. All data is relative: sensation to the sentient being, reason to the intelligent being.
4. We try to avoid regress by positing hypotheses, the truth of the hypotheses not yet determined. We cannot accept as true the conclusions following from them.
5. There is a vicious cycle in attempting to establish the sensible by reason, since reason itself needs to be established on the basis of sense.

ARISTOTLE (384–322 B.C.)

(Greek philosopher: pupil of Plato; tutor of Alexander the Great)

Animal Classifications

Animals containing blood
  birds
  amphibians
  reptiles
  fishes
  whales
Animals that are bloodless
  cephalopods
  higher crustaceans
  insects
  testaceans (a collection of all lower animals)

Attitudes, Vices, Virtues

Activity or Attitude

1. Facing death
2. Experiencing pleasure/pain
3. Giving and taking money
4. Attitude toward honor/dishonor
5. Assertion
6. Giving amusement

Vice of Excess

1. Rashness
2. Self-indulgence
3. Prodigality
4. Empty vanity
5. Boastfulness
6. Buffoonery

Virtue

1. Courage
2. Temperance
3. Liberality
4. Proper pride
5. Truth telling
6. Ready wit

Vice of Defect

1. Cowardice
2. Insensibility
3. Meanness
4. Undue humility
5. Mock modesty
6. Boorishness

Four Causes

(causes or types of relationships that produce an effect or result)

material cause: that out of which something is made
efficient cause: that by which something is made
formal cause: that into which something is made

final cause: that for the sake of which
something is made

Political States

Good States

monarchies
aristocracies
polities (constitutional governments)

Bad States

tyrannies
oligarchies
radical democracies

Sciences

practical philosophy (ethics and
political science)
productive philosophy (rhetoric,
aesthetics, and literary criticism)
theoretical or speculative philosophy
(theological, physical and
metaphysical, and
biopsychological)

Spheres of the Universe

ocean
the firmament
water
air
fire
planetary spheres
fixed stars
Primum Mobile (prime mover;
outermost sphere)

Ten Fundamental Categories

*(By which everything in the universe
can be defined.)*

1. being
2. quantity
3. quality
4. relation
5. doing
6. suffering
7. having/possessing
8. position
9. place
10. time

Ten Fundamental Qualifications

*(to identify/analyze the full nature of an
object or being)*

(example: Socrates as the subject)

1. substance (man)
2. quantity (five feet tall)
3. quality (white)
4. relation (married)
5. place (Athenian Agora)
6. date (400 BC)
7. position (sitting)
8. state (sober)
9. action (drinking hemlock)
10. passivity (convicted)

Three Dimensions of Man

man the artist or artisan, producer of
all sorts of things
man the moral or social being, who
can do right or wrong, achieve or
fail to attain happiness
man the learner, acquiring
knowledge of all sorts

DEMOCRITUS (C. 460–370 B.C.)

(Greek philosopher)

Fragments

Inherent properties of atoms:

size
shape
solidity
Qualities attributed because of
sensations within organisms:
color
sweetness
bitterness

EMPEDOCLES

Four Elements

earth
fire
water
wind/air

EPICTETUS (c. 60–c120)

*(Greek Stoic philosopher and teacher,
mainly in Rome)*

Three Theses

1. Every creature strives for its own natural good.
2. Because man's essence lies in his soul, his natural good is moral or spiritual.
3. Undeveloped when he comes into the world, man must use discipline to achieve his natural good.

EPICURUS (c. 342–270 B.C.)

(Greek philosopher)

Three Needs of Man

equanimity
bodily health and comfort
the exigencies of life

GAIUS (c. 110–180)

Classification of things by law

(Roman jurist)

divine right (divini juris)
human right (humani juris)
  public right (publici juris)
  individual right (res singulorum)
categories governed by other legal systems:
movable and immovable property
other natural resources

possession of intangible things
possession of tangible things
religious things
the human body
things common to all
things that cannot be possessed;
    things that belong to no one
water
wild animals

HIPPOCRATES (c. 460–c. 377 B.C.)

("Father of Medicine"; Greek physician)

Four Humors

sanguine (blood) or cheerful
phlegmatic (phlegm) or unexcitable
choleric (yellow bile) or quick to anger
melancholic (black bile) or depressed

PLINY (23–79)

*(Roman naturalist, encyclopedist,
and writer)*

Natural History

*(arrangement of the 37 books of his
Historia Naturalis)*

1. Preface, contents in detail
2. The world, godhead, stars, planets, meteors, sun, climate, tides, volcanoes, fire (cosmography, astronomy, meteorology)
3–6. Physical and historical geography: places and people (geography, ethnography, anthropology)
7. The human race, birth and death, oddities and freaks, women, bodily capacities (man, inventions)
8. Land animals
9. Sea creatures
10. Birds

ANICIENT SCHEMES
OF KNOWLEDGE

Pliny (cont.)

EASTERN/
NONWESTERN
SCHEMES OF
KNOWLEDGE

11. Insects
12–19. Trees, vines and wine, crops and agriculture (botany)
20–32. Medicines and drugs (medicine, pharmacology, magic)
33–34. Metals (metallurgy)
35. Painting (fine arts)
36–37. Minerals, mountains, gems, jewelry (mineralogy)

PYTHAGORAS (C. 582–500 B.C.)

Cycle of Life

(six phases in cycle of existence)

birth
growth
decay
death
absorption
metamorphosis

SEVEN WONDERS OF THE ANCIENT WORLD

1. Great Pyramid of Cheops
2. The Hanging Gardens of Babylon
3. The Statue of Zeus at Olympia
4. The Temple of Diana at Ephesus
5. The Tomb of King Mausolus at Halicarnassus
6. The Colossus of Rhodes on the Isle of Rhodes
7. The Lighthouse on the Isle of Pharos

SEVEN LIBERAL ARTS

Quadrivium:

arithmetic
astronomy
geometry and geography
music and poetry

Trivium:

grammar
logic and metaphysics
rhetoric

SOCRATES (C. 469–399 B.C.)

(Athenian philosopher)

Definition of Holiness

1. The Form, holiness, exists as an objective entity.
2. This Form is a universal, the same in everything holy.
3. It is the essence or essential cause of holy things.
4. It serves as a universal and objective standard for judging what things are holy and what things are not.

EASTERN / NONWESTERN SCHEMES OF KNOWLEDGE

AL-KHWARIZMI, MUHAMMAD (C. 780–850)

(Arab mathematician and astronomer)

Encyclopaedia

1. Indigenous or Arab knowledge
   Jurisprudence (I-XI)
   Scholastic philosophy (XII-XVIII)
   Grammar (XIX-XXX)
   Secretarial duties (XXXI-XXXVIII)
   Prosody and poetic art (XXXIX-XLIII)
   XLIV-LII History of Persia, Arabia, Islam, Greece, and Rome
2. Foreign knowledge
   Philosophy (I-III)

Logic (IV-XII)
Medicine (XIII-XX)
Arithmetic (XXI-XXV)
Geometry (XXVI-XXIX)
Astronomy (XXX-XXXIII)
Music (XXXIV-XXXVI)
Mechanics (XXXVII-XXXVIII)
Alchemy (XXXIX-XLI)

Key to the Sciences

Indigenous sciences
  Quranic jurisprudence
  theological philosophy
  Arabic grammar
  secretarial duties
  poetry and prosody
  history
Foreign sciences
  philosophy
  logic
  medicine
  arithmetic
  geometry
  astronomy
  music
  mechanics
  alchemy

CABALA OR KABALA

*(also spelled Cabbala or Kabbala; the
system of Jewish Mysticism; literally,
"received knowledge, tradition")*

En-Sof—the absolute and infinite God,
hidden from mankind but manifested
through ten *Sefirot* or Spheres, whose
order is:

1. Keter ("crown")
2. Khokhmah ("wisdom")
3. Binah ("intelligence")
4. Khesed ("lovingkindness")
5. Gevurah ("power")
6. Tiferet ("beauty")
7. Netzakh ("eternity")
8. Hod ("splendor")
9. Yesod ("foundation")
10. Malkhut ("kingdom")

I CHING—THE TAO OF ORGANIZATION

Table of Contents

1. The Creative
2. The Receptive
3. Difficulty
4. Immaturity
5. Waiting
6. Contention
7. The Army
8. Closeness
9. Small Development
10. Treading
11. Tranquillity
12. Obstruction
13. Association with Others
14. Great Possession
15. Humility
16. Delight
17. Following
18. Degeneration
19. Overseeing
20. Observing
21. Biting Through
22. Adornment
23. Stripping Away
24. Return
25. No Error
26. Great Acumulation
27. Nourishment
28. Great Surpassing
29. Double Pitfall
30. Fire (Clinging)
31. Sensing
32. Constancy
33. Withdrawal
34. Great Power
35. Advance
36. Damage to Illumination
37. People in the Home
38. Disharmony

EASTERN/
NONWESTERN
SCHEMES OF
KNOWLEDGE

EASTERN/
NONWESTERN
SCHEMES OF
KNOWLEDGE

I-Ching (cont.)

MEDIEVAL SCHEMES
OF KNOWLEDGE

39. Halting
40. Solution
41. Reduction
42. Increase
43. Removal
44. Meeting
45. Gathering
46. Rising
47. Exhaustion
48. The Well
49. Revolution
50. The Cauldron
51. Thunder
52. Mountain
53. Gradual Progress
54. Marrying a Young Woman
55. Abundance
56. Travel
57. Wind
58. Pleasing
59. Dispersal
60. Discipline
61. Sincerity in the Center
62. Small Excess
63. Settled
64. Unsettled

IBN QUTAIBA (BORN C. 828)

Encyclopaedia

   I Power
  II War
 III Nobility
 IV Character
  V Learning and eloquence
 VI Asceticism
 VII Friendship
VIII Prayers
 IX Food
  X Women

SHANKARA (C. 789–821)

*(Hindu Vedantist philosopher
and teacher)*

Qualifications for Success in Liberation

1. Discrimination between things permanent and transitory
2. Indifference to enjoyment of the fruits of one's actions
3. The six accomplishments:
   a. S'ama (tranquillity)
   b. Dama (self-control)
   c. Uparati (cessation of mental action)
   d. Titiksa (forbearance; patient endurance of all suffering)
   e. S'raddha (faith)
   f. Samadhana (deep concentration)
4. Yearning to be liberated (mumuksuta)

MEDIEVAL SCHEMES OF KNOWLEDGE

ST. AUGUSTINE (354–430)

Divisions of Pagan Knowledge

(De doctrina christiana)

works of mankind
  on their own
    luxuries
    utilitarian
  in collaboration with demons
    magic
    soothsaying
    omens
    superstitious practices
natural works, and those divinely
      inspired
  by reasoning
    logic
    rhetoric
    mathematics

via the senses
history
  natural history
  astronomy
  useful arts
    crafts
    professions
    sports

St. Isidore (c. 560–636)

Encyclopedia

The liberal arts
Medicine
Jurisprudence; time; brief world
  chronicle
The Bible
The heavenly hierarchy
The Church and heresies
People; language; statecraft
An etymological dictionary
Man
Zoology
Heaven; the atmosphere; seas and
  oceans
Geography
Cities and towns; building
Geology; weights and measures
Agriculture and horticulture
Warfare; public games
Ships; houses; costume
Food; tools; furniture

Hugues de Saint-Victor (c. 1096–1141)

Classification of Knowledge

theoretical
  theology
  physics
  mathematics
practical
  solitary
  private
  public

mechanical
  fabric-making
  armament
  agriculture
  hunting
  medicine
  theatrics
logical
  grammar
  argument
    demonstration
    probable argument
      dialectic
      rhetoric
    sophistic

Bartholomaeus Anglicus

Encyclopedia Plan

*(De proprietatibus rerum, 1220–1240,
most popular encyclopedia in Europe for
three centuries)*

God and the angels
The soul
The body and its anatomy, diseases, etc.
Astrology, astronomy, time
Matter, form, air
Birds and insects
Water and fishes
Geography
Geology
Trees and herbs
Animals
Colours, scents, flavors, liquors
Weights and measures, numbers,
  sounds

Thomas of Cantimpre (c. 1228–1244)

Encyclopedia

(De natura rerum)

Man; anatomy, soul, monsters
Animals: quadrupeds, birds, ocean

monsters, fresh- and salt-water fish, snakes, worms
Botany; trees, aromatic trees, aromatic herbs
Sources of water
Metals and precious stones
The atmosphere
The seven planets; the motion of the spheres
The four elements

VINCENT OF BEAUVAIS (C. 1244)

Speculum Maius: "The Greater Mirror"

I. Speculum naturale (Mirror of nature)
   God, divinity, angels, devils
   The Creation: the first 3 days— used as a vehicle for physics, geography, geology, agriculture, alchemy
   Botany
   The Creation: 4th-6th days— astronomy, weather, birds, fishes, animals (in the order in which they appeared on earth according to Genesis), and animal husbandry
   Man: soul and body
   God and man
   A resume of the Speculum historiale

II. Speculum doctrinale (mirror of learning)
   Language (and glossary), grammar, logic, rhetoric
   Ethics, family life and economics, politics, law
   Crafts, architecture, war, sports, navigation, hunting, agriculture, applied medicine
   Medicine, physics, mathematics, metaphysics, theology

III. Speculum historiale (mirror of history)
   Summary of the Speculum naturale and of the Speculum doctrinale
   A world history to 1244, based mainly on Pierre le Mangeor's Historia scholastica (c. 1160), covering Biblical, secular and cultural matters
   Speculum morale
   —Ethics, astrology, and theology (based principally on St. Thomas Aquinas)

DOMENICO BANDINI (C. 1335–1418)

(Fons memorabilium universi)

Encyclopedia

Part I. Theology
1. God
2. The angels
3. The soul
4. Hell, the Devil, and his demons (includes added treatise on the art of magic)

Part II. The Universe and Astronomy
1. The world
2. The heavens
3. The stars and constellations
4. The planets
5. The seasons and chronology

Part III. The Elements
1. The elements in general
2. Fire
3. Air
4. Weather
5. Birds; animal husbandry
6. Seas and oceans
7. Lakes, rivers, marshes, streams and fountains
8. Fish

Part IV. The Earth and its Geography

1. Provinces and regions, including the theory of politics and government
2. Islands
3. Cities and towns, ancient and modern
4. Notable buildings and miscellaneous items
5. People and customs
6. Mountains
7. Trees and vines; wine-making
8. Herbs, vegetables, etc.
9. Quadrupeds
10. A tractate on the eating of flesh, fish, and fowl
11. Reptiles and worms
12. Gems and precious stones
13. Metals and alchemy

Part V. Man and his Conduct

1. Famous and illustrious men
2. Philosophical sects and world chronicle to 1315
3. Theological and moral virtues and vices
4. Some medical remedies
5. Heresies and heretical sects
6. Famous women

**FRANCIS BACON
(1561–1626)**

Taxonomy of Knowledge

*(published in 1620 as plan for
"The Great Instauration")*

External Nature
  astronomy
  meteorology
  geography
  the greater masses: fire, air, water, and earth
  species: mineral, vegetable, and animal
Man
  anatomy
  physiology
  structure and powers
  actions: voluntary and involuntary
Man's Action on Nature
  medicine
  surgery
  chemistry
  vision and visual arts
  hearing, sound, and music
  smell and smells
  taste and tastes
  touch and the objects of touch (including physical love)
  pleasure and pain
  the emotions
  the intellectual faculties
  food, drink, etc.
  the care of the person
  clothing
  architecture
  transport
  printing, books, and writing
  agriculture
  navigation
  other arts of peace
  the arts of war
  the history of machines
  arithmetic
  geometry
  miscellaneous history of common experiments that have not grown into an art

---

**JOHANN AMOS COMENIUS
(1592–1670)**

*(Moravian educational reformer
and bishop)*

Ianua Linguarum Reserata :
"The Gate of Tongues Unlocked"

Origin of the world
Elements, firmament, fire, and meteors

MEDIEVAL SCHEMES
OF KNOWLEDGE

Johann Amos
Comenius (cont.)

MODERN SCHEMES
OF KNOWLEDGE

Waters, earths, stones, metals
Trees, fruits, herbs, shrubs
Animals
Man and his body
Qualities or accidents of the body
Diseases, ulcers, wounds
Senses (external and internal)
Mind, will, affections/emotions
Mechanical arts
House and its parts
Marriage and family
Civic and state economy
Grammar, dialectic, rhetoric
Arithmetic and geometry
Ethics
Games
Death and burial
Providence, God, angels

MODERN SCHEMES OF KNOWLEDGE

ENCYCLOPAEDIA METROPOLITANA PLAN

(Samuel Coleridge 1772–1834)

First Division
  Pure Sciences (2 volumes)
    Formal
Universal Grammar
Logic: Rhetoric
Mathematics
  Real
Morals
Law
Theology
Second Division
  Mixed and Applied Sciences
      (6 volumes)
  Mixed
Mechanics
Hydrostatics
Pneumatics
Optics
Astronomy
  Applied

Experimental Philosophy
  Magnetism:
    Electromagnetism
  Electricity, Galvanism
  Heat
  Light
  Chemistry
  Sound
  Meteorology
  Figure of the Earth
  Tides and Waves
The Fine Arts
  Architecture
  Sculpture
  Painting
  Heraldry
  Numismatics
  Poetry
  Music
  Engraving
The Useful Arts
  Agriculture
  Horticulture
  Commerce
  Political Economy
  Carpentry
  Fortification
  Naval Architecture
  Manufactures
Natural History
  Inanimate: Crystallography,
    Geology, Mineralogy
  Insentient: Phytonomy,
    Botany
  Animate: Zoology
Application of Natural History
  Anatomy
  Materia Medica
  Medicine
  Surgery
Third Division
  Biographical and Historical (5
    volumes)
  Biography chronologically
    arranged, interspersed with
    introductory Chapters of
    National History, Political

Geography, and Chronology, and accompanied with correspondent Maps and Charts. The far larger portion of History being thus conveyed, not only in its most interesting, but in its most philosophical, because most natural and real form; while the remaining and connecting facts are interwoven in the several preliminary chapters.

Fourth Division

Miscellaneous and Lexicographical (12 volumes)

Alphabetical, Miscellaneous, and Supplementary: containing a Gazetteer, or complete Vocabulary of Geography, and a Philosophical and Etymological Lexicon of the English Language, or the History of English Words—the citations arranged according to the Age of the Works from which they are selected, yet with every attention to the independent beauty or value of the sentences chosen, which is consistent with the higher ends of a clear insight into the original and acquired meaning of every word.

ROGET'S THESAURUS

(Peter Mark Roget's Original Categories, 1853)

Class I. ABSTRACT RELATIONS
  Section I. EXISTENCE
    1. Being, in the Abstract
    2. Nonexistence
    3. Formal Existence
    4. Modal Existence
  Section II. RELATION
    1. Absolute Relation
    2. Continuous Relation
    3. Partial Relation
    4. General Relation
  Section III. QUANTITY
    1. Simple Quantity
    2. Comparative Quantity
    3. Conjunctive Quantity
    4. Concrete Quantity
  Section IV. ORDER
    1. Order in General
    2. Consecutive Order
    3. Collective Order
    4. Distributive Order
    5. Order as Regards Categories
  Section V. NUMBER
    1. Number, in the Abstract
    2. Determinate Number
    3. Indeterminate Number
  Section VI. TIME
    1. Absolute Time
    2. Relative Time
    3. Recurrent Time
  Section VII. CHANGE
    1. Simple Change
    2. Complex Change
  Section VIII. CAUSATION
    1. Constancy of Sequence
    2. Connection between Cause and Effect
    3. Power in Operation
    4. Indirect Power
    5. Combinations of Causes
Class II. SPACE
  Section I. SPACE IN GENERAL
    1. Abstract Space
    2. Relative Space
    3. Existence in Space
  Section II. DIMENSIONS
    1. General Dimensions
    2. Linear Dimensions
    3. Centrical Dimensions
  Section III. FORM
    1. General Form
    2. Special Form
  Section IV. MOTION
    1. Motion in General
    2. Degrees of Motion

3. Religious Sentiments
4. Acts of Religion
5. Religious Institutions

MACMILLAN VISUAL DICTIONARY TOPICS

Astronomy
Geography
Vegetable Kingdom
Animal Kingdom
Human Being
Farming
Architecture
House
House Furniture
Gardening
Do-It-Yourself
Clothing
Personal Adornment
Personal Articles
Communications
Road Transport
Rail Transport
Maritime Transport
Air Transport
Office Supplies
Office Automation
Music
Creative Leisure Activities
Team Sports
Water Sports
Aerial Sports
Winter Sports
Equestrian Sports
Athletics
Combat Sports
Leisure Sports
Indoor Games
Measuring Devices
Optical Instruments
Health and Safety
Energy
Heavy Machinery
Weapons
Symbols

RANDOM HOUSE WORD MENU
(Stephen Glazier, 1992)

Part One: Nature
  Chapter 1 The Human Body
      Anatomy
      Medical Problems
      Health, Fitness, and
        Enhancement
      Hair and Grooming
      Physical Appearance
  Chapter 2 Living Things
      Biology
      Animals
      Plants
      Simpler Life Forms
  Chapter 3 The Earth
      Geology
      Geography
      Minerals, Metals, and Rocks
      Landscapes and Seascapes
      Weather and Natural Phenomena
Part Two: Science and Technology
  Chapter 4 The Sciences
      Physics
      Astronomy and Space Science
      Mathematics
      Chemistry
      Medicine
      Measures and Weights
  Chapter 5 Technology
      Machinery and Fabrication
      Structural Components
      Building and Construction
        Materials
      Tools and Hardware
      Knots
      Containers
      Weapons and Armaments
      Electricity and Electronics
      Telecommunications
      Computers
  Chapter 6 Transportation
      Aircraft
      Automobiles
      Railroads

MODERN SCHEMES
OF KNOWLEDGE

LIBRARIES BOOK CLASSIFICATION

Dewey Decimal System

000–099	General Works (encyclopedias, etc.)
100–199	Philosophy, Psychology, Ethics
200–299	Religion and Mythology
300–399	Social Sciences
400–499	Philology/Language
500–599	Pure Science
600–699	Technology
700–799	Fine Arts
800–899	Literature
900–999	History, Geography, Biology, Travel

LIBRARY OF CONGRESS SYSTEM

A	General works, polygraphy
B	Philosophy, psychology, religion
C	Auxiliary sciences of history
D	Universal history
E-F	American history
G	Geography, anthropology, recreation
H	Social sciences
J	Political science
K	Law
L	Education
M	Music
N	Fine arts
P	Language and literature
Q	Science
R	Medicine
S	Agriculture
T	Technology
U	Military science
V	Naval science
Z	Bibliography and library science

MODERN SCHEMES
OF KNOWLEDGE

PHILOSOPHY

BACON, FRANCIS (1561–1626)

*English essayist, philosopher,
and statesman)*

False Ideas Which Handicap Man

(Francis Bacon's Novum Organum, 1620)

1. Idols of the Tribe (conventional beliefs which satisfy the emotions)
2. Idols of the Cave (erroneous conceptions resulting from individual predilections)
3. Idols of the Market Place (confused ideas resulting from the nonsensical or loose use of language)
4. Idols of the Theatre (various systems of philosophy or other dogmatic, improperly founded assertions)

BRANCHES OF PHILOSOPHY

epistemology (theory of knowledge, truth, theory, method, evidence, analysis)

metaphyics (theory of existence, essence, space, time, self, God, cause)

logic (theory of argument, validity, proof, definition, consistency)

aesthetics (theory of beauty, art, taste, standard, judgment, criticism)

analytic philosophy (theory that process of analysis is central to philosophical method)

cosmology (study of origin and general structure of the universe)

ethics (theory of good, right, duty, responsibility, utility)

DESCARTES

Classification of Ideas

1. Innate ideas originate from within, such as idea of self.
2. Adventitious ideas come, or seem to come, through the senses.
3. Factitious ideas are made up from the elements of the ideas of other things.

HEIDEGGER, MARTIN (1889–1976)

(German philosopher and writer)

Three Fundamental Features of Man

1. factuality (he is already involved in the world)
2. existentiality (he is a project and a possibility)
3. fallenness (he has tendency to become a mere presence in the world, failing to make the most of his possibilities)

KANT, IMMANUEL (1724–1804)

(German philosopher)

Four Sets of Principles

Quantity: axioms of intuition
Quality: anticipations of perception
Relation: analogies of experience
Modality: postulates of empirical thought

Four Antinomies of Reason

1. The world has a beginning in time, and is limited with regard to space.
2. Everything compound consists of simple parts, and nothing exists anywhere but the simple, or what is composed of it.
3. There is freedom in the world, and

not everything takes place according to the laws of nature.

4. There exists an absolutely necessary being belonging to the world either as part of it, or as the cause of it.

Arguments for God

(Kant says the latter argument is not valid and that the former two arguments depend on the latter.)

1. Cosmological: If there exists anything, there must exist an absolutely necessary Being.
2. Physico-Theological: Concludes from order, beauty, and fitness of the world to a sublime and wise intelligence as its cause.
3. Ontological: Holds that to deny the existence of the most real Being is to utter a contradiction, which follows only if existence is taken to be a predicate, property, or characteristic similar to all others (e.g. whiteness).

KIERKEGAARD, SOREN (1813–1855)

(Danish philosopher and theologian)

Three Groups of Men

1. aesthetes: want entertainment, pleasure, freedom from boredom
2. ethical men: live for the sake of duty, taking on obligations in order to be bound to discharge them
3. religious men: live in order to obey God

LOCKE, JOHN (1632–1704)

(English philosopher)

Qualities of Objects

(John Locke's "An Essay Concerning Human Understanding," 1690)

Primary Qualities
  solidity
  extension
  figure
  mobility
  number
Secondary Qualities
  color
  odor
  sound
  taste

NIETZSCHE, FRIEDRICH (1844–1900)

(German philosopher)

Slave/Master

1. resentful/expresses anger directly
2. reactionary (negative)/creative (positive)
3. other-directed/self-directive
4. other-worldly/this-worldly
5. self-deceptive/self-aware
6. humble (meek)/proud (not vain)
7. altruistic/egoistic
8. prudent/experimental
9. democratic (self-indulgent)/aristocratic (value hierarchy)
10. confessional/discrete (masked)
11. morality of principles/morality of persons
12. weak-willed/strong-willed
13. good (weakness) vs. evil (strength)/good (strength) vs. bad (weakness)

PHILOSOPHIES OF THE BRANCHES OF KNOWLEDGE

Philosophy of art
Philosophy of education
Philosophy of history
Philosophy of law
Philosophy of linguistics
Philosophy of logic
Philosophy of man
Philosophy of mathematics
Philosophy of mind
Philosophy of nature
  philosophy of biology
  philosophy of physics
Philosophy of politics
Philosophy of religion
Philosophy of science

PHILOSOPHICAL SCHOOLS

Ancient and medieval schools

Aristotelianism
Atomism
Eleaticism
Epicureanism
Platonism
Pythagoreanism
Realism
Scholasticism
Skepticism
Sophists
Stoicism

Modern schools

Analytic and Linguistic philosophy
Empiricism
Existentialism
Idealism
Materialism
Phenomenology
Positivism and Logical Empiricism
Pragmatism
Rationalism
Utilitarianism

SPINOZA, BARUCH (1632–1677)
(Dutch philosopher)

Stages of Intellectual Salvation

1. On the level of imagination, where our intellectual life begins, we combine and fuse images, achieving a mixture of specious and true universals. The mind can order these and the foundation of scientific knowledge discovered. One begins to free oneself from the excessive temporality of the flux of images.
2. One arrives at science, ratio as Spinoza calls it. Since scientific laws apply to all times and places, the person who is able to understand this lives in more than just his/her own time and place. The person lives more broadly and deeply.

TILLICH, PAUL (1886–1965)
(U.S. philosopher and theologian, born in Germany)

Three Types of Anxiety
("The Courage to Be," 1952)

1. ontic anxiety, the anxiety of fate and death
2. moral anxiety, the anxiety of guilt and condemnation
3. spiritual anxiety, the anxiety of emptiness and meaninglessness

WHITEHEAD, ALFRED (1861–1947)

(English philosopher and mathematician, in the U.S. after 1924)

Categories of Existence

(Alfred North Whitehead, "Process and Reality," 1929)

1. actual entities
2. prehensions
3. nexus (plural of nexus)
4. subjective forms
5. external objects
6. propositions
7. multiplicities
8. contrasts

WITTGENSTEIN, LUDWIG (1889–1951)

(Austrian philosopher)

Method for Overcoming Puzzlement

1. One selects a set of concepts which may cause difficulty, leading us to make paradoxical statements with respect to them.
2. One examines repeated instances of the normal use of these concepts in an effort to banish the philosophical puzzlement.
3. One reveals the nature of the language games being played in the instances of usage by inventing new language games for purposes of comparison.
4. When we see that everything is open to view, and there is nothing further to explain, it is a sign that, with respect to the concepts in question, we have overcome our intellectual bewitchment.

BIBLIOGRAPHY

Benne, B. *Waspleg and Other Mnemonics.*
Dallas: Taylor Publishing, 1988.

Blocksma, Mary. *Reading The Numbers: A
Survival Guide to the Measurements,
Numbers, and Sizes Encountered in
Everyday Life.* New York: Penguin
Books, 1989.

Boswell, John and Dan Starer. *Five Rings,
Six Crises, Seven Dwarfs, and 38 Ways
to Win an Argument.* New York: Penguin Group, 1990.

Bragonier Jr., Reginald and David Fisher.
What's What. Maplewood, NJ: Ham-
mond Incorporated, 1990.

Bridger, David, ed. *The New Jewish Encyclopedia.* New York: Behrman House,
Inc., 1962.

Butler, Penny. *Desk Companion.* New
York: Henry Holt and Company, 1992.

Carpenter, Clive. *Guinness Book of Answers.* New York: Facts On File, 1993.

Chapman, Robert. *Roget's International
Thesaurus, Fifth Edition.* New York:
HarperCollins, 1992.

Collison, Robert. *Encyclopaedias: Their
History Throughout the Ages.* New York:
Hafner Publishing Company, 1966.

Considine, Douglas M. *Van Nostrand's
Scientific Encyclopedia.* New York: Van
Nostrand Reinhold Company, 1976.

Copeland, Robert. *Webster's Sports Dictionary.* Springfield, MA: G. & C. Merriam
Company, 1976.

Corbeil, Jean-Claude and Ariane Archam-
bault. *Macmillan Visual Dictionary.*
New York: Macmillan Publishing Company, 1992.

Corbeil, Jean-Claude. *Facts on File Visual
Dictionary.* New York: Facts On File
Publications, 1986.

Cribb, Joe. *Eyewitness Books: Money.* New
York: Alfred A. Knopf, 1990.

Crim, Keith. *Dictionary of World Religions.*
New York: Harper Collins, 1989.

Crystal, David. *Cambridge Factfinder.*
New York: Cambridge University Press,
1993.

Darton, Mike and John Clark. *Macmillan
Dictionary of Measurement.* New York:
Macmillan Publishing Company, 1994.

Dempsey, Michael W. *Everyman's
Factfinder.* Melbourne and Sydney,
Australia: J.M. Dent PTY. Limited,
1982.

Dempsey, Michael W. *Everyman's
Factfinder.* Melbourne and Sydney,
Australia: J.M. Dent PTY. Limited,
1982.

Diagram Group, The. *Comparisons.* New
York: St. Martin's Press, 1980.

Diagram Group, The. *Cyclopedia.* Philadelphia: Running Press, 1993.

Diagram Group, The. *The Macmillan Visual Desk Reference.* New York: Macmillan Publishing Company, 1993.

Diagram Group, The. *The Rule Book.* New York: St. Martin's Press, 1983.

Elliott, Stephen P., Martha Goldstein, and Michael Upshall, eds. *Webster's New World Encyclopedia.* New York: Prentice Hall, 1992.

Emiliani, Cesare. *The Scientific Companion.* New York: John Wiley & Sons, Inc., 1988.

Falla, Jack. *Sports Illustrated Hockey: Learn to Play the Modern Way.* New York: Sports Illustrated Winner's Circle Books, 1987.

Farndon, J. *Dictionary of the Earth.* New York: Dorling Kindersley, 1994.

Franck, Irene M. *On the Tip of Your Tongue.* New York: Signet, 1990.

Glazier, Stephen. *Word Menu.* New York: Random House, 1992.

Gold, Sarah, ed. *New York Public Library Desk Reference.* New York: Prentice Hall General Reference, 1993.

Gregory, John. *Understanding Ballet From Classroom to Stage.* London: Octopus Books Limited, 1972.

Halsey, William D. *Merit Students Encyclopedia.* New York: Macmillan Educational Company, 1991.

Harvey, Jr., Edmund H. *Reader's Digest Book of Facts.* Pleasantville, NY: The Reader's Digest Association, Inc., 1987.

Headlam, Catherine. *Kingfisher Science Encyclopedia.* New York: Kingfisher Books, 1993.

Herbst, Dan. *Sports Illustrated Soccer: The Complete Player.* New York: Sports Illustrated Winner's Circle Books, 1988.

Isaacs, Neil D. and Dick Motta. *Sports Illustrated Basketball: The Keys to Excellence.* New York: Sports Illustrated Winner's Circle Books, 1988.

Jackson, Albert and David Day. *Tools and How to Use Them.* New York: Alfred A. Knopf, 1978.

Jordan, Pat. *Sports Illustrated Pitching: The Keys to Excellence.* New York: Sports Illustrated Winner's Circle Books, 1988.

Christensen, Kathryn. *Put on a Circus.* Larkspur, CA: Art's Publication, 1991.

Kindall, Jerry. *Sports Illustrated Baseball: Play the Winning Way.* New York: Sports Illustrated Winner's Circle Books, 1988.

Kinder, Hermann and Werner Hilgemann. *The Anchor Atlas of World History, Volume II.* New York: Doubleday, 1978.

Kipfer, Barbara Ann. *Roget's 21st Century Thesaurus.* New York: Dell, 1990.

Konigsberg, Ira. *The Complete Film Dictionary.* New York: Nal Books—New American Library, 1987.

Lewis, Peter. *Martial Arts of the Orient.* London: Multimedia Books Limited, 1992.

Lorimer, Lawrence T. *Academic American Encyclopedia.* Danbury, CT: Grolier, Inc., 1991.

_____. *Encyclopedia Americana.* Danbury, CT: Grolier Inc., 1993.

McArthur, Tom. *Worlds of Reference.* New York: Cambridge University Press, 1986.

McHenry, Robert, ed. *Encyclopaedia Britannica.* Chicago: Encyclopaedia Britannica, Inc., 1993.

McKeever, Susan and Martyn Foote. *Dorling Kindersley Science Encyclopedia.* New York: Dorling Kindersley, Inc., 1993.

Meserole, Mike. *The 1992 Information Please Sports Almanac.* Boston: Houghton Mifflin Company, 1991.

Microsoft, Inc. *Microsoft Encarta '95.* Redmond, Wa.: Microsoft, Inc., 1995.

Mitchell, James. *Random House Encyclopedia.* New York: Random House, 1990.

Morley, John V. *Diderot and the Encyclopaedists.* London: Macmillan Publishing Company, 1923.

Morris, Christopher. *Academic Press Dictionary of Science and Technology.* San Diego, CA: Academic Press (Harcourt Brace Jovanovich Publishers), 1992.

Mulvoy, Mark. *Sports Illustrated: Golf.* New York: Harper & Row, Publishers, 1983.

Parker, Sybil P. *McGraw-Hill Dictionary of Scientific and Technical Terms.* New York: McGraw-Hill Book Company, 1989.

Pheby, John. *Oxford-Duden Pictorial English Dictionary.* New York: Oxford University Press, 1984.

Philbin, Tom and Steve Ettlinger. *The Complete Illustrated Guide to Everything Sold in Hardware Stores.* New York: Macmillan Publishing Company, 1988.

Randel, Don Michael. *Harvard Concise Dictionary of Music.* Cambridge, MA: The Belknap Press of Harvard University Press, 1978.

Randy Pitman & Elliott Swanson. *Video Movies: A Core Collection For Libraries.* Santa Barbara, CA: ABC—CLIO, 1990.

Reid, Francis. *The Staging Handbook.* Pitman Publishing Limited, London: 1978.

Richard L. Frey et al. *The New Complete Hoyle Revised.* New York: Doubleday, 1991.

Sadie, Stanley. *The New Grove Dictionary of Music and Musicians.* London, England: Macmillan Publishers Limited, Grove's Dictionaries of Music, Inc., Peninsula Publishers Limited, 1980.

Science and Technology Department of the Carnegie Library of Pittsburgh. *The Handy Science Answer Book.* Detroit, MI: Visible Ink Press, 1994.

Siegel, Alice and Margo McLoone Basta. *The Information Please Kids' Almanac.* New York: Houghton Mifflin Company, 1992.

Sports Illustrated Staff. *Sports Illustrated 1992 Sports Almanac.* Boston: Little, Brown and Company, 1991.

Thompson, Oscar, ed. *The International Cyclopedia of Music and Musicians.* New York: Dodd, Mead & Company, 1975.

Zeleny, Robert O. *The World Book Encyclopedia*: Chicago: World Book, Inc., 1994.

Wilkinson, Bud. *Sports Illustrated Football: Winning Defense.* New York: Sports Illustrated Winner's Circle Books, 1987.

Wilkinson, Bud. *Sports Illustrated Football: Winning Offense.* New York: Sports Illustrated Winner's Circle Books, 1987.

Worrall, Mary. *Oxford Children's Encyclopedia.* Oxford: Oxford University Press, 1991.

Wurman, Richard Saul, Alan Siegel, and Kenneth M. Morris. *The Wall Street Journal. Guide to Understanding Money & Markets.* New York: Access Press Ltd. and Siegel & Gale, Inc. and Prentice Hall Press, 1989.

Zevin, Jack. *Kingfisher Illustrated History of the World.* New York: Kingfisher Books, 1993.

INDEX